THE BRICE FAMILY

WHO SETTLED IN
FAIRFIELD COUNTY, SOUTH CAROLINA
ABOUT 1785

BRUCE

AND RELATED FAMILIES

Compiled by

Betty Jewell Durbin Carson

HERITAGE BOOKS
2014

HERITAGE BOOKS

AN IMPRINT OF HERITAGE BOOKS, INC.

Books, CDs, and more—Worldwide

For our listing of thousands of titles see our website
at
www.HeritageBooks.com

Published 2014 by
HERITAGE BOOKS, INC.
Publishing Division
5810 Ruatan Street
Berwyn Heights, Md. 20740

Copyright © 2014 Betty Jewell Durbin Carson

Heritage Books by the author:

The Brice Family Who Settled in Fairfield County, South Carolina, about 1785 and Related Families
Durbin and Logsdon Genealogy with Related Families, 1626–1991
The Durbin and Logsdon Genealogy with Related Families, 1626–1991, Volume 2
Durbin and Logsdon Genealogy with Related Families, 1626–1994
Durbin and Logsdon Genealogy with Related Families, 1626–1998
Durbin-Logsdon Genealogy and Related Families from Maryland to Kentucky, Volumes 1–2
CD: The Durbin and Logsdon Genealogy with Related Families, 1626–2000, 3rd Revised Edition
History of Curtis Land, 1635–1683; with Excerpt on Francis Land
Our Ewing Heritage, with Related Families, Part One and Two, Revised Edition
Betty Jewell Durbin Carson and Doris M. Durbin Wooley
CD: Our Ewing Heritage, with Related Families, Revised Edition
Betty Jewell Durbin Carson and Doris M. Durbin Wooley

International Standard Book Numbers
Paperbound: 978-0-7884-5579-7
Clothbound: 978-0-7884-6057-9

FOREWORD

Credit from an unpublished short history compiled by Laurie Simonton Brice, must be acknowledged. He was b. April 18, 1916 and married on Sept. 7, 1943 Margaret Mac Hemminger (b. July 28, 1910) at Willington, SC by Rev. Virgil A. Dean. He was a direct descendant of John Brice (1756-1816), son of William Brice and Jane McClure of County Antrim, Ireland.

John Brice, known as John Brice, Jr. and Dumper's Creek John as well as John Garner Brice, married his cousin, Jannette Brice (1811-1897), a daughter of James Brice (1758-1845) and his second wife, Mary Cathcart (1778-1828). Their son, James Henry Brice (1834-1906) was the great grandfather of Robert Brice Land.

To make the Brice family genealogy more complete, data has been gathered dating back to Robert the Bruce, King of Scotland. The Coat of Arms on the cover is the Bruce copy. The Coat of Arms of the Brice, Bryce and Bruce families are almost identical. The one used by the Brice family is: a gold shield (OR) with a saltire cross of red (gules), also a chief of red with a red bordure around the shield. The crest is a cubic arm erect proper grasping a scimitar argent. On Rev. Edward Brice's tomb it differs slightly and the motto is "Do Well Doubt Nought." This Coat of Arms could not be located in any books on Heraldry, but several are nearly the same.

Betty Jewell Durbin Carson

368 Sease Hill Road
Lexington, SC 29073
June 1, 2010

1

BRICE FAMILY NAME

The name of Brice or Bryce is sometimes said to have been derived from the Welsh ap or ab-Rice, meaning "son of Rice or Rees." It is also believed to have been derived from an ancient baptismal name and adopted as a surname by the sons of one whose Christian name was Brice.

In all probability, there are Brices whose name was derived in such manner but the majority of Brices are of Scotch descent and their name had its origin in Scotland. South Carolina Brices, who first settled in Fairfield County, agree that their name was Bryce in Scotland while Brice is the Irish and American form. There is a legend in the Brice family which seems to be more than reasonable and which, if true, establishes the name as one of great significance from the early beginning of Scotland's colorful history.

The family Brice legend told that the name comes from De Bruys, the same family which gave Robert Bruce, King of Scotland. Robert De Bruys, a noble Norman knight, who accompanied William the Conqueror in 1066, because of ability was sent into Scotland to take over the country. It was he who established the royal house of Bruce.

The surname of BRUCE so celebrated in the history of Scotland, is of territorial origin, from the Chataeu d'Adam at Brix, between Cherbourg and Valognes. The ruins of the extensive fortress built in the 11th century by Adam de Brus, and called after him, still remain. The name was brought to England in the wake of the Norman Conquest of 1066. The first Robert de Brus on record in Britain was probably the leader of the Brus contingent in the army of William The Conqueror in 1066. He appears to have died about the year 1094. A son of this Robert de Brus, was the first of the family connected with Scotland. The first people in Scotland to acquire fixed surnames were the nobles and great landowners, who called themselves, or were called by others, after the lands they possessed. Surnames originating in this way are known as territorial. Formerly lords of baronies and regalities and farmers were inclined to magnify their importance and to sign letters and documents with the names of their baronies and farms instead of their Christian names and surnames. The abuse of this style of speech and writing was carried so far that an Act was passed in the Scots parliament in 1672 forbidding the practice and declaring that it was allowed only to noblemen and bishops to subscribe by their titles. Leading figures of the name include Robert the Bruce (1274-1329) was the hero of the Scottish War of Independence and King of Scots, victor of Bammackburn (1314) and the bane of the English. Alexander, 6th Baron of Balfour of Burliegh (1849-1921) was the British Statesman, and Lord in Waiting to Queen Victoria. Surnames before the Norman Conquest of 1066 were rare in England having been brought by the Normans when William the Conqueror invaded the shores. The practice spread to Scotland and Ireland by the 12th century, and in Wales they appeared as late as the 16th century. Most surnames can be traced to one of four sources, locational, from the occupation of the original bearer, nicknames or simply font names based on the first name of the parent being given as the second name to their child.   Origin of Name:

From the French town of Brix Plant Badge: Rosemary   **Robert I of Scotland**

Robert I (11 July 1274 – 7 June 1329) usually known in modern English as **Robert the Bruce** (Medieval Gaelic: *Roibert a Briuis*; modern Scottish Gaelic: *Raibeart Bruis*; Norman French: *Robert de Brus* or *Robert de Bruys*) was King of Scots from 1306 until his death in 1329.

His paternal ancestors were of Scoto-Norman heritage (originating in Brieux, Normandy)[3], and his maternal of Franco-Gaelic[4]. He became one of Scotland's greatest kings, as well as one of the most famous warriors of his generation, eventually leading Scotland during the Wars of Scottish Independence against the Kingdom of England. He claimed the Scottish throne as a four-greats-grandson of David I of Scotland.

His body is buried in Dunfermline Abbey, while his heart is buried in Melrose Abbey. His embalmed heart was to be taken on crusade by his lieutenant and friend Sir James Douglas to the Holy Land, but only reached Moorish Granada, where it acted as a talisman for the Scottish contingent at the Battle of Teba.

Background and Early Life

Robert was the first son of Robert de Brus, 6th Lord of Annandale and Marjorie, Countess of Carrick,[5] daughter of Niall, Earl of Carrick. His mother was by all accounts a formidable woman who, legend would have it, kept Robert Bruce's father captive until he agreed to marry her. From his mother, he inherited the Gaelic Earldom of Carrick, and through his father a royal lineage that would give him a claim to the Scottish throne. Although his date of birth is known,[6] his place of birth is less certain, but it was probably Turnberry Castle in Ayrshire.[1][7][8]

Very little is known of his youth. He could have been sent to be fostered with a local family, as was the custom. It can be presumed that Bruce may have been raised speaking all the languages of his lineage and nation[4] and may have spoken Galwegian Gaelic, Scots and Norman French, with literacy in Latin. Robert's first appearance in history is on a witness list of a charter issued by Alasdair MacDomhnaill, Lord of Islay. His name appears in the company of the Bishop of Argyll, the vicar of Arran, a Kintyre clerk, his father and a host of Gaelic notaries from Carrick.

He saw the outcome of the 'Great Cause' in 1292, which gave the Crown of Scotland to his distant relative, John Balliol, as unjust. As he saw it, it prevented his branch of the family from taking their rightful place on the Scottish throne.[9] Soon afterwards, his grandfather, Robert de Brus, 5th Lord of Annandale—the unsuccessful claimant—resigned his lordship to Robert de Brus, Bruce's father. Robert de Brus had already resigned the Earldom of Carrick to Robert Bruce, his son, on the day of his wife's death in 1292, thus making Robert Bruce the Earl of Carrick. Both father and son sided with Edward I against John whom they considered a usurper and to whom Robert had not sworn fealty.[10]

In April 1294, the younger Bruce had permission to visit Ireland for a year and a half, and, as a further mark of King Edward's favour, he received a respite for all the debts owed by him to the English Exchequer.

In 1295, Robert married his first wife, Isabella of Mar the daughter of Domhnall I, Earl of Mar and his wife Helen .

Some sources claim that Helen was the daughter of the Welsh ruler Llywelyn ap Iorwerth, Prince of North Wales, Llywelyn 'The Great' (1173–1240) and his spouse Joan, Lady of Wales, an illegitimate child of King John of England. However, as both Llywelyn and Joan were dead by 1246, that theory would most likely be incorrect. However, there are suggestions that Helen may have in fact been the daughter of Llywelyn's son Dafydd ap Llywelyn and his Norman wife Isabella de Braose, of the south Wales dynasty of Marcher Lords.

Beginning of the Wars of Independence

Robert the Bruce and Isabella of Mar

In August 1296, Bruce and his father swore <u>fealty</u> to <u>Edward I of England</u> at <u>Berwick-upon-Tweed</u>, but in breach of this oath, which had been renewed at <u>Carlisle</u>, the younger Robert supported the Scottish revolt against King Edward in the following year. Urgent letters were sent ordering Bruce to support Edward's commander, <u>John de Warenne, 7th Earl of Surrey</u> (to whom Bruce was related) in the summer of 1297; but instead of complying, Bruce continued to support the revolt against Edward. On 7 July, Bruce and his friends made terms with Edward by a treaty called the <u>Capitulation of Irvine</u>. The Scottish lords were not to serve beyond the sea against their will, and were pardoned for their recent violence in return for swearing allegiance to King Edward. The Bishop of Glasgow, James the Steward, and Sir Alexander Lindsay became sureties for Bruce until he delivered his infant daughter <u>Marjorie</u> as a hostage.

Shortly after the <u>Battle of Stirling Bridge</u>, Bruce again defected to the Scots; he laid waste to Annandale and burned the English-held castle of <u>Ayr</u>. Yet, when King Edward returned to England after his victory at the <u>Battle of Falkirk</u>, <u>Annandale</u> and <u>Carrick</u> were excepted from the Lordships and lands which he assigned to his followers; Bruce was seen as a waverer whose allegiance could be acquired.[citation needed]

<u>William Wallace</u> resigned as <u>Guardian of Scotland</u> after the <u>Battle of Falkirk</u>. He was succeeded by Robert Bruce and <u>John Comyn</u> as joint Guardians, but they could not see past their personal differences. As a nephew and supporter of King John, and as someone with a serious claim to the Scottish throne, Comyn was Bruce's enemy. In 1299, <u>William Lamberton</u>, <u>Bishop of St. Andrews</u>, was appointed as a third, neutral Guardian to try to maintain order between Bruce and Comyn. The following year, Bruce finally resigned as joint Guardian and was replaced by Sir Gilbert, 1st Lord <u>de Umfraville</u>, Earl of Angus (in right of his mother, Maud, Countess of Angus).

In May 1301, Umfraville, Comyn and Lamberton also resigned as joint Guardians and were replaced by Sir <u>John de Soules</u> as sole Guardian. Soules was appointed largely because he was part of neither the Bruce nor the Comyn camps and was a patriot. He was an active Guardian and made renewed efforts to have King John returned to the Scottish throne.
In July, King Edward I launched his sixth campaign into Scotland. Though he captured <u>Bothwell</u> and <u>Turnberry Castle</u>, he did little to damage the Scots' fighting ability and, in January 1302, agreed to a nine-month truce. It was around this time that Robert the Bruce

submitted to Edward, along with other nobles, even though he had been on the side of the patriots until then.

There were rumours that King John would return as to regain the Scottish throne. Soules, who had probably been appointed by John, supported his return, as did most other nobles. But it was no more than a rumor and nothing came of it.

However, though recently pledged to support King Edward, it is interesting to note that Robert the Bruce sent a letter to the monks at Melrose Abbey in March 1302 which effectively weakened his usefulness to the English king. Apologising for having called the monks' tenants to service in his army when there had been no national call-up, Bruce pledged that, henceforth, he would "never again" require the monks to serve unless it was to "the common army of the whole realm", for national defence. Bruce also married his second wife that year, Elizabeth de Burgh, the daughter of Richard de Burgh, 2nd Earl of Ulster. By Elizabeth he had four children: David II, John (died in childhood), Matilda (who married Thomas Isaac and died at Aberdeen 20 July 1353), and Margaret (who married William de Moravia, 5th Earl of Sutherland in 1345).

In 1303, Edward invaded again, reaching Edinburgh, before marching to Perth. Edward stayed in Perth until July, then proceeded via Dundee, Brechin and Montrose, to Aberdeen, where he arrived in August. From there, he marched through Moray to Badenoch, before re-tracing his path back south to Dunfermline. With the country now under submission, all the leading Scots, except for William Wallace, surrendered to Edward in February 1304. John Comyn, who was by now Guardian, submitted to Edward.

The laws and liberties of Scotland were to be as they had been in the days of Alexander III, and any that needed alteration would be with the advice of King Edward and the advice and assent of the Scots nobles.

On 11 June 1304, with both of them having witnessed the heroic efforts of their countrymen during King Edward's siege of Stirling Castle, Bruce and William Lamberton made a pact that bound them, each to the other, in "friendship and alliance against all men." If one should break the secret pact, he would forfeit to the other the sum of ten thousand pounds. The pact is often interpreted as a sign of their deep patriotism despite both having already surrendered to the English.

With Scotland defenseless, Edward set about destroying her as a realm. Homage was again obtained under force from the nobles and the burghs, and a parliament was held to elect those who would meet later in the year with the English parliament to establish rules for the governance of Scotland. For all the apparent participation by Scots in the government, however, the English held the real power. The Earl of Richmond, Edward's nephew, was to head up the subordinate government of Scotland.

While all this took place, William Wallace was finally captured near Glasgow and was hanged, drawn and quartered in London on 23 August 1305.

In September 1305, Edward ordered Robert Bruce to put his castle at Kildrummy, "in the keeping of such a man as he himself will be willing to answer for," suggesting that King Edward suspected Robert was not entirely trustworthy and may have been plotting behind his back. However, an identical phrase appears in an agreement between Edward and his lieutenant and life-long friend, Aymer de Valence. Even more sign of Edward's distrust occurred when on October 10, 1305, Edward revoked his gift of Gilbert de Umfraville's lands to Bruce that he had made only six months before.[11]

Robert Bruce as Earl of Carrick and now 7th Lord of Annandale, held huge estates and property in Scotland and a barony and some minor properties in England and had a strong claim to the Scottish throne. He also had a large family to protect. If he claimed the throne, he would throw the country into yet another series of wars, and if he failed, he would be sacrificing everyone and everything he knew.

The killing of Comyn in Dumfries

Bruce, like all his family, had a complete belief in his right to the throne. However his actions of supporting alternately the English and Scottish armies had led to a great deal of distrust towards Bruce among the "Community of the Realm of Scotland". His ambition was further thwarted by the person of John Comyn. Comyn had been much more resolute in his opposition to the English; he was the most powerful noble in Scotland and was related to many more powerful nobles both within Scotland and England. He also had a powerful claim to the Scottish throne through his descent from Donald III on his father's side and David I on his mother's side. He was also the nephew of King John.

According to Barbour and Fordoun, in the late summer of 1305 in a secret agreement sworn, signed and sealed, John Comyn agreed to forfeit his claim to the Scottish throne in favour of Robert Bruce upon receipt of the Bruce lands in Scotland should an uprising occur led by Bruce.[12] However any Comyn claim to the throne would be tenuous in the extreme and the claim is almost certainly a matter of Bruce propaganda.

Whether the details of the agreement with Comyn are correct or not, King Edward moved to arrest Bruce while Bruce was still at the English court. Fortunately for Bruce, his friend, and Edward's son-in-law, Ralph de Monthermer learnt of Edward's intention and warned Bruce by sending him twelve pence and a pair of spurs. Bruce took the hint,[13] and he and a squire fled the English court during the night. They made their way quickly for Scotland and the fateful meeting with Comyn at Dumfries.

According to Barbour, Comyn betrayed his agreement with Bruce to King Edward I, and when Bruce arranged a meeting for February 10, 1306 with Comyn in the Church of Greyfriars in Dumfries and accused him of treachery, they came to blows.[14] Bruce killed Comyn in Dumfries [15] before the high altar of the church of the monastery. The Scotichronicon says that on being told that Comyn had survived the attack and was being treated, two of Bruce's supporters, Roger de Kirkpatrick and John Lindsay, went back into the church and finished Bruce's work but Barbour tells no such story.

Bruce hurried from Dumfries to Glasgow, where, kneeling before Bishop Robert Wishart he made confession of his violence and sacrilege and was granted absolution by the Bishop. The clergy throughout the land was adjured to rally to Bruce by Wishart.[16] In spite of this, Bruce was excommunicated for this crime.[17] Realising that the 'die had been cast' and he had no alternative except to become king or a fugitive, Bruce asserted his claim to the Scottish crown.

Coronation at Scone – King Robert I

Barely seven weeks after Comyn was slain in Dumfries, Bruce was crowned King of Scots at Scone, near Perth on 25 March with all formality and solemnity. The kingly robes and vestments which Robert Wishart had hidden from the English were brought out by the Bishop and set upon King Robert. The bishops of St. Andrews, Moray and Glasgow were in attendance as well as the earls of Atholl, Menteith, Lennox, and Mar. The great banner of the kings of Scotland was planted behind his throne.[18]

Isabella MacDuff, Countess of Buchan and wife of John Comyn, Earl of Buchan (a cousin of the murdered John Comyn), who claimed the right of her family, the MacDuff Earl of Fife, to crown the Scottish king for her brother, Duncan (or Donnchadh) – who was not yet of age, and in English hands – arrived the next day, too late for the coronation, so a second coronation was held and once more the crown was placed on the brow of Robert Bruce, Earl of Carrick, Lord of Annandale, King of the Scots.

From Scone to Bannockburn

In June 1306, he was defeated at the Battle of Methven and in August, he was surprised in Strathfillan, where he had taken refuge.[citation needed] His wife and daughters and other women of the party were sent to Kildrummy in August 1306 under the protection of Bruce's brother Nigel Bruce and the Earl of Atholl and most of his remaining men.[19] Bruce, with a small following of his most faithful men, including James Douglas, Lord of Douglas, Bruce's brothers Thomas, Alexander and Edward, as well as Sir Neil Campbell and the Earl of Lennox, fled to Rathlin Island off the northern coast of Ireland.[20]

Edward I marched north again in the spring. On his way, he granted the Scottish estates of Bruce and his adherents to his own followers and published a bill excommunicating Bruce. Bruce's queen, Elizabeth, his daughter Marjorie, and his sisters Christina and Mary were captured in a sanctuary at Tain, and sent to harsh imprisonment, which included Mary being hung in a cage in Roxburgh Castle, and Bruce's brother Nigel was hanged, drawn and quartered. But, on 7 July, King Edward I died, leaving Bruce opposed by his son, Edward II.

Bruce and his followers returned to the Scottish mainland in February in two groups. One, led by Bruce and his brother Edward landed at Turnberry Castle and began a guerrilla war in southwest Scotland. The other, led by his brothers Thomas and Alexander, landed slightly further south in Loch Ryan; but they were soon captured and like his brother Nigel shared the fate of Wallace in being hanged, drawn and quartered.

In April, Bruce won a small victory over the English at the <u>Battle of Glen Trool</u>, before defeating <u>Aymer de Valence, 2nd Earl of Pembroke</u> at the <u>Battle of Loudoun Hill</u>. At the same time, James Douglas made his first foray for Bruce into south-western Scotland, attacking and burning his own castle in Douglasdale. Leaving his brother Edward in command in <u>Galloway</u>, Bruce travelled north, capturing <u>Inverlochy</u> and <u>Urquhart</u> Castles, burning <u>Inverness Castle</u> and <u>Nairn</u> to the ground, then unsuccessfully threatening <u>Elgin</u>.

Transferring operations to <u>Aberdeenshire</u> in late 1307, he threatened <u>Banff</u> before falling seriously ill, probably owing to the hardships of the lengthy campaign. Recovering, leaving <u>John Comyn, 3rd Earl of Buchan</u> unsubdued at his rear, Bruce returned west to take <u>Balvenie</u> and <u>Duffus</u> Castles, then Tarradale Castle on the <u>Black Isle</u>. Looping back via the hinterlands of Inverness and a second failed attempt to take Elgin, Bruce finally achieved his landmark defeat of <u>Comyn</u> at the <u>Battle of Inverurie</u> in May 1308, then <u>overran Buchan</u> and defeated the English garrison at <u>Aberdeen</u>.

He then crossed to <u>Argyll</u> and defeated another body of his enemies at the <u>Battle of Pass of Brander</u> and took <u>Dunstaffnage Castle</u>, the last major stronghold of the Comyns.[21]

Bruce reviewing troops before the Battle of Bannockburn.

In March 1309, he held his first Parliament at <u>St. Andrews</u>, and by August, he controlled all of Scotland north of the <u>River Tay</u>. The following year, the clergy of Scotland recognised Bruce as king at a general council. The support given to him by the church in spite of his ex-communication was of great political importance.

The next three years saw the capture and reduction of one English-held castle or outpost after another: <u>Linlithgow</u> in 1310, <u>Dumbarton</u> in 1311, and <u>Perth</u>, by Bruce himself, in January 1312. Bruce also made raids into northern England and, landing at Ramsey in the <u>Isle of Man</u>, then laid siege to <u>Castle Rushen</u> in Castletown capturing it on 21 June 1313 to deny the island's strategic importance to the English. In the spring of 1314, <u>Edward Bruce</u> laid siege to <u>Stirling Castle</u>, whose governor, <u>Philip de Mowbray</u>, agreed to capitulate if not relieved before 24 June 1314. In March 1314, <u>James Douglas</u> captured <u>Roxburgh</u>, and <u>Randolph</u> captured <u>Edinburgh Castle</u>. In May, Bruce again raided England and subdued the Isle of Man.

The eight years of exhausting but deliberate refusal to meet the English on even ground have caused many to consider Bruce as one of the great guerrilla leaders of any age. This represented a transformation for one raised as a <u>feudal knight</u>. Bruce secured Scottish <u>independence</u> from England militarily — if not diplomatically — at the <u>Battle of Bannockburn</u> in 1314.

Freed from English threats, Scotland's armies could now invade northern England. Bruce also drove back a subsequent English expedition north of the border and launched raids into Yorkshire and Lancashire.

Ireland

Main article: Irish Bruce Wars 1315–1318

Buoyed by his military successes, Bruce's forces also invaded Ireland in 1315, purportedly to free the country from English rule (having received a reply to offers of assistance from Donal O'Neil, king of Tyrone), and to open a second front in the continuing wars with England. The Irish even crowned Edward Bruce as High King of Ireland in 1316. Robert later went there with another army to assist his brother.

To go with the invasion, Bruce popularised an ideological vision of a "Pan-Gaelic Greater Scotia" with his lineage ruling over both Ireland and Scotland. This propaganda campaign was aided by two factors. The first was his marriage alliance from 1302 with the de Burgh family of the Earldom of Ulster in Ireland; second, Bruce himself on his mother's side of Carrick, was descended from Gaelic royalty – in Scotland. Thus, lineally and geopolitically, Bruce attempted to support his anticipated notion of a pan-Gaelic alliance between Scottish-Irish Gaelic populations, under his kingship.

This is revealed by a letter he sent to the Irish chiefs, where he calls the Scots and Irish collectively *nostra nacio* (our nation), stressing the common language, customs and heritage of the two peoples:

> Whereas we and you and our people and your people, free since ancient times, share the same national ancestry and are urged to come together more eagerly and joyfully in friendship by a common language and by common custom, we have sent you our beloved kinsman, the bearers of this letter, to negotiate with you in our name about permanently strengthening and maintaining inviolate the special friendship between us and you, so that with God's will our nation (*nostra nacio*) may be able to recover her ancient liberty.

The diplomacy worked to a certain extent, at least in Ulster, where the Scots had some support. The Irish chief, Donal O'Neil, for instance, later justified his support for the Scots to Pope John XXII by saying "the Kings of Lesser Scotia all trace their blood to our *Greater Scotia* and retain to some degree our language and customs."[22]

The Bruce campaign to Ireland was characterised by some initial military success. However, the Scots failed to win over the non-Ulster chiefs, or to make any other significant gains in the south of the island, where people couldn't see the difference between English and Scottish occupation. Eventually it was defeated when Edward Bruce was killed at the Battle of Faughart. The Irish Annals of the period described the defeat of the Bruces by the

English as one of the greatest things ever done for the Irish nation due to the fact it brought an end to the famine and pillaging brought on the Irish by both the Scots and the English.[23]

Diplomacy

Robert Bruce's reign also witnessed some diplomatic achievements. The Declaration of Arbroath of 1320 strengthened his position, particularly *vis-à-vis* the Papacy. Pope John XXII eventually lifted Bruce's excommunication. In May 1328 King Edward III of England signed the Treaty of Edinburgh-Northampton, which recognised Scotland as an independent kingdom, and Bruce as its king.

Death

The alleged death mask of Robert Bruce, Rosslyn Chapel (1446), Scotland

Robert died on 7 June 1329, at the Manor of Cardross, near Dumbarton[24] He had suffered for some years from what some contemporary accounts describe as an "unclean ailment". The traditional view is that this was leprosy, but this was not mentioned in contemporary accounts, and is now disputed with syphilis, psoriasis, motor neurone disease and a series of strokes all proposed as possible alternatives.[25]

Robert is buried in Dunfermline Abbey.

His body lies buried in Dunfermline Abbey, but according to a death bed decree Sir James Douglas removed and carried his heart *'against the enemies of the name of Christ'* , in Moorish Granada, Spain to atone for his murder of John Comyn in the church of Greyfriars in Dumfries. Douglas carried the King's heart in a casket of which Sir Symon of Locard (Lockhart) carried the key. The decree overrode an earlier written request, dated 13 May 1329 Cardross, that his heart be buried in the monastery at Melrose. Douglas was killed in an ambush whilst carrying out the decree. On realising his imminent death Douglas is said to have thrown the casket containing Bruce's heart ahead of him and shouted "Onward braveheart, Douglas shall follow thee or die." According to legend *(Fordun Annals)*, the heart was later recovered by Sir William Keith and taken back to Scotland to be buried at Melrose Abbey, in Roxburghshire, following his earlier decree. In 1920 the heart was discovered by archeologists and was reburied, but the location was not marked.[26] In 1996, a casket was unearthed during construction work.[27] Scientific study by AOC archaeologists in Edinburgh, demonstrated that it did indeed contain a human heart and it was of appropriate age. It was reburied in Melrose Abbey in 1998, pursuant to the dying wishes of the King.[26]

Family and Descendants

Robert Bruce had a large family in addition to his wife, Elizabeth, and his children. There were his brothers, Edward, Alexander, Thomas, and Neil, his sisters Christina, Isabel
(Queen of Norway), Margaret, Matilda, and Mary, and his nephews Donald II, Earl of Mar and Thomas Randolph, 1st Earl of Moray.
In addition to his legitimate offspring, Robert Bruce had several illegitimate children by unknown mothers. His sons were:

Sir Robert (died 12 August 1332 at the Battle of Dupplin Moor);

Walter, of Odistoun on the Clyde, who predeceased his father;

Niall, of Carrick, (died 17 October 1346 at the Battle of Neville's Cross).

David II, who, as an infant, succeeded his father to the throne.

His daughters were;

Elizabeth (married Walter Oliphant of Gask);

Margaret (married Robert Glen), alive as of 29 February 1364;

Christian of Carrick, who died after 1329, when she was in receipt of a pension.

Robert's only child by his first marriage, Marjorie Bruce, married Walter Stewart, 6th High Steward of Scotland (1293–1326). She died on 2 March 1316, near Paisley, Renfrewshire, after being thrown from her horse while heavily pregnant, but the child survived. He was Robert II, who succeeded David II and founded the Stewart dynasty.

Bruce's descendants include all later Scottish monarchs (except Edward Balliol whose claim to be a Scottish monarch is debatable) and all British monarchs since the Union of the Crowns in 1603. A large number of families definitely are descended from him [28] but there is controversy about some claims.[29]

Ancestry

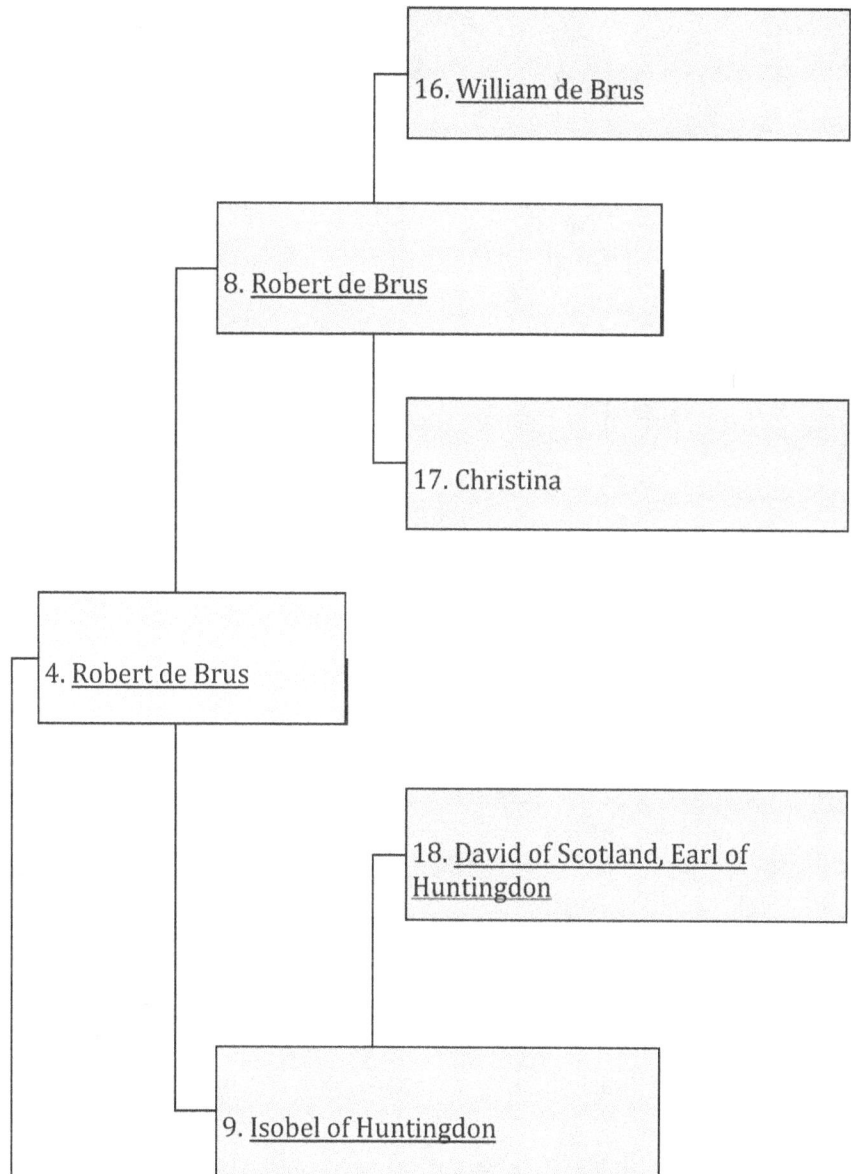

16. William de Brus

8. Robert de Brus

17. Christina

4. Robert de Brus

18. David of Scotland, Earl of Huntingdon

9. Isobel of Huntingdon

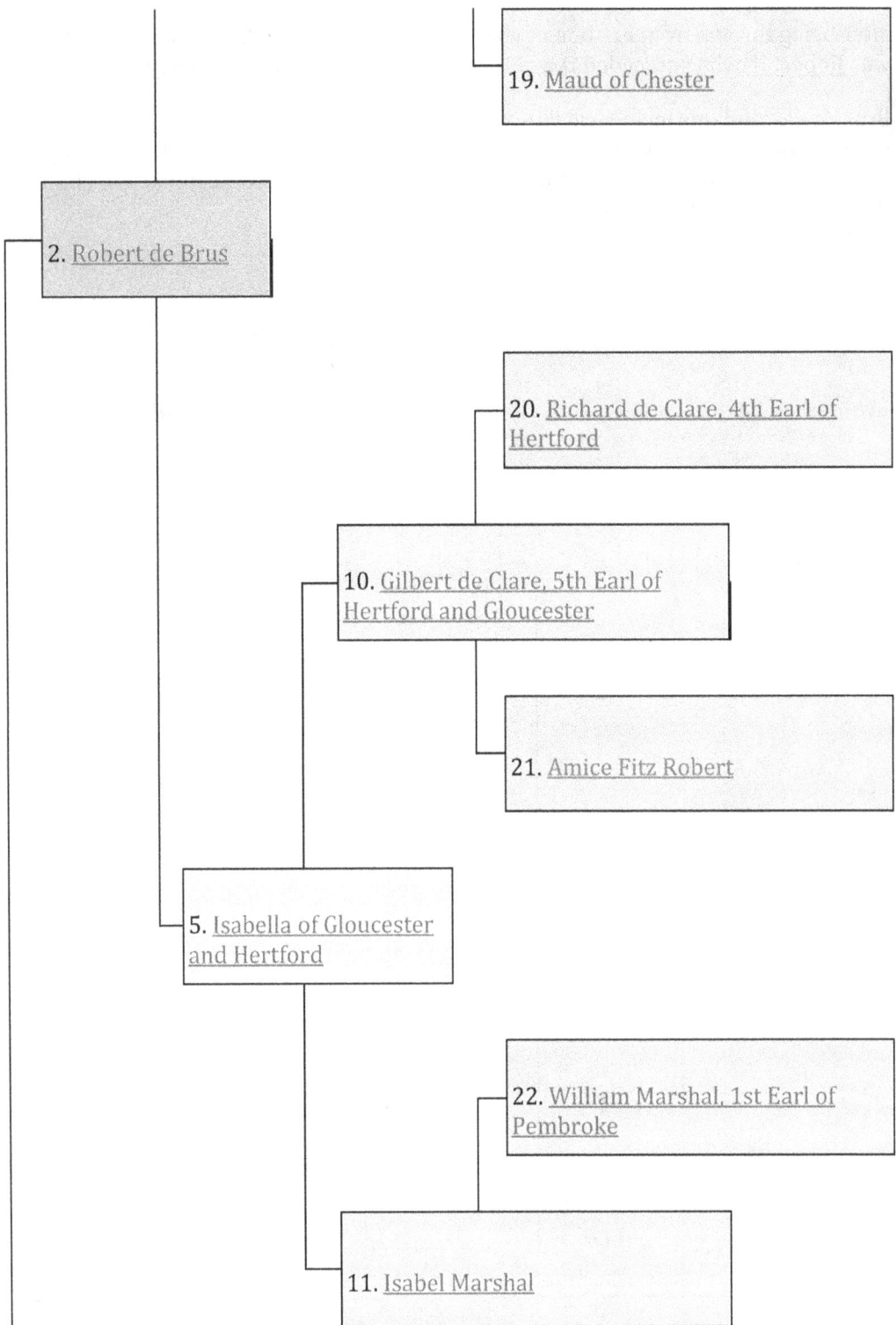

19. Maud of Chester

2. Robert de Brus

20. Richard de Clare, 4th Earl of Hertford

10. Gilbert de Clare, 5th Earl of Hertford and Gloucester

21. Amice Fitz Robert

5. Isabella of Gloucester and Hertford

22. William Marshal, 1st Earl of Pembroke

11. Isabel Marshal

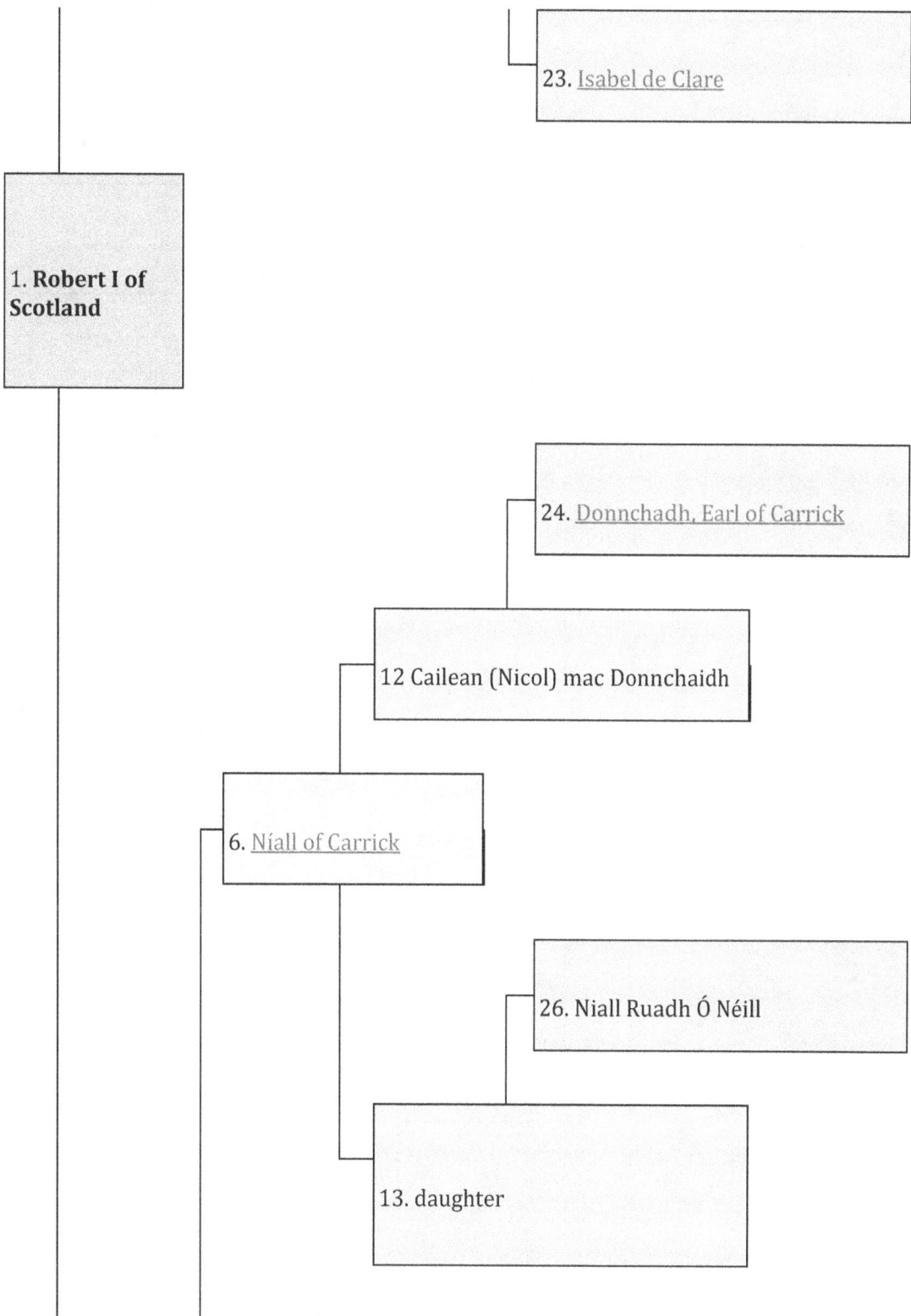

23. Isabel de Clare

1. **Robert I of Scotland**

24. Donnchadh, Earl of Carrick

12 Cailean (Nicol) mac Donnchaidh

6. Níall of Carrick

26. Niall Ruadh Ó Néill

13. daughter

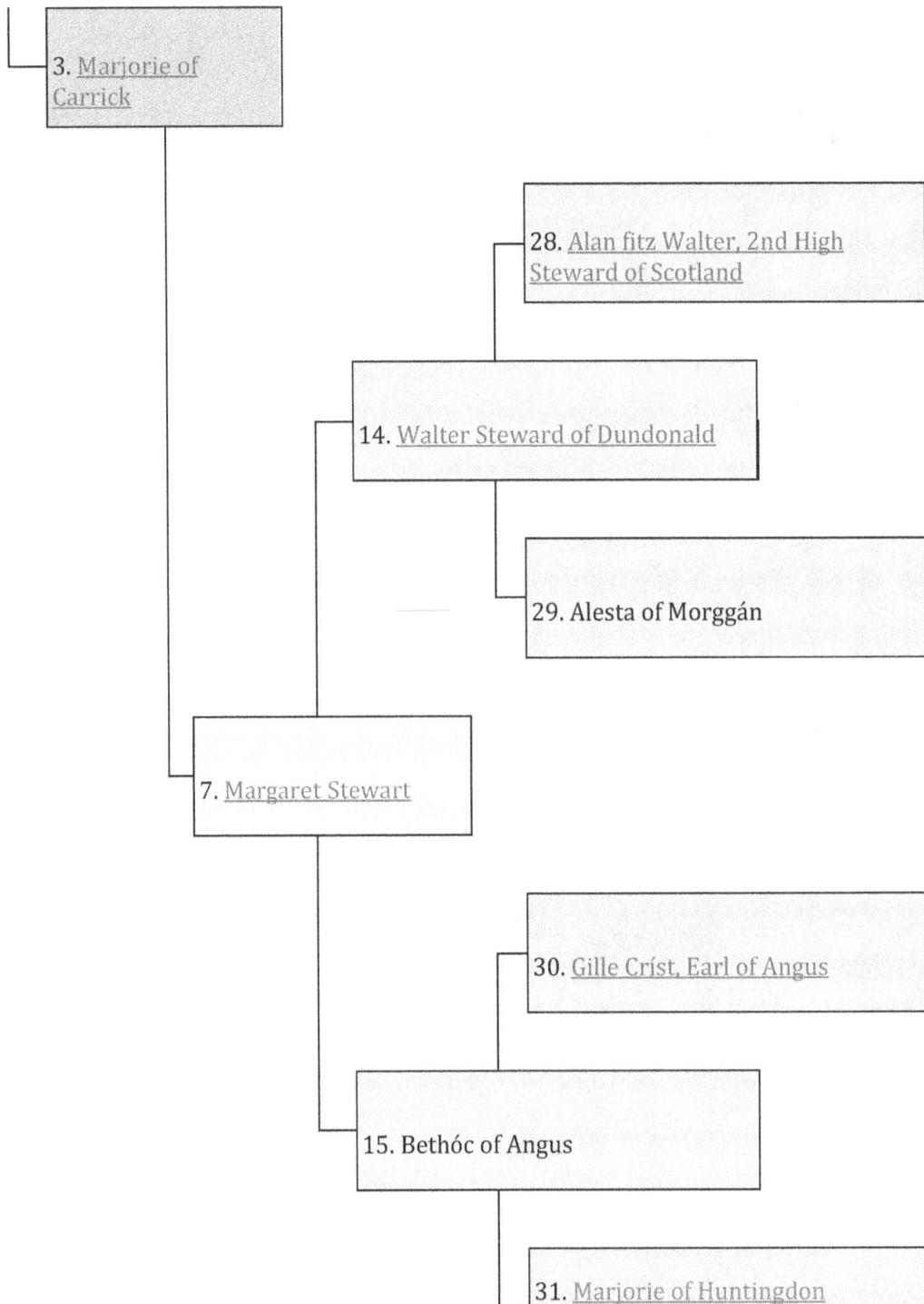

3. Marjorie of Carrick

28. Alan fitz Walter, 2nd High Steward of Scotland

14. Walter Steward of Dundonald

29. Alesta of Morggán

7. Margaret Stewart

30. Gille Críst, Earl of Angus

15. Bethóc of Angus

31. Marjorie of Huntingdon

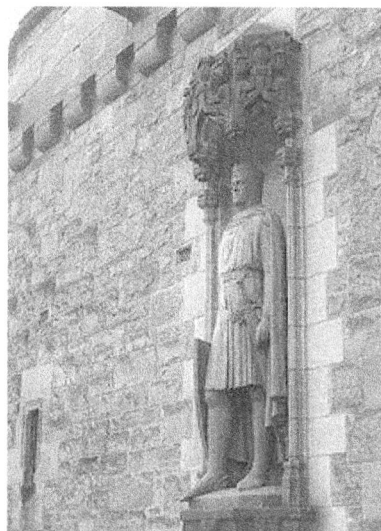

Statue of Robert the Bruce   Robert The Bruce at the entrance to Edinburgh Castle

The tomb of Robert I in Dunfermline Abbey was marked by the addition of large carved stone letters spelling out "King Robert the Bruce" around the perimeter of the bell tower. In 1974 the Bruce Memorial Window was installed in the north transept, commemorating the 700th anniversary the year of his birth. It depicts stained glass images of the Bruce flanked by his chief men, Christ, and saints associated with Scotland.[30]

A 1929 statue of Robert the Bruce is set in the wall of Edinburgh Castle at the entrance, along with one of William Wallace.

A statue of the Bruces stands outside Stirling Castle.

Banknotes

From 1981 to 1989, Robert the Bruce was portrayed on £1 notes issued by the Clydesdale Bank, one of the three Scottish banks with right to issue banknotes. He was shown on the obverse crowned in battle dress, surrounded by thistles, and on the reverse in full battle armour in a scene from the Battle of Bannockburn.[31] When the Clydesdale Bank discontinued £1 banknotes, Robert The Bruce's portrait was moved onto the bank's £20 banknote in 1990 and it has remained there to date.[32]

Aircraft

The airline <u>British Caledonian</u>, named a <u>McDonnell Douglas DC-10-30</u> (G-BHDI) after Robert the Bruce.[33]

Legends

According to a legend, at some point while he was on the run during the winter of 1305–06, Bruce hid himself in a cave on <u>Rathlin Island</u> off the north coast of Ireland, where he observed a spider spinning a web, trying to make a connection from one area of the cave's roof to another. Each time the spider failed, it simply started all over again until it succeeded. Inspired by this, Bruce returned to inflict a series of defeats on the English, thus winning him more supporters and eventual victory. The story serves to explain the maxim: "if at first you don't succeed, try try again." Other versions have Bruce in a small house watching the spider try to make its connection between two roof beams [2]; or, defeated for the seventh time by the English, watching the spider make its attempt seven times, succeeding on the eighth try[citation needed].

But this legend appears for the first time in only a much later account, "Tales of a Grandfather" by <u>Sir Walter Scott</u>, and may have originally been told about his companion-in-arms Sir <u>James Douglas</u> (the "Black Douglas"). The entire account may in fact be a version of a literary <u>trope</u> used in royal biographical writing. A similar story is told, for example, in Jewish sources about <u>King David</u>, and in Persian folklore about the Mongolian warlord <u>Tamerlane</u> and an ant.[34]

The Bruce in Fiction

The revolt of Robert the Bruce is the topic of <u>Mollie Hunter</u>'s 1998 book *The King's Swift Rider*, written from the point of view of a bold young Scot and future monk who joins the rebellion as a noncombatant.

In the 1995 film <u>*Braveheart*</u>, Robert the Bruce is portrayed by Scottish actor <u>Angus Macfadyen</u>. The film incorrectly showed him taking the field at <u>Falkirk</u> as part of the English army; he never betrayed <u>William Wallace</u> (despite having changed sides). Wallace is also alleged to have been a complete supporter of Robert the Bruce, but Wallace was a supporter of the Balliol claim to the throne which Bruce consistently opposed.

Scottish author <u>Nigel Tranter</u> wrote a trilogy, considered largely accurate, based on the life of King Robert: *Robert the Bruce: The Steps to the Empty Throne*; *Robert the Bruce: The Path of the Hero King*; and *Robert the Bruce: The Price of the King's Peace*. This has also been published in one volume as <u>*The Bruce Trilogy*</u>.

Chronicles of the reign of Robert the Bruce (or Robert de Brus) are published in a series titled *Rebel King, Hammer of the Scots* (2002); *Rebel King, The Har'ships* (2004); and *Rebel King, Bannok Burn* (2006). Two more volumes are planned. Historical fiction, but very close to Scottish history, this most comprehensive series on Robert's reign starts in January 1306 and will carry through Robert's death in 1329.

Katherine Kurtz and Deborah Turner Harris wrote a fantasy fiction series (*The Temple and the Stone* and *The Temple and the Crown*) linking Robert the Bruce with the Knights Templar.

The 1996 concept album of the German power metal band Grave Digger, Tunes of War includes a song named The Bruce.The whole album is about the Scottish struggles for independence from England.

The third volume of Jack Whyte's Templar Trilogy called "Order in Chaos" is largely set in Scotland during the rise of The Bruce. It winds up its story just after the battle at Bannockburn. It covers a lot of the challenges and politics of that era.

Notes

1 *a* *b* Robert's absolution for Comyn's murder, in 1310, gives Robert as a layman of Carrick, indicating Carrick / Turnberry was either his primary residence, or place of birth. Lochmaben has a claim, as a possession of the Bruce family, but is not supported by a medieval source. The contemporary claims of Essex / the Bruce estate at Writtle Essex, during the coronation of Edward, have been discounted by G. W. S. Barrow.

2 Robert The Bruce. Publisher: Heinemann. ISBN 0-431-05883-0

3 "Robert the Bruce's family was Norman, and can be traced back to Brieux in Orne, France".

4 *a* *b* G. W. S. Barrow,Robert Bruce: and the community of the realm of Scotland (4th edition ed.), p. 34 :- "This was indeed a marriage of Celtic with Anglo-Norman Scotland, though hardly in the protagonists themselves, since Majorie was descended from Henry I, her husband from Malcom Canmore. But Annandale was settled by people of English, or Anglo-Scandinavian speech, and thoroughly feudalized. Carrick was historically an integral part of Galloway, and though the earls had achieved some feudalization, the society of Carrick at the end of the 13th century remained emphatically Celtic."

5 Magna Carta Ancestry: A Study in Colonial and Medieval Families By Douglas Richardson, Kimball G. Everingham

6 King Robert the Bruce By A. F. Murison

7 Geoffrey le Baker's: Chronicon Galfridi le Baker de Swynebroke, ed. Edward Maunde Thompson (Oxford, 1889)

8 Scottish Kings 1005 – 1625, by Sir Archibald H Dunbar, Bt., Edinburgh, 1899, p.127, where Robert the Bruce's birthplace is given "at Writtle, near Chelmsford in Essex, on the 11th July 1274". Baker, cited above, is also mentioned with other authorities.

9 Scott, Robert the Bruce, p 29.

10 Fordun, Scotichronicon, p 309

11 Scott, Robert the Bruce, p 72.

12 Fordun, Scotichronicon, p 330; Barbour, The Bruce, p 13.

13 Ronald McNair Scott (1988). Robert the Bruce, King of Scots. Canongate: p.72

14 Barbour, The Bruce, p 15.

15 http://www.undiscoveredscotland.co.uk/dumfries/dumfries/

16 Scott, Robert the Bruce, p 74

17 The History Channel 17 May 2006

18 Scott, Robert the Bruce, p 75

19 Scott, RonaldMcNair, Robert the Bruce, pp 84–

85 **20** Scott, Robert the Bruce, pp 84–85.

21 Barrow, Geoffrey Wallis Stuart (2005). *Robert Bruce : and the community of the realm of Scotland* (4th edition ed.). Edinburgh University Press. ISBN 0748620222.. (Retrieved from Google Books)

22 Remonstrance of the Irish Chiefs to Pope John XXII, p.46

23 The Annals of Connacht

24 The exact location is uncertain and it may not have been very near the modern village of Cardross, although it was probably in Cardross Parish. Barrow suggests that it was at present-day Mains of Cardross farm on the outskirts of Dumbarton, beside the River Leven. [1]

25 Kaufman MH, MacLennan WJ (2001-04-01). "Robert the Bruce and Leprosy". *History of Dentistry Research Newsletter*. http://www.rcpsg.ac.uk/hdrg/April015.htm. Retrieved 2010-02-28.

26 *a b* Burial Honors Robert the Bruce

27 "Melrose Abbey". news.bbc.co.uk. http://www.bbc.co.uk/history/scottishhistory/earlychurch/trails_earlychurch_melroseabbey.shtml. Retrieved 2008-06-20.

28 Lauder-Frost, Gregory, FSA Scot,Darr *Some Descendants of Robert the Bruce*, in *The Scottish Genealogist*, vol. LI, No.2, June 2004: 49–58, ISSN 0300-337X

29 John McCain, veteran war hero: yes. But a descendant of Robert the Bruce? Baloney

30 "Dunfermline Abbey History". The Church of Scotland.
http://www.dunfermlineabbey.co.uk/index.php?ID=1853&CATEGORY=4-History. Retrieved 2008-10-20.

31 "Clydesdale 1 Pound obverse, 1982". Ron Wise's Banknoteworld.
http://aes.iupui.edu/rwise/banknotes/scotland/ScotlandP211a-1Pound-1982-donatedJRT_f.jpg. Retrieved 2008-10-20.; "Clydesdale 1 Pound reverse, 1982". Ron Wise's Banknoteworld. http://aes.iupui.edu/rwise/banknotes/scotland/ScotlandP211a-1Pound-1982-donatedJRT_b.jpg. Retrieved 2008-10-20.

32 "Current Banknotes : Clydesdale Bank". The Committee of Scottish Clearing Bankers. http://www.scotbanks.org.uk/banknotes_current_clydesdale_bank.php. Retrieved 2008-10-20.

33 "McDonnell Douglas DC-10-30 aircraft". Airliners.net.
http://www.airliners.net/photo/British-Caledonian/McDonnell-Douglas-DC-10-30/0920403/L/. Retrieved 2008-10-20.

34 silkroaddestinations.com – Uzbekistan, Shakhrisabz

References

Barrow, G. W. S. (1998), *Robert Bruce & the Community of the Realm of Scotland*, Edinburgh: Edinburgh University Press, ISBN 0852245394.

Bartlett, Robert (1993), *The Making of Europe, Conquest, Colonization and Cultural Change: 950–1350*, Princeton: Princeton University Press, ISBN 069103298X.

Bingham, Charlotte (1998), *Robert the Bruce*, London: Constable, ISBN 0094764409.

Brown, Chris (2004), *Robert the Bruce. A Life Chronicled*, Stroud: Tempus, ISBN 0752425757.

Brown, Chris (2008), *Bannockburn 1314*, Stroud: History, ISBN 9780752446004.

Dunbar, Archibald H. (1899), *Scottish Kings 1005–1625*, Edinburgh: D. Douglas, pp. 126–141, with copious original source matériéls.

Loudoun, Darren (2007), *Scotlands Brave*.

Macnamee, Colm (2006), *The Wars of the Bruces: England and Ireland 1306–1328*, Edinburgh: Donald, ISBN 9780859766531.

Oxford Dictionary of National Biography,
http://www.oxforddnb.com/public/dnb/3754.html.

Ó Néill, Domhnall (1317), "Remonstrance of the Irish Chiefs to Pope John XXII",
CELT archive, http://www.ucc.ie/celt/published/T310000-001/.

Nicholson, R., *Scotland in the Later Middle Ages*.

Geoffrey the Baker's: Chronicon Galfridi le Baker de Swynebroke, ed. Edward
Maunde Thompson (Oxford, 1889).

H. A. L. Fisher in his book "James Bryce" states Bryce is possibly a corruption of Bruce. The
Coats of Arms of the Brice, Bryce and Bruce families are almost identical. The one now
used by the Brice family is: a gold shield(OR) with a saltire cross of red (gules), also a chief
of red erect proper grasping a scimeter argent. The motto is "Do Well Doubt Nought."
This Coat of Arms was copied from the tomb of the Rev. Edward Brice and as described has
not been located in any books on Heraldry; however, several are practically the same.
These along with the Bruce families are given here to show more clearly the similarity of
the names.

ARMS: Or, on a saltire gules, a thistle slipped proper, on a chief of the second a maple-leaf between two shamrocks, also proper

CREST: On a wreath of the colours, a lion rampant azure, charged on the shoulder with a maple-leaf, and holding between the paws a caduces or

MOTTO: "Faimus" (we have been)

Bruce (Variation 2)

(2)

ARMS: Or a saltire and chief gules, in the dexter canton an escutcheon arg. Charged with a chief sable

CREST: On a cap of dignity, an arm from the shoulder couped fesswise holding a scepter ensigned on the point with an open crown as that worn by Robert I of Scotland, all proper

SUPPORTERS: Dexter, a knight in armour, the vizor open and a plume of feathers in his helmet, holding a scepter in his right hand, all proper; sinster, a lion rampant azure, aramed and langued gules, crowned with the crown of Robert I and gorged with that of David II, chained with an antique chain, or

MOTTOS: Over the crest – "Fuimus" (we have been); under the shield – "Do well and doubt not"

CREATION: Bt. (NS) 29 September 1628

DO WELL DO VBT NOUGHT

NEARE THIS LYETH THE BODY OF
THAT FAITHFVLL ⅁ EMENENT SER=
VANT OF GOD Mr EDWARD BRICE WHO
BEGVN PREACHING OF THE GOSPELE
IN THIS PARISH 1613 CONTINVEING
WITH QUIET SVCCES WHILE 1636
IN Wᴴ HE DYED AGED 67 ⅁ LEFT
TWO SONS ⅁ TWO DAVGHTERS
HIS SON ROBERT BRICE ESQʳ AF=
TER ACQVIREING A FORTVNE DYED
IN DVBLIN 22 OF NOVᴇʳ 1670
AGED 63 ⅁ LEFT 3 SONS ⅁ 3 DAV=
GHTERS. HIS ELDEST SON RONDALL
BRICE ESQˢ DYED IN DVBLIN A MEM=
BER OF PARLEAMENT FOR LISBVRNE
18 OF SEPᴇʳ 1697 AGED 51 ⅁ LEFT
TWO SONS ⅁ TWO DAUGHTERS

Templecorran Cemetery

This old cemetery at Ballycarry includes the ruins of Ireland's first Presbyterian Church within its boundaries, as well as the grave of the first Presbyterian minister in Ireland, Rev. Edward Brice, who died in 1636. Some 50 graves of general historical note are marked as part of the Templecorran Cemetery Project and guided tours for groups can be arranged by the Ballycarry Community Association.

Ballycarry (from the Irish: *Baile Cora*, Ulster Scots: *Braid Islann*) is a village in County Antrim, Northern Ireland. It is situated midway between Larne and Carrickfergus overlooking Islandmagee. It is within the Larne Borough Council area. In the 2001 Census it had a population of 981 people.

Burke's Encyclopedia of Heraldry gives Brice; alias Bruce (Kilroot, Ireland; confirmed at the Lyon office, Edinburgh, 10 June 1693) OR, a saltire gules, within a bordure wavy of the last; on a chief of the second a mullet in the dexter chief point of the first. Crest: a cubic arm erect proper grasping a scimeter argent hilt & pommel argent (no motto). In Burke's General Armory we find: Bruce: of Airth & Stenhouse County Stirling, bart, 1629. OR a saltire and chief gules in the dexter chief point a shield argent and chief sable. Crest: cap of maintenance, a dexter arm armed from the shoulder resting on the elbow and holding in the hand a scepter all proper. Motto: Fuimus and Do Well Doubt Nought. Of this grant Burke's Encyclopedia says: This branch is descended from Bruce of Stenhous, a younger son of Robert Bruce of Airth, and now represented by Sir Michael Bruce, bart. This edition says the scepter of the crest is ensigned on the point with an open crown as that worn by Robert First of Scotland. The supporters are: on the right a knight in armor with a sword by his side, a plume of feathers in his helmet, visor open etc., holding in his hand a scepter; on the sinister the supporter is a lion rampart proper armed and langued gules crowned with Robert First's crown and gorged with David Second's chain and with an antique chain OR. Mottoes: Fuimus and Do Well Doubt Noughtt. Fairbairne in his book "Family Crests" gives: Bryce (Scotland) a dexter arm holding in the hand a cutlass proper. Motto: Do Well, Doubt Nought; also Bruce (Samuel, Esquire of Norton Hall, Camden, Glouc.) a horse's head couped argent. Motto: Do Well and Doubt Nough; Brice (Ireland) a cubic arm erect proper grasping a scimeter argent, hilt & pommel OR (no motto). Brice (Ireland) an arm holding a cutlass, all proper. Motto: Do Well and Doubt Nought. Burke's Encyclopedia of Heraldry gives Bruce (Kennet, founded by Thomas De Bruys, of Kennet, brother of David Bruce of Clackmannon, who succeeded in 1405, now represented by Robert Bruce of Kennet, Esq.) OR a saltire and chief gules, the last charged with a mullet argent. Crest: a hand holding a scepter proper. Motto: Fuimus.

From the above descriptions, it appears that the names Brice, Bryce and Bruce had their beginning in Scotland from the name De Bruys. At any rate, a family evidently strong in moral and physical strength, fortitude, and courage has made its way from Scotland via Ireland to South Carolina. Three brothers John, James, and William Brice, sons of William and Jane McClure Brice of County Antrim, Ireland, landed in Charleston and made their way to what is now Fairfield County. These brothers were direct descendants of the famous Rev. Edward Brice of Scotland who emigrated to County Antrim, Ireland.

Rev. Edward Brice

He was born at Airth, Stirlingshire, about 1569, and is named Bryce in the Scottish records, but Brice in the Irish records. He entered Edinburgh University about 1589, and studied under Charles Ferme (or Fairholm). He laureated 12 August 1593. On 30 December 1595 he was admitted by the Stirling presbytery to the parochial charge of Bothkenner. He was translated to Drymen on 14 May 1602, and admitted on 30 September by the Dumbarton presbytery.

At the synod of Glasgow on 18 August 1607 he bitterly opposed the appointment of John Spottiswoode as permanent moderator, in accordance with the king's recommendation, adopted by the general assembly at Linlithgow on 10 December 1606. On 29 December 1613 Archbishop Spottiswoode and the presbytery of Glasgow deposed him for adultery. Robert Echlin, bishop of Down and Connor then gave Brice the cure of Templecorran (otherwise known as Ballycarry or Broadisland) in County Antrim in 1613 (may be 1614, New Style. William Edmunstone, laird of Duntreath, Stirlingshire, who had joined in the plantation of the Ards, County Down, in 1606, was now at Broadisland, having obtained a perpetual lease of on lands there on 28 May 1609.

The tradition is that Brice preached alternately at Templecorran and Ballykeel, Islandmagee. In September 1619 Echlin conferred on him the prebend of Kilroot. The *Ulster Visitation* of 1622 says that Brice 'serveth the cures of Templecorran and Kilroot—church at Kilroot decayed—that at Ballycarry has the walls newly erected, but not roofed.' In 1629 Brice is described as aged man and in 1630, when present on a communion Sunday at Templepatrick, he was unable to preach as appointed. Henry Calvert (or Colwort), an Englishman, was brought in by Lady Duntreath of Broadisland, as assistant to Brice; in June 1630 Calvert became minister of Muckamore (or Oldstone), County Antrim.

On Echlin's death, 17 July 1635, Henry Leslie succeeded as bishop, and held his primary visitation at Lisburn in July 1636, and requiring subscription from all the clergy. Brice and Calvert were among the five who refused compliance, two others being James Hamilton and John Ridge.[1] A private conference produced no result, and though on 11 August Leslie made concessions on the conduct of services, the subscription was still refused. Accordingly on 12 August sentence of perpetual silence within the diocese was passed, Brice, probably as the oldest, being sentenced first. Brice died soon after, and the presbyterians appointed no regular successor to him till 1646. His tombstone at the ruined church of Ballycarry says that he died, aged 67, and left two sons and two daughters. His eldest son, Robert, acquired a fortune at Castlechester, then the point of departure for the Scottish mail; pennies are extant with his name, dated Castlechester, 1671.

Notes

Dictionary of National Biography articles for Hamilton and Ridge.

This article incorporates text from the entry **Brice, Edward** *in the* Dictionary of National Biography *(1885–1900), a publication now in the* public domain.

Rev. Edward Brice, the first Presbyterian minister in Ireland, came to Ballycarry in 1613 and ministered in the Templecorran Church, now in ruins. He was originally from Stirlingshire in Scotland and was brought to the village by William Edmondstone, who settled there in 1609. Brice was one of several Scottish clergymen who were forbidden to preach by the Established Church authorities in the 1630s.

Ballycarry (from the Irish: *Baile Cora*, Ulster Scots: *Braid Islann*) is a village in County Antrim, Northern Ireland. It is situated midway between Larne and Carrickfergus overlooking Islandmagee. It is within the Larne Borough Council area. In the 2001 Census it had a population of 981 people.

The life of Edward Brice is described by Rev. Samuel D. Alexander in his book "History of the Presbyterian Church in Ireland" which was condensed from the standard work of Reid and Killen. In writing of the large number of newcomers to northern Ireland, the author says, "Among these better emigrants were several ministers from England and Scotland, who may be regarded as the founders of the Presbyterian church in Ireland. The first of these, in point of time, was Edward Brice, for many years minister of Drymen, in Sterlingshire; but having steadily opposed the proposition to make Archbishop Spotswood permanent moderator of the Synod of Clydesdake, he was soon obliged to leave his church and country, and settled near his old friend and neighbor William Edmonstone in the district of Broadisland, in the county of Antrim. He was admitted by Bishop Echlin, of Down, himself a Scotchman, and afterwards raised to the nominal rank of a prebendary, but without relinquishing his prior settlement or his former mode of preaching, which is described by Livingston as dwelling chiefly on "the life of Christ in the heart and the light of His Word and Spirit on the mind."

"Upon the visitation of Bishop Leslie at Lisburn in July 1636, according to the command of the convocation, he called upon his clergy to subscribe to the Catholic canons (rituals and beliefs). Five of the ministers refused, viz: Brice of Broadisland, Ridge of Antrim, Cunningham of Holywood, Colvert of Oldston, and Hamilton of Ballywalter. The Bishop, not wishing to lose these faithful men, held a private conference with them, hoping to induce them to conform to the canons, but failing in this, at the suggestion of Bishop Bramhall, he summoned his clergy at Belfast on the 10th of August, and opened the visitation by preaching from the ominous text: But if he neglect to hear the church, let him be unto thee as a heathen and a publican." Matt. XV: 1-17.

"Leslie having concluded his discourse, the five non-conforming ministers were called forward; and the Bishop, complaining that he had been misrepresented in a former private conference with them, proposed to debate the matter publicly on the next day, which was at once accepted, and Hamilton was appointed to conduct it in their name. It was accordingly begun before a large assembly of nobility and gentry and clergy of the diocese. It was conducted in the form of syllogistic reasoning, in which Hamilton displayed great readiness and acuteness, and the Bishop more moderation than could have been expected from his sermon; but, as it too often happens in public debates, the controversy merged into the discussion of some of the less important points of difference. The discussion was interrupted by Bramhall on account of the liberty allowed the minister, and Leslie adjourned it until the next day; but at the suggestion of the Bishop of Derry, it was not resumed, but at the time appointed, the brethren refusing to subscribe to the canons, received their sentences of deposition.

"Those severe proceedings hastened the intended voyage to New England, and the midst of their preparations Brice of Broadisland, one of the deposed ministers, departed his life. The number proposing to sail was one hundred and forty.

"These seven Englishmen and Scotchmen were the pioneers of evangelical religion in the north of Ireland, and began those labors which resulted in a general awakening and conversion and the ultimate foundation of the Presbyterian church in Ulster."

Since the Brice record in Ireland as listed by Dr. Herron is not complete and since Rev. Samuel D. Alexander in "History of the Presbyterian Church in Ireland" states that one hundred forty people intended to sail for New England when Rev. Edward Brice of Broadisland died (1636), we can assume that members of this Brice family came to America before the three brothers arrived in Fairfield County, South Carolina. No doubt this accounts for Brices and Bryces found in New York, Pennsylvania, Maryland, Virginia and other states during the early development of the United States. In all probability some members of these other families have records of their Brice ancestry.

Additional information on the Brice family in Ireland is found in the "History of Carrickfergus," new edition by Mrs. McCrum, Belfast, 1909. This author states, "Rev. Edward Brice, Presbyterian minister of Drimen, was obliged to flee from Scotland for opposing John Spotswood (Catholic church), Bishop of Glascow, who had been appointed moderator of the Synod of Clydesdale. About 1611 he settled in the parish of Templecoran, alias Broadisland, preaching there and in the church of Ballyheild, Island Magee, alternately. August 12th, 1636, he was deposed in Belfast by Henry Lesly, Bishop of Down, for refusing to conform to the canonical forms of Episcopacy. He died in the same year, aged 67, leaving two sons and two daughters.

"His eldest son Robert, resided at Castle Chichester. In November 1676, he died in Dublin, aged 63. By his wife Elizabeth, who died January, 1704, he had three sons and three daughters, one of whom was married to Thomas Knox, the first of the Northland family, who came to Ireland. Hugh, son of Robert, died 1687, aged 24. In 1675, his brother Rondall was High Sheriff of County Antrim and in 1692 was one of the representatives for the borough of Lisburn.   In September 1697, he died in Dublin, leaving two sons and two daughters. An Edward Brice, who is alleged to also have been a son of Robert, was a Colonel in the army and settled in Belfast, where he died at an advanced age, June 28, 1726.

"About 1720, a Captain Charles Brice resided at Castle Chichester. He is said to have married a Miss Curry by whom he had three sons viz: Edward, Robert, and Arthur, and two daughters, one of whom married a Mr. Ennis of Dromantine, County Down. Charles is reported to have died about 1746. Edward married Catherine, daughter of George Spaight, Carrickfergus, in September 1779. Their daughter, Prudence, was married to George Bateson of London. In 1761, Edward was surveyor of the port of Belfast and agent for the French prisoners kept in that town. He died in Castle Chichester July 1796. Robert enetered into the Royal Navy, was promoted to the rank of Admiral and was also created a Baronet. He married in England, Miss Kingsmill, by whom he obtained a large fortune on assuming her name, which name his brother Edward took soon after. Sir Robert died at Sidmonston, Hampshire, November 22, 1805, in his 75th year. He left no issue. Arthur was an officer in the guards and retained the name of Brice. Edward, who, it is presumed was the son of Rondall, married Jane, daughter of Richard Dobbs, by whom he had two sons, Edward and Alexander, and several daughters. He was High Sheriff of County Antrim. He died in 1742, aged 83. His son, Edward, in 1748, married first, Rose, daughter of A. Stewart, Ballingtoy, by whom he had the late Edward Brice and several other children. He married secondly, Dec. 1758, Jane Smith, alias Adair, daughter of William Adair, army agent in London, by whom he had several children, one of whom was married to Sir John Anstruther. He died in Old Bond Street, London, in 1804. Edward, who succeeded to the family estate, married Theodora, daughter of Thomas Mullins, afterwards created Lord Ventry. She died in Dublin in 1807, he died 1815, leaving four sons and four daughters.

"Henry Maxwell of Fennbroque, eldest son of Henry by Jane, a daughter of Robert Eckin, Bishop of Down and Connor, married for his second wife, Dorothy, daughter of Robert Brice of Kilroot, Esquire, by whom he had Robert, his heir; Edward, Colonel of the 67th regiment of foot; and one daughter, Margaret, married to James Adair of London; by whom she had James, one of his Majesty's Sergeants at Law, and the Recorder for the City of London. In 1831 Edward Brice of the above family, changed his name to that of Bruce. In 1823 died in London, aged 51, Sir Robert Kingsmill of Belfast, Esquire, by Catherine, daughter of George Spaight, Esquire. He succeeded his uncle, Sir Robert Kingsmill, the first Baronet, who died in 1805. The Earl of Donegall had been first elected, but was not approved of by the privy council. Willoughby Chaplin and Edward Brice then set up for mayor and both were returned but neither approved. A third election was then held by George Spaight, Deputy Recorder, at which Mr. Brice was returned by said return, which came to a trial on 23rd of November, but the council ruled Willoughby Chaplin continued."

Chichester Castle stood in the city of <u>Chichester, West Sussex</u>).[1] Shortly after the <u>Norman Conquest of England</u>, <u>Roger de Montgomerie, 1st Earl of Shrewsbury</u>, ordered the construction of a castle at Chichester. The castle at Chichester was one of 11 fortified sites to be established in Sussex before 1100. The Rape of Chichester, a subdivision of Sussex, was administered from the castle and was split off from the larger Rape of Arundel; a Rape was an administrative unit invented by the Normans.[2] Situated in the north-east corner of Chichester, the castle was protected by the city walls. As it was an urban castle inserted into a pre-existing settlement, buildings were probably cleared to make way for the castle. Chichester Castle was of timber construction; although some timber castles were rebuilt in stone, there is no evidence that this was the case at Chichester Castle.[3]

Although originally built by the Earl of Shrewsbury, the Earls of Sussex owned the castle in the period 1154–1176, after which it passed into possession of the Crown.[1] Early in the 13th century, Chichester Castle was used as a court and jail. Chichester and Oxford Castle were some of the earliest urban castles to be used for this purpose, but gradually most urban castles were also used in this way.[4] In 1216, the castle was captured by the French and recaptured by the English in the spring of 1217.[3] The same year, Henry III ordered the castle's destruction.[1] Between 1222 and 1269, Richard, 1st Earl of Cornwall, gave the site to the order of Greyfriars for them use as the site of a friary. The remains of the motte are still visible today in Priory Park;[3] the motte is protected as a Scheduled Monument.[1][5]

Soon after the Norman Conquest Earl Roger de Montgomery ordered the construction of a motte-and-bailey castle.

It was built in the north-east corner of the city, partly enclosed by the city wall and probably required the destruction of several properties already there.

The remains of the raised mound (motte) are still visible today in Priory Park. The keep was probably made of timber, as there is no reference to it being made of stone, and no evidence has been found.

In 1192, when King Richard was captured in Austria, we know that the castle was stored with barley, beans and bacon. This was probably in anticipation of a siege by the forces of Prince John, the King's brother.

In 1216 the castle briefly surrendered to the French, but the following Spring it was recaptured and demolished it to its foundations on the orders of King Henry III.

As some time between 1222 and 1269 the site of the castle was given by Richard, brother of King Henry, to the Franciscan Friars to build a new friary.

<u>Noviomagus Reginorum</u> – the Roman town of Chichester; the castle was situated in the northern part of the Roman military settlement.

Notes

^ *a b c d Chichester Castle*, Pastscape.org, http://www.pastscape.org/hob.aspx?hob_id=1386089, retrieved 21 May 2009

^ Jones (2003), p. 173.

^ *a b c* Chichester District Council, *Castle*, Chichester.gov.uk,

http://www.chichester.gov.uk/index.cfm?articleid=1940, retrieved 21 May 2009

^ Drage (1987), p. 127.

^ Chichester District Council, *Priory Park*, Chichester.gov.uk,

http://www.chichester.gov.uk/index.cfm?articleid=5724, retrieved 22 May 2009

Castler Chichester, Whitehead

Francis Joseph Bigger, M.R.I.A.

(From Belfast News-Letter, Saturday, October 21, 1922)

The only "relic of old decency" remaining at present in the popular and favourite water-place of Whitehead is Castle Chichester. It is not old as the pyramids of Egypt or the

Irish Round Towers go, but it is over 300 years since its hoary stones were first set up with mortar where Islandmagee joins the mainland. One, Moses Hill, a lieutenant in Sir Arthur Chichester's troop of horse, is credited with its construction, doubtless to maintain and confirm Chichester's new acquisition of the fertile slopes of Islandmagee, for the MacDonnell power was not entirely broken in the Glens nor their claims abated. Moses had suffered rout and defeat at their hands, and Chichester's brother had lost his head in the woods of Altfracken to a MacDonnell sword stroke, no matter how his alabaster effigy in Carrick's old church might look to the contrary. Sir Moses, as he became, thus exercised a careful discretion, little knowing that by so doing, he was helping to establish his race so firmly in Ulster that in future years the best of "the ransomed hills of Down" from Lagan water to Newry river were to be the heritage of the Marquis of Downshire, for a few generations at any rate, until they would fall back again into the hands of those who tilled them.

Sir Moses called his stronghold, Castle Chichester, after his chief, just as Chichester called his big mansion at Carrickfergus, Joymount, in honor of his commander Lord Mountjoy, as the great fort on the banks of Lough Neagh was also named. Charlemont was named after Sir Charles Blount, afterwards Lord Mountjoy, and we have other more recent similar appellations, such as Jennymount and Dollymount. This Islandmagee Castle was sometimes called the Marshalls Castle, Sir Moses Hill being Provost Marshall of Ulster. A manor was created and known as the Manor of Castle Chichester, including the lands of Portmuck, Islandmagee, Drumalis and Olderfleet. Some trade grew up around the Castle in the seventeenth century principally with Scotland, and mails were frequently dispatched to Portpatrick, on the coast of Galloway, and cattle shipped there for such commodities were more plentiful in Ulster. across The less legimate trade was carried to the caves and ports of Islandmagee and was as profitable, or more so, than the open ventures under the walls of Castle Chichester. The caves of Island-magee were well known to Sir Moses, for he had stampeded there to hide in safety for sometime, after the successful MacDonnell onslaught at Altfracken. Hill's cave is still known, and there are Hill's in Islandmagee at the present day, but the Magees were wiped out at the Gobbin Cliffs in 1641.

Sir William Brereton mentions having passed over from "the Portpatrick" to Island-magee in 1635, just as many thousands of Scotch settlers did for years and years of that century, to inhabit the fertile lands of Antrim and Down, and trade in the fast rising town of Belfast. Robert Brice occupied the Castle for sometime, being a prosperous trader with the land of his origin, issuing trade tokens in 1671 with the inscription "Robert Brice, Castle Chichester." He died in 1676, after adding to his wealth by a prosperous sojourn in Dublin, being succeeded by his son Hugh. Robert's father was the Rev. Edward Brice, the first Presbyterian minister of Ballycarry. He showed an easy aptitude, ably assisted by the education and upbringing of a comfortable manse, of meeting a situation of much promise, and adapting himself thoroughly to prosperous business activities. In 1720 Charles Brice was in the Castle, and the last Brice who resided, and died there in 1796, was Edward Brice, Surveyor of the Port of Belfast. Subsequently it was occupied as a coast guard station before it became what it is now, simply a feature of the landscape.

Tidbits

In 1581 a John Malone was Shrive of Dublin. He afterwards became Alderman. He had three daughters, one named Rose married John Brice, oldest son of John Brice, Alderman of Dublin.

From a book "James Bryce" we find "Middle of the seventeenth century in Cambuslang, Lanarkshire, one Robert Bryce (the name is possibly a corruption of Bruce) whose son Archibald settled at Dechmont Hill, Lanarkshire, as a small laird owning his own land, there died in 1738 leaving among other children, a youngest son, John. He lived at Airdrie not far from Glasgow, was an Elder of the established church—married Robina, daughter of James Allen of Airdrie a wool miller of a family once affluent but impoverished in religious wars of 17th century. The issue was Rev. James Bryce—the grandfather of this subject. Rev. James Bryce married Catherine Annan of Auchtormuchty. Of their sons, Reuben John became head of the Belfast Academy then one of the foremost boy's schools in northern Ireland as well as Minister of a Presbyterian church in the city; Robert grew up to a well-known physician in Belfast, James became a distinguished geologist and mathematical master in Glasgow. William became a homeopathic physician of repute in Edinburgh, while Archibald Hamilton, youngest of the seven sons, lived to rule over the Edinburgh Collegiate School. The most eminent were Reuben John and James."

"The Personal Experiences of Mrs. Campbell Bryce During the Burning of Columbia, South Carolina by General W. T. Sherman's Army Feb. 17, 1865" was published in Philadelphia in 1899. There is a record of some of this family going to South America about the time of The War Between the States. Time has not permitted an investigation of this Bryce family.

Archaeology

Neolithic artefacts found in the village suggest ancient settlement, while the Lislaynan ecclesiastical settlement looks back to a thousand years of Christian witness. There was also a Norman settlement in the area, at Redhall, and at Brackenberg, now the centre of modern Ballycarry. An early Christian stone coffin lid which was uncovered at Redhall in the 18th century, was reinstated in the Templecorran cemetery and displays an early Christian cross engraved within an arc.

Community

The town is home to Ballycarry Presbyterian Church. Founded in 1613, Ballycarry is the oldest congregation in the Presbyterian Church in Ireland. The present church building dates from 1830. The Old Presbyterian (Non-Subscribing) Presbyterian Congregation also traces its roots back to 1613, and this congregation remained strongest in 1829 when the Presbyterian Church was split over the Subscription Controversy, the Non-Subscribers leaving open the issue of subscription to the Westminster Confession of Faith. The Old Presbyterian Church is located on the Main Street in the village. The most imposing church building is that of St. John's Parish Church, the Church of Ireland congregation, built in the 19th century by the Ker family of Redhall.

Ballycarry Community Association organises the Broadisland Gathering community festival held each year on the first Saturday in September and associated dates. The Gathering highlights the strong Ulster Scots heritage of the community and includes dancing, music, pipe bands, discussions, re-enactment, exhibitions and the Aul Kinntra Fair, revived from the 1930s but dating back to the 17th century. Chief guests at the Gathering have including Rt. Hon. Dr. John Reid, when Secretary of State for Northern Ireland.

Ballycarry has a vibrant community association, which succeeded in attracting funding for a modern community centre in the village in 2001. The Association includes representatives from all local groups in the village including the three local churches, sports clubs, fraternities and social groups. In 2009 many events are being held in Ballycarry to celebrate the 400th anniversary of the community being established in 1609.

The Settlement Story   This article was originally published in The Ulster-Scot

Part One   The Dawn of the Ulster-Scots

2006 will be a big year for Ulster-Scots. It's the 400th anniversary of one of the most important events in Ulster-Scots history - the Hamilton and Montgomery Settlement of 1606 - yet like much of our history, it's a story that hardly anyone knows about. The Ulster-Scots Agency aims to change that. Here's a summary of the story:

Before the Plantation of Ulster, two Ayrshire Scots - James Hamilton and Hugh Montgomery - pioneered a massive migration from the Lowlands of Scotland to County Antrim and County Down. Starting in May 1606, over ten thousand mainly Presbyterian Lowland Scots made the short voyage across the North Channel, transforming barren Ulster into an industrial powerhouse. Their success inspired King James VI of Scotland and 1 of England's Virginia Plantation of 1607 and his Ulster Plantation of 1610. Their achievement was "The Dawn of the Ulster-Scots".

The lands they came to had been devastated and depopulated by the wars of the late 1500s. Records say that Antrim and Down were "wasted". The owner of the lands, Con O'Neill, had been imprisoned in Carrickfergus Castle by the late Queen Elizabeth 1 and was probably destined for execution. So Hugh Montgomery hatched an elaborate plan to both free O'Neill and to gain a Royal pardon for him from the newly-crowned King James 1 (formerly King James VI of Scotland) - and Montgomery's payment was to be half of O'Neill's lands. However James Hamilton found out and intervened in the negotiations - and won one third of the lands for himself.

Hamilton was from Dunlop in Ayrshire, was an academic and had been a founder of Trinity College in Dublin. His new territory included the entire River Bann and the area around Coleraine, as well as a major part of County Down which took in Bangor, part of Comber, Killyleagh, Dundonald and some of the Ards Peninsula. Montgomery was the Sixth Laird of Braidstane and had been a mercenary in the wars in Holland. His new territory included

Newtownards, Donaghadee, part of Comber, Greyabbey and a large portion of the Ards Peninsula. Hamilton and Montgomery can rightly be called "The Founding Fathers of the Ulster Scots".

The thousands of settlers they brought over absolutely transformed the region. The success of their settlement in Antrim and Down must have reassured King James VI & 1 of his Plantation in Virginia (at Jamestown) in 1607, and without doubt inspired the Plantation of the rest of Ulster which started in 1610.

As our American cousins head towards their own "Jamestown 400" celebrations in 2007, it is right that Ulster-Scots celebrate the success of the Hamilton & Montgomery Settlement of 1606. The Agency will be co-ordinating a series of events, publications and initiatives during the New Year, so watch this space – and contact us to ask how you can get involved!   (This article was originally published in The Ulster-Scot, December 2005)

Part Two   Who were Hamilton and Montgomery?

Ayrshire - the birthplace of the Founding Fathers.   James Hamilton (1559 - 1644) and Hugh Montgomery (1560 - 1636), the Founding Fathers of the Ulster-Scots, were born in Ayrshire just as the Reformation took hold in Scotland. The Scots Confession was written in 1560 at the direction of the Scottish Parliament and was drawn up by John Knox and five other ministers inside four days. It was promptly ratified as the first confession of faith of the Reformed Church of Scotland.   Ayrshire, just across the North Channel from Co Antrim, had long been a hotbed of activity. "The Lollards of Kyle", followers of John Wycliffe, had been active there since the late 1400s. One of them - Murdoch Nisbet - had translated the New Testament into Scots and sought refuge from persecution, probably in Ulster, for around 10 years. Robert the Bruce, William Wallace and Robert Burns were all either born or spent time in the Kyle district of Ayrshire. And even though they were Ayrshire neighbours, James Hamilton and Hugh Montgomery could hardly have been more different.

James Hamilton - Minister's Son, Academic and Agent.

The Hamiltons had arrived in Scotland around 1215 AD - Roger de Hamilton found favour with the Scottish king Alexander II and married the daughter of the Earl of Strathern. Their son Gilbert married King Robert the Bruce's niece Isabella and obtained a grant for a barony in Lanarkshire. There he established the town called Hamilton which today has a population of around 50,000 people. The Hamiltons continued to have close links with the Scottish royal family for centuries to come.

Rev. Hans Hamilton (1536 - 1608) was the first Protestant minister in Dunlop, Ayrshire. Dunlop is in the East Ayrshire council district, and if you visit the historic Main Street today you can still see his church, his mausoleum and also the significantly-named Clandeboye School buildings, all of which date from the early 1600s. He and his wife Jonet had six sons - James, Archibald, Gawin, John, William and Patrick - and one daughter, Jean.

Their eldest son, James Hamilton (1559 - 1644), was educated at St Andrews University where the first martyr of the Scottish Reformation, Patrick Hamilton, had been burned at the stake on February 29th 1528. Having built a reputation as "one of the greatest scholars and hopeful wits of his time", James became a teacher in Glasgow. Around 1587 he left Scotland by ship and due to storms unexpectedly arrived in Dublin. He decided to stay there and established a school, employing fellow Scot James Fullerton as his assistant. One of their pupils was the young James Ussher, who went on to become the Archbishop of Armagh, and who famously calculated that the first day of Biblical creation was Sunday 23 October 4004 BC! Fullerton and Ussher are buried alongside each other in Westminster Abbey in London.   In 1591, Queen Elizabeth 1 established Trinity College in Dublin, and the first Provost noted that Hamilton had "...a noble spirit... and learned head..." and persuaded the two Scots to become Fellows of the College. Hamilton was made Bursar there in 1598.

Both men were agents for King James VI of Scotland, providing him with information about Elizabeth 1's activities in Ireland, and perhaps even tampering with the mail to keep the King, and themselves, informed. They were so successful that they gave up their academic positions to take up appointments at the royal court. Hamilton was appointed Scottish agent to the English court of Elizabeth 1st, was involved in the negotiations for James VI's succession to the English throne, and eventually brought official news of Elizabeth's death to Scotland. Fullerton was knighted when King James VI of Scotland became King James 1 of England - at the Union of the Crowns - in 1603.

So James Hamilton had great influence with the new King James 1 - influence which he would soon use to gain lands in Ulster.

Hugh Montgomery – Aristocrat and Soldier

Roger de Montgomerie came to England from Normandy with William the Conqueror. His grandson, Robert, travelled to Scotland and became the First Laird of Eaglesham, Ayrshire, in 1106 and married Marjory, the daughter of Walter the Steward (of the House of Stewart). Over the following centuries the Montgomeries would also acquire the titles of Eglinton, Ardrossan, Coilsfield (Tarbolton), Annick Lodge (Kilwinning) and Skelmorlie(Largs).

In 1452 Robert Montgomerie acquired the title of first Laird of Braidstane, an area in   the bailliary of Kyle in Ayrshire. Braidstane is close to the small town of Beith in the North Ayrshire council district. Adam Montgomery was the Fifth Laird of Braidstane, and his son, Hugh Montgomery (1560 - 1636), was primarily an aristocrat and a soldier. He had been educated at Glasgow Colledge and went to France where he spent some time at the royal court. He then moved to Holland and became Captain of Foot of a Scottish Regiment, under William 1 of Orange-Nassau (King William III's great grandfather) fighting against the army of King Philip II of Spain – whose troops included an Englishman called Guy Fawkes!

When his father died, Hugh returned to Scotland to become the Sixth Laird of Braidstane and married Elizabeth Shaw, daughter of the Laird of Greenock. His fighting skills were used again when he became involved in the generations-old feud between the Montgomeries and the Cunninghams (led by the Earl of Glencairn). Hugh Montgomery claimed that one of the Cunninghams had insulted him, and challenged him to a duel, but Cunningham fled - first to London and then to Holland. Montgomery tracked him down to the Inner Court of the Palace at The Hague, drew his sword and with a single thrust aimed to kill him. Luckily for Cunningham, the sword hit the buckle of his belt and saved his life - but Montgomery, thinking he had killed Cunningham, put away his sword and while he was leaving the Palace was arrested and imprisoned in the Binnenhof.

Stationed there was a Scottish soldier - Sergeant Robert Montgomery - who came to visit Hugh in prison, and they came up with a jailbreak plan. Robert arrived at the prison dressed as a wealthy Laird with property in Scotland, to court the daughter of the prison Marshall in order to get the key to Hugh's cell. The plan was so successful that within a few days they were married in the prison, with Hugh Montgomery performing the ceremony according to Scottish law. The wedding guests had drunk so much wine that Hugh, Robert and his new wife were able to slip away unnoticed to a pre-arranged ship which took them to Leith, near Edinburgh.

Part Three Jailbreak, Rivalry and Plot!

The Union of the Crowns
   The Coronation of King James VI of Scotland as King James I of England on the 25th July 1603 brought huge change to the British Isles. The new King and his associates now had greater power at their disposal and could implement new policies across these islands. To understand the impact this was to have on life in Ulster we need to go back in time...

East Ulster: Waste and Desolate
For centuries east Ulster had been different from the rest of the Province. The Norman Lord, John de Courcy, arrived in Ulster in 1177 and the Earldom of Ulster (essentially counties Antrim, Down and part of County Londonderry) was established around 1205 with its headquarters at Carrickfergus Castle. 100 years later a branch of the O'Neills advanced from mid Ulster into south Antrim and north Down and laid claim to the areas known as Lower (North) Clandeboye, Upper (South) Clandeboye and the Great Ardes.   Throughout the 1500s Ulster was embroiled in conflict. Queen Elizabeth I intended to tame the Province by sending armies across the water to fight the Gaelic chieftains of the time. Yet these wars weren't as "black-and-white" as we might imagine today - for a variety of reasons some of those Gaelic chieftains became allies of the English.

Scorched Earth and Failed Settlements in Antrim & Down
   In County Down, Sir Brian Phelim O'Neill had been knighted in 1568 for his service to the Crown against Shane O'Neill - yet in 1571 Elizabeth granted a sizeable amount of Sir Brian's lands to Sir Thomas Smith, to settle the area with English gentlemen. Smith passed the opportunity on to his son of the same name, who shortly after was murdered by one of O'Neill's supporters. The Thomas Smith settlement scheme had failed.

By 1572 it was clear to O'Neill that he had fallen out of favour and he adopted a "scorched earth" policy, burning the major buildings - Grey Abbey, Movilla Abbey, Newtownards

Priory, Black Abbey, Holywood Priory and Comber Abbey - to prevent any incoming English army using them as garrisons. Subsequently, Elizabeth directed the Earl of Essex to sail to Ulster in 1573 with the lofty ambition of taking control of the lands from Belfast to Coleraine. Essex's campaign was brutal - he captured Sir Brian O'Neill and had him, his family, and their attendants executed in 1574. After yet another brutal massacre - on 26th July 1575 on Rathlin Island - Elizabeth brought Essex back to England. Essex's settlement plans had also failed.

Across the North Channel, King James VI of Scotland's own efforts at settlement had also been unsuccesful. He had tried to establish settlements of Lowland Scots in Kintyre and Lewis in 1598 but, under attack from the local clans, many of these settlers fled across the North Channel to seek refuge in County Antrim.

So, for the 34 years between 1572 and the beginning of the Hamilton and Montgomery Settlement of 1606, the east of Ulster was depopulated, wasted and desolate.

Con O'Neill's "Grand Debauch"

Sir Brian Phelim O'Neill's lands eventually passed to his son Niall in 1575 and were described by Sir Henry Sydney in that year as "...all waste and desolate...". Next they were passed on to Niall's son, Con Niall MacBrian Fertagh O'Neill. In 1586, Con signed his entire estates over to the Queen, who then re-granted them to him in 1587 for his "faithful services and allegiance". Con lived in the ancient Norman fortress Castle Reagh, also known as Castle Clannaboy, a massive structure 100 foot square, with turrets on the corners, dominating the Castlereagh Hills and overlooking what was then the small village of Belfast.

Around Christmas of 1602, Con held what has been described as "a grand debauch" at Castle Reagh, and when the wine ran out he sent his servants to Belfast for more. As they were returning they quarrelled with some of Sir Arthur Chichester's troops and had the wine confiscated. Con was furious and sent them back to attack the English soldiers, some of whom were killed in the skirmish. Con was arrested, found guilty of "levying war against the Queen" and was imprisoned in Carrickfergus Castle. Although the conditions of his imprisonment were later relaxed, and he was occasionally allowed to walk through Carrickfergus with a guard, he was ultimately destined for execution - Chichester having generously offered to hang him without trial.

The Carrickfergus Jailbreak

When Elizabeth I died and James VI of Scotland became James I of England, many in Ulster saw this new era as an opportunity. James, the first Stuart on the English throne, angered Chichester by regranting the Gaelic lords of west Ulster their lands; he also lost no time in granting the MacDonnells of North Antrim the territory of the Glens and the Route. James Hamilton and Hugh Montgomery were aware of the opportunities in Ulster and had influence with the new Scottish King. Their time would soon come.

Another who saw an opportunity was Ellis O'Neill, Con's wife. She made contact with Hugh Montgomery to see if he could use his influence with the new King to secure a Royal pardon for Con. If he succeeded, Hugh Montgomery's reward was to be half of Con's wasted lands in County Down. Montgomery agreed. Hugh Montgomery then entered into a plan with his Ayrshire neighbour, Thomas Montgomery of Blackstone, who is described in The Montgomery Manuscripts, the family records, as "...a discreet, sensible gentleman...". Thomas was owner of a ship (or 'sloop') which traded between Scotland and Carrickfergus, and he was to implement a jailbreak plan very similar to one Hugh had used to escape from Holland a few years before.

In July, 1604, Thomas arrived in Carrickfergus and noted the identity of the Provost Marshall, who was also the jailer of the town. He then courted the Provost's daughter, Annas Dobbin, in order to befriend her father. After an evening of well-planned drunken revelry in the Castle jail, Thomas got a rope to Con, possibly inside a hollowed-out cheese. Con escaped from his cell, used the rope to scale the castle wall, boarded the boat at the harbour below, and he and Montgomery fled to Scotland.

Arriving at the coastal town of Largs in Ayrshire, in the shadow of the Montgomery clan castle of Skelmorlie, they were met by a welcoming party led by Hugh's brother-in-law, Patrick Montgomery, and they all travelled to the castle home of Hugh Montgomery, the Sixth Laird of Braidstane. The Montgomery Manuscripts say that Con "...was joyfully and courteously received by the Laird and his Lady with their nearest friends. He was kindly entertained and treated with a due deference to his birth and quality, and observed with great respect by the Laird's children and servants..."

When the deal - a Royal pardon for O'Neill (with half of his lands going to Montgomery as a reward) - had been finalised at Braidstane, Con and Hugh travelled to London to win the King's approval.

James Hamilton Intervenes

But little did O'Neill and Montgomery realise what was about to happen. In August 1604 James Hamilton discovered their plan.

Hamilton's close associate, Sir James Fullerton, was an advisor to the King and had been granted Olderfleet Castle, near Larne, in September 1603. He convinced the King that O'Neill's lands were much too large to be split between O'Neill and Montgomery alone and that it would be better if they were divided into three portions - with one third for James Hamilton. The King agreed to the new plan; after all, settlement had never worked before and he had nothing to lose by allowing Hamilton and Montgomery to invest their own finance and energy in the wasteland of east Ulster. When O'Neill and Montgomery arrived in London, the King presented them with the new scheme. Montgomery, realising what had happened and no doubt outraged, kept his composure and agreed to the revised plan.

On 31st April, 1605, the tripartite deal was agreed, but Hamilton's actions seem to have united Montgomery and O'Neill for a time. Even though Con's life had been spared and his Royal Pardon had been granted, and Hugh Montgomery had secured substantial lands in County Down, they had both lost out on their original deal. The Hamilton Manuscripts, the Hamilton family's record of the settlement, state that O'Neill and Montgomery left London together, travelled back to Edinburgh and Braidstane, and then across to Ulster. Con returned to a hero's welcome in Castle Reagh.

Before leaving London, Montgomery had renewed his relationships with some of the King's advisors and in doing so created an opportunity for his brother George to benefit in some way. George had been made Dean of Norwich by Elizabeth I, and after her death he was appointed as King James' personal chaplain. Six weeks later, as a direct result of Hugh's influence on the Royal advisors, George Montgomery was made Bishop of Derry, Raphoe and Clogher on 13th June 1605 – the first Scottish bishop in Ireland. His portrait can be seen in Clogher Cathedral.

Hamilton, delighted by his own success, travelled to Dublin to present the outcome to Sir Arthur Chichester, "the most important Englishman in Ireland". Chichester was aghast at the amount of land which had been granted by the Scottish King to his fellow countrymen Hamilton and Montgomery - perhaps because he wanted O'Neill's lands for himself? If Chichester's offer to Queen Elizabeth I (to hang O'Neill without a trial) had proceeded, he would have been in a prime position to confiscate all of O'Neill's lands for himself. However the Queen was dead, and he had now been sidelined by the new King and his ambitious Scottish associates.

The relationship between Hamilton and Montgomery from this point on has been described as "mutual hatred". These two Ayrshire neighbours, the minister's son and the Laird's son, who had grown up only five miles from each other, were now bitter rivals for supremacy in Ulster. Perhaps their rivalry and determination were factors in the unprecedented success of the settlement.

Three-way negotiations and the Gunpowder Plot

With the agreement signed, O'Neill, Hamilton and Montgomery began to trade and sell with each other in a complex set of transactions from June 1605 until May 1606. Half way through this period, back in London, one of the most famous events in world history took place - the Gunpowder Plot. Guy Fawkes and Hugh Montgomery had fought on opposing sides during the wars in Holland in the late 1500s; Fawkes was there from 1594 - 1604 and held a post of command in the Spanish army when they seized Calais in 1596, and Montgomery was Captain in a Scottish regiment under William I of Orange from circa 1582 - 1587.

On 5th November, 1605, Fawkes' Gunpowder Plot was foiled and he was arrested. An emergency session of the King's Privy Council was held early that morning, and Fawkes was brought in under arrest. When questioned by the King and the Privy Council (all of whom had originally been with James at his court in Scotland) as to how he could conspire such a hideous treason, Fawkes replied that his intentions were "...to blow the Scotsmen present back to Scotland...".

Fawkes and the other conspirators were found guilty and were hung, drawn and quartered in London in January 1606. If the Gunpowder Plot had succeeded in killing the King and replacing him with a new monarch, the Hamilton & Montgomery Settlement may never have happened at all, and neither would James' Plantation of Virginia in 1607, his Plantation of Ulster in 1610, and his Plantation of Nova Scotia in 1621. The course of modern history would have been radically altered.

The Settlement Begins

The trading continued through late 1605 and early 1606; Hamilton passed the Masserene area of Antrim over to Chichester, and acquired lands around Coleraine as well as the lucrative fishing rights to the River Bann, which infuriated Sir Randal MacDonnell of North Antrim. By April, 1606, Hamilton had sold off all his interests in County Antrim in order to concentrate on County Down.

King James' "Union of the Crowns" policies continued, and on 12 April, 1606, he issued a proclamation announcing a new flag for his combined kingdoms.

With their new areas now assigned, Hamilton and Montgomery sent communications to Scotland to find willing tenants to farm the lands. Both men convinced their extended families to join them in the settlement scheme and, in May 1606, the first waves of settlers - farmers, stonemasons, builders, carpenters, textile workers, merchants and chaplains - sailed across the narrow channel of water and arrived in Ulster to form the backbone of the new Ulster-Scots community there.   (This article was originally published in The Ulster-Scot, March 2006)

Part Four   May 1606 - The Settlement Begins

May 1606

The first boats sailed from Portpatrick in May and arrived at Donaghadee. These were not the warrior emigrants which Queen Elizabeth I had sent during the 1500s to tame a hostile land. These settlers were an entire cross-section of Lowland Scottish society from large landholders to small tenant farmers, with their families in tow. They were attracted to Ulster by James Hamilton and Hugh Montgomery's offer of low rents for relatively large areas of available land. They were ready to create a new society.

They were wise to begin the Settlement in May; even today the North Channel can be a difficult crossing during the winter months. This also gave them a full summer to prepare for their first winter, always the most difficult time of year in a new land, never mind a land which was as devastated as east Ulster was.

Where did they come from?

Hamilton and Montgomery brought their own extended families from Ayrshire, and in Montgomery's case some of the family's existing tenants on the Montgomery estates in Scotland were tempted across the water to begin a new life in Ulster. Word spread like wildfire and soon the entire west of Scotland was aware of the new opportunity, right up into the Mull of Kintyre and eventually across the Lowlands into what was still then Border Reiver territory. In his book "Albion's Seed", Professor David Hackett Fischer includes a map which shows where the earliest settlers came from – the map on this page shows these locations (reproduced below with Professor Fischer's personal permission).

The sea crossing was not as much of a challenge as we might think. Travel today to where many of the settlers came from - the Ayrshire coast near Ardrossan and Largs - and look across to Arran, Bute and Kintyre. If you travel along the coastal road from Stranraer towards Dumfries you'll see it again – narrow stretches of water with outcrops of land, peninsulas and large islands just a boat trip away. These people were familiar with short sea crossings, it was part of their culture. (In fact, the crossing from Portpatrick to Donaghadee is shorter than the crossing from Ayr to Campbeltown on the Mull of Kinytre.)

What did the settlers find when they arrived?

The first sight of east Ulster must have been a shocking experience for the settlers. This was not a landscape of well-tilled agricultural land, it was a wasted and devastated former war zone.

The Montgomery Manuscripts famously record that "...in the spring time, Anno. 1606, those parishes were now more wasted than America... 30 cabins could not be found, nor any stone walls, but ruined roofless churches, and a few vaults at Gray Abbey, and a stump of an old castle in Newton, in each of which some Gentlemen sheltered themselves at their first coming over...". Sir Brian O'Neill's scorched earth policy of 1572 had been highly effective.

So the settlers started work, repairing the few ruined stone buildings which remained and preparing the lands for farming. Montgomery had "a low stone walled house" built near the harbour at Donaghadee and sent both the building materials and workers over from Scotland. This house is believed to be the original building on the site of The Manor House in Donaghadee today.

Next he repaired the stump of the old Castle in Newtown (Newtownards) - Castle Gardens Primary School and the new CastleBawn retail development in Newtownards are both references to Hugh Montgomery's repaired castle. Next were the adjacent Newtownards Priory ruins, for which he imported timber from Norway and slates from Scotland. He doubled the Priory in size and added the bell tower. He built a "great school" in Newtown to teach Latin, Greek and Logicks, including a green where the students could play golf, football and archery.

Montgomery acquired lands at Grey Abbey in 1607, "wholly repaired" the Abbey and installed Rev David McGill of Edinburgh as Curate there. Grey Abbey and Newtownards Priory survive to this day and are maintained by the Environment & Heritage Service.

Where did the Settlers live?

The initial settlements were Donaghadee, Newtownards and Bangor, and later included Greyabbey, Comber and Killyleagh. Con O'Neill's lands had been divided among O'Neill, Hamilton and Montgomery on the basis of townlands, with the main tenants granted up to 1000 acres each. The smaller tenants who came across were granted portions of these lands, usually in amounts of between two and four acres each, at a price of 1 shilling per acre each year. The map shown here shows the distribution of the initial 1606 Hamilton & Montgomery lands.

The main landholders built stone houses for themselves, whilst the smaller tenants built cottages from sods and saplings, with rushes for thatch and bushes for wattle. Wood was cut from the forests in the Lagan Valley and was transported to the new settlement to help in the building of houses and farms.

Meanwhile, back in Scotland... The Fight of the Earls!

Back in Scotland, the Montgomery/Cunningham struggle for precedency in Scotland (which had begun in 1488) once again flared up. On 1st July 1606 the heads of the families - the two Earls themselves - had a "violent tumult" close to the Scottish Parliament and Privy Council in Perth. The Montgomery Manuscripts tell us that "...the fight lasted from seven until ten o'clock at night... and it was not until the year 1609 that a reconciliation could be effected..."

Yet events back home don't seem to have disturbed Hugh Montgomery's planning and he forged ahead with the new Ulster settlement. His brother, the newly appointed Bishop of Derry, Raphoe and Clogher - George Montgomery - arrived in west Ulster in Autumn 1606, and copied what Hugh was doing in the east. He advertised his newly acquired church lands to Scots living in Glasgow, Ayr, Irvine and Greenock, and the first Scottish settlers began to arrive in Donegal and the North West in the spring of 1607. Around the same time other Scots started to arrive in Derry and Lifford.

Behind every good man...

Hugh Montgomery's wife, Elizabeth, organised most of the progress on the Montgomery estates in east Ulster. She had watermills built and established textile manufacturing of linen, woollen and tartan cloth. She offered new settlers a house, a garden plot and fodder for the winter in return for their labour. The fallow land was planted and the result was two consecutive bumper crops, giving the Settlement the prosperity it needed to survive and the appeal to attract more and more Scots across the North Channel.

A market was established in Newtown, with Scottish merchants coming across the North Channel to sell their goods to the Ulster-Scots. Records say that many of these traders were able to travel to the market in Newtown and be back in Scotland for bedtime. Sir Thomas Craig, still regarded as one of the finest legal minds Scotland has ever produced, wrote in 1606 "every day I see a stream of emigrants passing over to Ulster from my homeland".

May 1607 - Jamestown, Virginia

King James I may well have been inspired by the immediate success of the Hamilton & Montgomery Settlement. On December 20th 1606 three ships – the Godspeed, the Discovery and the Susan Constant – left London with the King's blessing, bound for Virginia. They arrived with 104 male settlers and established the first permanent English settlement in the New World on May 13th 1607 - exactly one year after the Scots arrived in Ulster. They founded the settlement of Jamestown, in honour of the King.

September 1607 - The Flight of the Earls

Back in west Ulster, Bishop George Montgomery was becoming embroiled in a series of disputes - as the only Scottish bishop in Ireland he has been described as having a "zeal" compared to the "sluggishness" of the other bishops. George Montgomery claimed far more land than the church could prove that it owned, including about half of the Earl of Tyrone's estate. This dispute was one of the factors which would result in the Flight of the Earls from Rathmullan in September 1607.

Arise, Sir James Hamilton

Hugh Montgomery had already been knighted by the King sometime between April and November of 1605 (ie around the time of King James approving the three-way division, and appointing George Montgomery as Bishop). Delighted by the achievements in east Ulster, King James I knighted Hamilton in 1608, but the year was also one of sorrow - his father, Rev Hans Hamilton, died at Dunlop, Ayrshire on 30th May.

September 1610 - The Plantation of (the west of) Ulster commences

Sir Arthur Chichester - no doubt still angered by losing out on Con O'Neill's lands in east Ulster, and greatly irritated by the rapid success of the Hamilton & Montgomery Settlement - saw the Flight of the Earls as another opportunity. On 17th September 1607, just 13 days after the Earls had left, Chichester brought forward two plans as to how their forfeited lands could be developed. These proposed schemes would eventually become the Plantation of Ulster (covering the counties of Armagh, Fermanagh, Cavan, Donegal, Tyrone and Londonderry) which would begin in September 1610.

Hamilton was concerned with the plans for the Plantation. He travelled to England in October 1609 and May 1610 - as a result he purchased some of the lands in County Cavan which had been set aside for Scottish planters.

1611 – The Plantation Commissioners Report

With the Plantation of Ulster underway, the Plantation Commissioners visited the Hamilton & Montgomery Settlement in 1611. Montgomery's Newtownards was described as "...a good town of a hundred houses or there abouts all peopled by Scots..."

They wrote that "...Sir James Hamylton, Knight, hath buylded a fayre stone house at the towne of Bangor... about 60 foote longe and 22 foote broade; the town consists of 80 newe houses, all inhabited with Scotyshemen and Englishmen...". The site of this house is now Bangor Town Hall and North Down Heritage Centre. Part of the permanent exhibition is the original 1625 Hamilton estate "Raven Maps", drawn by Thomas Raven.

1613 - The First Royal Borough, The First Presbyterian Minister

By 1613 it was clear that the Settlement had been a transformation. Inside only seven years, from what had been wasted and depopulated land, Newtown was made a Royal Borough, with Sir Hugh Montgomery nominated as Newtown's first Provost, and the right to send two members to Parliament.

Yet the progress of the Settlement was not just physical, economic and political. One of Hugh Montgomery's major tenants was Sir William Edmonston, Laird of Duntreath in Scotland. (His father, Sir James Edmonston, had narrowly escaped execution for his involvement in a plot to kill the young King James). Sir William moved from his Donaghadee lands to Ballycarry in County Antrim, and brought the 44 year old Rev Edward Brice across from Stirlingshire. Brice was the first Presbyterian minister in Ulster, arriving in 1613.

And so begins the next great chapter in Ulster-Scots history - the arrival of the Presbyterian ministers - all rooted in the Hamilton & Montgomery Settlement of 1606, "The Dawn of the Ulster-Scots."   (This article was originally published in The Ulster-Scot, May 2006)

Part Five   The Arrival of the Presbyterian Ministers

Intro   People often think that all Ulster-Scots are Presbyterians. This part of our story shows us that in the early years of the 1600s the Ulster-Scots settlers, both people and ministers, worshipped and ministered within the Established Church (the Church of Ireland) - a period often described as the"Prescopalian" era (ie both Presbyterian and Episcopalian). Even through the religious difficulties and theological differences which lay ahead, large numbers of Ulster-Scots have always been members of the Church of Ireland, right up to the present day. You don't have to be a Presbyterian to be an Ulster-Scot!

The Attraction of Ulster
By now the Settlement was a spectacular success. Many of Hamilton and Montgomery's family connections and major tenants were now pushing westward into new territory in King James I's Plantation in the west of Ulster - a pattern which around 250,000 of the settlers' descendants would continue centuries later in the New World of North America.

For example, James Hamilton's brother John acquired lands in County Armagh and founded Markethill, Hamiltonsbawn and Newtownhamilton. The Co. Londonderry villages of Eglinton and Greysteel were named after Sir Hugh Montgomery's cousin and the head of the Montgomery family, the Earl of Eglinton, whose nickname was Greysteel.

The economic success of the Settlement, whilst good news for Ulster, was causing significant economic problems back home in Scotland. Huge numbers of tenant farmers had left for Ulster, particularly from the large estates in the West of Scotland. The Scottish Secretary of State wrote "...the West country people of the common sort do flock over in so great numbers that much lands are lying waste for lack of tenants...". The attraction of Ulster was causing so much difficulty that the Scottish Privy Council ruled that no tenants were to migrate without their landlord's permission. There weren't even enough boats to meet the demand, and this allowed the shipowners to raise their prices. Again the Scottish Privy Council stepped in, to introduce fare controls.

The appeal of Ulster was to be a major factor in Scottish emigration for centuries. In fact, from 1650 to 1700, only 7,000 Scots emigrated to America, yet between 60,000 and 100,000 emigrated across the North Channel to Ulster. The Scots settlers seem to have agreed with Sir Arthur Chichester when, comparing the New World with Ulster, he said "I had rather labour with my hands in the plantation of Ulster than dance or play in that of Virginia."

The Scum of Both Nations...?

For all of its economic success, the spiritual condition of the Settlement may not have been quite so positive. Two of the early Scottish Presbyterian ministers who came to Ulster, Rev Robert Blair and Rev Andrew Stewart, wrote bleak accounts of what they found when they arrived.

Blair wrote that "...the case of the people through all that part of the country was most lamentable, they being drowned in ignorance, security and sensuality... the most part were such as either poverty, scandalous lives...".

Stewart famously wrote that "...from Scotland came many and from England not a few, yet all of them generally the scum of both nations, who, for debt, or breaking and fleeing from justice, or seeking shelter, came hither, hoping to be without fear of man's justice in a land where there was nothing, or but little, as yet, of the fear of God... void of Godliness who seemed rather to flee from God in this enterprise..."

... Or Worthy and Godly?

When most authors and historians quote Blair and Stewart, they stop with the two statements above.

However, Blair went on to write that "...among these, Divine Providence sent over some worthy persons...". Stewart went on to write "...yet God followed them when they fled from Him...", and The Montgomery Manuscripts record that "...among all this care and indefatigable industry for their families, a place of God's honour to dwell in was not forgotten nor neglected...". John Harrison, in his 1888 book The Scot in Ulster, wrote that "...Hamilton and Montgomery looked after the spiritual wants of the emigrants in County Down...".

Faith and church life clearly played a significant role in the early Settlement in Ulster.

The Divine Right of Kings and The Geneva Bible

At this time the Established Church (the Church of Ireland) held precedence, yet Sir Arthur Chichester wrote that the churches in Ulster were few, none were in good repair and that many of the clergy were absent. It has been said that there weren't three sufficient preaching Bishops on the whole island.

However across the water in Scotland, the Calvinism of the Presbyterians had been legally established in 1567, the year that King James came to the throne of Scotland. Thanks to Reformers like John Knox, Presbyterianism had won the hearts of the people. Many of the ministers who were graduating from Scottish universities, and many professors at the universities, were committed Presbyterians. Yet some of the Bishops within the Scottish Kirk were opposed to Presbyterianism and remained loyal to King James.

King James, as Head of State, was therefore also Head of the Established Church and he believed that Presbyterianism was destructive and anarchical. He was a firm believer in an idea known as the "Divine Right of Kings", and as such was deeply unhappy with the popular Bible of the time, the Geneva Bible, which was used in the Scottish Kirk but not in the Church of England.

The reason for this was that the Geneva Bible included footnotes written by John Calvin, John Knox and other Reformers. King James saw these footnotes as highly dangerous - they opposed the idea of the "Divine Right of Kings" and encouraged resistance to tyrants. Because the Geneva Bible was so popular (there had been 144 printings of it between 1560 and 1644) James saw these footnotes as a direct threat to his position both as Head of State and Head of the Established Church.

So King James ruled the Geneva Bible "seditious" and made it a criminal offence to own one, and he commissioned a new Bible - the Authorised Version or King James Bible, stripped of these dangerous footnotes - with the intention that it would replace the Geneva Bible. The Authorised Version was first published in 1611, yet it would be 40 years before the Geneva Bible was unseated as the most popular edition. King James also worked personally on his own version of the Psalms, entitled The Psalms of King David, translated by King James.

He was assisted by Sir William Alexander, (left) the author of The Great Day of the Lord's Judgement (Sir William Alexander will reappear in the next part of our story). The Authorised Version is rightly regarded today as perhaps the finest of all Bible translations, yet it is interesting to see some of the motivation which lay behind it. King James I's ambitious desire to be Head of both Church and State were soon to cause great turmoil in Scotland and Ulster.

The First Two Ministers Arrive

Sir James Hamilton had already brought Rev John Gibson to Ulster in 1609 to minister in Bangor, but it was 1613 when the first acknowledged Presbyterian minister arrived in Ulster. Driven from Scotland by Archbishop Spottiswoode (King James' main supporter in Scotland) Rev Edward Brice came from Stirlingshire to Broadisland (Ballycarry), on invitation from one of Sir Hugh Montgomery's first tenants, Sir William Edmonston. Edmonston may have been a cousin of Sir James Hamilton, and had just moved from his initial Ulster lands near Donaghadee to a larger estate in east Antrim.

Next, in 1615, Sir James Hamilton brought Rev Robert Cunningham to Holywood; he had formerly been a chaplain to a Scottish regiment under the Earl of Buccleugh in Holland, and married one of Sir Hugh Montgomery's daughters. Then events in Scotland took a serious turn for the worse for the Presbyterians.

The Five Articles of Perth

On 25th August 1618 King James exerted his power, and, in an effort to conform Scottish worship to the pattern of the Anglican Church and to impose bishops on the Presbyterians, his "Five Articles" were imposed upon a reluctant General Assembly at Perth. (these were - kneeling during communion; private baptism; private communion for the sick or infirm; confirmation by a Bishop; the observance of Holy Days). This coincided with a great storm directly over the Assembly building. When these "Five Articles of Perth" were made law on 4th August 1621 by the Scottish Parliament in Edinburgh, an even greater storm took place and made the entire city as dark as night, with thunder, lightning and hail - a day which became known as "Black Saturday".   The Scottish people now called their bishops "Tulchan Bishops" - tulchan being a Scots language term for a fake calf, designed to deceive a cow into giving milk. The people clearly felt they were being deceived by the actions of the King and his Bishops.

The First Wave of Ulster-Scots Ministers

These "Five Articles" were met with fierce opposition across Scotland, and ignited a new exodus of clergymen and settlers across the water. The initial wave of ministers who came to Ulster was: 1619 Rev John Ridge (Antrim) an English Puritan 1621 Rev James Glendinning (Carnmoney, Carrickfergus, Oldstone) 1621 Rev Henry Colwert (Broadisland, Oldstone) an English Puritan 1621 Rev George Hubbard (Carrickfergus) an English Puritan 1620? Rev David McGill (Greyabbey) personal Chaplain to Sir Hugh Montgomery and son of Lord Nisbet, the Lord Advocate of Scotland 1620 John MacLellan / McClelland (Newtownards) First Principal at Sir Hugh Montgomery's school in Newtownards and also a part-time minister. Sir Hugh's eldest daughter married John's close relative Sir Robert MacLellan around 1620. 1623 Rev Robert Blair (Bangor) Blair's first wife was Beatrix Hamilton, a sister of Jenny Geddes (who famously threw the stool at the Bishop in Edinburgh in 1637).   His second wife was Sir Hugh Montgomery's daughter Catherine, who he married in 1635. 1625 Rev George Dunbar (Larne) 1625 Rev Josias Welsh (Templepatrick) John Knox's grandson 1625 Rev James Hamilton (Ballywalter) Sir James Hamilton's nephew, who married one of Sir Hugh Montgomery's daughters 1627 Rev Andrew Stewart (Donegore) 1630 Rev John Livingstone (Killinchy)

Other Ministers of the era, listed in The Hamilton Manuscripts and the Ulster Visitation Book of 1622, include: Rev John Bole (Killyleagh) Rev George Porter (Ballyhalbert) Rev John Leathem (Holywood)

These ministers were theologically Presbyterian and were welcomed by the Ulster-Scots settlers, yet they preached and worshipped within the Established Church and its buildings. The Bishops in Ulster tolerated the Presbyterians for a time, and perhaps even initially welcomed the influx of new people and new clergy. The Bishops were also flexible in the ordination ceremonies of these new ministers, and in fact many of the new Bishops coming to Ulster were Scots. Bishop George Montgomery was Sir Hugh Montgomery's brother (he was transferred from Derry, Raphoe and Clogher in January 1610 to become Bishop of Meath). His replacement was fellow Scot Bishop Andrew Knox, formerly Bishop of the Isles.

During the reign of King James VI & I, at least 65 Scottish ministers served in Ireland, and 12 Scottish bishops, seven of whom were in Ulster dioceses.

The Rebuilding of the Churches In many instances the Scottish ministers and their new congregations set about restoring and rebuilding the ruined churches which had been destroyed by the English/Gaelic wars of the late 1500s, renewing worship in them for the first time in many decades. Montgomery repaired or built: • Donaghadee Parish Church • Portpatrick Parish Church • Newtownards Priory • Grey Abbey • Comber Parish Church (2/3 of the cost) Kilmore Parish Church Montgomery presented these six churches with a large bell, a Geneva Bible and a Common Prayer Book - all of which had his Braidstane coat of arms stamped on them. Hamilton repaired or built: • Bangor Abbey • Holywood Priory • Comber Parish Church (1/3 of the cost) • St Andrews, Ballyhalbert • Whitechurch, Ballywalter • Dundonald, St Elizabeth's • Killinchy Parish Church • Killyleagh Parish Church • Innishargy Church

The Death of Con O'Neill & The Death of King James During this period of great change, in 1618, Con O'Neill died. By the time of his death Con had sold off most of the 68 townlands he had agreed in the deal with Hamilton and Montgomery back in 1605, and may only have had as few as six townlands left in his estate. Con was buried near Holywood, but no known grave remains today. The Montgomery Manuscripts tell us that the local people fondly described Con as "the ould King." (page 83)

On 27th March 1625 the other "ould King"in our story, King James VI & I, also died. In the months that followed, great religious revivals would sweep through the West of Scotland and East Ulster, through the work of the ministers listed above.

However, when King James' son took the throne and was crowned as King Charles I in February 1626, life for the Presbyterians in Scotland and Ulster was to become worse than ever before...

(With thanks to Rev Dr Joseph Thompson of the Presbyterian Historical Society for his assistance with this article)
   (This article was originally published in The Ulster-Scot, July 2006)

Part Six   Three Ulster-Scots Spiritual Revivals, the Death of Montgomery and the "Eagle Wing" sets sail

Intro

King James was dead and his son, King Charles I, was now on the throne. James VI & I's death on 27th March 1625 coincided with remarkable spiritual renewal in Ulster and Scotland. In his History of Protestantism, Rev J A Wylie wrote that: "...the year of the king's death was rendered memorable by the rise of a remarkable influence of a spiritual kind in Scotland, which continued for years... preachers had found no new Gospel, nor had they become suddenly clothed with a new eloquence; yet their words had a power they had formerly lacked; they went deeper into the hearts of their hearers, who were impressed by them in a way they had never been before... the moral character of whole towns, villages and parishes was being suddenly changed..."

For Wylie, the key to the revivals was this: "...it was distinctly traceable to those ministers who had suffered for their faith under James VI..."   Unsurprisingly, the ministers involved in the revivals, and the regions where revival was so strongly experienced, were both closely linked to James Hamilton and Hugh Montgomery.

1. Stewarton, 1623 – 1630

The village of Stewarton is just two miles from James Hamilton's home village of Dunlop, and close to the Montgomery family castles of Eglinton, Giffen, Hessilheid and Braidstane. Rev William Castlelaw was then the minister in Stewarton; the previous minister had been Sir Hugh Montgomery's uncle, Rev Robert Montgomerie. Robert later moved to Ulster to become minister in Newtownards by 1630.

Rev Castlelaw's neighbour and colleague Rev David Dickson from Irvine had been banished to the north of Scotland in January 1622 for his opposition to King James' "Five Articles of Perth". However he was allowed to return to Ayrshire in June 1623 thanks to the support of Sir Hugh Montgomery's cousin and head of the Montgomery family, the Earl of Eglinton (above), and in particular the Earl's wife Anna. Eglinton Castle became a refuge for many of Scotland's persecuted Presbyterian ministers. Dickson began a weekly service in Irvine on Monday mornings, and within a few weeks thousands of people were flocking from all over Scotland to listen to his preaching.

Dickson was soon joined by Rev Robert Blair, the man Sir James Hamilton had brought to Ulster to become the minister in Bangor. The revival swept across the entire Stewarton parish, along the valley where the Annick Water or Stewarton Water runs and into the homelands of Hamilton and Montgomery. The Stewarton Revival lasted until around 1630, and its impact was to be felt for generations to come - the entire region would soon become a hotbed of Covenanter resistance to the Established Church.

2. SixMileWater, 1625 – 1634

The second revival took place in Ulster, in the area of South Antrim along the course of the Sixmilewater, in what had once been Sir Brian O'Neill's lands of Lower Clandeboye. Scotsman Rev James Glendinning had been preaching in Carrickfergus amongst the English settlers of the town without success. He was visited in 1625 by Rev Robert Blair, who had sailed across Belfast Lough from Bangor to hear him preach. Blair advised him to move to Oldstone to preach among the Scots settlers - this advice brought immediate results.

Crowds flocked to hear Glendinning, who was soon joined by Rev Josias Welch (Templepatrick - John Knox's grandson), and then in turn by Rev John Ridge (Antrim), Rev Robert Blair (Bangor), Rev Robert Cunningham (Holywood) and Rev James Hamilton (Ballywalter).

They established a monthly lecture meeting in Antrim on the last Friday of the month, in the house of a Scots settler called Hugh Campbell, which lasted from 1626 - 1634, and was attended by large crowds of Ulster-Scots. Religious revival swept the region. Glendinning left the area, and additional help then came to Sixmilewater in the form of Rev Henry Colwert (Oldstone), Rev George Dunbar (Larne) and in 1630 by Rev John Livingstone (Killinchy). Of these ministers, Cunningham, Blair and Livingstone had all been brought to Ulster by Sir James Hamilton.

In October 1632, Rev John Livingstone wrote to Anna, Countess of Eglinton (she had been involved in the Stewarton Revival) to tell her that there were crowds of around 1500 people regularly attending the communion services in Ulster.

3. Kirk O' Shotts, 1630
The Kirk of Shotts is only around 35 miles from Stewarton. The minister in 1630 was a Rev Hance. Hance had been assisted by some of the local Ladies, Countesses and Marchionesses who were supporters of the Presbyterian ministers.
In return for their help they asked him to hold a large communion service at Shotts on Sunday 20th June 1630, attended by other ministers of their choosing. The same familiar group of ministers were invited - Rev Robert Blair, Rev David Dickson, the renowned Rev Robert Bruce (Edinburgh) and a young John Livingstone (aged 27, the chaplain to his future wife's close relative Sarah Maxwell, Countess of Wigtown, but not yet ordained as a minister). The service attracted an enormous crowd, who remained at the church overnight, singing psalms and praying.

The next day the young Livingstone was due to preach a sermon, but he became nervous and tried to run away. However he returned and preached in the churchyard (below) to the assembled crowd for an hour and a half when a heavy rain shower began, but he preached on through for another hour regardless. 500 people in the crowd were converted.

1620 – 1630   1621 - Sir William Alexander is Granted Nova Scotia, Canada
On September 10 1621, King James signed a land grant to his old friend, and his partner on the Psalms project, Sir William Alexander. This was for an area larger than Great Britain and France combined, "between our Colonies of New England and Newfoundland, to be known as New Scotland ". In Latin the name of this land was Nova Scotia.

1622 - The Marriage of Hugh Montgomery & Jean Alexander
The following year, Sir William Alexander's daughter Jean married Sir Hugh Montgomery's eldest son Hugh. As a wedding present Sir Hugh built a large manor house

for the newlyweds just outside Comber, and named it Mount Alexander in honour of Sir William. It was made from the stone from the ruins of Comber Abbey, which, like Bangor Abbey, had been burned by Sir Brian O'Neill in 1572. Only a few walls from Mount Alexander survive today, as part of a farm.

1622 - Hamilton & Montgomery Become Viscounts

On 3rd May 1622, Sir Hugh Montgomery was made the first Viscount of the Great Ardes by King James; the next day, Sir James Hamilton was made the first Viscount Clandeboye.

1625 - Hamilton & Montgomery's Land Disputes

Hamilton & Montgomery's relationship was deteriorating fast and legal actions caused by boundary disputes were relentless. The estimated cost of these legal cases was £1400 - approximately £200,000 in today's money! These disputes would reach such a low point that in 1625 Hamilton called in the cartographer Thomas Raven to map all of the Hamilton estates. These maps are on display at North Down Heritage Centre in Bangor.

Portpatrick, Donaghadee, Ballymena, Ballygally, Killyleagh

Sir Hugh Montgomery bought Portpatrick from the Adairs of Kilhilt in 1626; he also tried to rename Donaghadee as "Montgomery" and Portpatrick as "Port Montgomery". With the income, the Adairs bought Ballymena from the MacQuillans and named the area "Kinhiltstoun" for a time. Sir Hugh's brother in law James Shaw moved to Ballygally and built Ballygally Castle in 1625. Around this time Sir James Hamilton moved from Bangor to Killyleagh Castle.

The Death of the Wives

Sir James Hamilton's second wife Ursula - from whom he was divorced - died in 1625. Ursula was the sister of Bishop George Montgomery's wife Elizabeth. Sir Hugh's great companion in the Settlement project, his wife Elizabeth, died in the late 1620s (exact date unknown). She was buried inside the Priory in Newtownards, without memorial. In 1630, during a visit to the Earl of Eglinton in Ayrshire, Sir Hugh remarried. His new spouse was Rev Livingstone's friend the Countess of Wigtown, Sarah Maxwell. She moved to Newtownards but stayed only a few months before returning to Scotland, vowing never to return to Ulster!

1631 - 1636 The Opposition of the Bishops

The three revivals were opposed by the Bishops of the Established Church in both Scotland and Ulster. After Blair and Livingstone had preached at Kirk O' Shotts, they were accused by the Scottish bishops of "exciting the people" - these charges were sent to Bishop Echlin in Ireland, who accused Blair and Livingstone of "making an insurrection". In Autumn 1631 Rev Blair, Rev Livingstone, Rev Dunbar and Rev Welch were all suspended from their ministries in Ulster.

The suspension was lifted briefly following an appeal to Archibishop Ussher, (James Hamilton's former pupil in Dublin) but it was reinstated in May 1632.   So Blair decided he would travel to London to appeal to King Charles I, carrying letters of support from a number of Scottish noblemen including Sir Hugh Montgomery's now-relative Sir William Alexander. Blair was given a letter of support from the King and he returned to Ireland.

However, the King's Lord Deputy in Ireland (Thomas Wentworth, the Earl of Strafford) and the new Archbishop of Canterbury (William Laud) were firm opponents of Presbyterianism. Nevertheless, the suspension of the four ministers was lifted in May 1634, but only for six months. In November 1634 not only were these ministers suspended again - this time they were permanently deposed.   Shortly after this action, Bishop Echlin fell ill. When his doctor asked what was wrong he replied "It's my conscience, man!". Lady Jean Montgomery (described in The Montgomery Manuscripts as a "vehement Presbyterian") said of Echlin "...I shall bear witness of it to the glory of God, who hath smitten this man for suppressing Christ's witnesses..."

A Letter to America
It was clear that life for the Ulster-Scots was going to get much worse. However, America offered the religious freedom they desired so Rev John Livingstone and his former teacher at Stirling (a Mr William Wallace) were chosen to make an advance trip to New England, to gather information and choose a suitable homeland in America for any future Ulster-Scots emigrants.

Livingstone wrote to John Winthrop, Governor of Massachussetts (left) in July 1634, but due to storms the attempted voyage was unsuccessful. However Winthrop's son visited Ulster in January 1635 and encouraged them to come to America.   The ministers began to make preparations, intending to set sail to America in the spring of 1636. Events would delay their planned departure date.

The Death of Hugh Montgomery Spring of 1636 was to be a time of great sorrow for the Ulster-Scots settlers and their ministers - they were devastated when one of the Founding Fathers of the Settlement, Sir Hugh Montgomery, died on 15th May 1636, aged 76. The Montgomery Manuscripts (available as digital CD Roms from the Ulster-Scots Agency) provide a detailed description of his funeral arrangements. The funeral followed the full Scottish ceremony for the burial of a Viscount - a Scottish state funeral in Newtownards for the Founding Father of the Ulster Scots.

The Ministers are all Deposed
To make matters even worse, in August 1636, all of the remaining Presbyterian ministers in Ulster - Rev Brice, Rev Ridge, Rev Cunningham, Rev Colwert and Rev Hamilton - were also deposed. Not only was Montgomery, the great figurehead, now dead, but the Ulster-Scots now had no ministers to pastor them.

The Funeral of Hugh Montgomery
Sir Hugh Montgomery's body was embalmed, rolled in wax and locked away until September. One week before the funeral, his body was taken outside Newtownards where it lay in State. He was buried in Newtownards Priory (above) on 8th September 1636, the building he had rebuilt in 1606 and where his first wife Elizabeth was already buried.

On the day of the funeral a great procession, all clothed in black, made the slow walk to the Priory. Carrying a large banner and large flag, the cortege of around 200 people included the Earl of Eglinton and scores of other noblemen who had travelled from Scotland to pay their respects. Even Montgomery's bitter rival, Sir James Hamilton, was there.

Perhaps Sir Hugh Montgomery's death was the factor which delayed the planned emigration to America. Rev Blair's wife and Rev Hamilton's wife were both daughters of Sir Hugh; Rev Livingstone and John McClelland were also related to Sir Hugh through marriage. It is highly likely that they would have wanted to see their father, father-in-law and Founding Father laid to rest before leaving for America.   Perhaps they were among the crowds in Newtownards that lined the streets as the funeral procession made its way through the town. Perhaps they stood outside the Priory during the funeral, where they might have gritted their teeth as their arch enemy Bishop Leslie preached the sermon. Perhaps they bristled at the irony of this when they saw the two Bible texts Sir Hugh had carved above the doorway there (Psalm 122v1 and Ecclesiastes 5v1) Perhaps, knowing that Sir Hugh's son would waver between the Established Church and Presbyerianism, they decided the time was now right to leave Ulster. And perhaps they slept on it...

Eagle Wing Sets Sail
  ... because the next morning, 9th September 1636, the Eagle Wing finally sailed from Groomsport.

On board were three of Sir James Hamilton's ministers (Rev Robert Blair, Rev John Livingstone and Rev James Hamilton) along with Sir Hugh Montgomery's schoolmaster and part-time minister in Newtownards John McClelland. With them was John Stewart, Provost of Ayr and 135 other Ulster-Scots emigrants, who had surnames like Campbell, Girwin, Brown, Stuart, Agnew, Calver and Summervil.

This was the first attempted voyage from Ulster to the New World of America. Adair's Narrative records that Livingstone and Blair had reservations about the journey. However the Eagle Wing left Ulster and sheltered off the Scottish coast, first at Loch Ryan and then near the Isle of Bute, before heading out across the North Atlantic. Around 1200 miles from Ireland they were struck by "a mighty hurricane" which smashed one of the master joists and the rudder. Adair wrote "...there were no waves there, but mountains of waters...".

After a stirring address from Blair, one of the crew volunteered to go over the side of the ship to fix the rudder, with a long rope tied around his middle. The repairs were made but the storm didn't cease. Livingstone proposed that they should wait for a further 24 hours, and if it was God's will He would end the storm and allow them to carry on; if not, they would take this as His sign to turn back. The storm continued, and they all agreed to turn back and head for Ulster. The trip home was completed in fine weather.

There were two deaths and one birth during the voyage, and on 3rd November 1636 the Eagle Wing docked in Carrickfergus. Sadly for Rev Blair and his wife Katherine (Sir Hugh Montgomery's daughter) their baby son William died on their return to Ulster.

Back to Scotland - for now...

The failed emigration was scorned by the Bishops in Ireland, and under further persecution the four ministers fled to Scotland - a Scotland where revolution was building and a National Covenant was being conceived. The Ulster-Scots ministers had little idea of what lay just around the corner...

(This article was originally published in The Ulster-Scot, August 2006)

Part Seven   Scotland's National Covenant, the Black Oath and the 1641 Massacre

Intro

The early years of the Settlement, referred to in The Montgomery Manuscripts as the "golden peaceable age", was over. Sir Hugh Montgomery was dead and had been succeeded by his son and namesake Sir Hugh Montgomery, 2nd Viscount Ards. The emigration attempt by Eagle Wing had failed and now all of the Presbyterian ministers were deposed. The once-depopulated Ulster was now filling up with mainly Scottish settlers in the east, and a combination of English and Scottish planters in the west. Tensions with the "native" population were rising...

The Ministers go back to Scotland

The four Ulster-Scots ministers who had commissioned Eagle Wing (Blair, Hamilton, McClelland and Livingstone) arrived back in Carrickfergus on 3rd November 1636. They remained in Ulster for a few months, avoiding the King's troops who were under orders to capture them.

As we've seen before, all four ministers had direct connections with Sir James Hamilton, who, according to The Hamilton Manuscripts, "...had secret friendly correspondence with the ministers and others that were persecuted for conscience sake; yea, some hid in his house when his warrants and constables were abroad looking for them..."

Blair lay low in Strandtown in Ballymacarrett, East Belfast (one of Hamilton's estates), in the house of an Archibald Miller, and preached every Sunday during the winter months. However in February 1637 a Mr Frank Hill of Castlereagh, on a visit to Dublin, informed on the ministers – fortunately they were tipped off by an Andrew Young and they escaped across the North Channel to Irvine in Ayrshire, where they stayed with their old friend Rev David Dickson. Shortly after this, the remaining Presbyterian ministers in Ulster also fled to Scotland.

Rev Robert Blair went to minister to a Scottish regiment in France, then came back to Ayr, and then to St Andrews in Fife where he joined with the renowned Samuel Rutherford. Rev John Livingstone became minister in Stranraer, and on some occasions as many as 500 Ulster-Scots sailed across to hear him preach. Rev John McClelland became minister in Kirkcudbright; Rev James Hamilton became a minister in Dumfries and then Edinburgh.

King Charles 1 and Archbishop Laud's attempt to impose the Prayer Book upon the church in Scotland met with outrage and fierce resistance from the Scottish population. On 23rd July 1637, Jenny Geddes (Rev Robert Blair's sister in law by his first wife) famously hurled a stool at Dean John Hanna in St Giles' Cathedral in Edinburgh and cried "Villain! Dost thou say Mass at ma lug?", an act which forced the Dean and Bishop to flee from the scene in the ensuing riot. The opposition from the people was so great that the Bishop of Brechin had to conduct services using the new Prayer Book with a pair of loaded pistols.   **1638 -**

National Covenant

The people of Scotland would not accept their church being ordered by the King and his Bishops. On Wednesday February 28th 1638, the Scottish National Covenant was read aloud at Greyfriars Church in Edinburgh, and was then signed by thousands of people from right across Scotland. This was the church where John Knox had once been taken for trial. Within months 300,000 people had signed the Covenant - a clear sign of rebellion against the King.

Back in Ulster, the King's Deputy, the Earl of Strafford, was deeply concerned that the Ulster-Scots would follow their kinsmen's example. Adair's Narrative records that "...Deputy Strafford, then ruling in Ireland, being a man not only opposite in his principles to the course now on foot in Scotland, but of a severe and jealous temper, began to be jealous of the whole Scotch nation in Ireland, and particularly the North, suspecting that they were on the same design with Scotland..." (page 59).

Strafford was aware that much of the trouble in Scotland was linked to the ministers who had returned there from Ulster - ministers who had lived on the estates of Sir James Hamilton and the late Sir Hugh Montgomery. Adair wrote that "...these two Scotch Lords (Ards and Claneboye)... found themselves and their estates in hazard..." (page 59)

1639 - The Black Oath

On May 21st 1639, Strafford launched his counter-strategy - to impose "The Black Oath" upon every Ulster-Scot over the age of 16. This oath required them to swear loyalty to King Charles I and to reject the Scottish National Covenant.

The penalties for not taking the Oath were severe; a report from the time said: "the Prelates did jointly frame and wickedly contrive with the earle of Strafforde, that most lawlesse and scandalous oath imposed upon the Scottish-British among us,... they were persecuted with so much rigour, that very many as if they had been traytours in the highest degree, were searched for, apprehended, examined, reviled, threatened, imprisoned, fettered together by threes and foures in iron yoakes, some in chaines carried up to Dublin, in Starre-chamber fined thousands beyond abilitie, and condemned to perpetuall imprisonment..."

Strafford had met with the Scottish Lords in Ulster a few months previously at Montgomery's home. Perhaps in today's language we would say that Strafford made them an offer they couldn't refuse. Under pressure, Viscount Clandeboye (Hamilton) and 2nd Viscount Ards (Montgomery) signed the petition in support of The Black Oath. No doubt Montgomery's wife - "Presbyterian Jean" - was furious. The Hamilton Manuscripts record how Hamilton personally forced the aged and blind Rev John Bole to take the Black Oath at Killyleagh. King Charles I then began to form an army to march on Scotland. The Covenanters responded by appointing Scotland's greatest soldier, the veteran General Alexander Leslie, to organise an Army of the Covenant to defend them.

1641 - Hamilton Returns to Dunlop, Ayrshire

Now an elderly man in his 82nd year, Sir James Hamilton returned to his home town of Dunlop in Ayrshire. There he erected two buildings - a mausoleum to his parents in the churchyard of the Kirk where his father, Rev Hans Hamilton, had been the minister. Attached to this mausoleum he built a school building which he named Clandeboye School. Both can still be seen today.

Clandeboye School is now used as a Sunday School room for the church, and inside it is a memorial plaque with the following inscription: "1641 - This school is erected and endowed by James Viscount Clandeboyes in love to this parish in which his father Hans Hamilton was pastor 45 years in King James the Sixt his raigne IcLV" The plaque is a copy of an inscription which was originally on the north gable of the building, and above it is the Hamilton coat of arms. Sadly the mausoleum has deteriorated over the years but there are major fundraising efforts ongoing to restore it to its former glory.

1641 - The Massacre

On 23rd October 1641 began one of the bloodiest chapters in Irish history, an event which Adair says had been in planning for eight years. Under the direction of Sir Phelim O'Neill, the native Irish population rose up against the English and Scottish settlers and planters, murdering thousands.

Adair also writes that the English were the primary target, and that the rebels "...first pretended a kindness to the Scotch nation in Ireland, and that their quarrel was only against the English that subdued them... but this was not to last long, for the Scotch neither expected nor found any kindness..."

At the time some estimated that 300,000 Irish Protestants had been murdered. Scholars now estimate that the figure was closer to 12,000, out of a total Ulster Protestant population of around 40,000*. The massacre had a massive impact upon the Ulster-Scots and Irish Protestants generally - and of course the name "P O'Neill" carries a significance to this day.

Hamilton & Montgomery's Armies

The Earl of Strafford had confiscated the arms and weapons owned by the Scots, leaving them defenceless. So Sir James Hamilton and Sir Hugh Montgomery (Jr.) each raised a regiment of 1,000 men, supplied with muskets and ammunition, to defend the Ulster-Scots settlers.

Many other Lords in Ulster did likewise, including Sir William and Sir Robert Stewart in the Laggan area of Donegal, Sir William Cole in Enniskillen and Sir Frederick Hamilton. Even at this, the Scottish forces were often outnumbered by as many as 4:1 - it was clear to the authorities in Scotland that the Ulster-Scots needed immediate assistance.

The Scots Army Arrives in Ulster

So, on 2nd April 1642, Major-General Robert Monro's Scottish Covenanter army of 2,500 men arrived at Carrickfergus. On 4th August a further 7,500 men arrived with General Leslie. With 10,000 Scottish Covenanter troops organised into 16 regiments, one of which was led by Montgomery's cousin the Earl of Eglinton, the Ulster-Scots would at last be defended. Their Presbyterian faith would be at the heart of this new era.

1640 – the first known use of the term "Ulster Scots"

Strafford's adviser in Ireland was Sir George Radcliffe. He had arrived with Strafford in 1633 and was perhaps the first Royal official to acknowledge that The Black Oath had not been a success. He could clearly see the commitment of the Scots in Ulster, and was deeply concerned at the possibility that the Covenanters, under the command of the Earl of Argyle, might come to Ulster.

On 8th October 1640 Radcliffe wrote: "...many thousands in the North never took the oath; and as I am certainly made believe, they now publicly avouch it as an unlawful oath; and for aught I see, they will shortly return, to any that dares question them, such an answer as Robert Bruce, Earl of Carrick, made to Sir John Comyn, who, charging him with breach of oath, taken at Westminster to King Edward, replies, with cleaving his head in two.   None is so dim-sighted, but sees the general inclination of the Ulster Scots to the covenant: and God forbid they should tarry there till the Earl of Argyle brings them armies [arms?] to cut our throats..."

This is the first known written record of the term "Ulster Scots", used to describe them by one of their committed enemies.

(with thanks to Anne Smyth of the Ulster-Scots Language Society for sharing her research on Radcliffe, and to Dr Lawrence Holden for sharing his research on Strafford)

Part Eight   The First Presbytery, the Covenant in Ulster and the Death of Sir James Hamilton

Intro

Sir James Hamilton was now an old man; he was living at Killyleagh Castle and had been through three marriages, with one son. However he was still in good health apart from some trouble with gout and kidney stones - The Hamilton Manuscripts say that he spent a lot of time each day in his house-gown. His old adversary Sir Hugh Montgomery had died in 1636, and Hamilton tried the following year to eclipse Montgomery's Donaghadee as Ulster's main port by building the Custom House and Tower House on the sea front of his own port of Bangor. The Tower House is now the Tourist Information Centre for North Down Borough Council.

1642 - The Army of the Covenant

In 1642 the 2,500 strong Army of the Covenant had arrived at Carrickfergus under the command of Major General Robert Monro. King Charles 1 was opposed to the Army going to Ulster at all, but Parliament forced his hand. The Hamilton Manuscripts say that Hamilton had "...lived to see the war of Ireland, and by his wisdom and power of his tenants, and the interest he had at Court, was very successful for the preservation of Ulster from the power of the enemy, as he was very charitable to distress'd people that came in great numbers from the upper countrys..."

The effects of the 1641 Massacre were everywhere to be seen - once again County Antrim had been devastated by warfare, but thanks to the regiments raised by Hamilton and 2nd Viscount Montgomery, the damage to County Down had been limited. The Scotch Army "...found much of the country wholly desolate, except some parts of the County of Down, where there had been two regiments formed by Lords Clandeboye and Ards... but generally in the country, through the county of Antrim, all was waste..." Adair p 90

A Presbyterian minister was appointed to each regiment in the Scotch Army, and on 10th June 1642, the first Ulster Presbytery was established at Carrickfergus, made up of five of these ministers and four ruling elders.They were soon joined by the chaplain to Hamilton's regiment (John Drysdale) and the chaplain to 2nd Viscount Montgomery's regiment (James Baty). A sculpture in Carrickfergus town centre commemorates this event, as does the magnificent "Carrickfergus Window" in Church House, Belfast.

The reaction among the Ulster-Scots people to the new Presbytery, and their new Scottish defenders, was spectacular. There was a flood of applications for elderships from all over County Antrim (Ballymena, Antrim, Cairncastle, Templepatrick, Carrickfergus, Larne and Belfast) and County Down (from Ballywalter, Portaferry, Newtownards, Donaghadee, Killyleagh, Comber, Holywood and Bangor). The demand was impossible to meet, so in July 1642 the Ulster Presbytery wrote to the General Assembly in Scotland to appeal for help. Help came quickly, in the form of two very familiar individuals, both of whom were old colleagues of Sir James Hamilton.

1642 - The Triumphant Return of Rev Robert Blair and Rev James Hamilton

Both military and spiritual help came across the water from Scotland. On 4th August 1642, General Alexander Leslie arrived with 7,500 soldiers. Then, in September 1642, the General Assembly in Scotland sent Rev Robert Blair (formerly minister of Bangor) and Rev James Hamilton (formerly minister of Ballywalter, Sir James Hamilton's namesake and nephew) back to Ulster. At this time Blair was Minister of St Andrews and Hamilton was Minister of Dumfries.

Having been driven out by the Bishops just six years previously (after the failure of the Eagle Wing) Rev Robert Blair and Rev James Hamilton had a deep knowledge of the Ulster-Scots and their experience, because they had stood shoulder-to-shoulder with these people in the early years of the Settlement. In fact, at least one historian of the period has said that it was Rev Robert Blair who was in fact the real leader of the Ulster-Scots. Blair and

Hamilton were soon joined by Rev Hugh Henderson of Dalry, Ayrshire, Rev William Adair of Ayr and Rev John Weir of Dalserf, Lanarkshire.

These ministers issued a call for public repentance to those people who had taken The Black Oath - to conforming clergy and congregations alike. Rev Blair oversaw these repentances in Bangor, Donaghadee and Killyleagh, assisted by Rev Hamilton. A national day of fasting was then held across Ulster on Sunday November 27th 1642. As Adair writes "...Thus these two ministers, Blair and Hamilton, who had a while before been deposed from their ministry by the bishops, are now employed as the instruments for first planting ministers in the country according to the purity of the Gospel - who were also useful in the army's Presbytery, and were the beginning of a settled ministry in the country..." p98

1642 - The English Civil War

   Back in London, relations between King Charles 1 and Parliament were deteriorating rapidly. He had dismissed the Parliament back in 1629 and ruled without them, but he needed their permission to raise an army to fight the Covenanters. Having been out of office for 11 years, Parliament got its revenge by recalling the King's advisor, that great enemy of the Ulster-Scots, the Earl of Strafford, from Ireland. Parliament accused Strafford of treason and had him executed in May 1641 (illustration below) - they also executed Strafford's great ally Archbishop Laud in 1645 - and also of course, King Charles I in 1649. These three most powerful opponents of the Ulster-Scots would each meet a grisly end.

In November 1641 Parliament demanded that the King's powers be reduced - in retaliation King Charles burst into the Houses of Parliament with 400 soldiers to arrest five leading MPs. However the MPs had been tipped off and had gone into hiding.

In Scotland, the wars against the Covenanters had been costly. King Charles was running out of money and he needed to raise funds, but Parliament refused his request for more money. The Covenanter Army then advanced south from Scotland and occupied much of Northern England. The situation was serious, and on January 1642 King Charles left London. Both the Parliament and the King then raised their own armies - the Parliamentarians and the Royalists - sowing the seeds of the English Civil War.

The Death of the 2nd Viscount Montgomery

   The 2nd Viscount Ards (also called Sir Hugh Montgomery) had, along with Hamilton and under great pressure from the King, betrayed the Ulster-Scots and Presbyterian cause in 1640 by accepting The Black Oath and by opposing Scotland's National Covenant, probably for fear of losing their estates. However the 2nd Viscount died suddenly on 15th November 1642. His widow, the renowned "Presbyterian Jean", perhaps got her own back on her husband when she later married the Covenanter hero   and the leader of the Army of the Covenant, Major General Robert Monro.

The 3rd Viscount Montgomery

   The 3rd Viscount Montgomery, also called Sir Hugh, was a young man of around 18 when his father died. He suffered from a strange wound which left a large open cavity in the left side of his chest, in which his heart could be seen and even touched. He was an expert fencer, musician and horseman; when he took over the command of his father's regiment he would play trumpet, drums and bagpipes for the soldiers. He later became the first Earl of Mount Alexander near Comber, County Down.

The Death of Sir James Hamilton

Then, early the following year, on 24th January 1643, Sir James Hamilton, the First Viscount Clandeboye and Founding Father of the Ulster-Scots, died aged 84. His death and burial have three things in common with Sir Hugh Montgomery's - Hamilton was buried inside a church he had rebuilt from ruins (Bangor Abbey, rebuilt in 1617); to which he had brought a Scottish minister of Presbyterian leanings (Rev Robert Blair in 1623); and without any gravestone or memorial.

(Gifford Savage, of the Friends of Bangor Abbey, recently showed me an old archive photograph of what is more than likely James Hamilton's coffin and tomb within the foundations of Bangor Abbey building. Sadly the tomb is no longer accessible to the public)

No information about Hamilton's funeral service is given in The Hamilton Manuscripts, but his rivalry with Montgomery lived on - in his will Sir James Hamilton threatened to disinherit any of his descendants who should marry a Montgomery!

1643 - Scotland's Solemn League and Covenant

On 25th September 1643, the Covenanters in Scotland formally allied themselves with the Parliamentary forces of England in a document known as the Solemn League and Covenant. From the spring of 1644, the Covenant was administered right across Ulster, from the east coast of County Down and Antrim to Ballyshannon and Ramelton in Donegal, overseen by Rev James Hamilton.

Against all the odds, the Ulster-Scots had succeeded - in forming their settlement in Ulster, their communities and a new church.

Conclusion

From their arrival at Donaghadee in May 1606, to the death of Sir James Hamilton in 1643, the Ulster-Scots had come through five decades of great opportunity and yet enormous turmoil. The success of the settlement in east Ulster provided "...the bridgehead through which the Scots were to come into Ulster for the rest of the century...".* So ends the story of the Hamilton & Montgomery Settlement - and so begins the epic story of the Ulster-Scots!

*from ATQ Stewart The Narrow Ground, page 38 - 39

Alexander Brice

This account does not give anything concerning Alexander Brice, brother of Edward who married Rose Stewart, and a grandson of Rondall Brice. However, Dr. Robert T. Herron of 6 Victoria St., Armagh, Ireland, who is a grandson of Dr. F. A. Brice (died 1813) of Cavan had a complete record of this branch of the family down to 1924 when he wrote to R. G. Brice of Charlotte, NC. Through the perusal of wills, land deeds, and other public documents in Dublin, Dr. Herron found that Alexander Brice was the father of one Nicholas Brice. Nicholas had two sons, Edward and William.

I.   Alexander Brice, b. Ireland

II.   Nicholas Brice, b. , Ireland
1.   Rev. Edward Brice, M.A. Ballycarry, born 1569 in Scotland, died 1636 aged 76; buried at Ballycarry, County Antrim, Ireland. Edward married Elizabeth, daughter of Rev. F. A. Arbuthnot, by whom he had a son, Dr. F. A. Brice.
   a.   Robert Brice, Castle Chichester, b. 1613, d. 1676, aged 63 years.
      (a)   Hugh Brice d. 1686, aged 24
      (b)   Rondall, b. 1646, d. 1697, married M. P. Lisburn, left two sons and two daughters
         aa.   Edward, b. 1669, d. 1742; married Jane Dobbs, daughter of Richard Dobbs.
                (1) Edward m. 1st Rose Stewart, dau. of A. Stewart, Ballingtoy; m. 2nd Jane Smith nee Adair, dau. of W. Adair, ArmyAgent, London
                  (aaa) Edward b. 1749, d. 1815, married Theodora, dau. of Thomas Mullins afterwards created Lord Ventury; left four sons and four daughters.
         bb.   Alexander, B. 1690, Ireland
                (aaa) Nicholas b. 1710, Ireland
                      William b. 1721-1810
                      Unknown son
      (c)   Edward, d. 1726

2.   William Brice b. 1721 Ireland, d. Apr 20, 1810, Fairfield County, SC married in 1749 Jane McClure of County Antrim, Ireland, and they had
       four sons:
   a.   John Brice (1747-1816)
   b.   James Brice
   c.   William Brice
   d.   Walter Brice

The first three named came to Charleston, South Carolina sometime between 1781 and 1786 and immediately set out up-country to establish homes among their Scotch-Irish friends. Land was selected near each other six to eight miles of Winnsboro in Fairfield County in a Presbyterian section which later became a center for education, religion, and culture. Here along with several other illustrious families, the Brices flourished, grew, and contributed greatly to the up-building of Fairfield County and South Carolina. Many descendants have distinguished themselves and their name in recent years in the practice of their professions while some are carrying on the traditions of the family from their Fairfield farms.

On February 14, 1763, Thomas Brice arrived at Charles Town, SC on the Brigt. Hope by way of Barbados (*South Carolina Gazette*, No. 1492, February 12 to February 19, 1763).

William Brice received a warrant for 100 acres on Turkey Creek, South Carolina. Petition dated Tuesday, 1 March 1768. "These Protestants lately arrived from Ireland in the Snow BETTY GREGG, John Monford, Commander petitioned. (*Citizens and Immigrants— SC 1768*, abstracted from contemporary records by Mary Bondurant Warren, 1980. Heritage Papers, Athens GA). This would show that this William arrived before the three sons above if the 1781 and 1786 dates are correct. A William Brice (Nr 11) served as a private and South Carolina Royalist, Muster, Lieut. Colonel Alexander Innes' Company, SC Royalists, Camden, SC, 24 Feb. 1781, 60 days, 24 Feb – 24 Apr 1781.

William Brice

William Brice (1760-1849) was the son of William Brice and Jane McClure of County Antrim, Ireland. William and his brother James Brice settled on Dumper's Creek, a branch of Little River. Another brother, James, settled in the New Hope community. William married Elizabeth Phillips (1765-1838). They had seven children to live to maturity.

BRICE, WILLIAM OF FAIRFIELD DISTRICT, FAIRFIELD COUNTY WILL TYPESCRIPT (MSS WILL: FAIRFIELD DISTRICT WILL BOOK R, VOL. 19, PAGE 259; ESTATE PACKET: FILE 92, PKG. 312) (2 FRAMES).

WILL OF

WILLIAM BRICE SENIOR

STATE OF SOUTH CAROLINA

FAIRFIELD DISTRICT

IN THE NAME OF GOD AMEN.

I William Brice Sen[r] of state and district aforesaid being of sound, and disposing mind and memory, do make and ordain this my last will and Testament in manner and form following..(That is to say) First I recommend my soul to God, and my body to the dust to be buried in a decent Christian manner. Item 1st It is my will that all my just debts be paid, and my funeral expenses 2[d] It is my will to give and bequeath to my daughter Jennet Brice the following named negroes. viz Norman Nelury, Winy and Sarah, also to furnisher her with a horse worth Seventy five dollars, also two Cows, and two feather beds and furniture, also one Beaurow & the loom 5[d] *It is my will to give and bequeath to my daughter Elizabeth Thomson one dollar.* It is my will to give and bequeath to my son John Brice the following named negroes viz Clarissa, Liga and Catharine. 5th It is my will to give and bequeath to my son William Brice the following negro , viz. Big Sam 6th It is my will to give and bequeath to my son Robert Brice the following parcels or tracts of land viz Five hundred and eighty two acres of land purchased from Jonathan Coleman, two hundred and twenty eight acres purchased of Robert Brice Jr. & thirty acres purchased from David Boyd I also allow him the following negroes viz Ben Rachel little Sam. old Fanny. Bob Iby and her five children Martin and Rose and their four children also I allow him all the stock, mules, horses, cows, hogs, and sheep also all the plantation tools wagons and riding carriage also two feather beds & furniture also the Book case & secretary Item 7th It is my will to give and bequeath to my daughter Jane *Douglas* ~~Brice~~ one dollar. 8th It is my will to give and bequeath to my son James Brice one dollar 9th It is my will to give and bequeath to my grand daughter Elizabeth Douglass the following named negro. viz Darkey. 10th It is my will that my son Robert Brice give to the old negro woman Fanny five dollars yearly during her life time 11th It is my will that all other furniture not mentioned. viz household and kitchen furniture to remain for the use of the place. Also the library to be devided betwixt my sons

John William & Robert, and my daughter Jennet. And lastly I

constitute and appoint my sons William Brice and Walter Brice

my Executors In Witness: Whereof, I have hereunto set my

hand and seal this 24th day of March in the year of our Lord

one thousand eight hundred & fifty three.

Signed and sealed in the presence   William ;⌣ Brice   L.S.
                                          his   mark
of and witnessed by us in the

presence of the Testator
                                    Proved (No Date)
Walter Brice
Robert Brice   Recorded Book 19
William Stevenson   Pages 259-260

                                    Apt. 92 File 312

66

John Brice

John Brice b. in Cammoney, Ireland , d. Fairfield County, SC (1756-1816), son of William Brice and Jane McClure (daughter of David McClure and Maud Wolfenden) of County Atrim, Ireland married **Mary Gardner or Garner** (1758-1836) as the spelling shows in the names of children. They had five children:

1.   Margaret Brice (1791-1855) never married.

2.   Jannet Brice (1792-1867) never married.

3.   James Garner Brice (1795-1864) married Margaret Bolick. They had two children:
   a.   Garner Brice married Margaret Clowney; they had one son, Robert Brice. This family moved to Dallas, TX many years ago.
   b.   Alice Jane Brice (1861-1926) married in Dec. 1877 John Spratt Clowney (1852-1929). They had nine children:
      (1)   James Brice Clowney (1878-1936) never married.
      (2)   Margaret Jennette Clowney b. Nov. 2, 1883 married Joe Clowney Bolick in Jan 1903.
         (a)   Joe C. Bolick, Jr. married
         (b)   Thomas Bolick married Agnes Hoffman
         (c)   Mamie Bolick married Charles Burley
         (d)   Frances Bolick married George E. Yongue
            (aa)   George E. Yongue, Jr. married Mary Ella Brice
            (bb)   Catherine Yongue never married
            (cc)   Louise Yongue
            (dd)   Charles Yongue
            (ee)   David Yongue
            (ff)   J. W. Yongue
            (gg)   Hesta Jane Yongue
         (e)   John Spratt Bolick married Doris Ringer
            (aa)   Barbara Sue Bolick
         (f)   Margie Bolick married Charles Locklier
            (aa)   Charles Bolick Locklier
      (3)   Susie Clowney b. Feb 8, 1855 married Joe Warren Milling (1881) on Dec. 24, 1905.
         (a)   Helen Milling b. July 12, 1914 married Carlisle Smoak on June 12, 1937
            (aa)   Susanna Smoak born 1946

(b) Joe W. Milling, Jr. born May 22, 1920 married on Sept. 13, 1941 Elenora Scease b. Dec. 15, 1920
    (aa) Joe III b. July 16, 1920
    (bb) Jimmy b. March 23, 1947
    (cc) Boyd b. July 17, 1949
    (dd) Robert b. June 6, 1950

(4) Eunice Marie Clowney b. April 8, 1887 married John Bolick in 1917.
    (a) Mabel Bolick married Fred McAlister
    (b) Mary Alice Bolick married Ernest Bullard
    (c) Robert Yongue Bolick
    (d) Martha Ellen Bolick married John Earnhart

(5) Julia Adelia Clowney b. Oct 1889 marries Samuel Marion Shirer.
    (a) John Marion Shirer married
    (b) Samuel Shirer
    (c) Clarence Shirer
    (d) William Shirer married

(6) Alice Irene Clowney b. Dec. 21, 1895 married Marshall Garth.
    (a) Alice Garth

(7) John Spratt Clowney (1897-1936) married Marie Crowder.
    (a) Mildred Clowney married J. T. Boulware
    (b) Roland Clowney married
    (c) Ida Clowney married
    (d) Alice Brice Clowney married Paul Weathers
    (e) Lois Clowney married Harry Serrington
    (f) John Spratt Clowney III—not married
    (g) Mary Julian Clowney married Mr. Killian
    (h) William E. Clowney not married

(8) Samuel Boyd Clowney (1899) married Molly Reardon
    (a) William Brice Clowney – married with children
    (b) Julean Clowney married Samuel Daily
    (c) Thomas Clowney married

(9) William Meador Clowney b. April 18, 1902 married on May 16, 1936 Annette Baker b. Nov. 15, 1915.
    (a) Jane Louise Clowney b. April 5, 1938
    (b) Benjamin Brice Clowney b. Dec. 18, 1940
    (c) William M. Clowney, Jr. b. March 23, 1943
    (d) Mary Sue Clowney b. May 18, 1945
    (e) Samuel Stanley Clowney b. Jan 17, 1947
    (f) James Edward Clowney b. May 30, 1948
    (g) Lenora Baker Clowney b. March 5, 1950

Hester Jane Clowney
John Spratt Clowney.

John Spratt Clowney (1852-1929) was the eldest son of Moses and Susannah Yongue Clowney. His name honors his paternal grandparents from County Down, Ireland: John Clowney and first wife Mary Margaret Spratt. John Spratt Clowney married Alice Jane Brice and they raised 9 children in Fairfield Co., South Carolina.

Robert Yongue Clowney
Margaret Rebecca Clowney.

Children of Moses Clowney and Susannah Elizabeth Yongue. The children's cheeks are painted pink, Margaret's medallion is painted gold, and the cord is painted red.

Susannah Elizabeth Yongue
Oct 25 1828 - Dec 10 1895

Moses Clowney
Nov 30 1822 - Feb 7 1894

Moses Clowney in what may have been an old uniform.

Some of the emulsion had been rubbed off this image, allowing one to see the black felt behind the glass. Notice the missing detail on the right side of the coat.   The cheeks had been hand painted.   It apperars that Moses had grey or blue eyes.   On the inside of the cover to this ambertype, under the felt, was a note by Meynel Clowney Cato, which says: Moses Clowney / Son of John Clowney / who emigrated to / America from County / Down Ireland / when he, Moses, was about / 18 yrs. old -- he was born / in 1820 in Ireland / Papa's (Samuel Thomas /Clowney) father.

Name: Moses Clowney
Born: Nov 30 1822   **Died**: Feb 7 1894
Burial location: Salem Presbyterian Church Cemetery, Fairfield County, South Carolina

Inscription: Moses Clowney Born Nov. 30, 1822 Died Feb. 7, 1894

Spouse: Susannah Elizabeth Yongue
Born: Oct 25 1828   **Died**: Dec 10 1895
Burial location: Salem Presbyterian Church Cemetery, Fairfield County, South Carolina

Inscription: S. E. Clowney Born Oct. 25, 1828 Died Dec. 10, 1895

Robert Cheyne Clowney

Robert Cheyne Clowney, born June 11, 1838 in County Down, Ireland. He came to America when just an infant, with his parents John and (2nd. Wife) Anna Boyd Clowney. They

71

settled about three miles southwest of Salem Presbyterian Church, on the old Ashford Ferry road near Strothers, S.C. in Fairfield County. Here he was reared and attended the old field schoolmasters and Mt. Zion College, Winnsboro, S.C.

When a young man, he went to Florida and was successfully engaged in the lumber industry. While there, war was declared. He immediately returned to his home and volunteered for service with the Little River Guards, in the 6th. Regiment under Col. William Bratton - (incidentally; he, and four brothers, namely: John Jr., Moses, Sgt. William James, and Capt. Samuel Boyd Clowney, all served as volunteers, in this struggle - all returned except John Jr., who was killed and his body never found).

After witnessing the fall of Fort Sumter their regiment moved on to Va., July 15, 1861, was placed under Gen. Longstreets command and fought in the 2nd. Battle of Manassas. Here Capt. Michael Brice was mortally wounded, and the company reorganized; whereby Lt. Robert Cheyne Clowney was promoted to Captain, on the battlefield. He continued serving under Gen. Longstreet's command in Va. and Md., also the memorable campaign in the mountains of east Tenn. during the years 1863-64. His horse was shot from under him; however, he received no serious injuries during his entire service. He, with the remainder of his company, were with Lee at the surrender at Appomatox Court House, on April 9, 1865.

In the fall of 1865, he married Miss Margaret Brice, daughter of Samuel and Dorcas Price Brice. They moved to the New Hope section of Fairfield, County, where he became a large land owner, successful planter and stock raiser.

He helped organize and build Mispah Presbyterian Church, where he served as elder until his death. He also gave liberally to the building and support of Bethlehem Methodist Church in his neighborhood.

His lovely home, which he bought from his father-in-law-, Samuel Brice who moved to Alabama, burned a few years after Capt. Clowney's death.

Capt. Robert Cheyne Clowney was a Mason. There was a chapter of The United Daughters of the Confederacy, named in his honor. He always took an active part in the religious, educational and economic life of his community and county. He represented Fairfield County in the Legislature for one term: 1878-1880 during the trying times of reconstruction.

Capt. Clowney died March 12, 1885 of pneumonia, and was buried beside his wife, (who had preceded him only two and a half years in death) at New Hope Associate Reform Presbyterian Church yard. Thus ended the short and promising career of a beloved husband, kind and generous father, and neighbor - a true friend to all mankind - leaving a large family, the eldest being only nineteen years of age.

NOTE: (cmb) Typeface and appearance are same as for Samuel Thomas Clowney eulogy which is accompanied by original written in Meynel Clowney Cato's hand; therefore, this more detailed document may be the original from which other versions - with different birth dates - were interpreted.

4.   William Brice (1800-1805)
5.   **John G. Brice** (1801-1878) known as John Brice, Jr. and Dumper's Creek John as well as John Garner Brice, married his cousin, Jannette Brice (1811-1897), a daughter of James Brice (1768-1845) and his second wife, Mary Cathcart (1778-1828). Eleven children were born to this union but three died as infants:

a.   John C. Brice (1832-1902) never married. He served in the Confederate Army as a private with Co. A Hampton's Legion which became Co. I, 2nd Calvary. M381, Roll 4.

b.   **James Henry Brice** (27 Jan. 1834-10 Dec. 1906) married Mary Emeline Douglass (26 Oct. 1839-10 Dec. 1920) , 15 Oct. 1867, Fairfield Co., daughter of Alexander and Jeanette Simonton Douglass. He served with Co. F, 12th S.C.V. In a letter of Oct. 4, 1938, Mrs. A. B. Douglas (Katherine Brice) of Rocky Mount, NC, told about the service in the Confederate Army of her father and uncles which includes my grandfather, James Henry Brice. Her statements agreed with the muster rolls in the S.C. Historical Commission except in the case of John C. Brice. She stated he served with the Quartermaster Corps whereas the record in Columbia stated the Calvary. She says "Father was a junior at Erskine College when Fort Sumter was fired on in April 1861. He left school and enlisted in the State troops in May and in June entered the Confederate Army. He was in the Battle of 1st and 2nd Manassas (Bull Run, the Yankees called it), the Battle of Chancellorsville, and was within sight of the house where Stonewall Jackson died; he was wounded in the Battle of the Wilderness and was captured at the Battle of the Crater, Petersburg March 25, 1865. I have his discharge signed by the Yankee general and his furlough when he was sent home after he was wounded as well as a number of other relics—including the sword used by Uncle William Brice." In a P.S. she states "I have Father's Literary Society pin that he had when he was at Erskine. It is a gold star with P.L.S. and motto Tentare est valere and also a Greek letter in each of the five points, and in the center the date 1842." (Philomathean Literary Society at Erskine was founded in 1842. The other Society was the Euphemian and since many Brices went to Erskine in the early days, it would be interesting to know the ones who joined each as there was intense rivalry between the two. Mrs. Douglas also said that John Simonton, Cousin Watt Simonton's nephew had something of the history of the Brice family from records in Ireland when he was there.

HONOR ROLL

STATE OF SOUTH CAROLINA,

County of _Fairfield_

TO THE COUNTY PENSION BOARD:

The undersigned applies for enrollment under the Act of 1919. I am the widow of _James_
H. Brice .... who enlisted in Company _F_ Regiment
of _12th_ Battalion of .... Captain _Hayne McMaster_ on the _5_
day of _Sept_ 1861, and served in that command until the _9th_ day of
April 186_5_ He was discharged from the service at _Appomattox Va._
on the _9th_ day of _Sept_ 1861 and was at that time a member of Company
_F_ Regiment of _12th_ Battalion of .... Captain _Hayne McMaster_
I was born _26_ day of _Oct_ 18_39_ I was married to him _12_ day of _Oct_ 186_7_
My husband did not desert the service of the Confederate States nor of this State. My husband died
on the _10_ day of _March_, 19_06_ My income from all sources does not exceed
$_____ The valuation of all my property does not exceed $_nothing_
I am _80_ years of age. I reside at _Winnsboro_ in _Fairfield_
County, S. C., and have lived there since the _____ day of _80 years_ 18_____
I have been on the pension roll of South Carolina in Class _____ I am not on the Pension roll of any other State, nor of the United States.

Sworn to and Subscribed before me this _1_
day of _Oct_ 19_19_   _Mary D. Brice_
W. L. Harvey   (Give full Christian name and Christian name of
Probate Judge.   husband.)
                                        James Henry Brice

STATE OF SOUTH CAROLINA.

County of _Fairfield_

Personally appeared before me _W. A. McDowell_
and _D. H. Robertson_
who being duly sworn, each of them deposes and says that they know _____
who is an applicant for a pension, and they have read the said application; that they know of their
own knowledge that her husband, named _James H. Brice_ was a
Soldier in Company _F_ Regiment of _12th_ and that he
rendered services as therein stated; that she has resided in this State _80_ years.

Sworn to and Subscribed before me this _1st_
                                        W. A. McDowell
day of _Oct_ 19_19_   Company _F_ Regiment _12th_
W. L. Harvey   _D. H. Robertson_
Probate Judge.   Company _G_ Regiment _68_

OFFICIAL INFORMATION FROM THIS OR ANY OTHER STATE.

I, _W. L. Harvey_ Probate Judge of _Fairfield_
County of South Carolina, submit the following evidence from official sources as to services rendered
by the applicant _Mary D. Brice_
....
....
....

To all of which I hereby certify:

Witness my hand and seal this _1_ day of _Oct_ 19_19_
                                        W. L. Harvey
                        Probate Judge of _Fairfield_ County

74

STATE OF SOUTH CAROLINA,

County of _Fairfield SC._

We, the undersigned County Pension Board of _Fairfield_ County, do certify that we have made a careful examination of the application of _Mary L Brice_. We are of the opinion that the said applicant is _____entitled to a pension thereunder for the following reasons:

(1) That her husband _Jos H Brice_ was _____a bona fide _____ in the late war between the States.

(2) That she is _80_ years of age, and was married prior to 1890, and was in Class _____.

(3) That her income does not exceed $ _None_.

(4) The value of all her property does not exceed $ _None_.

(Here state any other reasons which influenced the Board to grant or reject this petition.)
(Give physical condition of applicant.)

None

Give full Christian name of husband

Jos H Brice

COUNTY PENSION BOARD

H H Thomason Chm
D H Robertson
John W Lyons

The oldest family Bible of the John Brice family was destroyed after my great aunt Nancy Brice left the old home place and lived with the Blaines. The original home of John Brice was made of logs and his son, John Garner Brice, my great grandfather built a large home just below it in 1854. It was still standing in 1956 with 1854 on the guttering but it was in ruins.

The following article appeared in *The News and Herald*, Winnsboro about 1937. The author is unknown.

The John Brice Home

Steeped in the atmosphere of the ante-bellum South is the John Brice home on the Dumper's Creek road about 10 miles southwest of Woodward, one of the few remaining structures of this period that have defied the ravages of time in this region.

Built in 1854, the two-story house of typical Southern architecture stands sentinel over the romantic past so dear to the hearts of the older generation, and so intriguing to the imagination of youth, which know of the period only in song and story.

In imagination one may still see gaily plumaged peacocks strutting about the sweeping yards of lilac and hollyhocks. Located on a gentle swell, the southern gentry that lounged on the rambling porches to sip juleps and cut watermelons could see across waving fields of corn and flecked cotton acres. Identical porches, supported by towering columns, are at the front and rear of the stately old home. Granite steps have tumbled down, but still cling to the yard to speak eloquently of happier days. Two dormer windows at both the front and back lend a touch of distinction that gives personality. The trough-like gutters, fast falling into decay, guide the flow of rainwater from the steep roof into cemented storage cisterns.

The great stone fireplaces, some eight foot across, where the family group of four sons and three daughters gathered around blazing logs on dreary winter days, are still in use by the Negro family that occupied the place in 1956, and the original floors, showing the wear of light and heavy feet and numerous scrubbings, were still in good repair. A peg-legged meat cutting block reminds of days of plenty.

Most striking, however, is the wainscoting of walnut, built in panels, which underscores walls of bright patterns of paper, torn and hanging loose in places. The deep blue border overhead, still fresh and bright, amazes even the most casual visitor.

b.	**James Henry Brice** (1834-1906) and Mary Emeline Douglass (1839-1920) had five children:

(1)	Eugene Douglas Brice (26 Jul. 1868-1931) married on April 6, 1904 Laura Lee Jamison (1883-1955), daughter of Isaac Newton Jamison (1843-1908) and his wife Sarah Pauline Cherry (1845-1910) of Chester County.

   (a)	Mary Pauline Brice b. May 11, 1905, taught school in Chester.

   (b)	Maurice Brice b. July 23, 1906, taught school in Winnsboro.

   (c)	Walter Marion Brice b. Oct 26, 1906, unmarried lived in Winnboro.

   (d)	Eugene Douglas Brice, Jr. b. Feb 7, 1910 married Ola Mae Wood, no children; lived at North Charleston, SC.

   (e)	Anna Zelma Brice b. Jan. 3, 1912, worked for years in Clerk of Court, Winnsboro.

   (f)	James Cherry Brice b. June 12, 1914, umarried; served more than three and one half years in Pacific during World War II—including Australia, New Guinea, Biak and the Philippine Islands.

   (g)	Laurie Simonton Brice b. April 18, 1916 married on Sept. 7, 1943 Margaret Mae Hemminger (b. July 28, 1919) at Willington, SC by Rev. Virgil A. Dean.

      (aa)	Laurie Simonton Brice, Jr. b. April 25, 1948 at Hemingway, SC.

      (bb)	James Douglas Brice b. June 21, 1949 at Hemingway, SC.

   (h)	William Boyce Brice b. August 14, 1919; killed in the Battle of the Bulge in Germany on Dec. 16, 1944.

William Boyce Brice

No. 13366   Class of January 1943

Killed in Action, December 16, 1944, in Germany, aged 25 years

The story is soon told: William Boyce Brice, son of Eugene Douglas Brice and his wife, Laura J. Brice; born in Winnsboro, South Carolina, August 14,1919; graduated from Mt. Zion Institute, June 1936; spent two years at Erskin College; entered United States Military Academy and graduated in January, 1943; killed in action, Germany, December 16, 1944.

In high school he was the most popular among both teachers and pupils, receiving the medal for Best All Round Boy in school; at West Point was a member of Fishing Creek, Boxing, and Pistol Marksman, attained the high rank of Cadet Captain, was on the Board of Governors, First Class Club and also held the honor of "Mule Rider." His friends among the Cadets – and they were legion – called him "Willie B.", and men give nicknames only to those who they love. After gradution, he entered the Service of the United States as a Second Lieutenant, choosing the Infantry; training at Fort Benning, Georgia, he was promoted to First Lieutenant and stationed at Fort Jackson, Columbia, South Carolina, whence he was sent overseas in October, 1944; on December 16, 1944 in the <u>Battle of the Bulge</u>, he met a soldier's death in action.

Such is the all too brief story! It tells so little – is so cold and formal. Behind the facts, to those of us who know and loved him, it is the true reality – the fresh young life, the courage that knew no shadow of turning, the honor that never failed, the ability that gave promise of so much "Greater love hath no man than this, that he lay down his life for his friend." I who write these lines knew him "from his youth up." I was his Superin-tendent of Schools for eleven years, from his first grade through High School, in a small town. I know what I do speak. I never saw him do an ungenerous act or fail in that courtesy and courage that marks a gentleman, a gentleman born and a gentleman bred. William Boyce Brice came of good South Carolina ancestry. He fought, therefore, as a matter of course. He was "true to the instincts of his birth, and faithful to the teachings of his father." In "the short, sharp, agony of the Field", in a foreign land, he sealed his loyalty with his life.

G. F. Patton (General)

(From Vol. V, No. 1, April 1946 issue of *ASSEMBLY* publication of U.S. Military Academy, West Point, N.Y.)

A tomb is erected in the Associate Reformed Presbyterian cemetery, Winnsboro, in memory of William Boyce Brice, however, his body was first buried by the Germans in Germany but it was moved by the U.S. Army to the American Military Cemetery, Nouville En Condroz Belgium.

AMERICAN BATTLE MONUMENTS COMMISSION

WILLIAM B. BRICE

FIRST LIEUTENANT, U.S. ARMY

SERVICE # O-025756

422ND INFANTRY REGIMENT, 106TH INFANTRY DIVISION

Entered the Service from: South Carolina   Died: 16-Dec-44   Buried at: Plot B Row 27 Grave 6   Ardennes American Cemetery   Neupre, Belgium

Awards: Purple Heart

   (i)   Thomas Alexander Brice b. April 26, 1928 married on Dec. 20, 1952 to Muriel Florence Barnard of Barton, England.

      (aa)   Mary Florence Brice b. May 20, 1955.

(2)   Robert Henry Brice (1870-1946) married Annie Refo of the New Hope community on Nov. 15, 1900. Annie Refo Brice died when only 32 years of age.

(a) Infant deceased.

(b) Robert Henry Brice married and lived in Philadephia – no children.

(c) Georgia Brice married F. E. Harless of Bartow, Florida
They had one daughter.

(3) Jennette Brice (1873-1902), a nurse, died of typhoid fever on Oct. 12, 1902.

(4) Mattie Belle Brice (27 Nov. 1875-) married J. N. Hardin of Chester.

(a) Joe Neeley Hardin married and had three children; lived in New York.

(b) Harvey M. Hardin, minister and chaplain in Army, served overseas in World War II and the Korean Conflict; married and had children. One son attended West Point.

(c) Janet, lived in Lakeland, Florida;worked as secretary.

(d) Mattie Bell Hardin married and had children.

(e) Nora Hardin lived in Lakeland, Florida.

(5) **Lois Rebecca Brice** (1880-1918) married John Thomas Land of Chester County. See **Robert Brice Land.**

c. William S. Brice (1836-1899) never married. He served in the Confederate Army as a private with Co. B, 4th Calvary in the War Between the States. M381, Roll 4.

d. Nancy Emeline Brice (1840-1918) never married.

e. Mary Garner Brice (1840-1872) married Thomas E. Roddey of Rock Hill on Feb. 6, 1861. One daughter, Nettie, was born on Jan. 14, 1862.

(1) Nettie Roddey b. 1862, married David A. Miller on March 1, 1883.

(aa) David Alvin Miller b. Feb 12,1894, minister.

(bb) Thomas Roddey Miller b. Dec 31, 1896, was in the insurance business in Florence, SC. Served in State Legislature.

(cc) Robert Samuel Miller b. Sept. 2, 1903.

Mary Brice Roddey married the second time J. N. Steele on April 6, 1871 and they had one daughter, Leila Steele born March 11, 1872.

f. Walter Watt Brice (1842-1918) married on Dec. 22, 1870 Carrie Caldwell (1850-1908) of Chester County. He served in the Confederate Army as a private with Co. F 12th S.C.V. and was wounded at the Battle of the Wilderness.

428

1 PLACE OF DEATH

County _____ State _____ Register No. 86

Township _____ or Village

City Rocky Mount No. _____ St. _____ Ward

(If death occurred in a hospital or institution, give its NAME instead of street and number)

2 FULL NAME W. H. Brice

(a) Residence. No. 110 S. Church St. _____ Ward.

(Usual place of abode) (If nonresident give city or town and State)

Length of residence in city or town where death occurred _____ yrs. _____ mos. _____ ds. How long in U. S., if of foreign birth? _____ yrs. _____ mos. _____ ds.

PERSONAL AND STATISTICAL PARTICULARS

3 Sex — Male

4 Color or Race — White

5 Single, Married, Widowed, or Divorced (write the word) — Widower

5a If married, widowed, or divorced Husband of (or) Wife of — Carrie C. Brice

6 Date of Birth (month, day, and year) — July 30 1842

7 Age — 74 years — 7 Months — 7 Days — If LESS than 1 day, hrs. or min.

8 Occupation of Deceased
(a) Trade, Profession, or particular kind of work — None
(b) General nature of industry, business, or establishment in which employed (or employer)
(c) Name of employer

9 Birthplace (city or town) — Fairfield Co. S.C.
(State or country)

10 Name of Father — John G. Brice

11 Birthplace of Father (city or town) — Fairfield Co. S.C.
(State or country)

12 Maiden Name of Mother — Nettie Brice

13 Birthplace of Mother (city or town) — Fairfield Co. S.C.
(State or country)

14 Informant — Wm. B. Douglas
(Address) — Rocky Mount N.C.

15 Filed 4/15 1918 _____ Registrar

MEDICAL CERTIFICATE OF DEATH

16 Date of Death (month, day, and year) — Apr 7th 18

17 I HEREBY CERTIFY, That I attended deceased from Mch 25 1918 to Apr 7th 1918

that I last saw him alive on April 7 1918

and that death occurred, on the date stated above, at 11:48 a.m.

The CAUSE OF DEATH was as follows: Chronic nephritis

(duration) _____ yrs. _____ mos. _____ ds.

Contributory (SECONDARY)

(duration) _____ yrs. _____ mos. _____ ds.

18 Where was disease contracted if not at place of death?

Did an operation precede death? No Date of _____

Was there an autopsy? No

What test confirmed diagnosis?

(Signed) _____ M.D.

(Address) Rocky Mount N.C.

19 Place of Burial, Cremation, or Removal — Woodward S.C. Date of Burial 4/9 1918

20 Undertaker — Bullock Funeral Co. Address Rocky Mount N.C.

Regimental History Antietam after battle report:

Report of Maj. W. H. McCorkle, Twelfth South Carolina Infantry, of the battle of Sharpsburg and action near Shepherdstown. OCTOBER 1, 1862 SIR: I have the honor herewith to submit reports of the part taken by the Twelfth Regiment in the battles of Sharpsburg and Shepherdstown, on September 17 and 20, respectively: About 3 p.m. we arrived, with the Second Brigade, on the field of battle. Immediately, by order of Brig.-Gen. Gregg, skirmishers, under the command of Capt. John L. Miller, were thrown out. The position of the enemy being soon ascertained, they were called in, and a line of battle formed of three regiments, to wit, the Thirteenth, Twelfth, and First, the Twelfth being the center and the regiment of direction. In obedience to orders, we advanced to the top of the hill, in the cornfield, and there halted a few moments, when the firing commenced. The enemy now appearing in force on the opposite hill, and at the fence in the intervening ravine, the Twelfth, at once and alone, advanced down the hill and to the fence in front. In this charge we were subjected to a terrible cross-fire in front and from both flanks. After reaching the fence we were compelled to fall back to prevent being flanked on the right the enemy on the left having been   driven back. The enemy, being soon re-enforced, advanced toward us as far   as the fence.   Now we gain charged on them and drove them back a short distance, but were not   able to reach the fence, as in the first charge. There being a very heavy   flank movement on the right, we again fell back near the top of the hill.   Now the enemy advanced over the fence, when the Twelfth, again and for   the third time, charged upon them and drove them beyond the fence, with   great slaughter, putting them completely to rout as they ran through the   plowed ground and up the opposite hill.   In these charges the regiment suffered severely. In the last the loss was very   heavy. Here fell Col. Dixon Barnes, at the head of his regiment, gallantly   cheering his men on to victory, and here, also, fell Capt. F.A. Erwin and   Lieut. Stover, mortally wounded, both in the midst of their commands.   For particulars I refer to list of killed and wounded, marked D.*   Col. Barnes having fallen, I immediately assumed command. I remained   at the fence with the regiment until near sundown, when, there being no   appearance of the enemy, I fell back to the top of the hill, when I was   ordered to the rear of the fence occupied by Col. Edwards' regiment. Here   we remained during the night and until ordered to march on the night of the   18th.

SHEPHERDSTOWN.   On arriving on the battle-field on the morning of the 20th, the Twelfth   Regiment was formed into line of battle with the brigade. We were not   engaged in the fight, but were under a heavy shelling during the entire day,   and particularly while marching to our position. Here, being well protected   by a hill, this regiment suffered no loss but in 1 man slightly wounded.   In both the engagement I have great pleasure in testifying to the good   conduct of the officers and men of this regiment. They all fought with   remarkable gallantry, always ready to advance, and never faltering in any   instance, whether under shell or before musketry.   I have the honor to be, very respectfully, your obedient servant,   W.H. McCORKLE,   Maj., Comdg. Twelfth Regiment South Carolina Vols.   Lieut. Col. C. JONES.   Source: Official Records: Series I. Vol. 19. Part I, Reports. Serial No. 27   **Battles Fought**   Fought on 27 May 1862 at Hanover Court House, VA.   Fought on 3 May 1863 at Chancellorsville, VA.   Fought on 1 Jul 1863 at Gettysburg, PA.   Fought on 3 Jul 1863 at Gettysburg, PA.   Fought on 12 May 1864 at Spotsylvania Court House, VA.   Fought on 23 May 1864 at Jericho Ford, VA.   Fought on 12 Jun 1864 at Riddle Shop, VA.   Fought on 16 Aug 1864 at Petersburg, VA.   Fought on 2 Apr 1865 at Petersburg, VA.

(1)   Mary Kathleen Brice b. Nov. 17, 1874, d. Nov. 8, 1876.

(2)   Helen Brice b. June 23, 1879 married on May 8, 1906 to Dr. Philip Henry Eve of Beech Island, SC.

   (aa)   Katherine Brice Eve b. Jun 22, 1907, d. May 7, 1908.

   (bb)   Helen Caldwell Eve b. Nov. 12, 1908 married in 1936 to Chevis A. Garrett of Spartanburg.

   (cc)   Philip Henry Eve, Jr. b. Sept. 6, 1911

   (dd)   Edward Armstrong Eve b. Dec 12, 1912

   (ee)   Watt Brice Eve b. Oct. 7, 1915

(3)   Robert Baxter Brice b. Sept. 18, 1883, died 1884.

(4)   Katherine Brice b. Dec. 22, 1884 married Dec. 10, 1913 to Alexander Brown Douglas of Blackstock but their home was in Rocky Mount, NC.

   (aa)   Dorothy Douglas b. Sept. 9, 1914.

   (bb)   Alexander Brown Douglas, Jr. b. March 31, 1916.

       (5)   Frederick Neville Brice b. Sept 12, 1888, d. July 5, 1889.

g.   Margaret Jane Brice (1843-1911) married James M. Blaine and they had eight children.

       (1)   Ella Blaine married S. B. Clowney and had children.

       (2)   Carrie Blaine, former teacher at Mt. Zion, never married.

       (3)   Lula Blaine married W. L. Hicklin and had children.

       (4)   Margaret Blaine married F. M. Bell and had children.

       (5)   Janie Blaine married Rev. W. S. Hamiter of Chester—no issue.

       (6)   Nannie Blaine married S. J. Faris.

       (7)   John Melville Blaine married Lalatha Norris of Newton, GA on Nov. 12, 1919. He was graduated from Clemson College and served in the Spanish American War. Two children: John M. Blaine, Jr. and Margaret Blaine.

       (8)   Walter Blaine married Mary Augusta McFadden on Dec. 26, 19__. He had a brickyard at Blackstock for several years.

h.   Robert G. Brice (1846-1948)

i.   Martha E. Brice died 1848 aged 9 months.

j.   Sarah R. Brice (1849-1880) never married.

k.   David Y. Brice (1852-1854)

James Henry Brice was a private in the Confederate 12th Regiment South Carolina Infantry, Co. G.F., Roll M381, roll 4

Excerpts from Records of Court's Office—Winnboro

1794 – Pursuant to a warrant from John Will Esq. Com. of Land in the District of Camden dated the 7th day of November 1794 I have measured and laid out unto Matthew Miller and John Brice a tract of land containing 490 acres etc.---Nov. 26, 1794. Robert Kennedy, D.S.

1811 – John Brice bought from William Purvis 70 acres of land for $60.

1813 – John Brice bought 128 acres from Joseph Robinson for $450.

1826 – John Brice bough 157 acres from Samuel Cockrel for $1,884.

1830 – John Brice bought 2 acres for $25 on Dumper's Creek.

1833 – John Garner Brice, Jr. bought 83 acres in tracts from Hugh Murdock for $1,550 on Little River.

1835 – John Brice (son of John) paid $1,000 to James Brice, Sr. for 105 acres in one plot and another of 100 acres on Dumper's Creek.

1835 – John Cockrell sold to John Brice 325 ½ acres for $2,604 on Dumper's Creek and Shirley's Branch (a part of Little River).

1836 – Wiley W. Coleman sold to John Brice, Jr. for $1,500 – 97 acres.

1839 – John Brice paid $975 for 65 acres on Little River to Henry F. F. Coleman.

1819 – Stephen Noland sold to James G. Brice 120 acres for $1,200. Witnesses James Brice and D. R. Coleman – Recorded Jan 11, 1819.

1824 – Stephen Noland, Sr. sold to James G. Brice 120 acres for $500.

1837 – John Adger sold to James G. Brice 591 ¾ acres for $11,835 on Dumper's Creek of Little River.

Some land records show that Gardners were in the vicinity of John Brice but none shows who was the father of Mary Brice. John Brice who died in 1816 is buried next to Hubert Gardner (1726-1804) so it is possible he was Mary Brice's father. Robert Gardner and John Brice sold land together—James Gardner and Daniel Gardner bought land in 1805. Then in 1818 and 1820, James Gardner was selling land to William Adger and Nathaniel Majors. Since no other records were found, the Gardners may have gone westward. However, the search was not completed and notes show that Mary Gardner, wife of John Brice, came to this country when she was about 12 years of age. This would have been 1770. If this is true, earlier land records would not be found in Winnsboro.

Tombstone inscriptions of John Brice family found in the Jackson Creek Presbyterian cemetery, sometimes called the Stone Church, follow:
In memory of John Brice who died May 1st, 1816 in the 60th year of his age.
Sacred to the memory of Mary Brice consort of John Brice who departed this life 26th October 1836 in the 79th year of her age.
Sacred to the memory of William son of John and Mary Brice who departed this life A.D. 1805 in the 5th year of his age.

In memory of Margt. Brice daughter of John and Mary Brice who departed this life August 15th 1855 aged 64 years 9 months and 4 days.

In memory of James G. Brice son of John and Mary Brice. Died Dec. 22nd 1864 in the 69th year of his age.

In memory of Jannet Brice daughter of John and Mary Brice. Died Dec. 30th 1867 in the 75th year of her age.

Sacred to the memory of John G. Brice son of John and Mary Brice who was born June 17, 1801 and died Jany 4th 1878 aged 77 years 6 months and 18 days.

In memory of Jannette wife of John G. Brice born April 12, 1811. Died Sept. 28, 1807.

Sacred to the memory of Robert G. son of John and Jannet Brice who died May 28th, 1848 aged 2 years and 4 months.

Sacred to the memory of Martha E. daughter of John and Janet Brice who died December 31st, 1848 aged 9 months and 5 days.

Sacred to the memory of David Y. son of John and Jennet Brice who died April the 20th 1854 aged two years.

In memory of Sarah R. daughter of John G. and Jennette Brice. Born Oct. 28, 1849 Died Feb. 27, 1880.

In memory of William S. son of John G. and Janette Brice Born Nov. 26, 1836 Ded June 5, 1899.

In memory of John C. Brice son of Jno. G. and Jannette Brice Born July 31, 1832 Died Jan. 27, 1902.

Will of John Brice (Sr.)

State of South Carolina,
County of Fairfield . . .

IN THE NAME OF GOD AMEN:

I, JOHN BRICE being very weak in Body but of perfect mind and memory; thanks be given to God calling unto mind the mortality of my body and knowing that it is appointed for all men once to die, do make and ordain, publish and declare this to be my Last Will and Testament. That is to say principally and First of all I give and recommend my soul into the hand of Almighty God that give it and my Body I recommend to the earth from whence it came to be buried in decent Christian Burial at the discretion of my Executors, nothing doubting but by the mighty power of God at the General Resurrection I shall receive the same again, and as touching such worldy Estate wherewith it has pleased God to bless me in the I give, device and dispose of the same in the following manner and form.

And First of all I allow all my just debts to be paid off the whole of my Estate, Next I give and bequeath to my two only sons, James and John, two tracts of land which I now live upon to be equally divided at the discretion of my Executors. In the next place my wife Mary Brice to have a reasonable support off my two sons during life, Again I give to my two sons James & John all my plantation tools and loof plank, Again I give to my son James my gray mare and saddle, Next I give my daughter Margaret my Bay mare, and saddle, also I give to my daughter Jennet my sorrel horse and saddle and Thirty Dollars to be taken out of my stock of hogs and cattle, also I give to my son John one bay horse and bay colt, and saddle to be bought out of the balance of my stock, again I allow my daughter Jannet a spinning wheel to be bought out of the stock and the remainder of my whole stock & geese to be equally divided between my sons and daughters, also I leave my daughter Margaret a Loom and all the harness, also I live my furniture, also to each of my daughters, Margaret and Jennet – a bedstead and furniture, also to each of my sons James and John a bed and furniture, and the remainder of the household furniture and pots to be equally divided, and my incoming debts to settle off my Just debts as far as it will allow, also I allow all the corn and fodder for the use of the family and stock also I allow my son James to have the Bay mares cold, I likewise constitute, make and ordain my son James Brice and Nephew Robert Brice, the sole Executors of this my last Will and Testament.

Signed, Sealed and Delivered in the	His	
Presence of: -------	John Brice	(L.S.)
James Garner	Mark	
Wm. Brice	April 20th, 1816	
John Brice, Junr.	Will Book #7, Page 105	

WILL OF

JOHN BRICE

IN THE NAME OF GOD AMEN

I John Brice Being verry week in Body but
of perfect mind and memory thanks be given to God calling unto mind the mortality of my body and knowing that
it is appointed for all men once to die do make and
ordain this my last will and testament That is to say
principally and first of all I give and Recommend my
soul into the hand of Almighty God that give it and my
Body I Recommend to the earth from whence it Came to
be Buried in Decent Christian Burial at the Discretion of
my Executors nothing doubting but by the mighty power
of God at the General Resurrection I shall Receive the
same again, and as touching such worldly Estate wherewith
it has pleased God to Blefs me in this I give Devise and
dispose of the same in the following manner and form
And first of all I allow all my just debts to be paid off
the whole of my Estate Next I give and Bequeath to my
two only sons James and John Two tracts of Land which I
now live upon to be Equally divided at the Discretion of
my Executors,, In the next place I allow my wife Mary
Brice to have a Reasonable support off my two sons During
life Again I give to my two sons James & John all my
plantation tools and loofe plank again I give to my son
James my gray mare and saddle next I give my Daughter
Margaret my Bay mare and saddle also I give to my Daughter
Jinnet my sorrel horse and saddle and Thirty Dollars to be
taken out of my stock of hogs and Cattle also I give to
my son John one bay horse and Bay colt,, and saddle to
be Bought out of the Balance of my stock again I allow my
Daughter Jinnet a spinning wheel to be Bought out of the
stock and the Remainder of my stock—to whole stock/ & geese to
be Equally Divided between my sons and Daughters also I
leave my Daughter Margaret a Loom and all the harness
also I leave my son James A shot gun also I leave my wife
Mary Brice a bedstead and furniture also to Each of my

87

WILL OF JOHN BRICE

Daughters Margaret and Jinnet- a bed & stead and furniture,, also to each of my sons James & John a bed and
furniture,, and the remainder of the household furniture
and pots to be Equally Divided,, and my Incoming Debts
to settle off my Just Debts as far as it will allow also
I allow all the corn and fodder for the use of the
Family and stock also I allow to-the-Bay-mare-has my son
Jas Brice to hav the Bay mares colt I likewise Constitute
make and ordain my son Jas Brice and nephew Robert Brice
the sole Executors of this my last will and Testament
Signed Sealed and Deliverd In
the presence of
                        his
James S Gerner
        mark

Wᵐ.Brice   his
                              John   Brice   L S
John Brice Junr   mark

                    April 20th 1816

                              Proven 19th Nov. 1816
                              Jno. Buchanan J C O

                              Recorded in Will Book # 7
                              Page 105
                              Recorded May 29th, 1817
                              Apt.# 10   File # 57

Will of John G. Brice

State of South Carolina,
County of Fairfield . . .

I, John G. Brice, of the County of Fairfield in the State of South Carolina, being of sound and disposing mind do make, ordain, publish and declare this to be my last will and testament hereby revoking and making void all former wills by me heretofore made that is to say:

Item 1st. After my death I desire that my body be decently interred in a Christian like manner and that my funeral expenses and all just debts to be paid out of the first monies that may come into the hands of my Executors here after named.

Item 2nd. I will, device and bequeath to the heirs of the body of my son James H. Brice a certain tract or parcel of land situate in said County and State containing one hundred and sixty five acres, more or less, lying on Little River and bounded by lands of the said James H. Brice, John Simonton, Robert M. Stevenson and lands hereafter bequeathed to J. C. Brice.

Item 3rd. I will, device and bequeath to my son W. Watt Brice ten dollars in addition to what I have hereto fore given him out of my Estate.

Item 4th. I will, devise and bequeath to my son John C. Brice and William S. Brice the following tracts or parcels of land to wit – that known as the Dodd land containing in all – four hundred acres, more or less, situate in said County and State and lying on Bushy Fork and Dumpers Creek waters of Little River and bouded by lands of James H. Brice, James Stevenson, James Turner and others - - And should either of my said sons, John C. Brice and William S. Brice die without issue then and in that event the surviving one shall have and hold the lands of the deceased one and pay over to my son James H. Brice One Hundred Dollars to my son W. Watt Brice one hundred dollar to my wife Jennie Brice one hundred dollars, to my daughter Nancy E. Brice one hundred dollars to my daughter Margaret J. Blain one hundred dollars to my grand-daughter Mary Jennette Roddy fifty dollars and to my grand-daughter Lila Brice Steel fifty dollars.

Item 5th. I will, device and bequeath to my beloved wife Jennie (Jannette) Brice all my household and kitchen furniture of every description including books to hold during her life and at her death to be equally divided between my sons John C. Brice and William S. Brice and my daughters Nancy E. Brice and Sarah R. Brice.

Item 6th. I will, devise and bequeath to my said wife and to my daughters Nancy E. Brice and Sarah R. Brice the following tract or parcels of land to wit – the tract upon which I now reside called the home place; the Swan place the McMullen tract and part of the Turner tract, containing in all about six hundred acres, more or less, to hold jointly during the life time of my said wife Jennie Brice and at her death to become the absolute property of my said daughters Nancy E. Brice and Sarah R. Brice – and it is further my will that if either or both daughters Nancy E. and Sarah R. marry or any-thing occur to make a division of the land necessary then and in that event the same shall be appraised and valued by three or more disinterested persons chosen for that purpose who shall make a fair and impartial appraisement and division of the same, allowing to the elder the right of choise.

Item 7th. It is my will that if my daughter Sarah R. Brice die without issue then her portion of property bequeathed her herein shall be equally divided between my sons John C. Brice and William S. Brice and my daughter Nancy E. Brice.

Item 8th. It is my will that should my daughter Nancy E. Brice die without issue then and in that event I desire that the Estate bequeathed her herein be equally divided among all my lawful heirs, the child or children of a deceased parent to receive the portion that would have fallen to the parent if living.

Item 9th. I will and bequeath to my daughter Margaret J. Blain, the wife of James Blain five hundred dollars in addition to what I have already given her to be paid by my Executor hereinafter to be named as soon as it may be convenient for them to do so.

Item 10th. I will and bequeath to my grand daughter Mary Jennette Roddy five hundred dollars to be held in trust by my executors until the said Mary Jennette Roddy shall arrive at the age of twenty-one years or marry and become the mother of one child or children.

Item 11th. I will and bequeath to my grand daughter Lila Brice Steel five hundred to be held in trust by my Executors in the same manner and upon the same conditions as specified in Item 10th for my grand daughter Mary Jennette Roddy. It is further my will and desire that should either of my said grand daughters die without issue then the amount bequeathed the one so dying be equally divided among my lawful heirs in the manner as set forth in Item 8th.

Item 12th. It is my will that the legacies bequeathed to my grand daughters as set forth in Items 10th and 11th be paid out of the rents of the McCullen tract of land.

Item 13th. I will and bequeath to my sons John C. Brice and William S. Brice all the stock, horses, mules, cattle, hogs, sheep etc. and also all the farming implements, wagons and blacksmith tools of which I may die possessed.

Item 14th. I will and bequeath to my son James H. Brice the sum of ten dollars in addition to what I have already given him.

Item 15th. I do hereby nominate and appoint my sons W. Watt Brice and William S. Brice and Alexander S. Douglas the Executors of this my last will and testament.

In witness whereof I have hereunto set my hand and seal this the 30th day of April, A.D. 1875.

John G. Brice   (Seal)

The above and foregoing written instrument was subscribed by the said John G. Brice in our presence and acknowledged by him to each of us and he at the same time declared the above instrument so subscribed to be his last will and testament and we as the testators request and in his presence and the presence of each other signed our names as witnesses hereto.

T. J. Cameron
Daniel H. Cork
David H. Cork

Family of William Brice

William Brice (1760-1849) son of William Brice and Jane McClure of County Antrim, Ireland married Elizabeth Phillips (1765-1838). They had seven childrento live to maturity.

1.   Jennett Brice
2.   Elizabeth Brice (b. d. 1851) married in 1838 to Robert Murdock Stevenson (b. 1799 d.).
3.   John Phillips Brice (b. 1802, d. 1863) on August 10 1853 married Agnes C. Strong (b. d. 1902). John's tombstone list him as John Brice, Jr. son of William and Elizabeth Brice. Whe he died Letters of
Administration to his Estate refer to him as John Brice, Jr. It is not clear since he was the son of William. John and Agnes Brice had two children:
   a.   Christopher Strong Brice (1860-1910) who married on Sept. 10, 1884 Mattie J. Bell (b. 1862, d. 1913). They had the following children:
      (1)   Mark Livingston Brice b. July 13, 1885.
      (2)   Agnes Caroline Brice b. August 5, 1887, married Arch Alexander Douglas on April 24, 1917.
         (a)   Martin Alexander Douglas b. August 24, 1919
         (b)   Archabald Alexander Douglas b. Feb. 5, 1921
      (3)   Charles Bell Brice (b. 1889) married Elizabeth Williams on June 10, 1920.
      (4)   Isabelle Witherspoon Brice (July 1891-October 1891).
      (5)   Mary Chalmers Brice (b. 1894).
      (6)   Marian C. Brice (b. 1896).
      (7)   John Christopher Brice (b. 1901).
   b.   Johnnie Caroline Brice (1863-1893) married Rev. John T. Chalmers on Oct. 26, 1882.
      (1)   Eva Chalmers b. Nov 8, 1883.
      (2)   Mary Agnes Chalmers b. Feb. 4, 1885.
      (3)   Palmer Chalmers b. Nov. 26, 1886.
      (4)   Charlie Brice Chalmers Aug. 14, 1888-March 10, 1889.
      (5)   John T. Chalmers, Jr. July 20, 1890-Jan 11, 1890
      (6)   James C. Chalmers b. Feb. 2, 1892.
After the death of John Phillips Brice in 1863, his widow, Agnes Strong Brice, married Thomas P. Mitchell on Feb. 8, 1866 and they had the following children:
   a.   Willie Forest Mitchell b. June 3, 1867 and married on Dec. 30, 1897 to Burtie Brice, daughter of Thomas S. Brice.

b.   Martha E. Mitchell b. Nov. 18, 1868 and the family Bible shows Eunice M. Mitchell married Robert George Brice on May 8, 1889. It is presumed the initials of Miss Mitchell were somehow reversed.
   (1)   George Wallace Brice, b. Oct 3, 1891.
   (2)   Olive Brice, b. Dec. 16, 1893
c.   Marion Rebecca Mitchell b. August 27, 1870, married Rev. J. T. Chalmers on August 18, 1897.
4.   William Brice (b. d.) married Martha Eleanor Strong and they moved to Mississippi. The family prospered and during the War Between the States a battle was fought at Brice's Crossroads on June 10, 1864. In 1929, one acre was marked and designated as a battlefield site. Some of the family attended Erskine and married in South Carolina.
5.   Robert Brice (1809-1866) never married but he inherited most of the home place and must have been a large planter.
6.   Grace Jane Brice (1793-1857) married John Douglas on Feb. 11, 1819. From this marriage:
a.   William Douglas b. March 6, 1820, d. Feb. 29, 1896.
b.   Alexander Douglas b. Dec. 3,1821, d. 1897.
c.   John Douglas b. Sept. 16, 1823, d. Dec. 9, 1887.
d.   Grace Jane Douglas b. July 18, 1825, d. Oct. 14, 1854 married a Sloan.
e.   James Douglas b. Feb 10, 1829, d.
f.   Charles Douglas b. Feb. 10, 1829, d.
g.   Elizabeth Douglas b. Dec. 19, 1830,married T. W. Irwin.
h.   Robert Leroy Douglas b. May 31, 1835, d. 1866.
7.   James Brice married and moved into the Hickory Ridge section of Fairfield County. A number of this family spelled their name Bryce for sometime while most of them have used Brice in more recent years. Some of this family are buried in Jackson Creek Presbyterian Cemetery but Bryce is on their tomb. James must be buried in the Hickory Ridge section. There was a Thomas, John, and Charles Brice in this family.
   From Jackson Creek Presbyterian Cemetery (also called Stone church):
Sacred to the memory of/ William Brice Senr/who departed this life/ April 29th, A.D. 1849/ in the 89th year of his age./ He was a native of County Antrim, Ireland/ But for many years a Citizen of/ South Carolina./ He was many years a member of the/ Associate Reformed Church/ and adorned the doctrines he professed by a/ walk and conversation in conformity/ with the Gospel of Jesus Christ. He/ was a kind master, a good neighbor/ a devoted husband and indulgent Father. Mark the perfect man, and behold the upright/ for the end of that man is peace. Psalm 37 Ver: 37th./ Preserve O venerable pile,/ Inviolate thy Sacr'd trust/ To thy cold arms the Christian church/ Weeping commits his precious dust./

The pains of death are past/ Labour and sorrow cease/ And life's long war fare closed at last/ His soul is found in peace.

Sacred to the memory of Elizabeth Brice consort of William Brice who departed this life June 27th, 1838 in the 73rd year of her age. How still and peaceful is the grave, Where, life's vain tumults past, Th' appointed house, by Heav'n's decree Receives us all at last.

Sacred to the memory of Grace Brice daughter of William and Elizabeth Brice who departed this life September 14th, 1815 in the 11th year of her age.

Sacred to the memory of an infant child of William and Elizabeth Brice who departed this 1807.
(This last appears on two small stones so evidently twins were born in 1807 but did not live.)

Will of William Brice, Senior

STATE OF SOUTH CAROLINA,
FAIRFIELD DISTRICT . . . .

IN THE NAME OF GOD AMEN:

I, William Brice, Senr. Of State and District aforesaid, being of sound, and disposing mind and memory, do make and ordain this my last Will and Testament, in manner and form following, (that is to say)

First, I recommend my soul to God, and my body to the dust to be buried in a decent Christian manner.

Item 1st. It is my will that all my just debts be paid, and my funeral expenses.

2nd. It is my will to give and bequeath to my daughter Jennet Brice the following named negroes, viz—Norman Henry, Winy and Sarah, also to furnish her with a horse, worth seventy five dollars, also two cows, and two feather beds and furniture, also one Boaureau, & the loom.

3rd. It is my will to give and bequeath to my daughter Elizabeth Stevenson One Dollar.

4th. It is my will to give and bequeath to my son John Brice the following named negroes viz—Clarissa, Lige and Catharine.

5th. It is my will to give and bequeath to my son Robert Brice the following parcels or tracts of land viz—Five Hundred and Eighty Two acres of land purchased from Jonathan Coleman, Two Hundred and Twenty Eight acres purchased of Robert Brice, Jr. & Thirty acres purchased from David Boyd. I also allow him the following negroes viz—Bon, Rachel, little Sam, od Fanny, Bob Iby and her five children, Martin and Rose and their four children, also I allow him all the stock, mules, horses, cows, hogs, and sheep, also all the plantation tools, wagons and riding carriages, also two feather eds & furniture, also the Book Case and Secretary.

7th. It is my will to give and bequeath to my daughter Jane Douglas one dollar.

8th. It is my will to give and bequeath to my son James Brice One Dollar.

9th. It is my will to give and bequeath to my grand daughter Elizabeth Douglas the following negro viz—Darkey.

10th. It is my will that my son Robert Brice give to the old negro woman Fanny five dollars yearly during her life time.

11th. It is my will that all other furniture not mentioned viz—household and kitchen furniture to remain for the use of the place. Also the library to be divided betwixt my sons John, William & Robert and my daughter Jennet. And lastly I constitute and appoint my son William Brice and Walter Brice my Executors.

In Witness Whereof, I have hereunto set my hand and seal this 24th day of March in the year of our Lord one thousand eight hundred and forty three.

His
William Brice (L.S.)

Signed, and sealed in the Presence   Mark
Of and witnessed by us in the
Presence of the Testator. - - -   (Recorded Book 19, Pages 259-160)
Walter Brice
Robert Brice
William Stevenson

WILL OF
WILLIAM BRICE SENIOR

STATE OF SOUTH CAROLINA

FAIRFIELD DISTRICT

IN THE NAME OF GOD AMEN.

I William Brice Sen[r] of state and district aforesaid
being of sound, and disposing mind and memory, do make
and ordain this my last will and Testament in manner and form
following..(That is to say) First I recommend my soul to God,
and my body to the dust to be buried in a decent Christian
manner. Item 1st It is my will that all my just debts be
paid, and my funeral expenses. 2[d] It is my will to give and
bequeath to my daughter Jennet Brice the following named negroes. viz Norman Nelwy, Winy and Sarah, also to furnisher
her with a horse worth Seventy five dollars, also two Cows,
and two feather beds and furniture, also one Beaurow & the
loom 4th *It is my will to give and bequeath to my daughter Elizabeth Stevenson one dollar* It is my will to give and bequeath to my son John
Brice the following named negroes viz Clarissa, Lige and
Catharine. 5th It is my will to give and bequeath to my
son William Brice the following negro , viz. Big Sam 6th
It is my will to give and bequeath to my son Robert Brice
the following parcels or tracts of land viz Five hundred
and eighty two acres of land purchased from Jonathan
Coleman, two hundred and twenty eight acres purchased of
Robert Brice Jr. & thirty acres purchased from David Boyd
I also allow him the following negroes viz Ben Rachel little
Sam, old Fanny. Bob Iby and her five children Martin and
Rose and their four children also I allow him all the stock,
mules, horses, cows, hogs, and sheep also all the plantation
tools wagons and riding carriage also two feather beds &
furniture also the Book case & secretary Item 7th It is my
will to give and bequeath to my daughter Jane Brice Douglass one dollar.
8th It is my will to give and bequeath to my son James Brice
one dollar 9th It is my will to give and bequeath to my grand
daughter Elizabeth Douglass the following named negro. viz
Darkey. 10th It is my will that my son Robert Brice give to
the old negro woman Fanny five dollars yearly during her life
time 11th It is my will that all other furniture not mentioned,
viz household and kitchen furniture to remain for the use of the

96

place. Also the library to be devided betwixt my sons
John william & Robert, and my daughter Jennet. And lastly I
constitute and appoint my sons William Brice and Walter Brice
my Executors In Witness Whereof, I have hereunto set my
hand and seal this 24th day of March in the year of our Lord
one thousand eight hundred & fifty three.

Signed and sealed in the presence   William { his ⌣ Brice   L.S.
                                                    mark
of and witnessed by us in the

presence of the Testator
                                          Proved (No Date)
Walter Brice
Robert Brice   Recorded Book 19
William Stevenson   Pages 259-260

                                          Apt. 92 File 312

Beneath those rugged elms, that yew-trees shade,   Where heaves the turf in many a moldering heap.   Each in his narrow cell,   The rude forefathers of the hamlet sleep.

Old Stone Church is a church building built in 1802. When it was constructed, it was in the Pendleton District, South Carolina. When Pendleton District was divided in 1826, the church was in Pickens District. When Pickens District was split in 1868, it was in Oconee County, South Carolina. In 1968, this section of Oconee County was annexed back to Pickens County. The church is about mid-way between the centers of Pendleton and Clemson. It is now in the city limits of Clemson.

History

In 1790, the Hopewell Presbyterian Church, which was also called the Hopewell-Keowee Church, was built in the Pickens District. Hopewell was the name of General Andrew Picken's house on the Seneca River. Keowee was a common name for this section of the Seneca River in this period. The first church was a log building. Its location is on South Experimental Forest of Clemson University in Pickens County on Seed Orchard Road about 200 m west of West Queen St. This church burned in 1796. The ruins can be found at the edge of the forest. A monument was on the site until 1980 when it was moved to inside of Old Stone Church to prevent vandalism.[1]

The congregation was given a tract of land for the new church by John Miller, who was a printer in Pendleton. Miller had been a publisher in England. In 1775, he and two partners were tried for libel because of their publications of the Junius letters. They were found not guilty. In 1782, Miller came to Philadelphia, Pennsylvania. In 1783, he moved to Charleston, South Carolina and began publishing a newspaper, *Pendleton Messenger*. After the Treaty of Hopewell, he was given 640 acres (259 ha) on Eighteen Mile Creek near Pendleton by Governor Benjamin Guerard. He or his son later deeded about 16.9 acres (6.8 ha) to the Trustees of Hopewell Church.

The new church was constructed of field stone and mortar by John Rusk, who was the father of Texas Senator Thomas Jefferson Rusk, over the period from 1797 to 1802. It was a simple building with wooden pews and a pulpit. Early members of the church included Robert Anderson and Andrew Pickens.

In 1824, the congregation built a new church, Hopewell-Pendleton, in Pendleton. After the new church was built, The Old Stone Church was only used occasionally. The congregation in Pendleton is now known as the Pendleton Presbyterian Church. [2][3]

The Old Stone Church and Cemetery is on the National Register of Historic Places, No. 71000794. The South Carolina Department of Archives and History has additional pictures and information,[4] and copies of the nomination forms.[5]

REFERENCES

1. ^ Historical and Cultural Survey of the Clemson University Experimental Forest
2. ^ Holder, Frederick C., *Historic Sites of Oconee County, S.C.*, 2nd edition, Oconee County Historical Society, 1991, pp. 40-41.
3. ^ Brackett, Richard N., *The Old Stone Church*, Old Stone Church and Cemetery Commission & Pendleton District Historical and Recreational Commission, 1972.
4. ^ Pictures of the Old Stone Church.
5. ^ Old Stone Church and Cemetery nomination form.

Retrieved from "http://en.wikipedia.org/wiki/Old_Stone_Church_and_Cemetery"

Located off Highway 76 between Clemson and Pendleton, the Old Stone Church stands as one of the most interesting historical attractions in the Upstate. According to the legend, stones were gathered by farmers from their fields while women took sand in their aprons, to build the Old Stone Church. Built in 1797 on land donated by printer John Miller, the church was actually the second structure built by the religious community. The first building had been built in the early 1790's on the land of Ezekiel Pickens, son of General Andrew Pickens. It was called "Hopewell" after the Pickens estate nearby. A fire destroyed that wood church in 1796.   **John Miller**   The printer who donated the land, John Miller, came from England to Philadelphia in 1783. He moved to Charleston, South Carolina, and was appointed printer of the State of South Carolina. He founded the first daily newspaper in the state, the *The South Carolina Gazette and General Advertiser*. In 1795, Miller moved to Pendleton, South Carolina, a few miles from present day Clemson. There, he founded the Upstate's first weekly paper, *Miller's Weekly Messinger*. After the first church burned down, Miller donated seventeen acres for the building of another church. He is buried in the Church cemetery.

General Andrew Pickens   One of the original elders of the church was General Andrew Pickens. General Pickens had a distinguished history in Upstate South Carolina. He is responsible for treaties with the native Cherokee Indians, that resulted in many settlers being able to acquire land on which they began their new lives. General Pickens was so respected by the Cherokee, that they awarded him with the name Skyagunsat, the "Wizard Owl." General Pickens married Rebecca Calhoun, aunt of the great Senator John C. Calhoun. Their wedding in 1765 was said to be the largest wedding party ever assembled in the Upstate. It took place in the Long Cane area of Abbeville and the feasting lasted for three days. The pulpit and pews in the church were donated by General Pickens. General Pickens also owned a Bible, that was printed by Benjamin Franklin, Thomas Jefferson, himself, and his son Ezekiel. In his copy, Pickens recorded all of the dates of his family. He served several presidents in various capacities. His love of the wilderness led him to finally settle in a place called Tamassee, located in northern Pickens County. He served twice in the State legislature and was the first representative of his district to the United States Congress in Philadelphia. He died in 1817 at Tamassee and was buried in the Old Stone Church Cemetery. His tombstone reads: "General Andrew Pickens was born 13 September 1739, and died 11th August 1817. He was a Christian, a Patriot and a Soldier."

Dr. Thomas Reese The first pastor of the Old Stone Church was Dr. Thomas Reese. When the building of the church was begun in 1797, it was unclear when the construction would be completed. The church was built on a subscription basis: people donated funds to the church, and when the funds ran out, the building stopped until more money could be raised. Unfortunately, Dr. Reese did not live to see the completion of the church. He may have been the first person to be buried in the church cemetery. Dr. Reese's son is also buried there, but his story is very different from his father's. Sidney Reese shares the dubious distinction of being one of two people buried in Old Stone Church who died in duels. Sidney was killed over a quarrel on a trivial matter by a man named Michie. The other duel victim was Turner Byrum. Byrum was an ardent follower of John C. Calhoun. In a serious disagreement with B.F. Perry (a future governor of South Carolina), a duel resulted with Byrum being mortally wounded. He was buried at midnight during a heavy rainstorm.   **Clergy Hall** Dr. Reese's successor was the Reverend James McElhenny. McElhenny built a small two story-four room home near the Old Stone Church. He called this home Clergy Hall. It was his residence as well as that of his son-in-law, the Reverend Joseph Murphy. In an attempt to aid local farmers, Reverend McElhenny tried to introduce rice farming to the area. A mixture of the summer heat with the flooding of the fields led the Reverend and his son-in-law to catch malaria and die. After Murphy, the building was passed to John C. Calhoun and he added to the building, creating the magnificent Fort Hill Plantation. It is unclear how Calhoun ended up with Clergy Hall. While no pictures of Clergy Hall are known to exist, one can still see the walls of the original building at Fort Hill.   **John Rusk** The builder of the Old Stone Church was John Rusk. Rusk was an Irish stonemason who came to South Carolina from Ireland in 1791. He and his wife, Mary Sterritt, are buried in the cemetery. Originally, their graves were marked with simple field stones. In 1936 the state of Texas erected markers for them. Their son, Thomas Jefferson Rusk, had been very influential in Texas history. He left Pendleton in 1825 and eventually ended up in Texas. Thomas Jefferson Rusk served the state of Texas well. He was one of the drafters of Texas' Constitution, a signer of its Declaration of Independance from Mexico, the Secretary of War in Texas, the Commander-in-Chief of its Armies (succeeding Sam Houston), the first Chief Justice of the Supreme Court of Texas, and (along with Houston) the first Senator of Texas to the United States Senate.

General Robert Anderson One of the more interesting persons buried in the cemetary is Robert Anderson. General Anderson, a life long friend of General Pickens, served in the Revolutionary War, distinguishing himself in the Battle of Cowpens near present day Spartanburg. He volunteered for service and began as a sergeant in the Fifth S.C. Regiment. Anderson's personal life was just as interesting as his military. He was married three times. His first wife was Ann Thompson of Virginia. In his early career, Anderson was a surveyor and he was seperated from her for over two years. During that time, she, assuming that he had died, agreed to marry another man. When Anderson was finished with his work, he was returning home, when word reached him of Ann's impending marriage Anderson raced his horse to the church. While she was dressing, Ann looked out of the window and saw Anderson riding up. Saying to her maids, "Yonder comes Robert Anderson and I love his little finger more than I love the other man's whole body," she ran down the church stairs, climbed onto his horse and the two rode off to be married. They wed on November 4, 1765. Ann was the mother of his children. His second wife was Mrs. Samuel Maverick. Their marriage ended with her death in 1803. His third wife was Jane Reese, widow of Dr. Thomas Reese, first pastor of the Old Stone Church. Robert Anderson was originally buried on his plantation. However, his grave and those of his wives were moved to the Old Stone Church in 1933. A plaque and tombstone were dedicated to his memory. Many of his desendents were present at the dedication, including two of his direct great-great-great granddaughters. The plaque reads: "Robert Anderson (1741-1813): A distinguished soldier of the American Revolution, was a Captain in the Ninety-six Dist. of S.C. Militia 1775-1778 and in the upper Ninety-six S.C. Militia -- 1779-1781; promoted to rank of Colonel for valiant service at the battle of Cowpens Jan. 1781; chosen Brig. General of state militia just after close of war; County and City of Anderson named in his honor." Despite his great influence on the Upstate's history, there are no surviving images of General Robert Anderson.

Slaves in Church The Old Stone Church was the first church in South Carolina to allow slaves to be members. They were not only permitted to enjoy the church services, but were welcomed as members, sitting in the gallery at the rear of the church. The slaves entered the gallery from a staircase located on the rear wall. The staircase is shown here, prior to the rebuilding of the church that took place during the early 1960s. Even though the community was sparsely populated, the membership of the church grew rapidly. According to church records, by 1833, the roll of the church show one hundred and eleven whites and sixty-nine black members. This list did not include children and non-members. Adding these in, it would have placed the total at well over two hundred. Taken from the earliest Session Book is this note:

When 16 colored people were examined on their faith in Christ and fitness for membership, eight were received on condition they obtain certificates of good character from their masters, and eight are to wait for further instructions.

While members had to show good character prior to being accepted into the church, once in, they had to abide by the rules of the church. The following extract tells of a woman who did not.

Moses, Hannah, and Maria are reported to have forsaken the ordinance of this church. Whereupon they are cited to appear before the Session of this church and answer the charge. Mary, a servant of Mrs. Walker, having formerly been in the communion of this church and having been under suspension for the irregularity for forming a connection without a formal marriage, came before the Session and acknowledged her faults and professed her penitence for her former and careless manner of life, whereupon she is received under the care of this Session to be restored in due time as soon as it shall be satisfactorily ascertained that she shows her reformation to be genuine and permanent.

The Old Stone Church was not only used as a church. It served as a school, and in 1919, the first Sunday School in the Upstate was held at the Old Stone Church. The builders of the church knew that living this close to Indians was dangerous. The church could double as a fort if it were needed. Therefore, they built heavy wooden doors which could close over the glass windows to add protection.

Osenappa One of the legends surrounding the Old Stone Church is the story of Osenappa. While little is known of this Cherokee Indian, his impact on the life on Dr. Thomas Reese, the first paster of the church, must have been great. Osenappa was converted to Christianity by Dr. Reese, and he was very influential in converting other Indians. According to the story, it was Osenappa who supplied the Reese family with food and supplies in their early days. When an Indian uprising occurred, it was the actions of Osenappa that saved the Reese family. For a time, the Indian friend lived in the Reese household. Osenappa is buried in the Old Stone Church. His tomb is marked by a simple marker bearing his name and the date 1794. The family respected Osenappa so much, that George Reese, a son of Dr. Reese, named one of his sons Osenappa. Unfortunately, the boy only lived for seven months before he died of diptheria. His small tomestone reads "Osenappa, son of George and Anna Reese, Died at 7 Months."

Restoration In the 1960s, the church was completely restored. An earthquake sixty years before had severely damaged the structure of the chuch. To complete the restoration, it was necessary to take the church apart stone by stone and rebuild the entire structure. After several months of work, the building was completed. The inside of the church was restored to its original stark whites and deep browns. The magnificant pulpit was also restored. The present bulding is used for special services, and the Cemetery is still used be many upstate families and members of the two Presbyterian churches (the Pendleton Presbyterian Church and Fort Hill Presbyterian) that branched off of the original Old Stone congregation. The Church is used for weddings year round. It usually sees at least one wedding a week, for the entire year, and reservations have to be made a year in advance. The cemetery is open to the public and is a very interesting place to visit. As one walks the cemetery grounds, history is everywhere. During the early days of the church, the engraving of tombstones was an art. Many of the carvers put their names on the stones so that other families could see their work. In addition, the skill of these workers is evident today. Many of the markers can still be read, almost two hundred years later. The standing of the Old Stone Church is a testiment to a people not forgotton. As a writer said of the church "it has been an influence for the good of humanity, the preservation of the faith, once delivered to the saints and a dominate factor in those sturdy principles that have brought forth a citizenry of stalwart men and women, whose lives have been a decisive force in bringing this great nation to its present exalted position of leadership among the great powers of the world."

James Brice

James Brice (1768-1845) son of William Brice and Jane McClure of County Antrim, Ireland married Jane Wilson (1764-1804), a daughter of Robert and Agnes Wilson. The Wilson family was quite prominent and a number of them settled in Williamsburg County before the Revolutionary War. James Brice was married the second time to Mary Cathcart (1778-1828). He had six children by his first wife and five by his second wife.

1. Robert Brice (1791-1871) married Margaret Simonton (1801-1843) on Dec. 25, 1817. Robert Brice born 8 Oct 1791 in Fairfield County, South Carolina, son of James Brice, married Margaret Simonton 25 Dec 1817 in Fairfield County, S.C., and he died 2 Apr 1871 in Fairfield County. He is buried in New Hope A.R. P. Cemetery, Fairfield County, S.C. Margaret Simonton was born 20 Jun 1801 in Fairfield County. They had twelve children:

    a. Jane Wilson Brice born 15 Oct 1818 in Fiarfiled County, who married David Hemphill on July 14, 1836.
        (1) John Nixon Hemphill b. June 4, 1837, d. July 22, 1864
        (2) Margaret Brice Hemphill b. January 19, 1839
        (3) Robert Hemphill b. Oct. 11, 1840, d. June 13, 1862.

    b. Margaret Strong Brice b. July 29, 1820 married to Rev. L. McDonald on June 17, 1840. She died Jan. 29, 1842 aged 21 years and 6 months. They had one daughter Margaret Josephine McDonald b. April 27, 1841.

    c. John Alexander Brice b. Nov. 8, 1822, d. 1890, married on April 7, 1846 Margaret C. Bell (1825-1848) daughter of Charles & Jane Bell.
        (1) Carrie Brice (1848-1872) married William W. Ketchins.
            John A. Brice married on Aug. 19, 1851 Nancy McGinnis (1831-1878) daughter of Joseph and Pemelia McGinnis of Mecklenburg Co., NC.
        (2) Clarence Brice had a son, John A. Brice, who was secretary treasurer of the *Atlanta Journal* in Atlanta, Georgia.
        (3) Alice Brice married Dr. John M. Todd.
        John A. Brice married the third time on Jan. 15, 1879 to Mrs. Rebecca Brice Roseborough, widow of James L. Roseborough.

    d. James S. Brice b. Sept. 16, 1824, married on May 11, 1850 Celia M. Bell (1833-1852) daughter of Charles and Jane Bell. They had a daughter Margaret Celia Brice b. Sept. 3, 1851, d. Sept. 10, 1852. Later we find James Simonton Brice and his wife Elizabeth Moffatt in Tennessee. Incomplete list of children follows:
        (1) Robert Edgar Brice (Dec. 6, 1860-Dec. 2, 1916) married Minnie Bell Phillips on Sept. 5, 1886.
        (2) James M. Brice who edited the *News-Banner* in Union City, TN.
            "Last Saturday afternoon marked the change in the management of the *News-Banner* as the paper passed from the hands of J. M. Brice, into the hands of E. P. Waddell.

"Mr. Brice has been owner and manager of the *News-Banner* for 33 years having succeeded his Uncle Walter Brice to that position in 1888, at Troy. In 1909 Mr. Brice moved his paper to Union City.

"A history of the paper under the management of Mr. Brice is as follows: 'The end like change" is written on all creation's face. Human life and destiny is as changeful and transitory as the frosted ice-scapes on the winter's pane. If we leave our work just now, it but does antedate a time when fate shall bid us cease. Why should we repeine. We have enjoyed, we have reveled as a traveller in fairy land in the long work of our life. We are rich in experience if an naught else. We have lived to see the proud and haughty humbled in the dust and to see the humble and weak raised to the estate of might and power.

"If any one truth has been impression the more deeply upon us, it is that we are but tenants stopping but a little season or like travelers putting up for a night at an inn.

"We bought the *News-Banner* from our Uncle Dr. Walter Brice, paying him $700, and took charge the first Monday in April 1888. The world seemed exceeding bright and happy and a good place to be in as we journeyed to Troy that morning. It seemed full of a divine and glorious enchantment and illusion. We asked Dr. Brice to write a last article for the paper as Mr. E. P. Waddell, the new owner and editor of the *News-Banner* has asked us to do so.

"Dr. Brice had been its owner for nearly ten years. Dr. Brice possessed a cultivated intellect. He was a typical gentleman of the Old South. His home folks called him papa, his kinsmen Uncle Walter, his friends Dr. Brice, his enemies called him Bishop Brice referring to his courtly manners, his grace and poise and dignity. He was a fleshy florid man about 5 feet 9 and weighing 240 pounds. He had served in the Civil War as surgeon of the far-famed Avalanche. He was exceedingly courteous alike to poor and rich. He was a scholarly writer, using long rounded periods and it was he who first gave the *News-Banner* prestige in Obion county . ....

"His big brown kindly eyes had no more guile and deceit than those of a little child. He was immensely popular and possessed the supreme confidence of the people....

"While this "stopping" was in process, that fine old Scotch-Irish merchant, our grandfather, the late James S. Moffatt, dropped in and said that he desired the article printed that he handed us....

"We have stated that much fortune and misfortune have been ours but the greatest calamity that ever befell us was the death of our dear son Paul, who was with us for several years in the office. We have never taken much interest in the paper since his death and what we have done more by habit and discipline that aught else.

"Amid many fortunes and misfortunes, there is one very bright circumstance, the *News-Banner* hands over to the editor, E. P. Waddell, a paper possessing the confidence and respect, the esteem and patronage of the people of Obion county unimpaired. In an especial manner, the *News-Banner* possesses and has always possessed the good will, confidence and patronage of the country people. That we secured and held their confidence and respect and good will for more than a third of a century is as high an honor as could fall to us.

"The policy of the paper has been for good schools, for high professional ideals in pedagogy, for economical government, for lower taxes, for toleration and breadth in religious matters and in a general way for the development of a higher social life.
***

"We now say goodbye to our readers and we thank each one from the bottom of a grateful heart who ever said a kind word or did a favor either for the writer or for his paper.

James M. Brice"

(Asterisks denote places where material was left out to shorten the article.)

(3)   Martha Lee Brice married a Huff.

(4)   Charles Strong Brice, McAlester, Oklahoma.

(5)   William Bonner Brice b. Nov. 22, 1873 at Longview, Gregg Co., Texas. On March 31,1902 he married Anna Miller of Colorado Springs, Colorado.

    (a)   Charles Nisbett Brice b. Jan. 21, 1903.

    (b)   Brooks Arthur Brice b. March 11, 1904.

    (c)   William Bonner Brice, Jr. b. June 21, 1906.

    (d)   Clifford Verne Brice b. Dec. 18, 1909.

e.   Robert Wilson Brice b. July 2, 1826 married Anna Maria Steele on Mar. 18, 1850. "He was born at the home of his father, Robert Brice, near New Hope Church in Fairfield County, SC. His ancestors were all Scotch-Irish. His grandfather, James Brice, came from County Antrim, Ireland, about 1780, and settled on Little River. He married Jane Wilson, the daughter of Robert

Wilson, one of the leaders of the Whigs in his neighborhood, during the Revolutionary War.

"The mother of Robert Wilson Brice was Margaret Simonton, the daughter of John Simonton and Jeannette Strong. On both sides the parents of Mr. Brice were intelligent and pious, thrifty and industrious. His grandfather, James Brice, gave the land on which the New Hope church stands, and his father Robert Brice, was for many years an elder in the congregation. His grandfather, John Simonton, was also an elder in New Hope. When a boy, R. W. Brice attended the schools near his home, and was prepared for college by John JcClurkin, who for many years taught the school at New Hope.

"In the fall of 1840 he entered Erskine College, graduating in 1844. Even as a boy and young man, those noble traits of character which were displayed in his life afterwards, were plainly manifested, and he always exerted a good influence over his associates. He connected with the church while a student in college; and in Dec. 1844, when only a boy of eighteen, he began the study of Theology under his brother-in-law, Rev. L. McDonald, then pastor of Union Church in Chester County.

"The session of 1845-1846, he spent in the A.R. Seminary at Alleghany, PA, then presided over by Dr. John T. Pressly. On returning to the home of his father in the spring of 1846, he taught school for a time at New Hope, and then went to the Seminary at Due West, SC where he completed his course in the spring of 1848. He was received as a student by the First Presbytery in 1847, and was licensed in April 1848. After supplying some of the vacancies in the First Presbytery, he was sent to Kentucky in 1848, to supply some of the vacancies in that State. In the winter of 1849-50 he received a call from Hinkston, Kentucky, and in Jan. 1850, he also received a call to Hopewell, Chester County, SC. This latter call he accepted, and on May 31, 1850, he was ordained and installed as pastor of Hopewell, and there spent the remainder of his life, as the beloved pastor of this people. On Mar. 4, 1850, he was happily married to Anna Maria, the daughter of Rev. John and Jane C. Steele of Kentucky, who proved to be to him a helpmate indeed, and a model pastor's wife. To them was born a large family of children, all of whom have proved worthy children of a noble pair. As a pastor, Mr. Brice was greatly beloved by his congregation. His people placed implicit confidence and trust in him, for they found him to be a man without guile and without hypocrisy. His sermons were plain, expository and practical, and more than ordinarily interesting and instructive. Dr. R. Lathan, who was raised in Hopewell, says "He never preached a poor sermon—never an unstudied one." His custo was, during the winter months, to explain a Psalm and preach a sermon, and during the summer months to lecture on some book of the Bible, selected in regular order, and then after a short interval to preach a sermon. In this way he had explained the whole book of Psalms, and his lectures covered a good portion of the books of the New Testament. In his time Hopewell was literally a school house in which the Bible was taught. These faithful labors, together with regular pastoral visitation and catechizing were blessed to the odification of his congregation. In 1866 or 1867, Mr. Brice began to preach one third of his time at Old Purity, two miles south of Chester, and there in 1869 he organized the prescent A.R.P. church at Chester. He continued to minister to this new organization for one third of his time until October 1875.

"From the first to the last, Mr. Brice took an active interest in everything that pertained to the welfare of his denomination. He was constant in his attendance at Presybtery and Synod, and was an influential member of both these courts. He was Moderator of Synod at Sardis, NC in 1862, and at Hopwell, TN in 1874, and he was Treasurer of Synod's Home Mission funds from 1854 to 1878. In summing up the character of Mr. Brice, Dr. Lathan, who was in early life a member of his congregation, and for a while a student in his home, says in his history of Hopewell and its Pastors: "He was in the strictest sense of the word a model man. Nature had bestowed on him some rare gifts. His disposition was that of a high-toned Christian gentleman. In his nature there was nothing wild and fanciful. He was by every instinct of his being a matter of fact man. His passions were kept under perfect control. No man, so far as we know, ever saw him violently angry, nor did anyone ever hear him utter a hasty or rash sentence. All his convictions were reached calmly and conscientiously. Amid all the vicissitudes of life, he was, as near as mortal man can be, the same. His manners were plain but always gentlemanly.

"No man was better adapted to make himself friends, and no man was better fitted to retain them when made. Nature designed him to govern others, in that he was granted power to govern himself."
(From *The Centennial History of the Associate Reformed Presbyterian Church 1803-1903,* pp. 78-81)

(1) Janie C. Brice (1857-1907) married James McCalla Caldwell on Feb. 9, 1871.
    (a) Anna Brice Caldwell(1871 -) married William Stuart Hall on Sept. 19, 1894.
        (aa) William D'ormond Hall who married Claire Poole.
        (bb) James Caldwell Hall
        (cc) Robert Elliott Hall
        (dd) Anna Brice Hall

(ee)   Joseph Holmes Hall

(b)   Robert Brice Caldwell (1874 -) married Leila Hope Latham on Dec. 19, 1900. Their four children: Mary Simmons Caldwell, Leila Latham Caldwell, Susie Meek Caldwell, and Robert Brice Caldwell, Jr.

(c)   William Joseph Caldwell (1876-1879)

(d)   Janie Bothia Caldwell (1878 -) married James Baxter Westbrook on June 27, 1906. Children: Bothia Westbrook, Isabelle Westbrook and Janie Brice Westbrook.

(e)   **Florence Mcalla Caldwell** (1880 -) married **Robert James Lindsay** on Sept. 18, 1918.

     (aa)   **Robert James Lindsay, Jr.**

     (bb)   Stuart Hall Lindsay.

(f)   Mary McKenzie Caldwell (1881-1905).

(g)   Susan Hemphill Caldwell (1884 -).

(h)   William Frederick Caldwell (1886 -) married Juanita Wylie on Feb. 18, 1919.

James McCalla Caldwell (1888 -) married Naomi Harmon on Oct. 28, 1913.

     (aa)   James McCalla Caldwell.

     (bb)   Nellie Caroline Caldwell.

(i)   John Steele Caldwell (1889-) married Kathryn Cross on April 22, 1914.

     (aa)   John Steele Caldwell, Jr.

(j)   Kate Caldwell (1890-1895).

(2)   Margaret Simonton Brice (1852-1879).

(3)   Ashbel Green Brice (1854-1918) married Sallie Miller of Camden, AL on Dec. 18, 1883. No children.

A native and lifelong resident of Chester County, th elate Ashbel Green Brice was for four decades one of the most successful and most highly respected members of the Chester County Bar. He enjoyed a large and important practice, which was practically entirely in the realm of civil law. Mr. Brice was a man of deep public spirit and served his community in many positions of trust and responsibility, representing the county twice in the State Legislature, being for many years the chairman of the Chester City Board of Education, acting very effectively as a trustee of the Industrial and Mechanical College for Negroes, and holding high office in his church. In all of these fields of human endeavor, he rendered notable and unselfish service. He had a clear and logical mind and a sound and discriminating judgment; was conscientious, careful, and painstaking in everything he undertook; and a man of strong convictions, he stood at all times for law and order in all things. Though modest and retiring, he possessed great moral courage and consistently adhered to the highest ideals of his professon.

Ashbel Green Brice was born in Chester County, April 7, 1854, a son of Rev. Robert Wilson and Anna M. (Steele) Brice. . . . He was taught by his mother and did not attend school until after his sixteenth year when he began to prepare for college. . . . He studied for a while in the neighborhood schools and in the autumn of 1872 he entered the sophomore class at Erskine College. In the sophomore and junior years he stood first in his class, and in the senior year he won three of the five medals that had been offered to the class. After he was graduated, he taught school one year in Newberry County. In December 1876, he began the study of law in the office of Colonel James H. Rion, at Winnsboro. The following year he was admitted to practice and opened an office in Winnsboro; but, his father's health having failed, he soon returned to the old home, where he remained until his father's death in March 1879. He managed the farm during most of that year, but in Novembr 1878, he commenced law practice in Chester. In January 1879, he permanently located in that town... (Condenses from a rather long account in D. D. Wallace's *History of South Carolina*, Vol. 4)

(4)   Joseph Amanda Brice (1856-1887) married Dr. J. C. Galloway on Jan. 23, 1879.

    (a)   Julia Galloway married F. M. Kirkpatrick of Macon, GA.

        (aa)   Mary Kirkpatrick d. 1920.

        (bb)   Annie Kirkpatrick d. 1935.

(5)   Leila Mary Brice b. Dec. 9, 1857, d. Dec. 27, 1906 at Due West, SC.

(6)   Martha Frances Brice (1859-1909) married e. Brice McCaw of Chester on Jan. 12, 1881. They had three children.

(7)   John Steele Brice (1861 -) married Genevieve Fuller of Ninety Six in 1893. She died in 1897 and their only child died an infant.

    His second marriage was to Miss Claude Moore of York, SC.

    (a)   Claude d. as an infant.

    (b)   John Steele Brice, Jr.

    (c)   Robert William Brice.

    (d)   Adolphus Moore Brice.

    (e)   Ashbel Brice.

(8)   Anna M. Brice (1864 -) married Rev. J. W. Baird on June 4, 1891.

(a) Julia Warden Baird b. June 21, 1892 married on June 16, 1915 in Due West to Rev. Moses Ralph Gibson.

(b) Josie Brice Baird b. Nov. 26, 1893 married James W. Thompson Nov. 20, 1920.

(c) Elizabeth Steele Baird (1895-1896).

(d) Robert Cornelius Baird b. Dec 31, 1897 married Lela Roper on April 10, 1922.

(e) James Ashbel Baird b. Jan 27, 1899 married Marie McConnel Stroud on June 3, 1920.

(f) Anna Brice Baird b. July 27, 1902.

(9) Louisa Julia Brice (1868 -) married Rev. John Patterson Knox at Due West on Nov. 20, 1890. No children.

(10) Robert Hemphill Brice (1866-1899).

f. Christopher Simonton Brice b. April 25, 1828. D. 1900 married Margaret Gooch on Dec. 4, 1855. They had no children.

g. Walter Brice b. Feb. 7, 1830, M.D. in Troy, Tennessee married Mary E. Anderson on Feb. 7, 1854. Dr. Walter Brice served as a surgeon in the Confederate Army. Evidently he was married a second time because Rev. Robert S. Harris married Margaret Brice of Troy, a daughter of Dr. Walter Brice and Jane Bonar Moffatt.

(1) Robert Brice Harris b. 1900.

h. Charles Strong Brice b. Oct. 19, 1831 married Fannie Hinton. Charles was a lawyer in Chester.

i. Martha Brice b. August 25, 1833. d. 1922, married Prof. Joseph F. Lee on Dec. 23, 1853. Mrs. Lee died at the home of her son-in-law Rev. C. M. Boyd.

j. Sarah Amanda Brice b. Sept. 15, 1835, married Maj. A. B. Enloe of Troy, Tennessee on January 9, 1872.

k. Mary Elizabeth Brice b. May 18, 1838, married J. Israel Moffatt of Troy, Tennessee.

l. Thomas Scott Brice born 16 Sep 1840 in Avon, Fairfield County, South Carolina, and died 5 Mar 1913 in Shelby, North Carolina. He married Frances Eliza Adams on May 2, 1871.

(1) Eliza Burton Brice b. Jan. 19, 1873 married W. F. Mitchell.

(2) Mary Adams Brice b. July 13, 1874.

(3) Robert Hemphill Brice (1875-1877).

(4) James Mc .. Adams Brice (1877-1880).

(5) Thomas Leslie Brice b. April 25, 1888, married.

2. James Brice (b. d. 1844) never married.

3. William Brice (1793-1872) married Mary Simonton (1809-1890) on Oct. 6, 1829. The ceremony was performed by Rev. John Hemphill. William and Mary Brice had thirteen children.

    a. Margaret Brice b. Dec. 16, 1831, d. 1868, married Rev. D. P. Robinson May 24, 1849. The ceremony was performed by Rev. James Boyce.

        (1) William Brice Robinson b. March 1850.

        (2) Gardner Springs Robinson b. March 1852.

        (3) Mary Robinson b. 1854.

        (4) Lawrence Henry Robinson b. March 1852.

        (5) Margaret Frances Robinson b. Feb. 1864.

        (6) J. Lee Robinson b. July 12, 1867.

    b. Calvin Brice b. Oct. 5, 1832, d. 1905, married on Nov. 13, 1866 Nancy Ellen Wallace. The ceremony was performed by Rev. R. Ross.

        (1) Robert George Brice (1869-1900) married Eunice M. Mitchell on May 8, 1889.

            (a) George Wallace (1891-)

            (b) Olive (1893)

        May have been others.

This family corresponded with Robert T. Herron of Ireland and was getting the Brice records together.

        (2) William Brice

        (3) J. M. Brice

        (4) Evelyn Brice who married Thomas W. Brice, son of Maj. Thomas W. Brice and nancy Boyce Brice. Children are listed under Thomas W. Brice.

        (5) Ruth Brice married E. M. Kennedy of Blackstock.

        (6) Albert W. Brice married Tat Nicholson and they lived in the old home near Woodward.

        (7) A. Homer Brice was a graduate of Erskine in 1891. He served in the State Legislature; had a number of records of the Brice family. He never married and died in March 1956.

    c. Robert R. Brice b. Sept. 13, 1834; d. Apr. 25, 1861; never married.

    d. Jane W. Brice b. March 18, 1836 married J. C. Yonge on March 12, 1855. They had children.

    e. John P. Brice b. Dec. 27, 1837, d. July 24, 1861

    f. James A. Brice b. Nov. 22, 1839, died 1909. He married on Dec. 20, 1860 to Margaret Josephine McDonald (1841-1874) daughter of Rev. L. McDonald and his wife, Margaret Brice. The ceremony was performed by Rev. R. W. Brice.

        (1) Paul McDonald Brice (1861-1907) was a newspaper writer and editor.

(2)   William Oscar Brice (1866-1909) married Rachel Buchanan
        Thompson on Nov. 15, 1893.
        (a)   Palmer Matthews Brice (b. 1894) married Elizabeth Sloan,
                daughter of Mr. & Mrs. E. D. Sloan of Winnsboro. They had
                children.
        (b)   William Oscar Brice (b. 1894) married Rebekah Jennings of
                Winnsboro.
                (aa)   Peggy Brice married Charles Brown.
        Lieutenant General William Oscar Brice, U.S. Marine Corps who
was the second Marine aviator to attain this rank, has had a long,
colorful and distinguished career in the service of his country. The
son of Dr. William Oscar Brice and Rachel Thompson Brice, he was
born in Columbia in 1899. The family moved to Winnsboro six years
later. He was graduated from Mt. Zion Institute, where "Skinny" Brice
early exhibited his inbred loyalty to the "Rebel" cause by winning an
oratorical contest on the subject of "The Confederacy." He served at a
second lieutenant in World War I, which interrupted his studies at
The Citadal but he returned to finish his education, becoming a naval
aviator in 1924. Long before the second world war conflict began, he
was a member of the "Caterpiller" club, a real distinction in those
early days of air travel.
        General Brice has won a multitude of citations and decorations,
including the Legion of Merit presented by General Vandergrift.
During his first eighteen months in the Pacific war theater, when the
going was really tough, he displayed leadership, verve and daring of
the highest caliber and in 1943, Colonel Brice was awarded the
Distinguished Service Medal for outstanding leadership of all the
Allied search bombers and torpedo planes in the Solomons area. A
Presidential citation accompanied it and his unit was given credit for
inflicting tremendous losses on the Japanese.
        In 1944, Vern Haugland, famed Associated Press Correspondent,
writing of the Bonnie Blue Flag which waved over Brice's headquarters in the Solomons, said: "You don't have to have a Southern
accent to work under Colonel Brice but it helps. In Navy parlance,
Brice is the man who made the air safe over the Solomons and he has
commanded some of the nation's top aces, including Foss, Boyington,
and Hassen." Later in the war, the Winnsboro Marine officer did
another tour of duty in the Far East and he has been twice to Korea,
once during the "police action" and again since the "uneasy peace.
Earlier in this year he was elevated to his present rank, thus becoming

the second Marine aviator to attain this distinction in all American history. There are only four other Lieutenant Generals in the entire Marine Corps. Commandant Lemuel Shepherd is the only four star general (excerpt of news article in *The News and Herald*, Winnsboro).

History of Fairfield County South Carolina from "Before the White Man Came" to 1941 by Fitz Hugh McMaster has one chapter, XIII, titled Character Sketches of Winnsboro by W. O. Brice, 1907. In a foot note Mr. McMaster says "William Oscar Brice 1866-1909 is a worthy scion and flower and fruit of one of the oldest and most respected County families of Fairfield. It has been preeminent for culture and education and in the religious life of the county. In war and peace the Brice family did its full duty. William Oscar was born and reared in Winnsboro. He received his academic education here at Mt. Zion Academy, his collegiate education, at Erskine College."

- (c) Margaret Osmond Brice (b. 1903) lived in Dallas, Texas.
- (3) Robert Edwin Brice (1868-1916) married Carrie McMaster Flenniken Dec. 18, 1889.
  - (a) John Flenniken Brice b. Dec. 4, 1890.
  - (b) Margaret Josephine Brice b. July 25, 1893 married Charles Wilmot Brown July 2, 1913.
    - (aa) Josie Brice Brown born August 27, 1921.
  - (c) Robert Edwin Brice, Jr. born Jan. 30, 1897.
- (4) John Clifford Brice (1872-1915) married and had a son, John Clifford Brice, Jr.

After the death of Margaret Josephine Brice on June 5, 1874, James A. Brice married Jane Isabel Kennedy on Jan. 4, 1877. The ceremony was performed by Rev. W. L. Pressley.

- (5) Pressley Kennedy Brice b. Feb. 19, 1878 married Margaret T. Wahls in El Paso, Texas on Sept. 7, 1910.
  - (a) Margaret Brice b. July 3, 1911.
- (6) Moffatt Grier Brice b. Feb. 28, 1880, d. Dec. 10, 1899 after completing his junior year at Erskine College.
- (7) Mary Lavinia Brice b. April 8, 1882.
- (8) James Alexander Brice b. Nov. 1, 1884, d. March 9, 1920 married Sara Oakley in 1717. They had children.
- (9) Charles Simonton Brice b. July 6, 1887 married Louise Sparin at Fort Monroe, VA on Oct. 6, 1917.
  - (a) Charles S. Brice Jr. b. at Fort Monroe, VA on August 8, 1918.
- (10) John Payson Brice b. Sept. 22, 1889, d. 1891.

          (11)   Luther Kennedy Brice b. March 28, 1892, was a lawyer in Spartanburg.

          (12)   Julia Frances Brice b. April 26, 1895.

    g.   Martha Simonton Brice b. Nov. 12, 1841, d. 1878, married Dr. Thomas Barkley Madden on Jan. 19, 1868.

          (1)   Mary J. Madden b. April 6, 1870, d. April 27, 1910; married John E. Matthews of Columbia. They had children.

          (2)   William Campbell Madden b. May 21, 1872; lived in Winnsboro.

          (3)   Thomas Barkley Madden b. Sept. 21, 1874 served for some time at postmaster in Columbia.

          (4)   Robert Brice Madden b. Oct. 24, 1877, d. Sept. 12, 1878.

    h.   Mary E. Brice b. Nov. 30, 1843, d. 1895, married John Vinson on Sept. 4, 1867.

    i.   William W. Brice b. March 4, 1846, married by Rev. James Boyce to Hattie E. Vinson on Sept. 5, 1867.

          (1)   Mary E. Brice b. Oct. 9, 1869 was married on Oct. 5, 1887 to Josiah H. Moffatt at White Oak, in Fairfield County.

    j.   Sallie Agnes Brice b. June 7, 1848, married by Rev. J. M. Todd to J. M. Galloway (1847-1917) on Dec. 18, 1872.

          (1)   William B. Galloway b. Oct. 24, 1873, d. June 11, 1903

          (2)   Louis C. Galloway b. Sept. 3, 1875, d. 1940. Served as Professor of History at Erskine College.

          (3)   Robert S. Galloway b. Oct. 10, 1880.

          (4)   Mary E. Galloway b. Feb. 1, 1883.

          (5)   John C. Galloway b. Sept. 11, 1884.

          (6)   _ L. Galloway b. Oct. 14, 1890.

    k.   Walter H. Brice b. Dec. 21, 1850, d. Nov. 16, 1855

    l.   Infant son born Feb. 18, 1853.

    m.   Frances E. Brice b. Dec. 13, 1854, d. July 29, 1855.

4.   John Brice (1795-1869) never married.

5.   Nancy Brice (1802-1864) married John Simonton (1802-1864). W. B. Simonton was a son of this marriage. He was in Co. H, 12th S.C.V. and lost a leg at the Battle of Sharpsburg, Sept. 17, 1862.

6.   Walter Brice (1804-1871) married Martha Emeline Moore (1811-1898) on April 28, 1831. He became an outstanding medical doctor.

NAME OF SOLDIER: Brice, Walter H.

NAME OF DEPENDENT: Widow, / Minor,

SERVICE: Co. 1, 6th S. Car. Inf. S / Hosp. Corps, C.S.A.

DATE OF FILING	CLASS	APPLICATION NO.	CERTIFICATE NO.	STATE FROM WHICH FILED
1927 June 14	Invalids	1,833,368	A-12-10-27	S. C.
	Widow,			
	Minor,			

ATTORNEY:

[Veteran]: C 2,297,095

a.   James Michael Brice, M.D. b. April 27, 1832; Capt. Co. G 6th S.C.V. wounded at Seven Pines, killed at Fort Harrison, VA Sept. 30, 1864.

b.   Walter Scott Brice b. March 26, 1834, d. July 13, 1862 in Richmond, VA; Co. F, 12th S.C.V.

c.   Robert Wade Brice b. June 10, 1836, Confederacy, Co. H 6th S.C.V., d. 1910, captured at Vicksburg, Mississippi July 4, 1863; m. Martha Matilda Waters on Feb. 26, 1863. Buried Concord Presbyterian Church Cemetery, Woodward, Fairfield Co., SC.

Roll of Prisoners of War Captured at Vicksburg, Miss. In Hospital

Note.—The names of all Commissioned and Non-Commissioned Officers and Privates will be arranged separately, according to rank, in alphabetical order.

NO.	NAMES—In alphabetical order	RANK	REGIMENT	CO.	WHERE CAPTURED	WHEN CAPTURED	REMARKS
129	William Morris	Private	39th Reg. Georgia Inf.	E	Vicksburg Miss.	July 4, 1863	
130	B. L. Cullsburg	Sergeant	"	K	"	"	
131	Joseph L. Self	Private	"	"	"	"	
132	John M. Crawford	"	"	"	"	"	
133	Wm. W. Mitchell	"	"	"	"	"	
134	Willis N. Klickler	"	"	"	"	"	
135	James W. Warnock	"	"	"	"	"	
136	Robert M. Boice	"	"	"	"	"	"
137	W. F. Wood	"	"	"	"	"	
138	W. W. Shields	"	"	"	"	"	
139	James H. Kingkaik	"	"	G	"	"	
140	John C. McWillLin	"	"	"	"	"	
141	A. N. Boice	"	"	B	"	"	
142	John Davolin	"	"	"	"	"	
143	David Stevenson	"	"	"	"	"	
144	John Stevenson	"	"	"	"	"	
145	Arha H. Haggard	"	"	"	"	"	
146	Joseph Ellerer	Captain	36th Georgia Inf.	A	Vicksburg Miss.	July 4, 1863	
147	C. C. M. Boice	2d Lieut.	"	"	"	"	
148	Samuel Watkins	Private	"	"	"	"	
149	F. M. Morehead	"	"	"	"	"	
150	Silas George	"	"	"	"	"	
151	John F. Long	"	"	"	"	"	
152	Hugh Tapp	"	"	"	"	"	
153	John C. Smith	"	"	"	"	"	
154	George P. Way, field	"	"	"	"	"	
155	Joseph S. Ezzard	"	"	"	"	"	
156	Wm. K. Wells	4th Sergt.	"	F	"	"	
157	B. S. Chapman	Private	"	"	"	"	
158	S. P. Chanon	"	"	"	"	"	
159	William Batton	"	"	C	"	"	
160	Owen Reid	"	"	"	"	"	
161	William Columna	"	"	"	"	"	

2967

Robert Brice, Jr.
Fairfield District
S.C.

R. Filed Nov 20, 1865,

(13th Ex.) Worth over $20,000

Recom'd by the Gov.

Pardoned Same day

(1)   Walter Scott Brice b. Jan. 1, 1864, d. Oct. 22, 1882.
    (2)   Ida Marshall Brice b. March 30, 1866, d. 1896 married John James
            Waters on Jan. 5, 1886.
        (a)   Matilda Waters
        (b)   Elizabeth Waters
        (c)   Robert Brice Waters
        (d)   John James Waters, Jr.
    (3)   Richardson Walker Brice (1864 -) married Nancy Jane Mobley on
            Nov. 7, 1894. She was the daughter of Edward P. Mobley and lived at
            Wedgefield, SC
        (a)   Robert Wade Brice b. Oct. 6, 1895 married Henri Wertz of
                Sumter on March 4, 1918.
        (b)   Marion Mobley Brice married on Nov. 3, 1919 to Mary Belle
                Welch of Sumter. They had children.
        (c)   Marshall Moore Brice finished Clemson in 1917, married
                Margaret Gibbes Harris of Staunton, VA on June 7, 1913.
        (d)   Kathryn Mollichamp Brice died in infancy.
        (e)   Edward Pickett Mobley Brice.
        (f)   Walter Scott Brice.
        (g)   Matilda Watson Brice b. July 14, 1804
    (4)   James Lunsford Brice b. Oct. 17, 1871, married Jennie Eliza Bishop on
            June 27, 1911.
        (a)   Jennie Laurence Brice
        (b)   James Lunsford Brice, Jr.
    (5)   Robert Wade Brice b. July 15, 1874, d. March 1, 1910, married Carrie
            H. Suydam on June 15, 1898.
        (a)   Charles McDonald Brice b. Nov. 3, 1900, married June 19, 1920
                to Harriette Black of Waxhaw, N.C.
            (aa)   Harriette Brice b. June 1921.
            (bb)   Charles M. Brice, Jr. b. April 23, 1923.
        (b)   Ida Marshall Brice b. Nov. 29, 1901.
        (c)   Cornelia Suydam Brice b. Jan. 14, 1804.
        (d)   Robert Wade Brice, III b. July 13, 1906.
        (e)   Frances Brice b. August 14, 1919.
    (6)   Michael Moore Brice, b. 1875
    (7)   Wilson McDonald Brice b. 1881
d.   John Moore Brice b. March 7, 1839, Co. H 6th S.C.V.; wounded on June 7, 1862,
        killed June 3, 1864 at Gains Mill, VA.
e.   Thomas William Brice b. Nov. 22, 1841; d. 1908; served in Major Hampton's
        Legion. He married Nancy Eugenia Boyce.

HONOR ROLL

STATE OF SOUTH CAROLINA,

County of *Fairfield*

TO THE COUNTY PENSION BOARD:

The undersigned applies for enrollment under the Act of 1919. I am the widow of *R. Wade Brice* who enlisted in Company *H 6th* Regiment of .... Battalion of ...., Captain *Means* on the *11th* day of *April* 186*1*, and served in that command until the *31st* day of *May*, 186*2*. He was discharged from the service at *Chester SC* on the *28th* day of *April*, 186*5*, and was at that time a member of Company *H 2nd* Regiment of *Cavalry* Battalion of .... Captain *Macfie*

I was born *8th* day of *Nov* 18*37*. I was married to him *26th* day of *Feb* 18*63*. My husband did not desert the service of the Confederate States nor of this State. My husband died on the *16th* day of *March* 19*10*. My income from all sources does not exceed $*750 00* The valuation of all my property does not exceed $*6000 00*

I am *82* years of age. I reside at *Woodward* in *Fairfield* County, S. C., and have lived there since the *8th* day of *November* 18*37*.

I have been on the pension roll of South Carolina in Class *C no. 4* I am not on the Pension roll of any other State, nor of the United States.

Sworn to and Subscribed before me this *24* day of *Oct* 19*19*

....
W. L. Gourley
Probate Judge.

Martha Matilda Brice
(Give full Christian name and Christian name of husband.)
R. Wade Brice

STATE OF SOUTH CAROLINA.

County of *Fairfield*

Personally appeared before me *Jno. A Stewart* and *Jas R Stirling* who being duly sworn, each of them deposes and says that they know *Martha Matilda Brice* who is an applicant for a pension, and they have read the said application; that they know of their own knowledge that her husband, named *R Wade Brice* was a *private* in Company *H, 6* Regiment of *S C V*, and that he rendered services as therein stated; that she has resided in this State *82* years.

Sworn to and Subscribed before me this *24th* day of *October* 19*19*

....
W. L. Gourley
Probate Judge.

Jno. A. Stewart
Company *A* Regiment *18 Miss*

Jas. R. Stirling
Company *B* Regiment *4th S C C.*

OFFICIAL INFORMATION FROM THIS OR ANY OTHER STATE.

I, *W. L. Gourley* Probate Judge of *Fairfield* County of South Carolina, submit the following evidence from official sources as to services rendered by the applicant *Mrs Martha Matilda Brice*

To all of which I hereby certify:

Witness my hand and seal this *25* day of *Oct* 19*19*

W. L. Gourley
Probate Judge of *Fairfield* County

121

STATE OF SOUTH CAROLINA,

County of _Fairfield_

We, the undersigned County Pension Board of _Fairfield_ County, do certify that we have made a careful examination of the application of _Martha Rush Rice_ We are of the opinion that the said applicant is _____ entitled to a pension thereunder for the following reasons:

(1) That her husband _R. Wade Rice_ was _____ a bona fide _____ in the late war between the States.

(2) That she is _82_ years of age, and was married prior to 1890, and was in Class _____

(3) That her income does not exceed $ _none_

(4) The value of all her property does not exceed $ _500_

(Here state any other reasons which influenced the Board to grant or reject this petition.)

(Give physical condition of applicant.) _None feeble_

Give full Christian name of husband. _____

COUNTY PENSION BOARD

H.H. Fleming
John M. Lyles
D.H. Robertson

HONOR ROLL

WIDOW

Application Under Act of 1919

CLASS _C_

No. _4_

APPLICATION OF _Mrs. Martha M. Rice_

POSTOFFICE _Washington S.C._

COUNTY _Fairfield_

APPROVED

State Pension Board

"Maj. Thos. W. Brice, a gallant Confederate veteran and a well known farmer and business man, died at his home at Woodward early yesterday morning, after a serious illness of about two weeks. The funeral service will be held at noon today at Concord Presbyterian church and the remains laid to rest in Concord burying ground.

"Maj. Brice was born in the New Hope section of Fairfield County No. 22, 1841, and was therefore, in his sixty-seventh year. His education was obtained at Erskine College, from the halls of which institution he went forth in the spring of 1861 to take up arms for the South. He enlisted in the Hampton Legion and after a year's valiant service was transferred to Co. D, Sixth S.C. Vols. As first lieutenant. He was severely wounded in the eye at the Battle of Campbell's Station near Knoxsville in November, 1863, but after a few month's disability pluckily returned to the service.

"At the conclusion of hostilities Maj. Brice returned home, to take up along with other brave men of that time the work of rebuilding the South. He was a successful farmer and business man and by his industry and ability amassed a comfortable estate. He was possessed of the complete confidence of friends and neighbors, and his name has always been a synonym for honesty of purpose. He was never an aspirant for public lffice, but as illustrative of the affection and esteem in which he was held by the people all over his county he was selected as one of Fairfield's delegates to the Constitutional Convention of 1895, which framed the constitution under which the people of South Carolina are now living.

"His wife, who was Miss Nancy Boyce, a sister of Maj. W. W. Boyce, of Rock Hill, preceded him to the grave by about two years. He leaves five sons and a daughter to mourn his loss. Messrs. Saml. M., Laurie, and T. W. Brice of Woodward; Jos. J. Brice of Knoxville, TN; Jas. G. Brice of Montgomery, AL; and Mrs. E. H. Hardin of Chester."

(Newspaper clipping on the death of Maj. T. W. Brice)

(1)   John Moore Brice, M.D. (1867-1907) married Bessie Moore Hardin on Feb. 21, 1894.
    (a)   Rebecca Boyce Brice b. 1897, d. 1904.
    (b)   Nancy Moore Brice b. Sept. 26, 1899.
    (c)   Thomas Hardin Brice b. June 27, 1902.
    (d)   John William Brice b. May 5, 1905.
(2)   Thomas William Brice, Jr. (1872-1956) married Evelyn Brice, a daughter of Calvin and Ellen Wallace Brice.
    (a)   James Brice.
    (b)   Evelyn Brice married.

        (c)   Robert Miller Brice, Fairfield Auditor, married Carolyn Arnette.

             (aa)   Ellen Wallace Brice married William Buchanan of Winnsboro.

             (bb)   Emily Brice married.

             (cc)   Thomas William Brice, Jr.

(3)   Samuel McDonald Brice (1876-19_) married Elizabeth Doughtery on April 16, 1902 at North, Orangeburg Co., SC.

      (a)   Joseph Miller Brice, M.D. b. Feb. 4 1903 married and lived at Kingstree, SC. Had several sons.

      (b)   Elizabeth Brice b. August 28,1905.

      (c)   Samuel McDonald Brice b. March 25, 1908 married and lived in Woodward, Fairfield County, SC.

      (d)   Ida Brice b. June 7, 1910.

(4)   Laurie (Lawrence) Michael Brice, married Macie McAliley of Chester on April 18, 1905.

      (a)   Lawrence Brice.

      (b)   Nancy Boyce Brice.

(5)   Nancy Boyce Brice (1880 -) married Edward Henry Hardin of Chester on Feb. 18, 1908.

      (a)   Rebecca Moore Hardin b. Feb 18, 1909.

      (b)   Nancy Boyce Hardin b. July 18, 1910, died May 24, 1912.

(6)   Joseph Walkup Brice.

(7)   James Boyce Brice.

f.   Rebecca Jane Brice b. Sept. 8, 1844, d. July 4, 1901, married James L. Rosborough on Oct. 20, 1869.

(1)   Mary Emeline Rosborough b. August 29, 1870 married Wade Hampton Macfie on April 27, 1896.

      (aa)   Evelyn Rosborough Macfie b. May 23, 1895 married David Aiken Crawford on Dec. 28, 1922. Their only child, David A. Crawford, was killed in the invasion of Europe in June 1944.

(2)   Agnes Rice Macfie b. Oct. 4, 1901 married T. W. Ruff.

(3)   Rebekah Brice Macfie b. Jan. 2, 1904.

(4)   Wade Hampton Macfie b. Nov. 23, 1906 married and lived in Winnsboro.

      (aa)   Wade Macfie.

      (bb)   David Macfie.

After the death of James L. Rosborough, Rebecca Brice Rosborough married John A. Brice, son of Robert Brice and Margaret Simonton. This ceremony was performed on Jan. 15, 1879.

(5)   Rebecca M. Brice b. June 7, 1881 married Reuben Rice Macfie on June 21, 1905.

    (aa)   Reuben Rice Macfie, Jr. b. July 1, 1906 married to Alva Stevenson of Winnsboro. They had children.

    (bb)   James McGregor Macfie b. Oct. 10. 1908.

    (cc)   Mary Jane Macfie b. March 6, 1911.

    (dd)   Margaret Simonton Macfie b. June 14, 1913.

    (ee)   Rebecca Brice Macfie b. June 9, 1917, married and had children.

    (ff)   Katherine Morgan Macfie b. Nov. 18, 1920.

Thomas William Brice married 2nd Jane Gubbin, 1889.

g.   Wilson McDonald Brice b. March 21, 1847, d. April 15, 1897.

h.   Samuel George Brice b. August 20, 1849, d. 1936, married Miss Miller. They had children. Tombs at New Hope Associate Reformed Presbyterian Cemetery lists two members of the family.

    (1)   Mabel Brice Glement b. March 17, 1883, d. Nov. 15, 1924.

    (2)   Eugene Harold Brice, M.D. August 30, 1890-Feby 13, 1916; buried at sea.

i.   David Lunsford Brice b. Oct. 21, 1852, d. Jan. 21, 1867.

Children of James Brice and Mary Cathcart:

7.   Samuel Brice moved to Alabama, however, there is a grave in New Hope Cemetery "To the memory of Samuel Cathcart Brice son of Samuel and Dorcas Brice July 11, 1847 – March 6, 1856." We presume that he married in Fairfield County before going to Alabama.

8.   Jeannette Brice (1811-1897) married her cousin, John G. Brice, also known as Dumpers Creek John. There children are listed under the John Brice family.

9.   David Brice (1816-1858) married Mary Yonge (1822-1884) on Mar. 11, 1842. Seven children were born to this union.

    a.   Laura G. Brice b. Dec. 25, 1842 married Samuel B. Lumpkin on July 7, 1864.

    b.   James Y. Brice b. Oct. 23, 1844.

    c.   Rebecca C. Brice b. Oct. 17, 1846, d. August 19, 1859.

    d.   David Brice b. August 13, 1849.

    e.   Edward L. Brice b. Sept. 11, 1851.

    f.   Florella M. Brice b. May 7, 1854.

    g.   Nannie M. Brice b. april 28, 1856.

10.   Mary Brice (b.   d.   ) married George Miller.

11.   Jane Brice (1814-1844) married Mr. Grissam and they had at least one son, Leroy Grissam.

Petition for Administration on Estate of James Brice, Senr.

The State of South Carolina,
Fairfield District . . . .   In the Court of Ordinary

To John R. Buchanan, Esq., Ordinary in andfor the District of Fairfield in the State aforesaid.

     The petition of John Simonton of the District and State aforesaid respectfully showeth—

     That James Brice late of the District and State Aforesaid departed this life on the 9th of Jany. Intestate.   That said intestate was possessed at the time of his death, of personal property supposed to be worth about seven thousand dollars; and also of considerable real estate.

     That he left the following persons his heirs at law viz—Robert Brice, William Brice, John Brice, Nancy Simonton, wife of your petitioner, Walter Brice, Samuel Brice, Jennett Brice, wife of John Brice, David Brice, Mary Miller, wife of George Miller, children of said intestate, and Leroy Grissam, son of Jane Grissam, deceased, who was a daughter of said James Brice, deceased.

     Your petitioner prays that Administration may be granted to him upon the personal Estate of said deceased.

     And your petitioner will pray—

Jany. 19th, 1845   John Simonton

Tomb Inscription of the James Brice Family

     Sacred to the memory of Jane Brice wife of James Brice who departed this life the 8th of Sept. in the year of our Lord 1804, in the 40th year of her age.

     Also, here lies James Brice Senior who departed this life on the 9th day of January A.D. 1845 aged 77 years. Let me die the death of the righteous, and let my last end be like this.

     Sacred to the memory of Mary Brice wife of James Brice who departed this life the 1st day of November 1828 in the 50th year of her age.

     (From New Hope Cemetery – the original James and his first and second wives— Many other Brices are buried there but the inscriptions are not included here)

ROBERT BRICE LAND GENEALOGY

John Baden

John Baden, Sr., b. 20 Sep 1732, d. 30 Sep 1824, married 12 Jan 1782, Willimina M. Maulden.[1] He was the son of Robert Baden and Martha Lawson and a brother to Thomas Baden.

John Baden, Jr. b.   , d. Jan. 1846, married 24 Mar 1814, Elizabeth Naylor.

John Thomas Baden, b. 1792, married 7 Dec 1813, Margaret Baden.[2]

Thomas George Baden, b. 1810, d. 1842, married 1853 Sarah Sabina b. 1811.

Jeremiah Smith Baden b. 1840, d. 30 Mar 1903 (Suwannee, FL); married Jul 1865 Angeline Lydia Barber b. 1843 Bryan Co., GA, d. 1823 Live Oak, Suwannee, FL.

Mary Harriet Baden b. 22 Oct 1885 (McAlpin/Suwannee, FL), d. 18 Nov 1962, married 25 Dec 1911 Marion Hampton Hicks b. 21 Nov 1889 New Bern/Suwannee, FL, d. May 1970 Clearwater/Pinellas, FL.

(aaa)   Vivian Olive Hicks b. 27 Apr 1914 Live Oak/Suwannee, LD; d. 26 Oct 2008 Dunedin/Pinellas, married **Joseph Lindsey Land** 1 Jun 1942, Clearwater/Pinellas, FL.

  (aaaa) **Robert Brice Land** b. 12 Jun 1843 Clearwater/Pinellas, FL, married Kathleen L. Wallace 29 Sep 1989 (Vol. 7061, Certificate 108176).

In a book compiled by Maurice Walter Frier, March 1978, Honolulu, Hawaii a grandson on the maternal side "My oldest sister Hilory (Mrs. J. A. Bishop, Riverview, FL) was born in his log cabin in Suwannee County, FL (Jeremiah Smith Baden). She said she remembered him well but knew little of any detail about him. In a later interview with Bessie she said he was from Maryland, he never spoke of his parents, no one ever heard him express a desire to visit his former home, those of his "far south" family knew nothing of his family in the "far north." Bessie and Hilory had been told he had taught school in Georgia before the War of the Rebellion, that he had met our Grandmother, Miss Angeline Lydia Barber, during the War and that he promised he would return and marry her when the war was over. He did just that for the license for the wedding was issued 14 Feb 1865. He was still fighting for the Yankee cause.

---

[1] Index to Marriages, Prince Georges County, Maryland.

[2] Margaret was a cousin.

Jeremiah Smith Baden enlisted in Chatham County, Georgia, served as 4th Corporal, Company L, Georgia 25th Infantry Regiment on 9 Aug 1861. Mustered out on 16 Nov 1861, Camp Wilson, Savannah, Georgia. (Roster of Confederate Soldiers of Georgia, 1861-1865).

He served in Company "E", 47th Georgia Regiment of Infantry. He saw military service as a Sergeant at Chickamauga, Chattanooga, Atlanta Campaign, and throughout the Caroline Campaign. In the last campaign, his unit was under the command of General Joseph E. Johnson who surrendered 26 April 1865, 17 days after General Lee (Confederate Army Records).

It is recorded in his Confederate Army Records, the papers on file in the courthouse in Suwannee County, FL for the settlement of his estate, and it is the same on Grandmother Baden's Confederate Pension Application Records [3158].

No explanation has been found as to why Jeremiah Smith Baden was left out in the will of his great grandfather John Baden, Jr., while his two brothers reaped so much. Jeremiah went south either on 8 December 1859, the day he became 21 or soon after. He has not been located on any census for 1860 either in Maryland, Washington, D.C. or Georgia nor on the 1870 census.

1.   Thomas Luther Baden b. 1868, Georgia, d.   , married Mary E. and was a woodsman.
2.   Susan Frances (Anna) Baden, b. 5 Sep 1871, Florida, d. 14 Jan 1960, married William Author Roberts, b. 31 Dec 1863, Florida, d. 30 Apr 1925.
3.   Idella Jeanette (Nettie) Baden, b. 12 Jun 1875, Florida, d. 15 May 1964, married 15 May 1896 Warren Walter "Mack" Frier, b. 23 Jan 1873, Florida,d. 5 Aug 1959.
4.   Isaac Barber Baden, b. Sept 1877, Florida, married Ola Sapp.
5.   James Edward Baden, b. Feb 1880, married Annie
6.   Will H. Baden, b. Oct 1881, Florida, married Willow Sapp
7.   Lily Belle Baden, b. 6 Oct 1883, Florida, d. 2 Feb 1919, married James Edard Vann, b. 22 Jan 1880, d. 23 Dec 1945.

8.   Mary Harriet Baden b. 22 Oct 1885, McAlpin/Suwannee Co., FL, d. 18 Nov 1962, Clearwater/Pinellas Co., FL. On 25 Dec 1911 she married Marion Hampton Hicks, b. 21 Nov 1889 New Bern/Suwannee Co., FL. He died May 1970 at Clearwater/Pinellas Co., FL.
a.   George Olin Hicks, b. 25 Nov 1912, Live Oak, FL.
        b.   Vivian Olive Hicks, b. 27 Apr 1914, Live Oak, FL; d. She died 26 Oct 2008, Dunedin/ Pinellas County, FL. On 1 Jun 1942, she married **Joseph Lindsey Land in Clearwater, FL.**

     c.   **Robert Brice Land is the son of Vivian Olive Hicks and Joseph Lindsey Land. He was born 12 Jun 1943, Clearwater/Pinellas County, Florida. He is a veteran of the Korean War.**

     3.   Elizabeth Inez Hicks, b. 10 Sep 1915, Live Oak, FL, married John Wilks, Jr. resided in Largo, FL.

     4.   Hilda Videl Hicks, b. 30 Aug 1917, Live Oak, FL, married James Eubanks.

     5.   James Lloyd Hicks, b. 10 Apr 1926, Largo, FL, married 10 Apr 1947, Janet Ruth Hancock.

Jeremiah and Angeline are buried in the Mt. Pisgah Church cemetery in Suwannee County, FL. His headstone announces he was born 8 December 1840, died 30 March 1903. This all tallies with his Army records and census records.

The application for Grandmother Baden's Confederate Pension Application had to be a sworn statement or it could not be accepted in Tallahassee, FL. It was a sworn statement and accepted.

Marriages

Angeline Barber and Jerry Baden Feb 16, 1865
William Roberts and Susana Baden Feb 14, 1886
Thomas Luther Baden and W.E. Eof alfard Nov, 1890
Mack W. Frier and Janet Baden May 16, 1894
Isaac B Baden and Ola Sap Jan. 8 1902
James Edward Vann and Isabel Baden 26, 1904
William Horas Baden and Willa Sapp 28, 1906
James Edward Baden and Annie Lee Sept, 1910.
Marion Hampton Hicks and Harriet Baden Dec 24, 1911

A. Edgar Baden   Deaths. — July, 13. 1874.
W. Osna Baden   Aug. 10. 1874
JerryMiah S. Baden   March 30. 1903
Pearl Roberts   Nov   1902
Jewel Angaline Baden   Nov Feb 21, 1908
Bell Vann   Feb. 2. 1919
William Angaline Baden   Nov, 17, 1923
William Harace Baden   March 29. 1946
Isaac Barber Baden May or June   1962

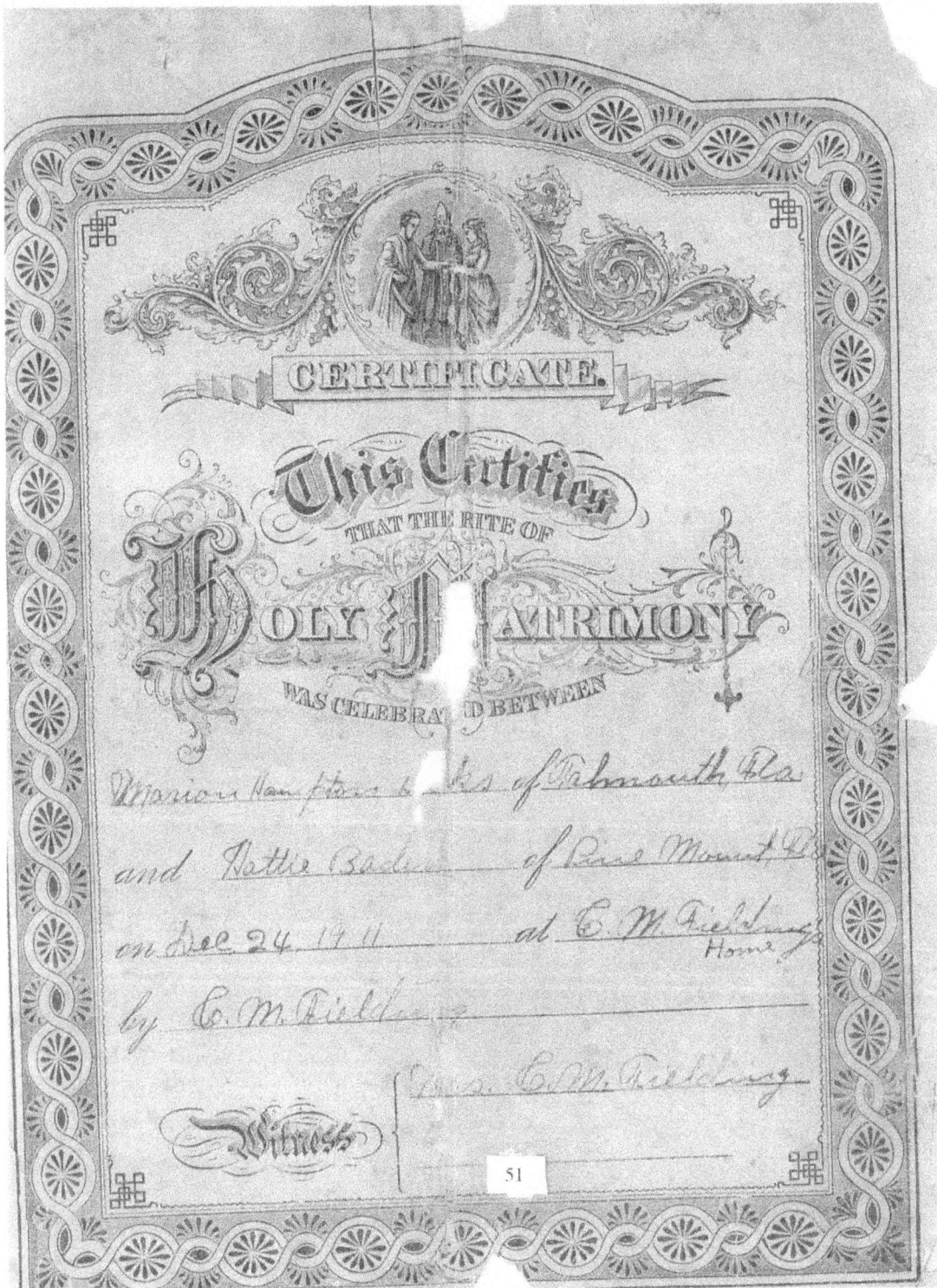

CERTIFICATE.

This Certifies

THAT THE RITE OF

HOLY MATRIMONY

WAS CELEBRATED BETWEEN

Marion Hampton _____ of Falmouth, Fla

and _Hattie Baden_____ of Pine Mount, Fl

on _Dec 24, 1911_____ at _C. M. Fielding's_
Home

by _C. M. Fielding_

Mrs C. M. Fielding

Witness

51

132

SCHEDULE I.—Free Inhabitants in _The 12th Militia Dist_ in the County of _Lumpkin_ State of _Georgia_ enumerated by me, on the _26th_ day of _August_ 1850. _Reid_ Ass't Marshal

Dwelling-houses numbered in the order of visitation	Families numbered in the order of visitation	The Name of every Person whose usual place of abode on the first day of June, 1850, was in this family.	Age	Sex	Color	Profession, Occupation, or Trade of each Male Person over 15 years of age.	Value of Real Estate owned	Place of Birth. Naming the State, Territory, or Country.	Married within the year	Attended School within the year	Persons over 20 who cannot read & write	Whether deaf and dumb, blind, insane, idiotic, pauper, or convict
1	61	61	Isaac Barker	49	m		Candle Maij B. M.	1000	Geo				
2			Frances "	47	f				"				
3			Susan "	27	f				"				
4			Israel "	23	m		Farmer		"				
5			Matha "	17	f				"				
6			Mary Ann "	14	f				"				
7			Caroline "	12	f				"		1		
8			Angeline "	7	f				"		1		
9	62	62	Riddich Cribbs	30	m		Farmer	300	Geo				
10			Susan "	32	f				"				
11			James "	6	m				"				
12			Shepherd "	6	m				"				
13			Ann C "	5	f				"				
14			Cornelia "	3	f				"				
15			Daniel & Mrs	2	m				"				
16	63	63	Obadiah Barker	25	m		"	300	Geo				
17			Nancy "	30	f				"				
18			Julian "	1/2	f								
19			Cordelia Barker	11	f								
20	64	64	Thomas Conady	48	m		"	500	Geo				
21			Sarah "	40	f				"				
22			Jane "	15	f				"				
23			John "	13	m				"				
24			Henry "	12	m				"		1		
25			William "	10	m				"				
26			Elizabeth "	8	f				"		1		
27			Sarah "	6	f				"				
28			Mary "	1	f				"				
29	65	65	James Thompson	28	m		"	300	Geo				
30			Rebecca "	27	f				"				
31			Wm C "	7	m				"		1		
32			Angeline "	5	f				"				
33	66	66	John Tipper	60	m		"	500	N 3				
34			Elizabeth "	50	f				Geo		1		
35			Catharine Thompson	24	f				"				
36			John Thompson	20	m		"		"			(?)	
37	67	67	James Thompson	40	m		"	300	Geo			(?)	
38			Susan Ann "	35	f				"			(?)	
39			Joshua "	13	m				"			10	
40			Elizabeth "	11	f				"				
41			Julian "	9	f				"		1		
42			Rebecca "	7	f				"				

52

Georgia ⎱ by W. H. Hayman Ordinary of Bryan Co
Bryan county ⎰ county to any Minister of the Gospel or Judge

Justice of the Inferior court or justice of the peace for said
County you are hereby authorised to Join in marriage Mr
Jeremiah S Baden and Miss Angeline Barber of said county
according to the Laws and constitution of this State for which
this Shall be your Sufficient License given under my hand and
private Seal of office this Feby the 14th 1865
                                    (LS) W H Hayman OBC
I hereby certify that Jeremiah S Baden & Miss Angeline Barber
were duly Joined in matrimony this day by me this Feby the 16, 1865
                                    James Shuman JP
Recorded Feby the 20th 1865 By W H Hayman Ordinary B C

_____

Georgia Bryan County By W H Hayman ordinary of said county
To any minister of the Gospel Judge Justice of the Inferior court or Justice
of the peace for said county you are hereby authorised to join in marriage
Mr A J Sapp and Miss Ann Brown of said county according to the con
stitution and Laws of said State for which this Shall be your Sufficient
License Given under my hand and private seal there being no Seal of office
the fourteenth day of April A D 1865
                                    (LS) W H Hayman OBC
the above Joined was duly Married by W B McHan upon
the 16th day of April 1865
                    Recorded this April the 17th 1865
            53   W H Hayman Ordinary B C

134

CONFEDERATE PENSION RECORD ABSTRACT

VETERAN'S NAME (LAST, FIRST, MIDDLE): BADEN, JEREMIAH S.			FILE NO. 3158
STATE GEORGIA	UNIT DESIGNATION(S): Co. E, 47TH GEORGIA		FLA. RESIDENT SINCE: NOT GIVEN
ENLISTMENT DATE: MARCH 1862	PLACE OF ENLISTMENT: NOT GIVEN	APPLICATION FILED:	CITY AND/OR COUNTY OF RESIDENCE: NONE FILED
DISCHARGE DATE: CLOSE OF WAR	PLACE OF DISCHARGE: NOT GIVEN	APPLICATION FILED:	CITY AND/OR COUNTY OF RESIDENCE:
DATE OF BIRTH: NOT GIVEN	PLACE OF BIRTH: NOT GIVEN	APPLICATION FILED:	CITY AND/OR COUNTY OF RESIDENCE:
DATE OF DEATH: 3-30-1903	PLACE OF DEATH: SUWANNEE COUNTY, FLORIDA	APPLICATION FILED:	CITY AND/OR COUNTY OF RESIDENCE:
WIDOW'S NAME (FIRST, MIDDLE, LAST): ANGELINA LYDIA BADEN		APPLICATION FILED:	CITY AND/OR COUNTY OF RESIDENCE:
DATE OF MARRIAGE: 2-14-1865	PLACE OF MARRIAGE: EDEN (BRYAN) GEORGIA	APPLICATION FILED: 8-4-1903	CITY AND/OR COUNTY OF RESIDENCE: COOPER (SUWANNEE Co.)
FLA. RESIDENT SINCE: 2-20-1867	DATE OF DEATH: BEFORE 1934 / AGE/YEAR (AS GIVEN ON APPLICATION): 60 IN 1903	APPLICATION FILED: 7-28-1909	CITY AND/OR COUNTY OF RESIDENCE: PINE MOUNT (SUWANNEE Co.)
		APPLICATION FILED:	CITY AND/OR COUNTY OF RESIDENCE:

STATE OF FLORIDA
DEPARTMENT OF STATE
Division of Archives, History and
Records Management
Form DS-AR 1 (10-74)

PAGES: 8

ARC 3-1 (21)
Ref. 104

NOTE:
The license was issued 14 Feb 1865
The marriage ceremony was performed 16 July 1865
M. Finis

54

The United States of America,

TO ALL TO WHOM THESE PRESENTS SHALL COME, GREETING:

Homestead Certificate No. 4884
Application 2852

Whereas there has been deposited in the GENERAL LAND OFFICE of the United States a CERTIFICATE of the Register of the Land Office at Gainesville, Florida, whereby it appears that, pursuant to the Act of Congress approved 20th May, 1862, "To secure Homesteads to actual settlers on the public domain," and the acts supplemental thereto, the claim of Jeremiah S. Baden has been established and duly consummated in conformity to law for the north half of the north-east quarter, the north-east quarter of the north-west quarter and the south-west quarter of the north-east quarter of section thirty-six, in township four south, of range fourteen east, of Tallahassee Meridian in Florida, containing one hundred and sixty acres and eighteen hundredths of an acre

according to the Official Plat of the Survey of the said Land returned to the GENERAL LAND OFFICE by the SURVEYOR GENERAL.

Now know ye, That there is therefore granted by the UNITED STATES unto the said Jeremiah S. Baden the tract of Land above described: TO HAVE AND TO HOLD the said tract of Land, with the appurtenances thereof, unto the said Jeremiah S. Baden and to his heirs and assigns forever.

In testimony whereof I, Grover Cleveland President of the United States of America, have caused these letters to be made Patent, and the Seal of the General Land Office to be hereunto affixed

Given under my hand, at the City of Washington, the twentieth day of June, in the year of Our Lord one thousand eight hundred and eighty five, and of the Independence of the United States the one hundred and Ninth.

[L.S.]

By the President: Grover Cleveland

By M. McKean, Sec'y.

S. H. Clark, Recorder of the General Land Office.

55

Jeremiah Smith Baden

&

Wife, Angeline Lydia (Barber)

Now know ye, That there is therefore granted by the UNITED STATES unto the said *Jeremiah S. Ogden*

the tract of Land above described: TO HAVE AND TO HOLD the said tract of Land, with the appurtenances thereof, unto the said *Jeremiah S. Ogden* and to his heirs and assigns forever.

In testimony whereof I, *Grover Cleveland* President of the United States of America, have caused these letters to be made Patent, and the Seal of the General Land Office to be hereunto affixed.

Given under my hand, at the City of Washington, the *twentieth* day of *June*, in the year of Our Lord one thousand eight hundred and *eighty five*, and of the Independence of the United States the one hundred and *ninth*.

By the President: *Grover Cleveland*

By *M. McKean*, Sec'y.

S. W. Clark, Recorder of the General Land Office

L.S.

138

DEATHS.

58

139

BIRTHS.

NAMES.

59

ANGELINE
BADEN
WIFE OF
J. S. BADEN
MAY 27 1843
NOV. 17 1928

REGISTRATION CARD — (Men born on or after April 28, 1877 and on or before February 16, 1897)

SERIAL NUMBER	1. NAME (Print)			ORDER NUMBER
U-2118	MARION (First)	HAMPTON (Middle)	HICKS (Last)	

2. PLACE OF RESIDENCE (Print)

BAY AVE. BUCKROE BEACH ELIZ. CO., VA
(Number and street) (Town, township, village, or city) (County) (State)

[THE PLACE OF RESIDENCE GIVEN ON THE LINE ABOVE WILL DETERMINE LOCAL BOARD JURISDICTION; LINE 2 OF REGISTRATION CERTIFICATE WILL BE IDENTICAL]

3. MAILING ADDRESS

BUCKROE BEACH BOX 117
[Mailing address if other than place indicated on line 2. If same insert word same]

4. TELEPHONE	5. AGE IN YEARS	6. PLACE OF BIRTH
	52	LIVE OAK (Town or county)
(Exchange) (Number)	DATE OF BIRTH NOV. 20 1889 (Mo.) (Day) (Yr.)	FLORIDA (State or country)

7. NAME AND ADDRESS OF PERSON WHO WILL ALWAYS KNOW YOUR ADDRESS

MARY HARRIET HICKS, BAY AVE, BUCKROE BEACH VA

8. EMPLOYER'S NAME AND ADDRESS

PERRY LOFTON JUDD, NEWPORT NEWS, VA.

9. PLACE OF EMPLOYMENT OR BUSINESS

DIKIE HOSPITAL HAMPTON ELIZ. CITY VA.
(Number and street or R. F. D. number) (Town) (County) (State)

I AFFIRM THAT I HAVE VERIFIED ABOVE ANSWERS AND THAT THEY ARE TRUE.

Marion Hampton Hicks
(Registrant's signature)

D. S. S. Form 1
(Revised 4-1-42)   (over)   16-22628-2

JOHN THOMAS LAND

World War II Draft Registration Card, 1717-1918

Death Certificate of John Thomas Land

He was the youngest of four children: Bea, James M., Eldridge Hall, John Thomas Land

Land, magh Lindsey   _John Thomas (name of property)_

Limer Margaret K   R B   Shocco

Lynch Jay Zilen   Sidney   Judkins

Latta Mary E   J P   Norlina

Lynch Geo W   Ed   Fishing Creek

Lynch Ben J   Sidney   Judkins

Lynch Ashley   June   "

Little _Murphy Coxyll_   River

Lynch ~~Wester~~ _Lola Cromell_   Fred _Baird_   "

North Carolina State Board of Health
BUREAU OF VITAL STATISTICS

Nº 145022

STANDARD CERTIFICATE OF BIRTH

1. PLACE OF BIRTH—
County .... Warren .... Registration District No. ...... 93-2673 ...... Certificate No. 6
Township .... River .... or Village ....
City .... Vaughan .... No. .... St. .... Ward
(If birth occurred in a hospital or institution, give its name instead of street and number)

If child is not yet named, make supplemental report, as directed

2. FULL NAME OF CHILD .... Joseph Lindsey Land

3. Sex	If plural births	4. Twin, triplet, or other	6. Premature	7. Are parents married Yes	8. Date of birth June 25, 1918
Male		5. Number in order of birth	Full term		(Month, day, year)

9. Full name	FATHER	18. Full maiden name	MOTHER
	John Thomas Land		Lois Rebecca Brice

10. Residence (usual place of abode) Vaughan
(If non-resident, give place and State)

19. Residence (usual place of abode) Vaughan
(If non-resident, give place and State)

11. Color or race White 12. Age at last birthday .... (years)

20. Color or race White 21. Age at last birthday .... (years)

13. Birthplace (city or place) S. C.
(State or country)

22. Birthplace (City or place) S. C.
(State or country)

14. Trade, profession or particular kind of work done, as spinner, sawyer, bookkeeper, etc. Truck Foreman

23. Trade, profession or particular kind of work done, as housekeeper, typist, nurse, clerk, etc. Housewife

15. Industry or business in which work was done, as silk mill, sawmill, bank, etc.

24. Industry or business in which work was done, as own home, lawyer's office, silk mill, etc.

16. Date (month and year) last engaged in this work .... 19........

17. Total time (years) spent in this work ....

25. Date (month and year) last engaged in this work .... 19........

26. Total time (years) spent in this work ....

27. Number of children of this mother (at time of this birth and including this child) (a) Born alive and now living ...... 4 ...... (b) Born alive but now dead .... (c) Stillborn ....

CERTIFICATE OF ATTENDING PHYSICIAN OR MIDWIFE

I hereby certify that I attended the birth of this child, who was born alive at 5:A. m. on the date above stated.

WHEN THERE WAS NO ATTENDING PHYSICIAN OR MIDWIFE, THEN THE FATHER, HOUSEHOLDER, ETC., SHOULD MAKE THIS RETURN.

(Signed) L. J. Picot .... M.D
or .... Midwife

Given name added from a supplemental report .... (Date of)

Address .... Littleton, North Carolina

Filed .... 19 ...... J. H. Harris .... REGISTRAR
.... REGISTRAR

THIS IS TO CERTIFY that the above is a true copy of the birth certificate

of Joseph Lindsey Land
filed in this office.

J.W.R. Norton
State Registrar.

FILE ...... 725 ...... PAGE 387

Date Issued: 11-24-1958

65

148

APPLICATION FOR MARRIAGE LICENSE   C. J. NO. 13503

Name J. L. Land   Address Aberdeen, N.C.

Age 23   Color white Birthplace Vaughan, N.C.

Married before? no Divorced? --- Where? -----   Occupation S.A.L.R.R.
and

Name Vivian Hicks   Address Clearwater, Fla.

Age 28   Color white Birthplace Live Oak, Fla.

Married before? no Divorced? --- Where? -----   Occupation bookkeeper

It is expected that John C. Brown

STATE OF FLORIDA.

COUNTY OF

Before me, the undersigned authority, personally appeared

_____ and

who being first duly sworn, deposes and say that ___he___ the parent___ of the said

_____

who is ___ years of age, and that ___he___ do___ hereby consent to the marriage of the said

to _____

_____

_____

Subscribed and sworn to before me this, the ___ day of ___, 19___

_____
(TITLE)

FORM V.S. NO. 48

Address Clearwater, Fla.

will perform the ceremony.

STATE OF FLORIDA.

COUNTY OF Pinellas

Before me, the undersigned authority, personally appeared the persons above named, who, being first duly sworn, depose and say that the information given by each of them as above set forth is true and correct, and that neither of them is married at this time and that they are not related within the prohibited degree.

J. L. Land

Vivian Hicks

Subscribed and sworn to before me this, the

1 day of June 19 42

John C. Brown
Notary Public

_____
(TITLE)

Marriage License

C. J. No. 13503

CENTRAL BUREAU OF VITAL STATISTICS

State of Florida, Pinellas County

To any Minister of the Gospel, or any Officer Legally Authorized to Solemnize the Rite of Matrimony:

Whereas, Application having been made to the County Judge of Pinellas County, of the State of Florida, for a license for marriage, and it appearing to the satisfaction of said County Judge that no legal impediments exist to the marriage now sought to be solemnized:

These are, therefore, To authorize you to unite in the

Holy Estate of Matrimony

J. L. Land   and   Vivian Hicks

and that you make return of the same, duly certified under your hand, to the County Judge aforesaid.

Witness my name as County Judge, and the seal of said Court, at the Courthouse in Clearwater, this 1st

day of June, A. D. 19 42   (SEAL)   Jack F. White, County Judge.

CERTIFICATE OF MARRIAGE

I Certify that the within-named J. L. Land

and Vivian Hicks were by me, the undersigned, duly united in the Holy Estate of Matrimony, by the authority of the within License.

Done this 1st day of June, A. D. 19 42, at Clearwater, Florida.

Witness Mrs. Johnny Williams   (SEAL)   John C. Brown - Notary Public
MINISTER OR LEGALLY AUTHORIZED OFFICER

Witness Johnny Williams   Clearwater, Fla.
ADDRESS

Returned this 1 day of June, A. D. 19 42, and recorded in Marriage Book 23, page 2

Jack F. White, County Judge.
J.B.

NOVEMBER 2009
KENTUCKY
Clerk of Circuit

67

150

FLORIDA CERTIFICATE OF DEATH

Vivian	Olive		Lane	Female
DATE OF BIRTH	AGE			DATE OF DEATH
April 2?, 1914	94			October 26, 200?
SOCIAL SECURITY NO.	BIRTHPLACE			COUNTY OF DEATH
265-54-0181	Live Oak, Florida			Pinellas

X Decedent's Home

1627 Paradise Lane Unit C — Dunedin

MARITAL STATUS: X Widowed

RESIDENCE STATE: Florida   COUNTY: Pinellas   CITY, TOWN: Dunedin

STREET ADDRESS: 1627 Paradise Lane Unit C   ZIP CODE: 34698

OCCUPATION: Bookkeeper   KIND OF BUSINESS: Retail Department Store

RACE: White

HISPANIC: X No

FATHER'S NAME: Marion Hicks   MOTHER'S NAME: Mary Harriet Boden

INFORMANT'S NAME: Bonnie Rosary   RELATIONSHIP: Daughter   STATE: Florida

CITY, TOWN: Dunedin   STREET ADDRESS: 1657 Paradise Lane Apt. C   ZIP CODE: 34698

PLACE OF DISPOSITION: Sylvan Abbey Memorial Park   LOCATION CITY OR TOWN: Clearwater   STATE: Florida

METHOD OF DISPOSITION: X Burial

LICENSE NUMBER: F043034

NAME OF FUNERAL FACILITY: Sylvan Abbey Funeral Home   STATE: Florida

CITY OR TOWN: Clearwater   STREET ADDRESS: 2853 Sunset Pt. Rd.   ZIP CODE: 33759

DATE SIGNED: 10/2?/200?   TIME OF DEATH: 0846

NAME OF ATTENDING PHYSICIAN: Gregory S. ____

STATE: Florida   CITY OR TOWN: Clearwater   STREET ADDRESS: 1969 Sunset Point Road Suite 15   ZIP CODE: 33765

DATE FILED BY REGISTRAR: November 05 2008

Barbara M. Sanders

Chief Deputy Registrar, Pinellas County

68

41488457

Hospital Birth Certificate

This Certifies

That _ROBERT BRICE LAND_ Was Born in the

Morton F. Plant Hospital
Clearwater, Florida

at _4:00A._ m. _Saturday, June 12th_ 19_43_

In Witness Whereof the said Hospital has caused this Certificate to be signed by its duly authorized officer and its Corporate Seal to be hereunto affixed.

Lilly C. Foley R.N.
SUPERINTENDENT.

J. Sidley Hood M.D.
ATTENDING PHYSICIAN.

Family History

Father's full name _Joseph Lindsay Land_

Residence _Clearwater Fla._

Birthplace _Vaughan, N.C._ Date _June 25th, 1918_

Mother's maiden name _Vivian Olive Hicks_

Birthplace _Live Oak Fla._ Date _April 27th 1914_

Place of marriage of parents _Clearwater Fla._

Date of marriage of parents _June 1st, 1942_

Form B—Hollister Birth Certificate, Design © 1925, Franklin C. Hollister, Chicago

"Remember thy Creator
in the days of thy youth"

69

152

Florida
State Board of Health

BUREAU OF VITAL STATISTICS
JACKSONVILLE

This is to Certify *that a* Birth Certificate *has been filed for*

Robert Brice Land   Sex Male

Child of: Born on   June 12, 1943

Mr. & Mrs. Joseph Lindsay Land   *This Record is filed in*
914 S. Turner St.   Book No.   1571
Clearwater, Fla.
                                     Page No.   20645

Henry Hanson   Edward M. L'Eagle
State Health Officer   Director Bureau of Vital Statistics

Dr. Walter Brice

Dr. Walter Brice, son of James and Jane Brice, was born Sept. 5, 1804. He lost his mother when three days old, was nursed and tenderly cared for by a colored woman, a servant of his father. He was born and raised on Little River, Fairfield District, near New Hope church.

He received the rudiments of his education from Mr. W. Young, who taught near his father's house, studied his languages under Mr. John Hemphill afterwards Judge Hemphill of Texas, pursued his education at Mount Zion College, Winnsboro, under Mr. Tuts. In 1825 he went to Jefferson College, Canonsburg, Pennsylvania, remained there until he graduated in October 1828 commenced the study of medicine the first of January 1829 under Dr. John Douglas of Chester County, attended two courses of lectures in Charleston, SC. He graduated March 1831.

▪▪▪

Dr. Walter Brice, Sr. died suddenly at his residence, Fairfield County, SC on the 7th December, 1871, of disease of the heart, in the 68th year of his age.

Rarely has any community sustained a greater loss in the death of a single individual. He was a descendant of a highly respectable family, born September 5, 1804, in the immediate vicinity in which he settled and died. His academic education was conducted under the superintendent of such men as the late Rev. Rodgers, Hon. Sam'l McAlilly, and Hon. John Hemphill. He graduated at Jefferson College, Pennsylvania in 1828 and at the medical college, Charleston, SC in 1831.

In the same year, he married Miss Emma Moore, and immediately commenced the practice of medicine. By his skill and .... attention to his profession, he soon acquired an extensive practice—too extensive indeed, for the physical abilities of any one man. But such were his sympathies with the sufferings of the afflicted, that he often denied himself needful rest to relieve their maladies, and minister to their comfort. The poor, in the bounds of his practice were never neglected. On the contrary, I am informed by some of that class that he not only relieved their maladies, but furnished such provisions as were needful to them when destitute. In short, he not only secured the confidence, respect and esteem, but also the love of all classes of the community, and died, it is believed, without an enemy.

Years since, he made a public profession of religion, and connected himself with the A.R.P. church at New Hope, of which Dr. Boyce was then the pastor, and from that period . . . his profession by a Christian . . . and conversation. He was fond of the Bible, and studied its contents, not only to conform his life to its sacred teachings, but that he might enjoy its comforts and consolations. His uniform practice was, I am informed, to read a chapter as soon as he arose and dressed. Some five years since his heart became organically diseased, and he was compelled to relinquish his practice; and from the nature of the disease, he knew that his time would probably be short. He set his house in order, and was constantly on the lookout for his departure. His language was, "I hope I am prepared, and when it shall please God to take me away, I am willing to go." Often he said that "he might die at any moment, and when death comes, it will do its work quickly." And so it was. He went but little into society, but he was always pleased to receive his friends, and entertained them with remarkable cheerfulness.

Indeed, the writer has been acquainted with him for thirty years and never saw him in any other mood than that of cheerfulness. But he is gone and I do not expect shortly to see his superior, taken all in all. He is missed in the community in which he dwelt. He is missed in the church in which he was a constant worshiper, when health permitted. And, above all, he is missed in his family. But "we sorrow not as those who have no hope," for if we believe that Jesus died and rose again, even so them also which sleep in Jesus, will God bring with him." May God be the stay and comforter of the widow and fatherless, and may this and bereavement be abundantly sanctified to the family, and to us all.

----L McDonald   (copied from a newspaper clipping)

The Dr. Walter Brice House is significant as an unusually intact example of the residence of a prominent Fairfield County planter and physician before the Civil War. Dr. Walter Brice (1804 - ca. 1871) attended Mt. Zion College in Winnsboro and Jefferson College in Canonsburg, Pennsylvania. He graduated from the Charleston College of Medicine in 1831. In 1860 he owned 52 slaves, real estate totaling $25,500, and personal property valued at $5,289. The house (ca. 1840) is a two-story, weatherboarded frame, L-shaped building with a side gabled roof and exterior end chimneys. A two-tiered, pedimented veranda on the center front features a plain balustrade and four wooden pillars on both levels with a diamond muntined window in the pediment. Multi-paned sidelights and transom frame the second floor entrance, while the first story door features an elliptical traceried fanlight with traceried sidelights above recessed panels. The Greek Revival elements reflect awareness on the part of the builder of the stylistic details that were popular at the time. The Dr. Walter Brice Office sits southeast of the house. It is a ten-foot-by-twelve-foot weatherboarded frame building with gabled metal roof, stuccoed end chimney, and boxed cornice. Listed in the National Register December 6, 1984.

New Hope A.R.P. Church and Session House were constructed ca. 1886. This church, with its decorated belfry and its intact session house, is significant as an interesting example of local interpretation of stylistic elements of religious architecture. The meeting house form church is a one-story, weatherboarded, frame church with an apsidal plan and a narthex pavilion. A bracketed belfry with bellcast roof, gablets, and finial surmounts the front-gabled roof. The gable end features a boxed cornice with returns and a blind oculus. Façade fenestration with shelf architraves has a double-leaf door surmounted by a ten-light transom flanked by single, large-paned, four-over-four, shuttered windows. Side elevations have windows identical to those of the façade. The interior walls are plastered above narrow-beaded-board wainscoting. The rear balcony displays a turned balustrade. Alterations include a 1970 left wing and the front steps. The session house is a ten by twelve foot weatherboarded frame building with a gable end roof with boxed cornices. Listed in the National Register December 6, 1984.

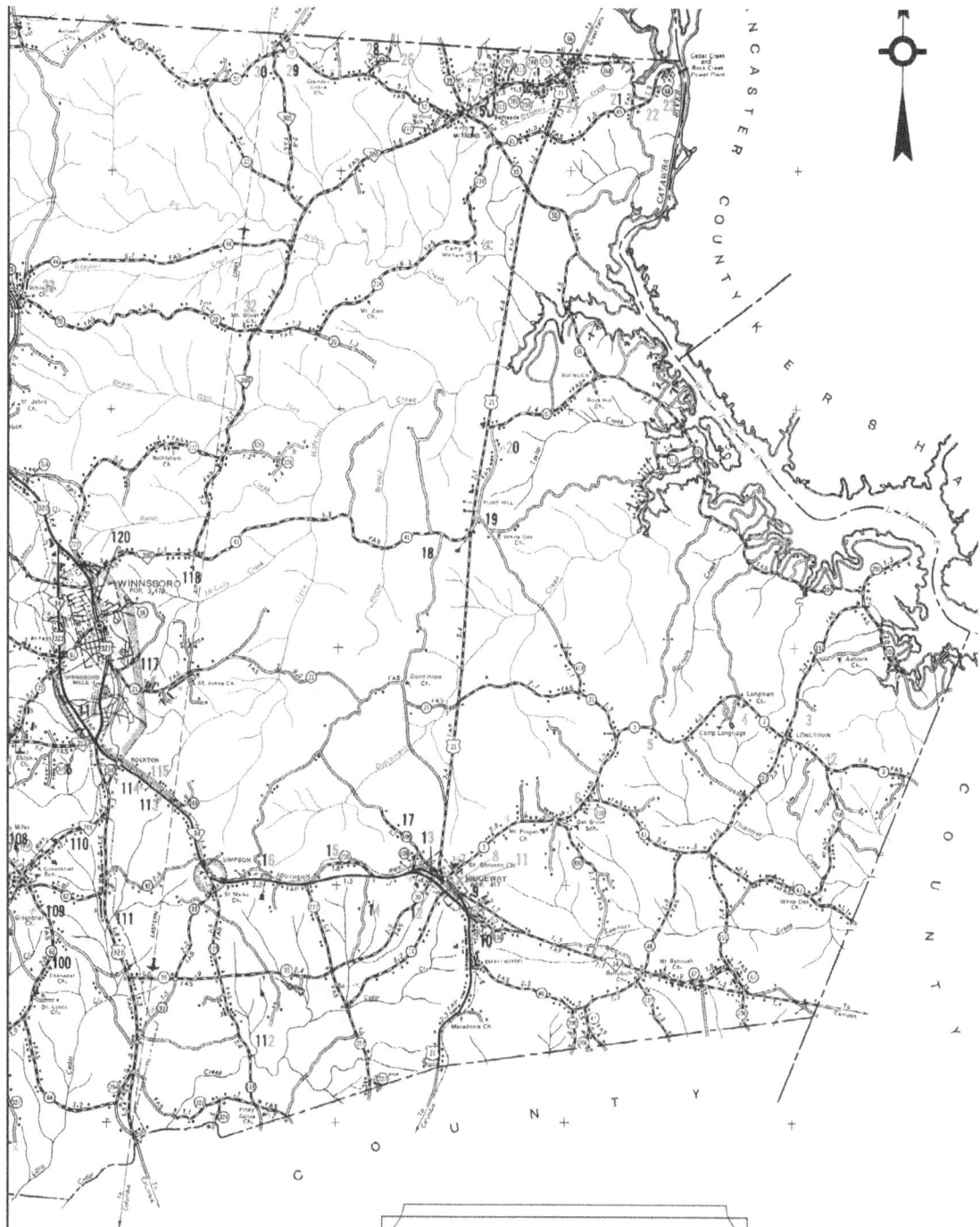

MAP
OF HISTORIC FAIRFIELD
SHOWING LOCATIONS OF PLACES OF

200

WILL OF
SAMUEL BRICE

In the name of God Amen

I Samuel Brice of the District of Spartanburgh and State of
South Carolina, being of Sound and disposing mind memory and
understanding praised be God for the Same, but being advanced
in life and calling to mind the uncertainty of life, do make
and declare this my last will and Testament in manner and form
following---That is to say after all my just debts and funeral
expences are paid, I give to my dear and beloved wife Nancy
Brice, during her natural life or widowhood all the benefits a-
rising from and privileges of my plantation, all my house hold
and kitchen furniture, together with one third part of the money
arising from the Sales of my perishable property.---

But in the event of her marriage She is only to enjoy the
privileges and advantages of the plantation to the amount of a
comfortable maintainance and support during her life.

I give and bequeath to my two well beloved daughters
Elizabeth Ann Brice, and Rachel Brice, my entire Tract of Land
to be equally divided between them together with the household
and kitchen furniture, herein before bequeathed to their mother,
and which is not to be their right untill after the decease of
their mother.--- Also I give and bequeath to my two beloved
daughters Elizabeth Ann and Rachel Brice the other two thirds
of the money which may arrise from the Sale of my perishable
property, together with two thirds of the money of which I may
die Seized and possefsed to be equally divided between them,
And I also bequeath my said daughters two thirds of amount of
the notes and accounts that may be due to me at my decease, to
be divided in like manner between them----and it is my desire
that my Executors hereinafter to be named do put the said two
thirds of money falling to my said daughters, out at interest
in safe hands untill my said daughters arrive at the age of
twenty one years, or untill the days of their marriage.

I desire that my Executors proceed to sell at a suitable
time after my decease all of my estate not hereinbefore disposed
of, upon such credit as their own discretion may dictate.----

WILL OF SAMUEL BRICE PAGE 2.

And it is my further desire and Special request that
they will favour the Interest of my surving family by procureing some suitable person to cultivate the farm to the best advantage, thereby promoting their wellfare in life through future
periods.----

And I do hereby nominate, constitute and appoint, my
friends Mr. Joseph Nesbitt and Mr. Elijah McMillan Executors to
this my last will and Testament, hereby revoking and making void
all former Wills and Testaments at any time heretofore by me
made, and do declare this to be my last Will and Testament.----

In Witnefs whereof I the said Samuel Brice, have hereunto set my hand and Seal.----This Twentyfifth day of July in
the year of our Lord one thousand eighteen hundred and forty
three

Signed sealed declared and)
published by the above named)
Samuel Brice, as and for his)
last will and testament in)   Samuel Brice (Seal)
the presence of us, who at   )
his request, and in his pre-)
sence have subscribed our   )
names as witnefses thereto.-)

John Smith

John Wingo Son of A

J. A. Miller

Recorded in Will Book D Page 173

Box 32 Package 29

Recorded October 19th 1849

M. Bowden O.S.D.

IN THE NAME OF GOD AMEN

I John Simonton Se^{nr} of the waters of Jacksons Creek, in the
District of Fairfield and State of South Carolina; being
frail and weak of body, but of Sound and disposing mind and
memory, and calling to mind the uncertainty of life and desirous
to dispose of all such worldly estate as it hath pleased God
to blefs me with, do make and ordain, this my last will and
Testament in manner and form following viz In the first place,
I give and bequeath my Soul to God who gave it, And my body to
the earth, to be buried in a decent & christian manner at The
discretion of my Executor

2d I allow all my Just debts paid, and for which, and defraying
my funeral expences, will hereafter be allowed - 3rd I give and
bequeath to my beloved wife Sarah Simonton all and Singular
the estate real and personal she was pofsefsed of before our
inter marriage, also Thirty Acres of land to be taken of the
land I bought from James Weldon, to be run parallel with her
line on the S E Side of the land bequeathed to her, my Negro
man Ryal, four hundred dollars in cash, waggon and harnefs,
Three horses, choice of Them That is now on the plantation
together with all the Stock sows & hogs, household and kitchen
furniture (except as will hereafter be otherwise disposed of)
to her and to her use and behoof and at her disposal forever,

4th I Give and bequeath to my Niece Letitia M Weldon who now
lives with me, one Feather bed Mattrefs and furniture

5th I have already given my Son Charles S Simonton who is now
dead eleven hundred dollars in cash in the year eighteen hundred
and thirty five As A recipt will Show dated in that year,
which I believed to be in full his part of my estate, I therefore
                                          son
now leave his heirs nothing except his /   John R Simonton
and daughter Margaret Simonton each I give and bequeath one
hundred dollars - 6th I give and bequeath to my other children
viz Robert Simonton William Simonton, Sarah Wilson, John
Simonton, Jennet Douglafs, Margaret Brice And Mary Brice an
equal distributive Share to each of them, of all the residue
and remainder of my estate, which consists only of the remainder

WILL OF
JOHN SIMONTON SENr

of the plantation I bought from James Weldon (which Said plantation I allow my Executor to Sell; and the money thens arising,
to be applied to the payment of money above devided and bequeathed
} And four Slaves Viz Lewis, Jack Hannah and Sarah, one horse
and Gig and all bonds, notes or Accounts due me at my decease
together with what money may be then on hand all of which
equally and fairly distributed to my Children within named
Viz Robert, William, Sarah, John, Jennet, Margaret, And Mary.
And Should my children not agree about the valuation of the
four Slaves within named, It is my will Should it be consiftent
with law that my Executor Sell them at private Sale; as also
the land and make title to it, all other parts or parcels of
my said estate they may Not Agree in retaining in any of their
hands I allow my Executor to Sell at publick out cry, 7th
It is my will that my Slaves, continue make, And, gather the
crop now intended or pitched, the proceeds thense Arisising
after leaving Sufficient of the same, for the support of my
said wife Sarah, her family, and Stock they insueing year, to
go to the payment of my Just debts, And funeral expences, the
balance of Money arising out the crop of cotton to be divided
that is to say one half to my wife Sarah the other half to be
equally divided among my children as above stated 8th I
give & bequeath to my Daughter Mary Brice Secotte Commentary
on the bible one Small trunk and my Armed chair, And the
balance of my books I allow my wife Sarah and my children to
divide as they may think proper, And lastly I do hereby
Constitute and appoint my son in law William Brice Executor
of this my last will and testament, hereby disannulling and
revoking all other and former wills by me heretofore made, And
declaring this and no other to be and contain my last will and
testament, In testimony whereof I have hereunto set my hand
and Seal this nineteenth day of February Anno Domini 1839
Signed Sealed published pronounced and delivered by the testator
to be and contain his last Will and testament in the presence
of us who in his presence & in the presence of each other have
hereunto set our names as witnefses

WILL OF

JOHN SIMONTON Sr.^{nr}

John Adger

James Boyce
          his
Robert X Bryson
          mark

John Simonton senr -- (L.S.)

Proved ....(unknown)

.................(unknown)

Recorded in book 19

Page 22 & 23 & 24 & 25

Recording date unknown

Apt. 72 File 30

WILL OF
JOHN STEVENSON

Fairfield

District

In the name of God Amen

I John Stevenson of the Destrict aforesaid being Weak of
body but of sound Judgment and memory I desire to make my
Will and leave Such things as god hath bestowed upon me
in the Manner and form as follows first I Bequeath my
Soul to god and my body to be desently interded ------
iprimifses I bequeath to my wife Jánnet Stevenson my negro
wench / named bet during her Widdow hood and to be at her
disposel.at her death and if the wench have any children
the ar to be Equly Divided amongst my children item. I
Bequeath to my Son William Sevenson that tract of land I
bought from Joel buttler item I Bequeath to my Son James
Stevenson Twenty Dollars/ item. I Bequeath to my Son Hugh
Stevenson one hundred dollars a dun mair Yormly sauld his
item I Bequeath to my son John Sevenson one hundred and
Eighty dollars- item

I Bequath to my three Sons Andrew Robert and Samuel Sten-
son the plantation and tract of Land I now live upon to be
Equly devided Amongs them Reserving What Will be sufficient
for . their Mother during her Widdewhood item I Bequeath to my
Daughter Margret Stevenson one hundred dollars further I alow
my Four Suns John Andrew Robert Samuel Stevenson to be
larned to Read and Writ as far as the rule of three
and my Daughter Marget to be Lerned to read the remander of
my Estate to be Divided amongst my children Lastly I nominate
and appoint my Wife Jinnet Stvenson John Simanton and John
Waugh- to be Executers of this my last Will and testmant as
Wittness my hand and Seal this fifth of March 1808

Witnefs present

William Waugh
   his
Henry X Marton   John Stevenson
   mark
   his
Mathew X Andrew
   mark

Proved 5th April 1808

Jno Buchanan J.C.p

Recorded July 17th 1809 in will bk
Page 449   Apt21 File 481

163

WILL OF
JOHN A ROSBOROUGH

In The Name of God Amen

I John A Rosborough of The Waters of Wateree in the District
of Fairfield and State of South Carolina, being frail and
weak of body, but of sound and disposing mind and memory, and
calling to mind the undertainty of life, and desirous to dispose of all such Worldly estate as it hath pleased God to
blefs me with, do make and ordain This my last Will and Testament in manner and form following, that is to Say.

first. I give and bequeath my Soul to God who gave it, and my
body to the earth to be buried in a decent Christian manner
at the discretion of my Executors

in the Second place, I allow all my Just debts to be paid, and
for the purpose thereof, I allow the proceeds of the present
crop. Together with Some Stock,(after leaving Sufficient for
the maintenance of my family) to be applied to the payment of
my Just debts, and if that---Should not be Sufficient for to
pay all my debts I allow the balance to be paid out of the
proceeds of the next crop ensuing Third, it is my Will that
my wife Jane B. Rosborough and all my children do continue to
live on and occupy the place or plantation whereon I now live,
untill my eldest Son James F. Rosborough attain the age of
twenty one years, and it is my will as soon as my Son James as
aforesaid arrives at the age of twenty one, my Executors do
Sell at publick Sale all the plantation ,whereon I now live
and all the Slaves I am now pofeofed of namely Jak, Liney
& child, Cynthe, Ofmind, George and Mary with their increase,
together with all other personal property that may be on the
place at that time, the proceeds thence Arising from the Sale
of the above described property with the moneys that may be
in hands if any then be, to be equally and fairly divided
between my beloved wife Jane B. Rosborough and my children
James F. Rosborough Burr C Rosborough and Martha I Rosborough
already born and Should my wife Jane B Rosborough live(who
share and share alike
is now pregnant) to be delivered of a child I allow him or
her as the case may be to be maintained and educated out of

WILL OF JOHN A ROSBOROUGH

my estate as my other children now born and to have an equal
share of My whole estate with my beloved wife Jane D Rosborough and children above named   Fourth, it is my will that all
my children be maintained and educated out of the proceeds of
the crop yearly made on the place and the Remainder of the
money that may be left yearly after paying for Schooling and
maintenance of my family, I allow it to be put to interest
yearly untill my Son James F Rosborough arrives at the age
of Twenty one and then divided as above directed Fifth, it
is my will Should any of my Slaves not Serve peaceably and
willingly with my family I allow my Executors to Sell them
at any time at publick Sale, and apply the proceeds of Such
Sale or Sales as within or heretofore directed.

Sixth it is also my will that my Executors or either of
them Shall and may Sign and execute titles to all my property real or personal when Sold as I have herein directed
Lastly I do constitute and appoint my FATHER in law John
Kennedy Se^{nr}. William 'Brice and Burr Cockerell - - - - - - -
- -- - - - - - -   Executors of this my last Will and Testament, hereby revoking all other and former WILLS by me heretofore made, and declaring this and no other to be and contain
my last Will and Testament

In testimony whereof I have hereunto Set my hand and Seal this
twenty Second day of August - - - - Anno Domini 1859

Signed Sealed published pronounced	John A Rosborough (L.S.
and declared by the Testator as and	Proved not found
for his last Will and Testament	Recorded not found
in the presence of us, who in his	In will book #19
presence and the presence of each	Page #1
other, have hereunto Set our names	Apt #71 File #3
as witnesses	

N.B. The word Share and Share
alike enterlined before Signed

    Robert Walker
        his
   Hugh A Boyd
       mark

    Robert W Marshall

WILL OF
SAMUEL W. GRIFSIN

SOUTH CAROLINA

FAIRFIELD DISTRICT

Know all men by these Presents, That I, Samuel W
Grifsin of the State and district aforesaid, being weak
of body, but of sound mind and judgement, I do hereby make
this my last will and testament, revoking all others heretofore made   I do in the first place bequeath my Soul to
God and in the next place my body to be interred in the
burying ground at New Hope Church. I do wish my property
disposed of in the following manner all of my estate real
and personal with the land that I am now living upon with t
the exception of one negro woman named Lizzir, and her ifsue
that I will hereafter dispose of. In the first place all of
my property, except the above named negro, to be sold at pub
lic auction and all of my just debts to be paid, the balance
of the money after paying my debts to be kept at interest
unto my son James Leroy comes to the age of twenty one years,
except so much as will be necefsary to pay for his raising
and education, I do wish him to get a collegiate education.
The above named Lizzir and her children to be and remain
about wherever my son is raised and to be kept unsold until
he comes of age, and then her and her ifsue and the balance
of the money belonging to my estate to be paid over to him
as he is my only child But if my son should not live to be
of twenty one years of age age I do allow that the property
that I got by wife Jane Brice, to fall back to the hairs
of James Brice Sen[r] and what property I had of my own to fall
into my own relations, the Executors to make titles to
my land when sold, I do appoint S Brice and John Simonton
as my Executors of this my last will and testament. as
witnefs my hand and seal this 14 November 1844.

Witnefs present

John Stevenson

Robert Brice   Sam[l] W. Grifsin (L S)

Thomas Chisolm
                                    Proven --Date not found

                                    Recorded in Will Book # 19
                Recording date unknown   Page 188

WILL OF
JANE S. CALDWELL

THE STATE OF SOUTH CAROLINA.

I Jane S. Caldwell of Fairfield District in the State aforesaid, being of Sound and disposing mind and memory, do make this my last will and testament in manner & form following. viz.

Item 1. I give and bequeath to my Son James Caldwell three negro Slaves, namely a man called Singo, xxx a woman called Lucy xxxxxxxxxxxxxxxxxxxxxxxxxxxxx Also one third of my flock of Sheep, all the blacksmith tools, the cotton gin and wheat thrasher, and half of my stock of cattle, two mules, called Peet and Mike and one horse called Jack, and one bedstead and bed and the usual bed clothes.

Item 2d. I give and devise to my daughter Eliza Caldwell, all the plantation and tract of land whereon I now reside, containing two hundred and forty nine and a half acres, situate in the District of Fairfield and State aforesaid, being all the land which was divided off and afsigned to me by the commifsioners under proceedings in the Court of Equity for partition of the Estate of my husband Robert Caldwell deceased, for and during the term of her natural life, but in case of her marriage, not to be in any wise subject or liable to the debts, contracts or incumbrances of her husband, and at the death of my said daughter, to the heirs of her body who may be then living, share and share alike; and in case my said daughter Eliza shall die without leaving ifsue of her body living at the time of her death; then said plantation and tract of land is to be equally divided between my three sons, James, William, and Robert, their heirs and afsigns in fee simple.

I also give and bequeath to my said daughter Eliza, two negro slaves, namely a woman called Ryna and a girl called Peggy, for and during the natural life of my said daughter, but in case of her marriage, not to be in any wise subject or liable to the debts contracts or incumbrances of her husband, and at the death of my said daughter, I give and bequeath said negro slaves and their ifsue and increase to the heirs of the body

of my said daughter who may be living at the time of her
death equally to be divided among them, the issue of a
deceased child, if any such, to represent the parent, &
take the share which the parent would be entitled to if
living: but in case my said daughter Eliza shall die without
leaving issue of her body living at the time of her death,
then I will and direct that said negroes & their increase be
sold, and the proceeds equally divided among all my children,
the issue of a deceased child, should there be any such, to
take the share which the parent would be entitled to if living,
& represent the parent, I also give and bequeath to my said
daughter Eliza, my new Buggy and harness, my loom & harness,
my cupboard and silver ware, all my kitchen furniture and all
my table furniture, my mantle clock, two mules called Bet
and Poll, and one third of my sheep.

Item 3^d. I give and bequeath to my daughter Jane Wylie, wife
of Vander A. Wylie, two negroes, namely, a woman called
Caroline and her daughter Martha, (together with their future
issue and increase,) for and during the natural life of my
said daughter Jane Wylie, but not in any wise to be subject
or liable to the debts, contracts or incumbrances of her present,
or any future husband, and at the death of my said daughter,
said negro slaves and their issue and increase, to be equally
divided among the heirs of her body who may be then living -
But in case my said daughter Jane Wylie shall die without leaving issue of her body living at the time of her death, then
I will and direct that said two negro slaves and their issue
and increase, be sold and the proceeds equally divided among
all my children, the issue of a deceased child, if any such,
to represent the parent, and take the share which the parent
would be entitled to if living - I also give and bequeath
to my said daughter Jane Wylie one cow, one foalding leaf
pine table, one short posted bedstead, one bed, 1 pair sheets,
1 corded counterpane, 1 bolster and pair of pillows -

Item 4th I give and bequeath to my son William Caldwell, a
negro boy called Little Sam and a girl called Mary, also one

WILL OF

JANE S. CALDWELL

bedstead and bed & the usual bedclothes, one cow, and one
Stock hog - and one sixth of the sheep.

Item 4<u>th</u> I give and bequeath to my son Robert Caldwell, a
negro man called Joe, and a negro boy called George, also one
cot and our bed & the usual bedcloathes, one cow, one stock
hog, and one sixth of the sheep.

Item 5<u>th</u> I give and bequeath all my plantation implements to
my son James & my daughter Eliza equally to be divided among
them.

Item 6<u>th</u> My son James is to have half the crop which shall be
made on my plantation this year; the other half of said crop
I give and bequeath to my daughter Eliza and my sons William
& robert, share and share alike. All my corn, wheat, fodder;
meat, and other provisions I wish to remain on the plantation
for the joint and common use of my daughter Eliza and my three
sons James, William and Robert.

Item 7<u>th</u> All the money on hand at the time of my decease,
I give and bequeath to my daughter Eliza and my two sons
William and Robert, share and share alike.

Item 8<u>th</u> All the rest of my household furniture not otherwise
disposed of, I give to my daughter Eliza.

Item 9<u>th</u> I give and devise to my son James Caldwell, all my
interest and share, as one of the heirs at law of my son
Henry S. Caldwell deceased, in the tract of land afsigned to
said Henry S. and James Caldwell by the court of Equity under
proceedings for partition of the Estate of my husband Robert
Caldwell deceased.

Item 10<u>th</u> All the rest residue and remainder of my Estate of
every kind and, discription whatsoever whether accruing to xxx
xxxx the Estate of my husband Robert Caldwell deceased, or
from the Estate of my deceased Sons Henry S. Caldwell and
Alexander M. Caldwell, I give, devise and bequeath to my
daughter Eliza, and my Sons James, William and Robert, share
and share alike.

Item, 11<u>th</u> I nominate and appoint my son James Caldwell and
my friend, John Simonton, John Brice of Dumpers Creek, and

WILL OF
JANE S. CALDWELL

James Johnston executors of this my last will and testament -
Part of the third line of the 1st item erased before the
execution.

In Witness whereof I have hereunto set my hand and seal this
third day of April 1847 -

In presence of us, who have subscribed as witnesses in her
presence

James R. Cockrell   Jane S Caldwell (L.S.)

James Gibson

David McDowell

Proved.......(unknown)

............(unknown)

Recorded in book 19

Pages 193 & 194 & 195

Recorded June 25, 1947

Apt. 85 File 295

wWILL OF
SAMUEL BRICE

In the name of God Amen

I Samuel Brice of the District of Spartanburgh and State of
South Carolina, being of Sound and disposing mind memory and
understanding praised be God for the Same, but being advanced
in life and calling to mind the uncertainty of life, do make
and declare this my last Will and Testament in manner and form
following----That is to say after all my just debts and funeral
expences are paid, I give to my dear and beloved wife Nancy
Brice, during her natural life or widowhood all the benefits a-
rising from and privileges of my plantation, all my house hold
and kitchen furniture, together with one third part of the money
arising from the Sales of my perishable property.----

But in the event of her marriage She is only to enjoy the
privileges and advantages of the plantation to the amount of a
comfortable maintainance and support during her life.

I give and bequeath to my two well beloved daughters
Elizabeth Ann Brice, and Rachel Brice, my entire Tract of Land
to be equally divided between them together with the household
and kitchen furniture, herein before bequeathed to their mother,
and which is not to be their right untill after the decease of
their mother.---- Also I give and bequeath to my two beloved
daughters Elizabeth Ann and Rachel Brice the other two thirds
of the money which may arrise from the Sale of my perishable
property, together with two thirds of the money of which I may
die Seized and possefsed to be equally divided between them,
And I also bequeath my said daughters two thirds of amount of
the notes and accounts that may be due to me at my decease, to
be divided in like manner between them----and it is my desire
that my Executors hereinafter to be named do put the said two
thirds of money falling to my said daughters, out at interest
in safe hands untill my said daughters arrive at the age of
twenty one years, or untill the days of their marriage.

I desire that my Executors proceed to sell at a suitable
time after my decease all of my estate not hereinbefore disposed
of, upon such credit as their own discretion may dictate.----

WILL OF SAMUEL BRICE PAGE 2.

And it is my further desire and Special request that they will favour the Interest of my surving family by procureing some suitable person to cultivate the farm to the best advantage, thereby promoting their wellfare in life through future periods.---

And I do hereby nominate, constitute and appoint, my friends Mr. Joseph Nesbitt and Mr. Elijah McMillan Executors to this my last will and Testament, hereby revoking and making void all former Wills and Testaments at any time heretofore by me made, and do declare this to be my last Will and Testament.---

In Witnefs whereof I the said Samuel Brice, have hereunto set my hand and Seal.---This Twentyfifth day of July in the year of our Lord one thousand eighteen hundred and forty three

Signed sealed declared and   )
published by the above named)
Samuel Brice, as and for his)
last will and testament in   )   Samuel Brice (Seal)
the presence of us, who at   )
his request, and in his pre-)
sence have subscribed our   )
names as witnefses thereto.-)

John Smith

John Wingo Son of A

J. A. Miller

Recorded in Will Book D Page 173

Box 32 Package 29

Recorded October 19th 1849

R. Bowden O.S.D.

172

WILL OF

Rebecca Moore

South Carolina)

Chester District)   I Rebecca Moore of the State and District aforesaid being in delecate health and infirm in body But of same mind and disposing Memory do make this my last Will & Testament

1ˢᵗ I desire, after my death, that my boddy should be in decently interwed and that all necessary funeral expenses should be defreyed out of my estate.

And if that all my just Debts should be paid

2ᵈ I Will and Bequeath to my Grandson Thomas W Moore Jᴿ and his heirs forever a negro boy named George about Eleven or Twelve years of age

3ᵈ I Will & Bequeath to my Grandson John Michael Moore (son of John Moore decd.) and his heirs forever a negro Boy named Washingyon about fourteen years of age

4ᵗʰ I desire and it is my Will that all my legatees who have received any portion of the funds arising from the payment of certain debt due me for the sale of a certain House and lot in the town of Columbia S.C. should be required to account to my estate for so much of such funds as has been received and that said funds when so accounted for shall be disposed agreeable to the provisions contained in the next clause of this my/last Will and Testament.

5ᵗʰ It is my Will and desire that the funds' refered to in the last clause te-gether with all the balance of My Estate shall be distributed as follows--To my son Thomas W Moore and his heirs forever one sixth. To my son in Law John Douglass and daughter Mary his wife to them and their heirs forever another one Sixth. To my Son in Law Walter Brice and daughter Emiline his wife to them & their heirs forever another one Sixth. To my Son in Law George W Hill and daughter Sarah A. his wife to them and their heirs forever another one Sixth. To my Grand Children (the Children of my son John Moore deceased) to them and their heirs forever another

one Sixth to be devided equally among them my siad Grand
Children Share and Share alike. And the remaining one
Sixth to my Grand Children (the Children of my deceased
daughter Rebecca Wade and Thomas Wade her Husband) to
them and their heirs forever to be equally divided between
them my said Grand children Share and Share alike. Reserving however hereafter at any time before my death the right
to myself of making any gifts or donations to any of my
children or Grand children that I may from time to time
think proper. Which said gifts or donations should there
be any are not to be accounted for by the party or parties
so receiving them in a final settlement of my estate

6th I nominate and appoint my son in Law Walter Brice and
my Son Thomas W. Moore my Executors and charge them with the
executions of this my last Will and Testament.

In witness whereof I have this day the twenty seventh of My May in the year of our Lord one thousand eight hundred and fifty one called upon John S. Wilson, John Nickles,
and Elihu Gladden, to witness this my last, Will and Testament and to them in the presence of each other I have signed
sealed and acknowledged this to be my last Will and Testament

                                        Rebecca Moore LS

J.S. Wilson
John Nickles
Elihu Gladden

Probated November 10, 1851
            Peter Wylie, Ordy.
Recorded in Book A-1 Page 96
Apartment No. 57-A
Package No. 1617

Series: S108092 Reel: 0013 Frame: 00311 Date: 1776 C. or later Description: BRICE, JAMES, ACCOUNT AUDITED (FILE NO. 744A) OF CLAIMS GROWING OUT OF THE AMERICAN REVOLUTION. Names indexed: BRICE, JAMES

Series: S213190 Volume: 0015 Page: 00007 Item: 001 Date: 1/9/1786 Description: BRICE, SAMUEL, PLAT FOR 160 ACRES ON NORTH FORK OF TYGER RIVER, SPARTANBURG COUNTY, NINETY SIX DISTRICT, SURVEYED BY ANDREW THOMSON. Names indexed: BRICE, SAMUEL; CALDWELL, JOHN; MCMAHAN, WILLIAM; MILLAR, MICHAEL; THOMSON, ANDREW Locations: MIDDLE TYGER RIVER; NINETY SIX DISTRICT; NORTH TYGER RIVER; SPARTANBURG COUNTY Document type: PLAT

Series: S213190 Volume: 0021 Page: 00142 Item: 002 Date: 8/3/1786 Description: NAZARETH CONGREGATION, PLAT FOR 8 ACRES, INCLUDING MEETING HOUSE AND BURYING GROUND, ON NORTH FORK OF TYGAR RIVER, NINETY SIX DISTRICT, SURVEYED BY ANDREW THOMSON. Names indexed: BRICE, SAMUEL; CALDWELL, JOHN; THOMSON, ANDREW Locations: MIDDLE TYGER RIVER; NINETY SIX DISTRICT; NORTH TYGER RIVER Document type: PLAT Topics: NAZARETH CHURCH

Series: S108092 Reel: 0013 Frame: 00321 ignore: 000 Date: 1776 C. or later Description: BRICE, SAMUEL, ACCOUNT AUDITED (FILE NO. 745) OF CLAIMS GROWING OUT OF THE AMERICAN REVOLUTION. Names indexed: BRICE, SAM

Series: S213192 Volume: 0044 Page: 00327 Item: 002 Date: 12/23/1816 Description: BRICE, THOMAS, PLAT FOR 202.5 ACRES ON JEMES CREEK, SPARTANBURGH DISTRICT, SURVEYED BY JAMES SELMAN. Names indexed: BRICE, THOMAS; PEARSON; SELMAN, JAMES; VERNON Locations: JEMMYS CREEK; NORTH TYGER RIVER; SPARTANBURG DISTRICT Document type: PLAT Series: S213192 Volume: 0048 Page: 00002 Item: 001 Date: 12/2/1825 Description: BRICE, WILLIAM M. M., PLAT FOR 60.5 ACRES ON BRANCH OF BENS CREEK, SPARTANBURG DISTRICT, SURVEYED BY JAMES LEONARD. Names indexed: BEACKMAN, WILLIAM; BRICE, WILLIAM M. M.; HAY, WILLIAM; JENKINS, H.; LEONARD, JAMES; RHAY, AMOS Locations: BENS CREEK; SPARTANBURG DISTRICT; TYGER RIVER Document type: PLAT

Series: S213192 Volume: 0055 Page: 00184 Item: 001 Date: 9/29/1849 Description: CARSON, TENCH C., PLAT FOR 45 ACRES IN GREENVILLE DISTRICT, SURVEYED BY WILLIAM P. MCBEE. Names indexed: BRICE, GEORGE; CARSON, TENCH C.; MCBEE, WILLIAM P. Locations: GREENVILLE DISTRICT Document type: PLAT

Series: S213192 Volume: 0055 Page: 00207 Item: 001 Date: 12/4/1849 Description: BRICE, JAMES R., PLAT FOR 5.8 ACRES IN ANDERSON DISTRICT, SURVEYED BY MARTIN S. MCCAY. Names indexed: BRICE, JAMES R.; FANT, J. R.; WHITE, HENRY; WHITE, THOMAS Locations: ANDERSON DISTRICT Document type: PLAT

Series: S213192 **Volume:** 0037 **Page:** 00200 **Item:** 004 **Date:** 12/6/1798 **Description:** SIMONTON, JOHN, PLAT FOR 90 ACRES ON BRANCH OF LITTLE RIVER, BRANCH OF BROAD RIVER, CAMDEN DISTRICT, SURVEYED BY MOSES HILL. **Names indexed:** CAMERON; HILL, MOSES; MILLING, HUGH; SIMONTON, JOHN; WALKER, RICHARD

Series: S108092 **Reel:** 0134 **Frame:** 00240 **ignore:** 000 **Date:** 1776 C. or later

Description: SIMONTON, JOHN, ACCOUNT AUDITED (FILE NO. 7015) OF CLAIMS GROWING OUT OF THE AMERICAN REVOLUTION. **Names indexed:** SIMONTON, JOHN

Death and Marriage Records

William White Brice married Margaret Clowney. Children include:
1. John Edgar Brice (1901-1956) married Marguerite Brannon. They had one daughter Peggy.
2. Charles W. Brice, Sr. married and lived in Chester County.
3. William White Brice, Chester
4. Albert W. Brice, Greenwood.
5. James C. Brice married Miss Scott. They had one son. J. C. Brice was superintendent of schools in Easley, SC.
6. Elizabeth Brice.
7. __ Brice married Harold Alexander of Chester.

Alexander Douglas b. Oct. 14,1799, d. July 18, 1863, married Jennette Simonton b. Sept. 8, 1799, d. Jan. 3, 1872.
1. Martha Simonton Douglass b. Jan. 2, 1826 married Rev. J. H. Peoples.
2. John S. Douglass b. May 15, 1828; married Margaret D. Boyce Jan 3, 1855 by Rev. Dr. James Boyce
    a. William B. Douglass b. April 11, 1856
    b. Laura Jennette Douglass b. Oct. 17, 1857
    c. Charles Alexander Douglass b. Jan. 31, 1859
    d. Nancy Caroline Douglass b. July 2, 1860, d. Oct. 28, 1861
    e. Lois Emeline Douglass b. March 23, 1862
    f. John Scott Douglass b. Nov. 17, 1863, d. Sept. 26, 1864
    g. James Calvin Douglass b. Feb. 27, 1866
    h. Martha Eugenia Douglass b. July 8, 1867
    i. Edgar Scott Douglass b. Dec. 7, 1868
    j. Ebenezer Erskine Douglass b. June 23, 1870
    k. Albert Gilmore Douglass b. Dec. 24, 1871
    l. John Walkup Douglass b. Nov. 9, 1873
    m. Joseph Simonton Douglass b. Feb. 8, 1879

3. Jane G. Douglass b. June 15, 1839
4. Alexander S. Douglass b. Dec. 25, 1833
5. Margaret S. Douglass b. Nov. 24, 1836
6. Mary E. Douglass b. Oct. 26, 1839, married James Henry Brice
7. Sarah E. Douglass b. Sept. 10, 1843

Margaret Simonton married Rev. E. E. Boyce
Ella Brice married Rev. S. L. Morris.

New Hope A.R.P. Church

New Hope A.R.P. Church and Session House were constructed ca. 1886. This church, with its decorated belfry and its intact session house, is significant as an interesting example of local interpretation of stylistic elements of religious architecture. The meeting house form church is a one-story, weatherboarded, frame church with an apsidal plan and a narthex pavilion. A bracketed belfry with bellcast roof, gablets, and finial surmounts the front-gabled roof. The gable end features a boxed cornice with returns and a blind oculus. Façade fenestration with shelf architraves has a double-leaf door surmounted by a ten-light transom flanked by single, large-paned, four-over-four, shuttered windows. Side elevations have windows identical to those of the façade. The interior walls are plastered above narrow-beaded-board wainscoting. The rear balcony displays a turned balustrade. Alterations include a 1970 left wing and the front steps. The session house is a ten by twelve foot weatherboarded frame building with a gable end roof with boxed cornices. Listed in the National Register December 6, 1984.

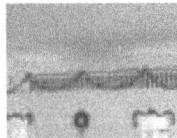

Rev. R. M. Stevenson, D.D. write a historical sketch of New Hope A.R.P. church. This appeared in the Oct. 31, 1943 Associate Reformed Presbyterian. He lists the professional men reared at New Hope: Ministers, R. W. Brice, J. R. Castles, C. E. McDonald, J. C. Douglass, J. W. Douglass, W. B. Douglass, C. A. Douglass, Scott Douglass, J. E. McDonald, W. L. McDonald and John Means Simonton. Physicians: Walter Brice, W. S. B. McClerkin, Henry Castles, Jr., J. Michael Brice, J. L. Thompson, J. C. S. Brice, W. F. Mitchell, J. E. Douglass, Sr., J. E. Douglass, Jr., John W. Douglass, and Eugene Brice. Dentists: R. T. Douglass and C. M. Douglass.

Erskine College: Calvin Brice's family: George, William, Homer, Bert, Evie, and Ruth. William Brice: Jane, Margaret, Sarah, Mary, John, Samuel, Robert and James. A.
C. S. Brice, Sr. – Ella
C. S. Brice, Jr. - Agnes

Clarence Brice – John A., Jr. and Lila
Mrs. Rebecca Rosborough Brice – Emmie Rosborough
John A. Brice, Sr. – Clarence, Caroline, Alice, Robie and Jennie
Robert Brice – Robert, Charles, Thomas, Margaret, Amanda and Mary
T. S. Brice – Lesslie, Burtie and Mamie
Dr. Walter Brice – Michael, Scott, Wade, John, Thomas and Rebecca
William Brice – John C. S.
S. G. Brice – Eugene and Bessie
John G. Brice – Watt and Mary
T. P. Mitchell – Johnnie and Chris Brice, William, Eunice, Bessie
John Simonton – Mary, Mattie, Margaret, Boyce, Robert and John
Robert Simonton – Marie, Joh Means, Bessie, Bertie and Martha
(The list includes many Douglasses, Stevensons, and others)

Dictionary of Given Names by Flora Haines Longhead gives (1) Brice (Ango Saxon) – A Breach
(2) Bryce (Celtic) – Speedy
(3) Bruce (Old French).
From Bruys in Normandy.

History of Fairfield County, South Carolina from "Before the White Man Came" to 1942 by Fitz Hugh McMaster gives a list of 102 farms out of a total of 738 in the county as listed in the census of 1850 that had a value of $7,000 or more. These included: John Brice $17,500; Walter Brice $19,800; Robert Brice $28,000; David Brice $11,900; James G. Brice $16,700; John Brice, Jr. $17,760. In 1860 there were 707 farms with 134 valued at $10,000 or more. These included: J. G. Brice $30,000; J. G. Brice $33,000; John Brice $33,620; Robert Brice $30,000; Dr. W. Brice $25,500; Robert Brice, jr. $55,680; John Brice, Jr. $24,000; Sam Brice $27,500; John A. Brice $17,665.

From the *News and Herald*, Saturday, Feb. 2, 1878: School Notice – A graded school in the English branches and arithmetic, for white children between the ages of six and sixteen years, will be opened at Mount Zion College, as follows: For the primary department – embracing children in primary grades as far as the third reader and the multiplication table – under Miss Blaine, at 10 o'clock A.M. on Monday next.

From *The State*, August 25, 1956: The Pentagon reported today that Lt. General William O. Brice will be promoted to a four star general and retired as of September 1.

The *Fairfield News and Herald*, Wednesday, August 9, 1882 reports that the 12th regiment survivors met and elected officers. Those included J. H. Brice, second vice president. Plans were made for their fourth annual reunion to be held at Rock Hill. The fifth annual reunion of the Sixth regiment was held in Winnsboro. The procession was formed under the command of Maj. Thomas W. Brice and marched to the court house. The address was by Jr. Sanders.

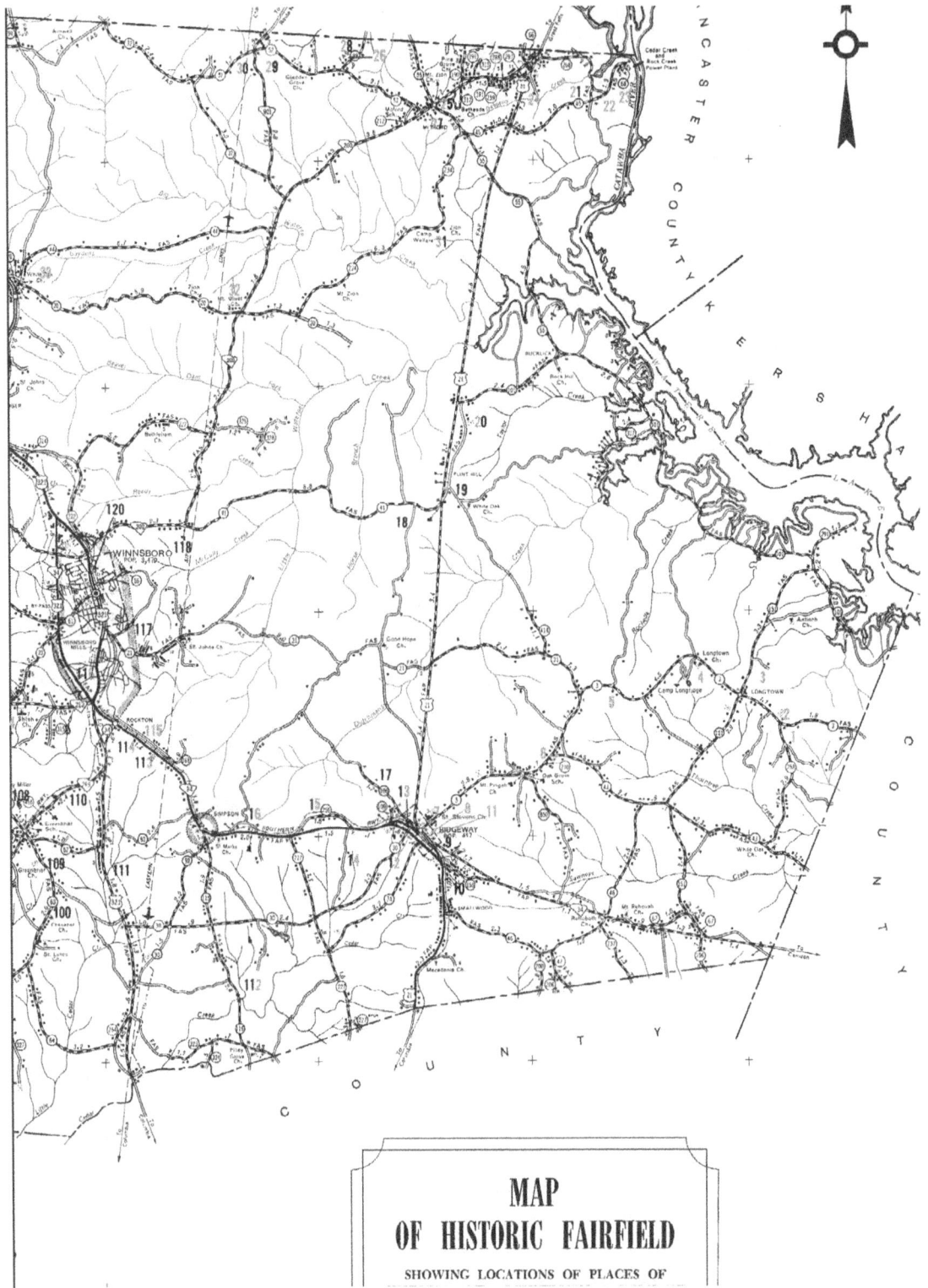

MAP
OF HISTORIC FAIRFIELD

SHOWING LOCATIONS OF PLACES OF

John J. Brice, Nephew

Walter Brice, County Antrim, brother of John, William, and James Brice, did not emigrate to this country; however, his son, John J. Brice and his family did come over in November 1840 and settled in the New Hope community. John J. Brice (1795-1863) and his wife, Mary (1796-1874) had one son, William, and several daughters: Hannah (1822-1874) did not marry and is buried at New Hope; Grace White Brice was born in County Antrim and died Jan. 15, 1856, aged 15 years, 11 months and 24 days and buried at New Hope so she must have been an infant when her parents came over in November 1840; Elizabeth Brice married F. Elder; Mary Brice married James Richey. The later Homer Brice explained that William was "Maggie Turner's father which means he is the grandfather of Mrs. O. C. Scarborough and John M. Turner." It is not known whether Elizabeth and Mary married in this country or in Ireland.

Francis Brice

S213184: Colonial Plat Books (Copy Series) BRICE, FRANCIS, PLAT FOR 100 ACRES ON EDISTO RIVER.

Series: S213019 **Volume:** 0009 **Page:** 00351 **Item:** 000 **Date:** 2/20/1760 **Description:** BRICE, FRANCIS, LAND GRANT FOR 100 ACRES ON BRICES BRANCH. **Names indexed:** BRICE, FRANCIS **Locations:** BRICE BRANCH **Document type:** LAND GRANT

Series: S111001 **Volume:** 0014 **Page:** 00043 **Item:** 005 **Date:** 5/5/1761 **Description:** BRICE, FRANCIS, MEMORIAL FOR 100 ACRES ON EDISTO RIVER. **Names indexed:** BRICE, FRANCIS **Locations:** BRICE CREEK; EDISTO RIVER **Document type:** MEMORIAL

S165018: Resolutions of the General Assembly RESOLUTIONS DIRECTING THE REMISSION OF A FINE ON FRANCIS BRICE FOR BREAKING THE QUARANTINE LAW, AND FOR ERECTING A FORTIFICATION TO PROTECT THE HARBOR AND ENTRANCE OF SANTEE RIVER. (2 PAGES)

In the House of Representatives April 30 1794

Resolved - as the Opinion of the Legislature that the
application of Francis Brice, Master of the Ship Major
Pinchney for a remission of the Penalty of Five
hundred pounds Sterling, for breach of Quarantine
should be made to his Excellency the Governor
who is satisfied of

In the Senate May 9. 1794

Resolved That the Governor be & he is hereby authorised to cause a battery to be erected on such place as shall on examination be found best adapted to defend the Harbour & entrance of Santee river, & that the faith of the State be & the same is hereby pledged to provide in the next Tax bill a sum not exceeding Fifty pounds for defraying the expence thereof. Ordered that the resolution be sent to the House of Representatives for their concurrence

By order of the Senate

Felix Warley C.S.

Rd [illegible] that Mr Fraser & Dr Mitchell [illegible]

Series: S111001 **Volume:** 0012 **Page:** 00175 **Item:** 001 **Date:** 5/4/1773 **Description:** BRICE, DANIEL, MEMORIAL FOR 200 ACRES IN TRYON COUNTY, N.C., SUMMARIZING A CHAIN OF TITLE TO A GRANT TO THOMAS PENNY OF OCT. 24,

1767. **Names indexed:** BRICE, DANIEL; PENNY, THOMAS; TRYON, GOV.; VARNOR, ALEXANDER **Locations:** CRAVEN COUNTY; JAMEYS CREEK; NORTH CAROLINA; TRYON COUNTY, NC; TYGER RIVER **Document type:** MEMORIAL

Series: S108092 **Reel:** 0013 **Frame:** 00307 **ignore:** 000 **Date:** 1776 C. or later
Description: BRICE, DANIEL, ACCOUNT AUDITED (FILE NO. 744) OF CLAIMS GROWING OUT OF THE AMERICAN REVOLUTION. He served two hundred seventy days as a horseman under Capt. John Collins and Col. Roebuck from 15 June 1780 to 1 June 1781. A.A.744; X1162. **Names indexed:** BRICE, DANIEL

James Brice served under Capt. Saddler during 1779 and during 1780 was at Fort Lacey, at Fort Congaree and lost a horse in Sumter's Defeat. A.A.744A.

Robert Brice enlisted in the First Regiment on 4 November 1775 under Capt. Roger Sanders, S.C. H.&G., I, 60; N.A.553.

Daniel Brice

Descendant Register, Generation No. 1

1. **Daniel BRICE** was born ABT. 1726, and died 1780 in the Revolutionary War. Annuitants Claims. He married **Rachel ???** WFT Est. 1739-1769. She was born WFT Est. 1703-1731, and died WFT Est. 1746-1820.

Descendant Register, Generation No. 2

2. **Samuel BRICE** (Daniel BRICE[1]) was born 1743, and died 8 Sep 1795, Spartanburg, SC. He married **Jean ???** WFT Est. 1756-1785. She was born WFT Est. 1722-1749, and died WFT Est. 1765-1837.

   Child of Samuel BRICE and Jean ??? is:

   + 3 i. William BRICE was born 1762 in SC, and died BEF. 1840.

   William Brice served as a private in Felder's Batt'n, Art'y, South Carolina Nil., Roll Box 24, p. 602.

3. **William BRICE** (Samuel BRICE[2], Daniel BRICE[1]) was born 1762 in SC, and died BEF. 1840. He married **Sarah REID** WFT Est. 1778-1810, daughter of David REID and Sarah COULTER. She was born ABT. 1762, and died BEF. 1840.

Children of William BRICE and Sarah REID are:

    4 i. <u>Jane BRICE</u> was born WFT Est. 1781-1809 in Spartanburg SC, and died WFT Est. 1786-1891.

    5 ii. <u>Dorcas BRICE</u> was born WFT Est. 1781-1809 in Spartanburg SC, and died WFT Est. 1786-1891.

    6 iii. <u>William Jr. BRICE</u> was born 1778 in Spartanburg SC, and died WFT Est. 1779-1868.

 + 7 iv. <u>Samuel C. Jr. BRICE</u> was born 1781 in Spartanburg SC, and died WFT Est. 1837-1873.

    8 v. <u>James Winder BRICE</u> was born 1791 in Spartanburg SC, and died WFT Est. 1792-1881.

Descendant Register, Generation No. 4

7. **Samuel C. Jr. BRICE** (William BRICE[3], Samuel BRICE[2], Daniel BRICE[1]) was born 1781 in Spartanburg SC, and died WFT Est. 1837-1873. He married **Elizabeth PRICE** 10 MAR 1814. She was born 1783 in SC, and died WFT Est. 1838-1878.

Children of Samuel C. Jr. BRICE and Elizabeth PRICE are:

 + 9 i. <u>John Coulter BRICE</u> was born 11 DEC 1814 in Wilkinson County, MS, and died 30 APR 1881.

  10 ii. <u>Nancy BRICE</u> was born 1824 in Mississippi, and died WFT Est. 1825-1918.

  11 iii. <u>Rosannah BRICE</u> was born 1826 in Arkansas Territory, and died WFT Est. 1827-1920.

  12 iv. <u>Samuel Clinton BRICE</u> was born 1828 in Gibsland, LA, and died WFT Est. 1829-1918.

  13 v. <u>Sarah G. BRICE</u> was born 1831 in Gibsland, LA, and died WFT Est. 1832-1925.

14 vi. <u>Margaret J. BRICE</u> was born 1833 in Gibsland, LA, and died WFT Est. 1834-1927.

15   <u>Elizabeth BRICE</u> was born 1836 in Gibsland, LA, and died WFT Est. 1837-1930.
vii.

9. <u>**John Coulter BRICE**</u> (Samuel C. Jr. BRICE[4], William BRICE[3], Samuel BRICE[2], Daniel BRICE[1]) was born 11 DEC 1814 in Wilkinson County, MS, and died 30 APR 1881. He married **Hetty FRAME** 9 NOV 1833 in Louisiana, daughter of Polly ???. She was born 5 SEP 1815 in Ohio, and died ABT. 1869.

Children of John Coulter BRICE and Hetty FRAME are:

  16 i. <u>Nancy Jane BRICE</u> was born 1834 in Bienville Parish, LA, and died WFT Est. 1835-1928.

+ 17 ii. <u>Nelson Alexander BRICE</u> was born 13 JAN 1836 in Louisiana, and died WFT Est. 1884-1928.

  18 iii. <u>Mary Elizabeth Brice BRICE</u> was born 1838, and died WFT Est. 1839-1932.

  19 iv. <u>Samuel L. BRICE</u> was born 1840, and died WFT Est. 1841-1930.

  20 v. <u>David Jasper BRICE</u> was born 1842 in Louisiana, and died WFT Est. 1843-1932.

  21 vi. <u>John Newton BRICE</u> was born 1842, and died WFT Est. 1843-1932.

  22 vii. <u>Rosannah BRICE</u> was born 1846 in Bienville Parish, LA, and died WFT Est. 1847-1940.

  23   <u>Sarah Margaret BRICE</u> was born 1848 in Louisiana, and died 1906.
  viii.

  24 ix. <u>Louisiana BRICE</u> was born 1850 in Louisiana, and died WFT Est. 1851-1944.

17. **Nelson Alexander BRICE** (John Coulter BRICE[5], Samuel C. Jr. BRICE[4], William BRICE[3], Samuel BRICE[2], Daniel BRICE[1]) was born 13 JAN 1836 in Louisiana, and died WFT Est. 1884-1928. He married **Amanda RAGSDALE** 24 FEB 1859 in Walker, Texas. She was born 1840 in Mississippi, and died 20 APR 1884.

Children of Nelson Alexander BRICE and Amanda RAGSDALE are:

   25 i. <u>Thomas Alexander BRICE</u> was born 1870 in Texas, and died WFT Est. 1871-1960.

+ 26 ii. <u>James Edward BRICE</u> was born 1872 in Zavala County, and died 1951.

   27 iii. <u>William Elonzo BRICE</u> was born 1874 in Frio County, Texas, and died WFT Est. 1875-1964.

+ 28 iv. <u>Pherabe Lee BRICE</u> was born 14 MAR 1876 in Loma Vista Tx, and died 9 DEC 1934 in Uvalde, Texas.

   29 v. <u>Lena BRICE</u> was born 1877 in Texas, and died WFT Est. 1878-1971.

+ 30 vi. <u>George Luis BRICE</u> was born 1879 in Zavala County, and died WFT Est. 1917-1970.

   31 vii. <u>Emmett Walter BRICE</u> was born 1882 in Zavala County, and died 1957. He married <u>Avarilla BARNES</u> WFT Est. 1899-1930. She was born 1883, and died 1958.

FISHING CREEK PRESBYTERIAN CHURCH AND GROUNDS

This tract of seven acres was deeded to the Rev. John B. Davies, pastor, and Major John Neely, elder, of the Fishing Creek Presbyterian Church Society, by John McFadden, October 6, 1826. It was part of 56 acres granted to George Kelsey, by George III., May 7, 1774.

Redrawn by Elmer Oris Parker from a plat by Thomas Reid, Deputy Surveyor.

Fishing Creek Presbyterian Church

A general view of the churchyard showing some of the older graves in the silent city of the dead

Elizabeth Hartness, wife of John Smith Hartness was a daughter of John Cooper and Elizabeth Walker, daughter of Robert and Jane Walker.

189

Approved to 1838

"Unworthy Communicants are said to eat
and drink judgment to themselves; which
I conceive, imports, 1. That the heart which
comes by unworthy communicating comes
upon the person himself, not on Christ,
whose body and blood he is guilty of;
for themselves had a relation not to others,
but to Christ.
They may eat judgment to Ministers and
Fellow Communicants, if they have a sin-
ful hand in bringing them to the table."
Thomas Boston.

What a solemn thought for Church-sessions!

The Records of the Session

of

Fishing Creek Church,

with

A brief statement of its origin and
progress compiled by its present
Pastor, John B. Davies, acting
as the clerk for the said Session

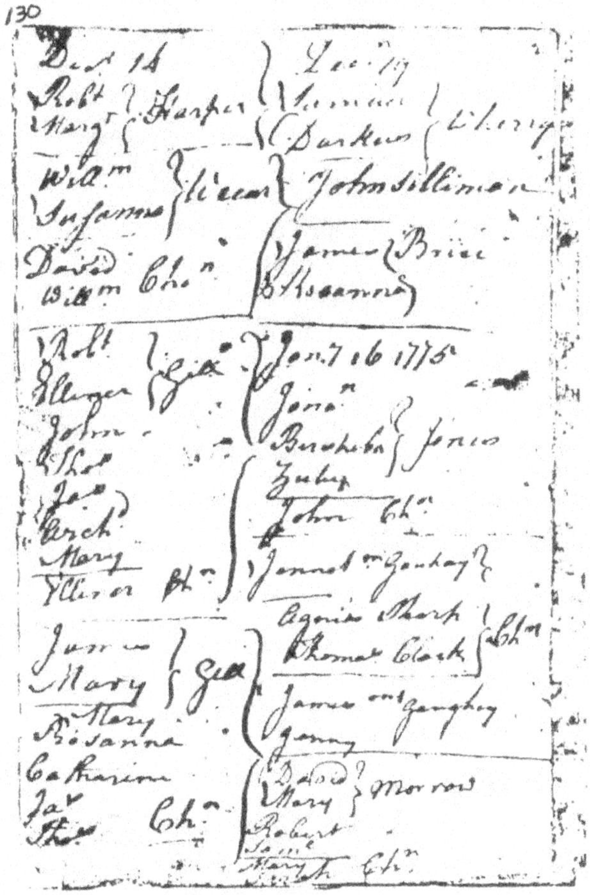
130

Dec 14
Robt / Marg^t } Harper
Willm / Susanna } McCan
David / Willm Ch^n
Robt / Ellinor } Gill
John / Thos / Jas / Arch / Mary / Ellinor Ch^n
Jas / Mary } Gill
Mary / Rosanna / Catharine / Jas / Thos Ch^n

Dec 19
Samuel / Darkus } Ukery
John Silliman
James / Rosanna } Brice
Jan 16 1775
Jon^n / Bershebe } Jones
Zuby / John Ch^n
Jennet McGaughey
Agnes Short / Thomas Clark } Ch^n
James McGaughey / Jenny
David / Mary } Morrow
Robert / Jane / Mary / Sarah Ch^n

James & Rosanna (Coulter) Brice

James Winder Brice (Jr.) (1825-1908) - tombstone reads " Born in Indian Territory ". He was a mason and emblem printed on face of above grand tomb. His wife's name was Maria (pronounces 'Mariah' He fought in the Civil War and was a Captain. That also is printed on his tombstone. I have good information on some of his life. He was a state representive in Louisiana around 1877 just after Reconstruction in the South was drawing to a close.   His daughter, Margaret Virginia Brice was the mother to my maturnal grandfather, Blanton Ponder Theus. She married a W.P. (William Ponder) Theus of Arcadia, La. in 1876, I believe. I have their old family Bible. She died when my g. father was around 2 yrs making it around 1897.   My mother, Ruth Louise Theus Carroll was born Oct 27, 1917 in Arcadia, La. Her brother James Ponder Theus died while service in the Marine Corp in New Zeland during WW II. He died from a broken neck while diving in shallow water hitting a stump or some hard object at age 18.   My older sister, Jennie Clare Carroll born Oct 17, 1944. Still living thanks to the Lord.   My middle sister, Sally Keith Carroll born September 23, 1945 and still living. Her son, David Ponder East born in May 29, 1975. no childen.   I was born, Frances Theus Carroll, on September 5, 1948 in Lake Charles, La. Two children. Jennie Marie McAfee Brady on September 30, 1969. she has only one daughter, Jordan Marie Borchers born January 13, 1995; Jesse Recoy Roth born July 31, 1982.   Blanton Ponder Theus (Born Nov. 19, 1895; died Oct 3, 1984) in Monroe, Louisiana.

Series: S213190 **Volume:** 0032 **Page:** 00400 **Item:** 001   **Date:** 5/23/1795   **Description:** BRICE, CALEB, PLAT FOR 490 ACRES ON LAKE SWAMP, CHERAW DISTRICT, SURVEYED BY ROBERT ELLISON FOR JAMES MARLOW ON SEPTEMBER 4, 1794.   **Names indexed:** BRICE, CALEB; CESSIONS, EDWARD; ELLISON, ROBERT; HIXEN, THOMAS; MARLOW, JAMES; NETTLES, JOSEPH; SCOFF, WILLIAM; WADKINS, SAMUEL   **Locations:** CHERAW DISTRICT; LAKE SWAMP   **Document type:** PLAT

Series: S213192 **Volume:** 0044 **Page:** 00327 **Item:** 002   **Date:** 12/23/1816   **Description:** BRICE, THOMAS, PLAT FOR 202.5 ACRES ON JEMES CREEK, SPARTANBURGH DISTRICT, SURVEYED BY JAMES SELMAN.   **Names indexed:** BRICE, THOMAS; PEARSON; SELMAN, JAMES; VERNON   **Locations:** JEMMYS CREEK; NORTH TYGER RIVER; SPARTANBURG DISTRICT   **Document type:** PLAT

FAIRFIELD COUNTY, SOUTH CAROLINA

LARGEST SLAVEHOLDERS FROM 1860 SLAVE CENSUS SCHEDULES

and SURNAME MATCHES FOR AFRICAN AMERICANS ON 1870 CENSUS

Transcribed by Tom Blake, August 2001

PURPOSE. Published information giving names of slaveholders and numbers of slaves held in Fairfield County, South Carolina, in 1860, is either non-existent or not readily available. It is possible to locate a free person on the Fairfield County, South Carolina census for 1860 and not know whether that person was also listed as a slaveholder on the slave census, because published indexes almost always do not include the slave census.   Those who have found a free ancestor on the 1860 Fairfield County, South Carolina census can check this list to learn if their ancestor was one of the larger slaveholders in the County. If the ancestor is not on this list, the 1860 slave census microfilm can be viewed to find out whether the ancestor was a holder of a fewer number of slaves or not a slaveholder at all. Whether or not the ancestor is found to have been a slaveholder, a viewing of the slave census will provide an informed sense of the extent of slavery in the ancestral County, particularly for those who have never viewed a slave census. An ancestor not shown to hold slaves on the 1860 slave census could have held slaves on an earlier census, so those films can be checked also. In 1850, the slave census was also separate from the free census, but in earlier years it was a part of the free census.   African American descendants of persons who were enslaved in Fairfield County, South Carolina in 1860, if they have an idea of the surname of the slaveholder, can check this list for the surname. If the surname is found, they can then view the microfilm for the details listed regarding the sex, age and color of the slaves. If the surname is not on this list, the microfilm can be viewed to see if there were smaller slaveholders with that surname. To check a master surname list for other States and Counties, return to Home and Links Page.   The information on surname matches of 1870 African Americans and 1860 slaveholders is intended merely to provide data for consideration by those seeking to make connections between slaveholders and former slaves. Particularly in the case of these larger slaveholders, the data seems to show in general not many freed slaves in 1870 were using the surname of their 1860 slaveholder. However, the data should be checked for the particular surname to see the extent of the matching.   The last U.S. census slave schedules were enumerated by County in 1860 and included 393,975 named persons holding 3,950,546 unnamed slaves, or an average of about ten slaves per holder. The actual number of slaveholders may be slightly lower because some large holders held slaves in more than one County and they would have been counted as a separate slaveholder in each County. Excluding slaves, the 1860 U.S. population was 27,167,529, with about 1 in 70 being a slaveholder. It is estimated by this transcriber that in 1860, slaveholders of 200 or more slaves, while constituting less than 1 % of the total number of U.S. slaveholders, or 1 out of 7,000 free persons, held 20-30% of the total number of slaves in the U.S. The process of publication of slaveholder names beginning with larger slaveholders will enable naming of the holders of the most slaves with the least amount of transcription work.

SOURCES. The 1860 U.S. Census Slave Schedules for Fairfield County, South Carolina (NARA microfilm series M653, Roll 1235) reportedly includes a total of 15,534 slaves, ranking it among the 30 highest County totals in the U.S. This transcription includes 65 slaveholders who held 50 or more slaves in Fairfield County, accounting for 5,926 slaves, or just over 38% of the County total. The rest of the slaves in the County were held by a total of 757 slaveholders, and those slaveholders have not been included here. Due to variable film quality, handwriting interpretation questions and inconsistent counting and page numbering methods used by the census enumerators, interested researchers should view the source film personally to verify or modify the information in this transcription for their own purposes. Census data for 1860 was obtained from the Historical United States Census Data Browser, which is a very detailed, searchable and highly recommended database that can found at http://fisher.lib.virginia.edu/census/ . Census data on African Americans in the 1870 census was obtained using Heritage Quest's CD "African-Americans in the 1870 U.S. Federal Census", available through Heritage Quest at http://www.heritagequest.com/ .

FORMAT. This transcription lists the names of those largest slaveholders in the County, the number of slaves they held in the County where the slaves were enumerated and the first census page of that County on which they were listed. The census shows no subdivisions within the County. Following the holder list is a separate list of the surnames of the holders with information on numbers of African Americans on the 1870 census who were enumerated with the same surname. The term "County" is used to describe the main subdivisions of the State by which the census was enumerated.

TERMINOLOGY. Though the census schedules speak in terms of "slave owners", the transcriber has chosen to use the term "slaveholder" rather than "slave owner", so that questions of justice and legality of claims of ownership need not be addressed in this transcription. Racially related terms such as African American, black, mulatto and colored are used as in the source or at the time of the source, with African American being used otherwise.

PLANTATION NAMES. Plantation names were not shown on the census. Using plantation names to locate ancestors can be difficult because the name of a plantation may have been changed through the years and because the sizeable number of large farms must have resulted in lots of duplication of plantation names. In South Carolina in 1860 there were 482 farms of 1,000 acres or more, the largest size category enumerated in the census, and another 1,359 farms of 500-999 acres. Linking names of plantations in this County with the names of the large holders on this list should not be a difficult research task, but it is beyond the scope of this transcription.

FORMER SLAVES. The 1860 U.S. Census was the last U.S. census showing slaves and slaveholders. Slaves were enumerated in 1860 without giving their names, only their sex and age and indication of any handicaps, such as deaf or blind Slaves 100 years of age or older were supposed to be named on the 1860 slave schedule, but there were only 1,570 slaves of such age enumerated, out of a total of 3,950,546 slaves. One holder, John Bratton, at page 47, reported a 100 year old male "African". Also, on page 51, Nancy Mays holds a black male slave of whom is written he is "100 or more years old. He was brought from Africa when a young man, about 70 years ago. His mind is good. He says he is prepared to die and next God." Freed slaves, if listed in the next census, in 1870, would have been reported with their full name, including surname. Some of these former slaves may have been using the surname of their 1860 slaveholder at the time of the 1870 census and they may have still been living in the same State or County. Before presuming an African American was a slave on the 1860 census, the free census for 1860 should be checked, as almost 11% of African Americans were enumerated as free in 1860, with about half of those living in the southern States. Estimates of the number of former slaves who used the surname of a former owner in 1870, vary widely and from region to region. If an African American ancestor with one of these surnames is found on the 1870 census, then making the link to finding that ancestor as a slave requires advanced research techniques involving all obtainable records of the holder.

MIGRATION OF FORMER SLAVES: According to U.S. Census data, the 1860 Fairfield County population included 6,373 whites, 204 "free colored" and 15,534 slaves. By the 1870 census, the white population had decreased 9% to 5,787, and the "colored" population had also decreased 9% to 14,101. (As a side note, by 1960, 100 years later, the County was listed as having 8,394 whites, about a 32% increase, while the 1960 total of 12,318 "Negroes" was about 22% less than what the colored population had been 100 years before.) Where did the freed slaves go? Charleston County saw an increase in colored population of almost two thirds between 1860 and 1870, so likely that is where many went. No other South Carolina County showed a significant increase. Between 1860 and 1870, the South Carolina colored population only increased by 4,000, to 416,000, a 1% increase. States that saw significant increases in colored population during that time, and were therefore more likely possible places of relocation for colored persons from Fairfield County, included the following: Georgia, up 80,000 (17%); Texas, up 70,000 (38%); Alabama, up 37,000 (8%); North Carolina, up 31,000 (8%); Florida, up 27,000 (41%); Ohio, up 26,000 (70%); Indiana, up 25,000 (127%); and Kansas up from 265 to 17,000 (6,400%).

PARTIAL SLAVEHOLDER LIST:

BRICE, Dr. Walter, 52 slaves, page 174

BRICE, James G., 55 slaves, page 138

BRICE, John A., 51 slaves, page 186

BRICE, Wm., 60 slaves, page 94

CALDWELL, James B., 96 slaves, page 117

MCCULLOUGH, Danl., 53 slaves, page 110

MEANS, Est. E., 69 slaves, page 145

MEANS, John H., 128 slaves, page 154

SIMONTON, John, 55 slaves, page 171

YONGUE, John L., 75 slaves, page 99

SURNAME MATCHES AMONG AFRICAN AMERICANS ON 1870 CENSUS:

(exact surname spellings only are reported, no spelling variations or soundex)

(SURNAME, # in US, in State, in County, born in State, born and living in State, born in State and living in County)

BRICE, 315, 89, 63, 101, 87, 63

CALDWELL, 1034, 170, 22, 212, 160, 22

MEANS, 238, 62, 15, 84, 57, 15

SIMONTON, 75, 3, 2, 6, 3, 2

YONGUE, 67, 67, 43, 64, 64, 43

Alexander Douglass

Alexander Douglass b. 1759, Galloway, Scotland, d. 21 Sep 1822, Fairfield County, SC married Grissell Grace Brown or Grissell Brown Grace, b. 1763 in Antrim County, Ireland.

1. Samuel Douglass
2. Mary Douglass b. 1788 in Antrim County, Ireland.
3. John Douglass b. 1789, Ballymena, Antrim County, Ireland.
4. James Douglass b. May 1793 in Fairfield County, SC.
5. William Douglass b. 1797 Fairfield County, SC.
6. Alexander Douglass, Jr. was born 13 Sep 1799, Fairfield County, SC. He died 3 Jan. 1863, Fairfield Co., SC. He married Jeannette Simonton born 8 Sep 1799, d. 3 Jan 1873, Fairfield County, SC.
   a. Martha Simonton Douglass b. 2 Jan 1827
   b. John Simonton Douglass b. 14 May 1828
   c. Grace Jane Douglass b. 28 Jun 1830
   d. Alexander Scott Douglass b. 25 Dec 1833
   e. Mary Emmeline Douglass b. 26 Oct 1839, d. 10 Dec 1920, married on 15 Oct 1867, James Henry Brice b. 27 Jan 1834, d. 1906, Fairfield County, SC
   f. Sara E. Douglass b. 10 Sep 1843

7. Charles Brown Douglass b. 6 Jan 1801

Gaston Family

Gaston J. Orleans married Olive Gaston; King P. of Naverre married Magdalene

Jean Gaston married Agnes Naverre

John Gaston (son of Jean Gaston and Agnes Naverre) married Ester Naugh
1.   John William Gaston, b. 1685, Caranleigh, Cloughwater, Antrim, Ireland, d. 1770 Caronleigh, Cloughwater, Antrim, Ireland, married in 1702 Mary Olivet Lemon, b. 1682 in Caronleigh, Cloughwater, Antrim, Ireland, d. 1752 Caronleigh, Cloughwater, Antrim, Ireland.
      a.   Hughston Gaston b. 1687 in Ballymena, Antrim, Ireland
      b.   Alexander Gaston b. 5 Feb 1702, Cloughwater, Antrim, Ireland
      c.   Mary Gaston b. 1712, Cloughwater, Antrim, Ireland
      d.   Robert Gaston b. 1720, Caranleigh, Cloughwater, Antrim, Ireland
      e.   Gage Gaston b. 1722, Caranleigh, Cloughwater, Antrim, Ireland
      f.   Janet Gaston b. 1726, Cloughwater, Antrim, Ireland, d. 28 Apr 1801, Chester Co., SC, married abt 1750 in Ireland, America, Indiana, USA Charles Strong b. Jan 1725, Antrim, Ireland, d. 1783, Camden, SC, son of John Strong and Elizabeth Wier.
           (1)   Robert Strong b. 1752, Antrim, Ireland
           (2)   Jane Strong b. 1757, Antrim, Ireland
           (3)   Christopher Strong b. 20 Jan 1760, Chester Co., SC
           (4)   Letitia Strong b. 1 Mar 1766, Chester Co., SC
           (5)   Margaret Strong b. 1768, Fishing Creek, Chester, SC, d. 11 Mar 1828, Fairfield County, SC married John Simonton 1 Jul 1785, Fishing Creek, Chester County, SC, b. 1760 Fishing Creek, SC; d. 31 Jan 1841, Fairfield County, SC.
               (a)   Charles H. Simonton
               (b)   Robert Simonton b. 19 Jul 1786, Tipton, TN
               (c)   Charles Strong Simonton b. 2 Mar 1788, Fairfield, SC
               (d)   William Simonton b. 3 Feb 1791
               (e)   Christopher Ross Simonton b. 27 Oct 1792
               (f)   Sarah Simonton b. 6 Mah 1795, Chester, SC
               (g)   John Simonton b. 6 May 1797, Chester, SC
               (h)   Jeannette Simonton b. 8 Sept 1799, Fairfield Co., SC
               (i)   Margaret Simonton b. 20 Jun 1801, Fairfield Co., SC
               (j)   Janet Strong Simonton b. ca 1805, Fairfield Co., SC
               (k)   Martha Simonton b. 8 Sep 1805, Fairfield Co., SC
               (l)   Alexander Gaston Simonton b. 12 Dec 1807
               (m)   Mary Simonton b. 16 Dec 1809, Cape Elizabeth, Maine
      g.   Elizabeth Gaston, b. 1727, Cloughwater, Antrim, Ireland
      h.   William Gaston, b. 1735, Cloughwater, Antrim, Ireland
      i.   Martha Gaston b. 1741, Ballamena, Antrim, Ireland

Some researchers list Mary Olivet Gaston married:

(1)   William Gaston b. 1685 in Caranleigh, Cloughwater, Antrim, Ireland

(2)   William Duc De Orleans b. France

(3)   John Gaston b. 10 May 1803 in Frosces, Antrim, Ireland
    a.   Joseph Gaston b. Ireland
    b.   Lee Gaston b. Ireland
    c.   Hugh Gaston b. ca 1700 in Ballymena, Antrim, Ireland
    d.   John Gaston b. 4 Apr 1703, Cloughwater, Antrim, Ireland

Simonton Family

A.   Theophilus Simonton b. 1675, Conestoga Manor Township, Lancaster, Pennsylvania, d. 1757, Rowan County, NC; married Mary Smith b. abt 1675, Delaware, d. 1767 Rowan County, NC.
1.   Thomas Simonton
2.   Theophilus Simonton b. 1701 Lancaster County, Pennsylvania
3.   Robert Simonton b. 1708 in Bedminster, Somerset, New Jersey
    a.   John Simonton b. 1760, Fishing Creek, Chester, SC, d 31 Jan 1841, Fairfield Co., married Margaret Strong, b. 1768 in Fishing Creek, d. 11 Mar 1818, Fairfield Co., daughter of Charles Strong and Janet Gaston.
        (a)   Charles H. Simonton
        (b)   Robert Simonton b. 19 Jul 1786, Tipton, TN
        (c)   Charles Strong Simonton b. 2 Mar 1788, Fairfield, SC
        (d)   William Simonton b. 3 Feb 1791
        (e)   Christopher Ross Simonton b. 27 Oct 1792
        (f)   Sarah Simonton b. 6 Mah 1795, Chester, SC
        (g)   John Simonton b. 6 May 1797, Chester, SC
        (h)   Jeannette Simonton b. 8 Sept 1799, Fairfield Co., SC
        (i)   Margaret Simonton b. 20 Jun 1801, Fairfield Co., SC
        (j)   Janet Strong Simonton b. ca 1805, Fairfield Co., SC
        (k)   Martha Simonton b. 8 Sep 1805, Fairfield Co., SC
        (l)   Alexander Gaston Simonton b. 12 Dec 1807
        (m)   Mary Simonton b. 16 Dec 1809, Cape Elizabeth, Maine

Robert Simonton is believed to be the oldest of the Simonton children that came to North Carolina. He first came to Anson Co NC in about 1750 and received a Grant of land recorded in 1754 in what was later to be known as York Co., South Carolina. It must be noted that land in 1750 was opened for settlement by Lord Granville who controlled or owned North Carolina in Anson County. Robert Simonton apparently allowed his Grand Nephew, John son of John who was the son of Theophilus Simonton II who died in Lancaster Co. PA in 1750. Robert Simonton allowed John to use this land until he had a family after which John Jr. settled with his family in Chester Co South Carolina.

To prove that Robert Simonton was in Lancaster Co. PA, he placed an advertisement in the Pennsylvania Gazette on the 19th of October, 1749 and on the 9th of November 1749 about a Irish Servant man named John Donesan about 24 years of age, red faced, short black hair, a lusty big fellow, speaks bad English and other clothing description with a reward of 3 pounds plus expenses for his return. This places Robert in Lancaster Co. PA In 1749. Robert was a pioneer in NC and SC. Roberts daughter Margaret who married Andrew Kerr and with a family of three, including one named William were in York Co. SC in 1786 as shown in court records, as well as wasThomas Simonton, Roberts son who was also shown in the York Co, SC court records in 1786. Robert owned the land in SC until the 20th May 1786, when he sold it to W M Berry.This land being located just north of the Catawaba Indian Lands in SC, and on the Catawaba River.

Robert probably did not live on this land in 1750 long and he relocated to Rowan Co NC on Fourth Creek near where his sisters and their husbands Andrew and Thomas Allison had located. This is the same area where his sister Mary and Samuel Thornton also received their land grant. When Robert came to Rowan Co, he purchased land from a John   Edwards, and from Robert Allison. Robert Allison could have been a brother to Thomas and Andrew Allison. Robert Allison apparently left the Rowan Co area and possibly went to Mecklenburg Co NC.

During Robert Simonton's time in Rowan Co He arranged for numerous properties to be purchased by various members of his family. He served as Captain of the Milita during the early days of North Carolina when Indians were a threat to Statesville. It appears that Robert was promoted to Major in 1760 for the N.C. Militia which is where the title of Major was then carried by Robert. Robert was too old to fight in the Revolutionary War, but he served as a "Juror" in Rowan Co at this time. Robert arranged for his brother William   to purchase land adjacent to Robert's and the Allison lands. He also assisted in the purchase of land by the Widow McKee (William Simonton's mother in Law) to purchase land just north of William Simonton's land.

Robert Simonton Esq. having been appointed a Justice of the Peace in the Granville District, and then also appointed as Captain of a Company in the Regiment of the Rowan Command of Colonel Alexander Osborn, in 1756 by his Excellency Arthur Dobbs Esq. Captain General and Governor in Chief in and over his Majesty's Province of North Carolina. Robert Allison, brother of Thomas and Andrew Allison, was appointed Lieutenant to Capt. Robert Simonton.

Robert was referred to as Major Robert Simonton during the time preceding the Revolutionary War as he served on what was called the Committee of Safety during the time before the War.

Robert Simonton sold his land in Statesville, Rowan Co to his brother William in 1787.   Deed records confirm this. A theory developed by the Historian William Watts, who died in 1997, was that when Iredell Co was formed from then Rowan Co in 1788, the first meeting of the people who formed this Co, met in the Robert Simonton house which was recently vacated by Robert due to his death and sold to William. The court Records refer to William Simonton's house, not his home.This would be reasonable since William at this time had a very large family and such a meeting would have crowded his home very much. The house that now exists in Statesville and is referred to as the William Simonton House,was the location of then Robert Simonton's home which was most probably a log cabin as were all other houses in 1788. It is probable that the current house now known as the William Simonton House was built to the approximate current shape and arrangement in about 1800. It is evident that a part of the foundation was the same foundation as an earlier house on this site.

It should be noted that this house, if not the oldest remaining house of this era, is one of several original houses and represents a legacy of the Simonton, Allison, Thornton families that were among the earliest pioneers of Statesville Rowan (now Iredell) Co.

Robert Simonton died in 1788, without a will and is shown as follows: May 6 1788;"Ordered that Administration on the Estate of Robert Simonton deceased, issue to

Thomas Simington, who qualified and gave Bond with Adam and Andrew Allison in the Sum of 3.000:0:0" Feb 11 1792: "Dr. the Administrator of Robert Simonton deceased to amount of Inventory and Legacies not charge insaid Inventory Cr. By amount of Legacies and Account paid Balance in the hands of the Administrators. L 2606 3 5   1714 3 3 ---------
L 892 . 2 This evidence of the death of Robert Simonton in Rowan (Iredell) Co was found in the McCubbins Papers, Rowan Co Library, NC. Records show that the Brand Robert used on his livestock was a crop and slit in each ear and the initials RS on the rump. After Robert died, his wife and Adam Simonton and his family and Ann Simonton m to Matthew Gaston, moved to Greene Co, Georgia.

North Carolina Land Grants in South Carolina:

Simonton, Robert: File No. 959 (236); Bk. 10, p. 432. Warrant: Unto Robert Simonton, 500 A on waters of Broad River . . . . 3 Apr 1752 Gab Johnston

500 A on S side Cataba River on Simontons Creek . . . 20 Feb 1754 Matt Rowan.

Father: Theophilus (Simontoun) Simonton I b: ABT 1685 in Ulster, Ireland   Mother: Mary Smith b: ABT 1690 in Glebe of Urney, Tyrone, Ulster, Ireland   Marriage 1 Margaret Gaston b: ABT 1715 in North Ireland
• 	Married: ABT 1733 in Lancaster Co, PA
Children
1. 	Margaret Simonton b: 1734 in Lancaster Co, Penn
2. 	Isabel Simonton b: 1738 in Lancaster Co, PA
3. 	Adam A. Simonton b: 29 Jan 1744 in Manor Township, Lancaster Co, PA
4. 	Ann Simonton b: 1746 in Lancaster Co, PA
5. 	Sarah Simonton b: ABT 1748 in Lancaster Co, PA
6. 	Mary Simonton b: ABT 1749 in Lancaster, Pennsylvania
7. 	William Simonton b: ABT 1750 in Lancaster Co, PA
> 	1. 	Theophilus Simonton III b: ABT 1756 in Rowan Co, NC; served in Iredell County, NC Sixth Company, 1812 and in the 7th Regt. (Pearson's) North Carolina Militia as a 1st Lieutenant in the War of 1812 (Roll Box 190, p. 602). He died in Oglethorpe, GA 20 Apr 1793 (Will Book "A", 1802-1822).
8. 	Thomas Simonton b: 1758 in Rowan Co, NC,

Rowan County, NC Tax List, Court, Governmental & Criminal Records: 1790-1909, U.S. Patent & Trademark Office Patents:
Simonton, Robert 	4 	163:1
Simonton, Theophilus 	Poles (polls) not returned

1732-1774: Colonial Soldiers of the South:
	Simonton, Robert (Cpt.) 635, Rowan County, NC

6. 	Adam Simonton lived in the Northwest part of Rowan County. He was born 29 Jan 1744, Rowan County, NC; died 5 Oct 1801, Greene County, Georgia. The Sharpe Map of Rowan shows him as the caretaker of a bridge in that area. Adam served under the command of General Rutherford in the Cherokee Expedition during the

Revolutionary War. A cash claim was approved by Committee on Claims in November of 1776. **DAR ID Number: 31162** "July 1776. Cherokee Indians were committing numerous depredations and occasional murders near the head sources of the Catawba River. Upon this information, Gen. Rutherford called out a brigade of militia from Guilford, Mecklenburg, Rowan, Lincoln and other western counties, composed of infantry and three corps of cavalry. Two skirmishes took place during this campaign, in which several Indians were killed and a considerable number made prisoners, among the latter, Hicks and Scott, two white traders, who had married Indians and espoused their cause.

" Blacksmiths John Dobbins, Adam Simonton and Joseph Foster procured part of their supply of iron and steel from the General Merchandise store located northwest of Salisbury. " Records of Alexander Lowrance show Adam Simonton made him two bells, fixed his axe and sharpened two plow irons for him. Artisans in the North Carolina Backcountry. Georgia Tax Index 1789. Adam Simonton, County:Greene, District: Carson B:198-199. 26 Sept 1794. Jacob Nichols to Leonard Robey 100 pds 200a on S. Yadkin & 5th Creek adj Thomas Hall, Adam Simonton, Jacob Nichols, **Joseph Kilpatrick.** Thomas Lazenby,, Tobias Robey 14 May 1795. Note: This is probably the grandfather of Martha Kilpatrick of the Keasler line. January 7, 1800- William McGough of Abbeville County S.C. sells to Adam Simonton of Green County, Georgia, 200 acres of land on Oghechee River, South Fork, bounding on the north of John King's land, on the east on Spellinan's land, and on the south by Baldqin's land and on the west 21 Sep 1786 Indenture between Micajah Williamson, Sr., and Sara, his wife of Wilkes County, Grantors, and Adam Simonton of Greene County, Grantee, for £100; 200 acres in Greene County, granted to said Williamson on 4 Jan 1785. Wit: James Adams, Susannah GILLIAM. Rec: 14 Oct 1789 1790 1795 Tax Lists, Greene County. Adam Simonton had two tracts of land of 260 and 340 acres on land classed as Oak and Hickory lands. He had three slaves. 5 Oct 1801 Abner Simonton joined Margaret and Robert Simonton in an application for appointment as Administrators of the estate of Adam Simonton, deceased, in Greene County, Georgia and in Jan 1803 receipted Margaret and Robert Simonton said administrators for $390 as part of legacy.

In addition to the cash claim approved by Committee on Claims in November of 1776, Adam Simonton received a land grant of 585 acres in Greene Co GA in 1789 for service in the Revolutionary War. Adam was first named as the executor of his mother Margaret Simonton's Will.
In the Bible of his son Felix which was held by Felix's son A. C Simonton and the contents testified to by Thomas Garrett in 1898 as to its authenticity, it was shown that Adam Simonton was born in PA in 1744. This meant that Robert Simonton, Adams father was married in PA to Margaret (believed to be Gaston). This also means that Robert lived on or near his father's estate in Conestoga Manor, Lancaster Co. PA in 1744.

Father: Robert SIMONTON b: 19 Jul 1726 in Lancaster, PA, USA   Mother: Margaret GASTON b: 1727 in Fishing Creek, SC, USA   Father: Robert SIMONTON b: Abt 1710 in Tyrone, Ulster, North Ireland   Mother: Margaret GASTON b: Abt 1715   Marriage 1 Margaret JOHNSON b: 11 Jan 1755

- Married: 26 Dec 1771 in Rowan Co, NC

- Married: 28 Dec 1810 in , Georgia

Children

1. Margaret SIMONTON b: 24 Dec 1772 in Rowan Co, NC
2. Robert SIMONTON b: 29 Oct 1774 in Rowan Co, NC
3. Abner A SIMONTON b: 2 Feb 1777 in Rowan Co, NC
4. Agnes SIMONTON b: 23 Apr 1779 in Rowan Co, NC
5. Joel SIMONTON b: 18 Nov 1781 in Rowan Co, NC
6. Mary SIMONTON b: 20 Nov 1783 in Rowan Co, NC
7. Felix SIMONTON b: 18 Dec 1785 in Rowan, NC, USA
8. Annie SIMONTON b: 10 Jan 1792 in GA
9. Ezekiel SIMONTON b: 24 Jul 1795 in GA
10. Thomas Hall SIMONTON b: 21 Oct 1817 in [city], [Newton], GA, USA

Sources: Title: OneWorldTree

Continuation of Robert Simonton and Margaret Benton or Gaston family:

7. Anna Simonton b. 1746, Rowan Co., NC
8. Sarah Simonton b. 1659, Antrim, Ireland
9. John Simonton b. 1760 Fishing Creek, SC

DAR Lineage Books list:

Adam Simonton 32, 59

James Simonton 37, 251

Volume IV:

Simonton, Sergt. Alexander

124	312, 313
129	177, 178
133	190

Simonton, James

| 150 | 293 |

Simonton, John

| 129 | 91 |

Simonton, Robert

| 123 | 89 |

Other children of Theophilus Simonton and Mary Smith:

4. Ann Simonton b. 1712 in Tyrone, Ulster, Ireland?

5. Isabel Simonton b. 1715

6. William Simonton b. 1716 in Derry Township, Lancaster, Pennsylvania

7.   John Simonton b. abt 1718, Lancaster, Pennsylvania

8.   Nathan Simonton b. 1720

9.   Smith Frame Simonton b. 1720

10.   Magdalene Simonton b. abt 1727, in Iredell County, NC.

The above families were taken from various submitters and may not be completely accurate.

Strong Family

Christopher Strong b. 1660, Scotland married Jeannette Symington, b. Scotland

1.   John Strong b. abt 1686, Scotland, d. 1750, Antrim, Ireland married Elizabeth Wier

      a.   Strong b. abt 1705, Antrim, Ireland

      b.   Robert Strong, b. abt 1707, Antrim, Ireland

      c.   James Strong b. 1709, Antrim, Ireland

      d.   John Strong b. abt 1711, Antrim, Ireland

      e.   Charles Strong b. Jan 1725, d. 1783

2.   James Strong b. 1709, Antrim, Ireland

SOUTH CAROLINA WOMEN WHO RECEIVED
REVOLUTIONARY INDENTS

This list has been compiled from the records in the nine volumes of STUB ENTRIES TO INDENTS and the three volumes of ACCOUNTS AUDITED of Revolutionary Claims against South Carolina, issued by the Historical Commission of South Carolina. Some of these women loaned money to the state, some furnished supplies or rendered other services.

A ********************** A

Indents Bk. I: Annas Mrs. Elizbth p.65. . . .Bk. B: Anderson Mrs. Ann 68. . . . Atchison Mary 52. .Axson Elizbth 3,42. .Accts. Aud. Vol. 1: Abney Martha 34. .. Aberlay Mrs. Ann 13. .Adams Mrs. Mary 66. . .Addison Mrs. Mary 103,105. . . Akin Mrs. Ann 120. . .Alcorn Mrs. Catherine 128. . .Allen Mrs. Agnes 175. . . Accts. Aud. Vol 2: Anderson Mrs. Rebecca 72. .Anderson Ruth 66,67. .Anderson Mrs. Margt wid. of Cpt. Geo. 64,65. . . .Anderson Mrs. Margt wid. of Thos. of Camden 112. .Allison Dorothy 4,5. .Allison Mrs. Sarah 10. .Allison Rachel 7,9.. Allston Elizbth 32. . . .Allston Mrs. Rachel 34. . .Altman Mrs. Sarah 35,37. . .. Andrews Mrs. Jane 127. . .Accts. Aud. Vol 3: Ayer Mrs. Frances 13. . .Ayers Mrs. Margt 15. .Bk. L-N:Altman Mrs. Sarah 3. . .Bk. R-T Adair Mrs. Elizbth 101. . .Adair Mrs. Sarah 162. .Andrews Mrs. Jane 67. . .Arnett Mrs. Jane 66. . . Bk. U-W: Adams Mrs. Sarah 25. . .Arnst Mrs. Maria 203. . .Atkins Mrs. Elisha 205. . .Austin Mrs. Elizbth 204. . . .Bk. Y-Z: Aberly Mrs. Ann 161. . .Alcorn Catherine 161. . .Allison Rachel 319. . .Anderson Mrs. Ann 104. . .Attoy Mrs. Mary 111. . .Bk. O-Q: Anderson Mrs. Sarah 273.   Anderson Sara 89.from Bk. B

B ************************ B

Indents Bk. I: Balls Mrs. Elizbth 66. . .Bair Mrs. Barbara 56. . .Barber Mrs. Mary 66. . .Barron Mrs. Rebecca 66. . .Beard Mrs. Mary 104. . .Bk. U-W: Box Mrs. Margt 248. . .Boyls Mrs. Martha 152. . .Bk. Y-Z: Baxter Mary 313. . .. Baynard Eliza 210. . .Berwick Mrs. Ann 217. . .Bolton Agnes 12. . .Brice Mrs. Margt (Lockhardt) 205. .Budd Susannah 62. . .Bugg Elizbth 126. . .Burke Elizbth 217. . .Bk. X. Pt. 1: Bayley Mrs. Lucy 146. . .Brandon Mrs. Agnew 142,198. . . Breed Mrs. Briscilla 142. . .Brown Mrs. Grizell 143. . .Bk. O-Q: Benbow Mrs. Martha 114. .Beverly Mrs. 309. . .Booth Mrs. May 179. . .Bowers Mrs. Sylvana 273. . .Bradley Mrs. Margt 46. . . .Brumfield Mrs. Elizbth 48. . .Bk. X. Pt. 2: Buzzard Elizbth 27. .Bk. L-N: Bagwall Mrs. Jane. .Brazell Hannah 6. . .Bridges Mrs. Mary 265. . .Brown Mrs. Sarah 262. . .Bryant Mrs. Sarah 264. . .Bk. R-T: Babb Mrs. Mary 164. . . .Babilitman Mrs. Zeba 9. . .Bonneau Mrs. Ann 106. . . Bowman Mrs. Sarah 165. .Box Mrs. Mary 163. .Boyd Mrs. Martha 9. . .Brazzel Mrs. Hannah 6. .Burns Mrs. Mary 166. . .Accts. Aud. Vol. 2: Babb Mrs. Mary 17. . .Bacot Mary 32. . .Ball Mrs. Elizbth 96. . .Bails Mrs. Elizbth 50-2. . .Bair Mrs. Barbara 52. . .Baird Mrs. Winifred 55. . .Baker Charlotte Bohun 71. . . Bampfield Mrs. Rebecca 127-30. . .Barber Mrs. Mary 142. . . .Bare Mrs. John Christopher 143. .Bk. B: Bacot Mrs. Mary 27. . .Baker Charlotte B.59. . .Baker Elizbth E. 137. . .Ball Elizbth 44. . .Bampfield Mrs. Rebecca 162,208. . .Barron Mrs. Sarah 127. . . .Batchelor Mrs. Mary 22. . .Bancart Mary 137. . .Beresford Dorothy 54. .Beresford Sarah 18,105,110. .Berwick Mrs. Ann 90. . .Boobe Sarah 56. . .Bounetheau Mrs. Mary 220. . .Bower Mrs. Katherine 139. . .Boyd Elizbth 153. . .Broughton Ann 20. . .Burrington Elizbth 127. . . .Butler Sarah 36. .Butler Jane 37.

90

Bowman, John
He served in the militia under Capts. Wilson and Anderson. In addition, he rented a wagon and team to the militia during 1781 and served eighty-four days in the militia as a horseman during 1782. A.A.657; F410; L599.

Bowman, Samuel
He served in the First Regiment under Capt. William Cattell during 1775 and was a sergeant under Capt. Charles Lining during 1780. Salley, Doc., p. 32; S.C.H.&G., I, 56; N.A.853; N.A.246.

Bowman, William
He served in the militia and was at the fall of Charleston. Yearbook, 1897.

Bowman, William
He served in the militia and was at the fall of Charleston. Yearbook, 1897.

Bowsman, John
See John Bowman.

Bowsman, Peter
He served in the Second Regiment.

Box, Edward   W25268
                                   BLWt 26455-160-55
d.   15 May 1857
m.   Nancy _____ , 7 March 1842
While residing in Laurens County, he enlisted under Capt. Robert Manfield and Col. Worton. (Moved to Tenn.)

Box, Lewis
He served as a captain under Major Hicks and Col. LeRoy Hammond. (Johnson, William, S10918); (Elkin, Joshua, S10694).

Box, Samuel   S3015
b.   1745, Orange District, S. C.
While residing in Orange District, he was drafted during 1776 under Capt. Sanders and Col. Moultrie and was in the battle at Fort Moultrie. In 1779, he was drafted under Col. Moultrie and Gen. Lincoln. He was taken prisoner in the fall of Charleston and held twenty-two days. Afterwards, he was drafted under Col. Maitland and was in the battle at Stono. Thereafter, he was under Capt. Elliott and Gen. Marion and was in several skirmishes. (Moved to N. C. and Tenn.)

Boxall, John
He enlisted in the Second Regiment on 4 November 1775. He was killed at Fort Moultrie on 28 January 1776. N.A.853.

Boyakin, Francis
See Francis Boykin.

Boyce, Alexander
He became a lieutenant in the Sixth Regiment during 1776 and was a captain on 27 June 1778. He died during November 1779 of wounds received at the siege of Savannah on 9 October 1779. Heitman, p. 114; S.C.H.&G., X, 229.

Boyce, John
He was in the battles at Kings Mountain, Cowpens and Eutaw Springs. In addition, he lost three fingers when attacked by 'Bloody Bill' Cunningham. Landrum, p. 351.

Boyce, Thomas
He served in the militia after the fall of Charleston. A.A.653; W353.

Boyce, William   W9561
m.   Elizabeth _____ , 1779
He served under Capts. William Kimball, Lewis, Armstrong, Col. Armstrong and Gen. Marion and was in the battle at Guilford Courthouse.

Boyce, William
He served under Capt. Isaac Ross, Col. Myddleton and Gen. Sumter during 1781. Salley, Doc., p. 83; A.A.5843A; M402.

Boyd, David
b.   1758
d.   3 December 1833
m.   Eleanor Crosson
He enlisted in the First Regiment on 4 November 1775 and was discharged on 11 August 1778. N.A.853; P.1.

Boyd, David   R1085
d.   1823/24
m.   Sarah Dobrey (Causthorn)
He first served in a Virginia unit. Thereafter, he served under Col. Pinckney in the First Regiment and was transferred to Capt. Clarke and sent to Augusta. During 1779, he was a footman under Capt. Hugh Whiteside and a horseman under Capts. Mills and Knox. In addition, he served under Col. LeRoy Hammond prior to the fall of Charleston. During 1780, he was under Gen. Sumter. During 1781, he was under Capts. George Cooper and Hugh Knox. (Moved to Ga.) C.S.; N.A.853; A.A.665; X374.

Boyd, Edward
He served under Capt. Isaac Ross, Col. Myddleton and Gen. Sumter. Salley, Doc., p.

Boyd, Evan
He made clothes for Col. Maham's regiment during 1781. C.S.; A.A.666; R378.

1781, he was under Capts. Foster and Barnett, Col. Henry Hampton and Gen. Sumter. He was in the battle at Eutaw Springs and was in many skirmishes. (Moved to Ga.) Salley, Doc., p. 54; A.A.791A; M290.

Brewster, William
He served in the militia. Ervin, p. 30.

Brewton, George
b.   21 February 1746
d.   28 August 1815
m.   Catherine_____
He enlisted on 24 February 1779 as a sergeant in the Second Regiment under Capt. Charles Motte. In addition, he served in the militia that year. Saffell, p. 291; N.A.853; A.A.738½; R366.

Breyler, Jacob
He served in the Second Regiment under Capt. Blake during 1778. S.C.H.&G., V, 16.

Brian, Barnaby
He served in the Second Regiment under Capt. Thomas Dunbar during 1779. Saffell, p. 293.

Brian, Hardy
See Bryant Hardy.

Brian, James
He served in the militia under Capt. William McKenzie, Col. William Hill and Gen. Sumter. M125.

Brian, Matthew
He served in the militia under Capt. James Giles, Col. Hill and Gen. Sumter during 1781. Salley, Doc., p. 67; Ervin, p. 83.

Brian, William
He enlisted in the Fourth Regiment on 14 February 1776. N.A.853.

Briana, John
He served in the militia under Col. Roebuck after the fall of Charleston. A.A.740; X3372.

Briant, Frances
He served in the militia during 1782. A.A.742; N92.

Briant, William
He enlisted in the Third Regiment on 22 April 1779. A.A.741A; N.A.853.

Brice, Daniel
m.   Rachel_____
He lost his life in service in 1780. Annuitants Claims.

Brice, Daniel
He served two hundred seventy days as a horseman under Capt. John Collins and Col. Roebuck from 15 June 1780 to 1 June 1781. A.A.744; X1162.

Brice, James
He served under Capt. Saddler during 1779 and during 1780 was at Fort Lacey, at Fort Congaree and lost a horse in Sumter's Defeat. A.A.744A.

Brice, Robert
He enlisted in the First Regiment on 4 November 1775 under Capt. Roger Sanders. S.C. H.&G., I, 60; N.A.853.

Brice, Samuel
He served under Col. Roebuck after the fall of Charleston. A.A.745.

Bricken, James
He served in the Charleston Militia Regiment under Capt. James Bentham and Col. Simons during 1778. S.C.H.&G., LIII, 14.

Brickford, John
He served as a carpenter's mate aboard the frigate South Carolina. A.A.477B; C670.

Bride, Thomas
He served as a horseman under Capt. Joseph Calhoun from 1780 to 1783. A.A.746; 1574.

Bridge, John
He enlisted in the Fifth Regiment on 25 June 1776. N.A.853.

Bridge, William
He enlisted in the Fifth Regiment on 28 July 1776. N.A.853.

Bridge, William
He served during 1779 and 1781 in the Colleton County Regiment under Captain William Clay. A.A.747; S217.

Bridges, Edward
He served in the cavalry under Colonel Wade Hampton. A.A.747A; C727.

Bridges, Francis
He enlisted on 7 July 1779 and served in the Second Regiment under Capt. Thomas Moultrie. Saffell, p. 292; N.A.853.

Bridges, James
He served as a spy on the Indian expedition during 1779 and as a captain of horse from 7 June 1780 to 7 April 1781 in Roebuck's regiment. A.A.748; X1771.

Sloane, John
He served in the militia as a horseman. A.A. 7089; I.184.

Slown, John
He served under Capt. Peter Burns, Col. Wade Hampton and Gen. Sumter. A.A.7089; M236.

Sly, Charles
He served twelve months aboard the brig _Polly_ during 1777 and 1778. A.A.7090; X304.

Smart, James
He served thirty-one days on foot under Lt. Jacob Buxton, forty days on horseback, and one hundred fifty-three days as a lieutenant in the militia during 1781 and 1782. A.A. 7091; X155; X3984.

Smart, Jeremiah
He was a mattross in the Fourth Regiment under Capt. William Mitchell during 1780. N.A. 246; N.A.853.

Smart, Nathan
He served forty-two days in the militia. A.A. 7092; V298.

Smart, William
He served one hundred fifty days as a horseman in the militia during 1781. A.A.5428; A.A.8568; X176.

Smellie, Patrick
See Patrick Smillie.

Smely, William
He served as an ensign in the Wadmalaw Island Company of the Colleton County Regiment of Foot during 1775. S.C.H.&G., II, 6.

Smiley, David
He served in the militia after the fall of Charleston. A.A.7094; U2.

Smiley, _____
See Smyly.

Smiley, John
He served two hundred seventy-seven days as a horseman in the militia during 1779, 1781, and 1782. A.A.7172; X189; X313.

Smiley, William
He served under Capt. James Giles, Colonel William Hill and Gen. Sumter. A.A.7095; M100.

Smiley, William
He served forty days riding express and twenty-three days with a Lt. Brice and Col. Bratton. A.A.7095; X1938.

Smiley, William
He enlisted in the Second Regiment on 7 August 1775 under Capt. Barnard Elliott. S.C.H. &G., XVI, 31; XVII, 100.

Smillie, Patrick
b. c. 1747, Scotland
He enlisted in the Rangers on 22 July 1775 under Capt. John Purvis and Col. Thomson. S.C.H.&G., I, 302; II, 185.

Smily, William
See William Smiley.

Smiser, Jacob
He was commissioned lieutenant on 6 December 1781 in the Second Regiment under Capt. William Fishburn. S.C.H.&G., XXXV, 115.

Smith, Aaron
While serving under Colonel Roebuck, he was wounded in the battle at Cowpens and died five days later. A.A.7098; X3703; (Smith, Samuel, S19098).

Smith, Aaron   BLWt 2264-200
b. 1758
d. 1817
m. _____ Wilde
He served as a captain in the militia during 1775 and became a first lieutenant in the Second Regiment on 18 March 1778. He served as a lieutenant in the Third Regiment during 1779 and was taken prisoner at the fall of Charleston. P.I.; Heitman, p. 501; S.C.H.&G., V, 149; A.A.7098; C115; Yearbook, 1893.

Smith, Aaron   R9718
d. 5 August 1850
m. Elizabeth _____, May 1810
He enlisted, while residing in Fairfield District, and served thirty days in the militia during 1782. A.A.7098; V289.

Smith, Abner
b. Ireland
He was wounded in the battle on Sullivan's Island. In addition, he served one hundred twenty-three days in the militia during 1782 and 1783. McCall, III, 209; O156.

Smith, Abraham   R9677
b. 12 March 1754, Neuse River, N. C.
He enlisted, near Fish Dam Ford during May 1777 or 1778, in the Third Regiment under Capt. David Hopkins. He was captured by the British and confined in Savannah. He was taken to Jamaica and kept until the end of the war. (Moved to Mo.)

Smith, Abram
He served twenty days in the militia under Lt. Jacob Buxton. A.A.7101; X3976.

Brices Who Fought in the Confederacy

South Carolina

Name:	**John C. Brice**
Side:	Confederate
Regiment State/Origin:	South Carolina
Regiment Name:	Cavalry Battalion, Hampton Legion South Carolina
Regiment Name Expanded:	Cavalry Battalion, Hampton Legion, South Carolina
Company:	A
Rank In:	Private
Rank In Expanded:	Private
Rank Out:	Private
Rank Out Expanded:	Private
Film Number:	M381 roll 4

Calvin Brice

Side Served:	Confederacy
State Served:	South Carolina
Service Record:	Enlisted as a Sergeant. Enlisted in Company C, 6th Infantry Regiment South Carolina. Surrendered Company C, 6th Infantry Regiment South Carolina on 9 Apr 1865 at Appomattox, VA.

John Brice

Side Served: Confederacy

State Served: South Carolina

Service Record: Enlisted as a Private. Enlisted in Company C, 6th Infantry Regiment South Carolina.

R Brice

Side Served: Confederacy

State Served: South Carolina

Service Record: Enlisted as a Private. Enlisted in Company C, 6th Infantry Regiment South Carolina.

Name: **C Brice**

Side Served: Confederacy

State Served: South Carolina

Service Record: Enlisted as a Private. Enlisted in Company D, 1st Cavalry Regiment South Carolina.

Name: C Brice

Side Served: Confederacy

State Served: South Carolina

Service Record: Enlisted as a Private. Enlisted in Company D, 10th Battn Cavalry Regiment South Carolina.

J Brice

Side Served:	Confederacy
State Served:	South Carolina
Service Record:	Enlisted as a Private. Enlisted in Company D, 6th Infantry Regiment South Carolina.

Thomas Brice

Side Served:	Confederacy
State Served:	South Carolina
Service Record:	Enlisted as a 2nd Lieutenant. Commission in Company D, 6th Infantry Regiment South Carolina.

W Brice

Side Served:	Confederacy
State Served:	South Carolina
Service Record:	Enlisted as a Private. Enlisted in Company D, 6th Infantry Regiment South Carolina.
Regiment:	6th Infantry Regiment South Carolina
Date of Organization:	8 Jul 1861
Muster Date:	9 Apr 1865
Regiment State:	South Carolina

Regiment Type:	Infantry
Regiment Number:	6th
Regimental Soldiers and History:	Regimental History Battles Fought Fought on 20 Dec 1861 at Dranesville, VA. Fought on 5 May 1862 at Williamsburg, VA. Fought on 31 May 1862 at Seven Pines, VA. Fought on 1 Jun 1862 at Seven Pines, VA. Fought on 17 Sep 1862 at Sharpsburg, MD. Fought on 6 May 1864 at Wilderness, VA. Fought on 12 Jun 1864 at Petersburg, VA. Fought on 27 Jun 1864 at Petersburg, VA. Fought on 30 Sep 1864 at Fort Harrison, VA. Fought on 7 Oct 1864 at Petersburg, VA. Fought on 10 Dec 1864 at Petersburg, VA.

W Brice

Side Served:	Confederacy
State Served:	South Carolina
Service Record:	Enlisted as a Private. Enlisted in Company D, 6th Infantry Regiment South Carolina.
Regiment:	6th Infantry Regiment South Carolina

Date of Organization:	8 Jul 1861
Muster Date:	9 Apr 1865
Regiment State:	South Carolina
Regiment Type:	Infantry
Regiment Number:	6th
Regimental Soldiers and History:	Regimental History Battles Fought

Fought on 20 Dec 1861 at Dranesville, VA.

Fought on 5 May 1862 at Williamsburg, VA.

Fought on 31 May 1862 at Seven Pines, VA.

Fought on 1 Jun 1862 at Seven Pines, VA.

Fought on 17 Sep 1862 at Sharpsburg, MD.

Fought on 6 May 1864 at Wilderness, VA.

Fought on 12 Jun 1864 at Petersburg, VA.

Fought on 27 Jun 1864 at Petersburg, VA.

Fought on 30 Sep 1864 at Fort Harrison, VA.

Fought on 7 Oct 1864 at Petersburg, VA.

Fought on 10 Dec 1864 at Petersburg, VA.

J Brice

Side Served: Confederacy

State Served: South Carolina

Service Record: Enlisted as a Private.   Enlisted in Company D, 6th Infantry Regiment South Carolina.

CONFEDERATE APPLICATIONS FOR PRESIDENTIAL PARDONS, 1865-1867

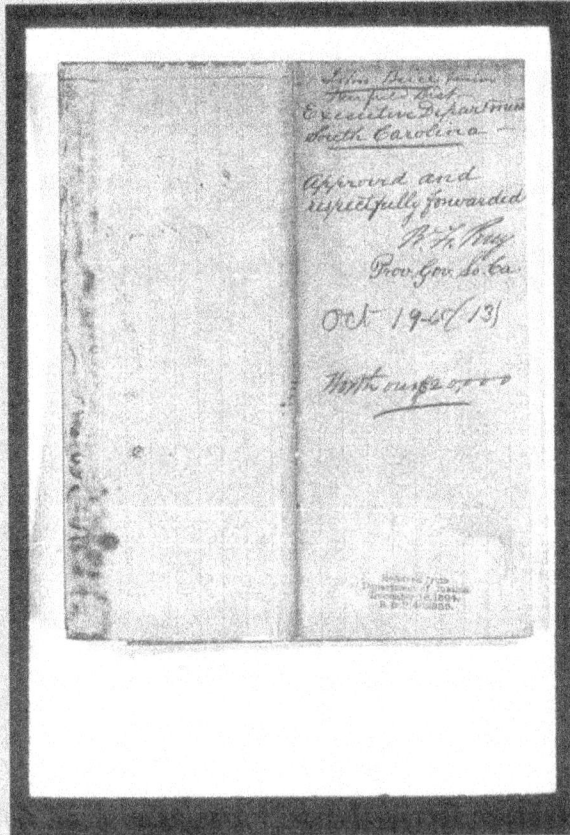

JOHN BRICE SENIOR -MAJOR- Co. D - 6TH SCV 1861- NOV 16, 1863 -WIA CAMBELLS STATION TENN

STATE: SOUTH CAROLINA
YEAR: 1865

SOURCE INFORMATION: WWW.ANCESTRY.COM DATABASE:
CONFEDERATE APPLICATIONS FOR PRESIDENTIAL PARDONS, 1865-1867

Name:	**James H. Brice**
Side:	Confederate
Regiment State/Origin:	South Carolina
Regiment Name:	12 South Carolina Infantry
Regiment Name Expanded:	12th Regiment, South Carolina Infantry
Company:	G,F
Rank In:	Private
Rank In Expanded:	Private
Rank Out:	Private
Rank Out Expanded:	Private
Film Number:	M381 roll 4
Name:	**Walter W. Brice**
Side:	Confederate
Regiment State/Origin:	South Carolina
Regiment Name:	12 South Carolina Infantry
Regiment Name Expanded:	12th Regiment, South Carolina Infantry
Company:	G,F
Rank In:	Private
Rank In Expanded:	Private
Rank Out:	Private
Rank Out Expanded:	Private

Name:	**James Brice**
Side:	Confederate
Regiment State/Origin:	South Carolina
Regiment Name:	3 Batt'n. South Carolina Inf.
Regiment Name Expanded:	3rd Battalion, South Carolina Infantry (Lauren's) (James')
Company:	D
Rank In:	Private
Rank In Expanded:	Private
Rank Out:	Private
Rank Out Expanded:	Private
Film Number:	M381 roll 4
Name:	**James P. Brice**
Side:	Confederate
Regiment State/Origin:	South Carolina
Regiment Name:	Infantry Regiment, Hampton Legion South Carolina
Regiment Name Expanded:	Infantry Regiment, Hampton Legion, South Carolina
Company:	F
Rank In:	Private
Rank In Expanded:	Private
Rank Out:	Private
Rank Out Expanded:	Private
Film Number:	M381 roll 4
Name:	**James A. Brice**

Side:	Confederate
Regiment State/Origin:	South Carolina
Regiment Name:	6 South Carolina Infantry
Regiment Name Expanded:	6th Regiment, South Carolina Infantry
Company:	H
Rank In:	Private
Rank In Expanded:	Private
Rank Out:	Private
Rank Out Expanded:	Private
Alternate Name:	Wm./Lucas
Film Number:	M381 roll 4
Name:	**J.T. Brice**
Side:	Confederate
Regiment State/Origin:	South Carolina
Regiment Name:	12 South Carolina Infantry
Regiment Name Expanded:	12th Regiment, South Carolina Infantry
Company:	G,F
Rank In:	Private
Rank In Expanded:	Private
Rank Out:	Private
Rank Out Expanded:	Private
Alternate Name:	**James H./Brice**
Name:	**J.M. Brice**

Side:	Confederate
Regiment State/Origin:	South Carolina
Regiment Name:	6 South Carolina Reserves (90 Days, 1862-3)
Regiment Name Expanded:	6th Regiment, South Carolina Reserves (90 days 1862-63)
Company:	I
Rank In:	Private
Rank In Expanded:	Private
Rank Out:	Private
Rank Out Expanded:	Private
Film Number:	M381 roll 4

Name:	**A. Brice**
Side:	Confederate
Regiment State/Origin:	South Carolina
Regiment Name:	3 South Carolina Infantry
Regiment Name Expanded:	3rd Regiment, South Carolina Infantry
Company:	K
Rank In:	Private
Rank In Expanded:	Private
Rank Out:	Private
Rank Out Expanded:	Private
Alternate Name:	**D.P./Brice**
Name:	**Alex Brice**

Side:	Confederate
Regiment State/Origin:	South Carolina
Regiment Name:	27 South Carolina Infantry
Regiment Name Expanded:	27th Regiment, South Carolina Infantry (Gaillard's)
Company:	C
Rank In:	Private
Rank In Expanded:	Private
Rank Out:	Private
Rank Out Expanded:	Private
Name:	**D.M. Brice**
Side:	Confederate
Regiment State/Origin:	South Carolina
Regiment Name:	5 South Carolina State Troops
Regiment Name Expanded:	5th Regiment, South Carolina State Troops
Company:	E
Rank In:	Second Lieutenant
Rank In Expanded:	Second Lieutenant
Rank Out:	Second Lieutenant
Rank Out Expanded:	Second Lieutenant
Name:	**D.P. Brice**
Side:	Confederate
Regiment State/Origin:	South Carolina

Regiment Name:	3 South Carolina Infantry
Regiment Name Expanded:	3rd Regiment, South Carolina Infantry
Company:	K
Rank In:	Private
Rank In Expanded:	Private
Rank Out:	Private
Rank Out Expanded:	Private
Name:	**John M. Brice**
Side:	Confederate
Regiment State/Origin:	South Carolina
Regiment Name:	3 Battalion, South Carolina Reserves
Regiment Name Expanded:	3rd Battalion, South Carolina Reserves
Company:	B
Rank In:	Private
Rank In Expanded:	Private
Rank Out:	Private
Rank Out Expanded:	Private
Name:	**Jesse R. Brice**
Side:	Confederate
Regiment State/Origin:	South Carolina
Regiment Name:	3 Battalion, South Carolina Reserves
Regiment Name Expanded:	3rd Battalion, South Carolina Reserves

Company:	B
Rank In:	Private
Rank In Expanded:	Private
Rank Out:	Private
Rank Out Expanded:	Private
Name:	**John M. Brice**
Side:	Confederate
Regiment State/Origin:	South Carolina
Regiment Name:	4 South Carolina State Troops
Regiment Name Expanded:	4th Regiment, South Carolina State Troops
Company:	H
Rank In:	Private
Rank In Expanded:	Private
Rank Out:	Private
Rank Out Expanded:	Private
Name:	**W.S. Brice**
Side:	Confederate
Regiment State/Origin:	South Carolina
Regiment Name:	4 South Carolina Cavalry
Regiment Name Expanded:	4th Regiment, South Carolina Cavalry (Rutledge's)
Company:	B
Rank In:	Private
Rank In Expanded:	Private

Rank Out:	Private
Rank Out Expanded:	Private
Name:	**C.S. Brice**
Side:	Confederate
Regiment State/Origin:	South Carolina
Regiment Name:	4 South Carolina Cavalry
Regiment Name Expanded:	4th Regiment, South Carolina Cavalry (Rutledge's)
Company:	H
Rank In:	Private
Rank In Expanded:	Private
Rank Out:	Private
Rank Out Expanded:	Private
Name:	**C.S. Brice**
Side:	Confederate
Regiment State/Origin:	South Carolina
Regiment Name:	10 Batt'n.South Carolina Cav.
Regiment Name Expanded:	10th Battalion, South Carolina Cavalry
Company:	D
Rank In:	Private
Rank In Expanded:	Private
Rank Out:	Private
Rank Out Expanded:	Private

Name:	**W.S. Brice**
Side:	Confederate
Regiment State/Origin:	South Carolina
Regiment Name:	10 Batt'n South Carolina Cav.
Regiment Name Expanded:	10th Battalion, South Carolina Cavalry
Company:	A
Rank In:	Private
Rank In Expanded:	Private
Rank Out:	Private
Rank Out Expanded:	Private
Name:	**W.S. Brice**
Side:	Confederate
Regiment State/Origin:	South Carolina
Regiment Name:	25 South Carolina Militia
Regiment Name Expanded:	25th Regiment, South Carolina Militia
Name:	**Alexander Brice**
Side Served:	Confederacy
State Served:	South Carolina
Service Record:	Enlisted as a Private. Enlisted in Company C, 27th Infantry Regiment South Carolina.
Sources:	425

Regimental History, First South Carolina Cavalry

Gettysburg after battle report:

Report of Col. John L. Black, First South Carolina Cavalry, of engagement at Brandy Station.   Culpeper County, Va., June 10, 1863.

Sir: I respectfully submit the following report relative to the movements of the regiment under my command, in the action near Brandy Station on the 9th: My regiment was formed at sunrise for the purpose of moving to a new camp. About this time, brisk firing was heard, and, being near Gen. Stuart's headquarters, I instantly reported there, and was ordered forward on the road leading to Rappahannock Station, and halted at a point designated by Lieut. [C.] Dabney, of Gen. Stuart's staff. I here found the first squadron of my regiment (Capt.'s [M. T.] Owen and [S. H.] Jones) dismounted and skirmishing with the enemy on my left. This squadron had been ordered to this point on the evening of the 8th, and remained there through the night.   I immediately dismounted a party of sharpshooters from the fifth squadron, and moved them forward to support this squadron, at the request of Maj. [C. E.] Flournoy, commanding [Sixth] Virginia Regt., drawn up on the right of the line; but about the time the second line came up, a report reached me that the enemy was advancing on the road from Kelly's Ford and Rappahannock Station.   Communicating with Maj. Flournoy, I at once withdrew my second line, and moved to the right, crossing the railroad, and selecting a position at the junction of the roads leading to Kelly's and Rappahannock Station Fords, not knowing at the time that Gen. Robertson's brigade was in front of me.   Soon after I had changed position, Capt. Owen, commanding my first squadron, retired from Maj. Flournoy's left. This was done by a misconstrued order, delivered by a courier. As the ammunition of this squadron was exhausted, I at once replaced it with my fifth squadron (Capt.'s [Niles] Nesbitt and Fox), which retired from this position, as I am informed, by the direction of the officer in charge of this part of the line.   At this time I was ordered to join Gen. Hampton's brigade, on the north side of the railroad. Here, by direction of Gen. Hampton, I dismounted first my fifth squadron, and deployed them as sharp-shooters, under Capt. J. R. P. Fox; afterward the fourth squadron, under Capt.'s [L. J.] Johnson and [J. S.] Wilson, in command of their respective detachments of sharpshooters; one company of the second squadron, under Lieut. [F. A.] Sitgreaves, the other company of this squadron (Capt. [E.] Sharpe) having been left deployed as flankers on the extreme right. These companies deployed and moved forward steadily, and although they, with the sharpshooters from the other regiments of the brigade, were charged by the enemy's cavalry, they held their ground and charged on foot in return, and held their position until ordered by Gen. Hampton to retire, which they did in proper order, coming out with very few rounds of ammunition in their boxes.   Before my sharpshooters could remount, I moved rapidly to the left, toward Brandy, as ordered, following Col. Young, of the Cobb Legion, to support him. This march was made in column of squadrons. As the head of the Georgia Legion was near Gen. Stuart's headquarters, the enemy was seen approaching on my then left. Col. Young immediately changed the head of his column to the left, and charged. A portion of the enemy's force turned to the right, along the railroad, to avoid Col. Young's column. I immediately changed the head of my column to the half left, and ordered my first squadron to charge, and immediately after ordered the second squadron to charge, changing its direction at right angles to the direction of the first, to intercept the enemy escaping in that direction. Both squadrons charged in gallant order, as well as the second squadron, which was in rear.   The companies in this charge were Capt.'s Owen, Jones, [J. D.] Trezevant, [T. W.] Whatley, Sharpe, and Fox (Lieut. [Frederick] Horsey commanding the latter, Capt. Fox having previously been severely wounded).   In this charge, the first squadron was separated from the others entirely. The second and third were checked by a cut in the railroad, but the men delivered the fire of their rifles on the retreating enemy with effect. The squadrons were soon joined by the first on the hill, as a support on the left of our batteries.   From this position I was ordered to rejoin Gen. Hampton south of the railroad, and, by order, changed position several times. The fourth change of position brought my regiment into line in the ravine between Gen. Stuart's headquarters and Brandy, on the east side of the run, my right resting on the road. Here I was directly in rear of our battery, on which the enemy were firing rapidly, and a storm of shells passed over the regiment, one exploding in the column as the regiment was coming into line, but, fortunately, inflicted little damage, though many exploded near by.   I was here ordered to move to the left, to support Brig.-Gen. [W. H. F.] Lee, and moved up the ravine for that purpose, and reported to Col. Chambliss, commanding Lee's brigade, before coming into action. Here I was ordered to return to Gen. Hampton, near Brandy, and from thence was ordered to hold the road leading from Brandy to Madden's, where I remained until ordered into camp.   There were 14 or more prisoners and as many horses captured by the regiment under my command. Some of the latter were turned over on the field, besides arms and equipments.   The loss of the regiment in action was 3 killed, 9 wounded (1 since dead), and 5 missing.   I regret to report the fall of Capt. Robin Ap. C. Jones, who fell, gallantly leading his company in the charge, near division headquarters. A gallant and accomplished officer, his loss cannot be easily repaired. Capt. J. R. P. Fox was severely wounded early in the action while in charge of the sharpshooters from his squadron, which he fought and managed well. I fear he fell into the enemy's hands in leaving the field.   Fully satisfied that every man under my command did his duty, and his whole duty, and at the same time proud that not a man who left camp with the regiment at sunrise left it during the day, without first being wounded or ordered off on duty, until marched back at night, I have the honor to be, respectfully, your obedient servant,

JNO. L. BLACK,   Col. First South Carolina Cavalry.

Capt. T. G. Barker,   Assistant Adjutant-Gen.

Source: Official Records: Series I. Vol. 27. Part II. Reports. Serial No. 44

Battles Fought

Fought on 4 May 1863 at Chancellorsville, VA.

Fought on 1 Aug 1863 at Brandy Station, VA.

Battle of Brandy Station

Brandy Station was the largest cavalry battle ever fought on the North American continent. of the 20,000 soldiers involved, about 17,000 were of the mounted branch. Brandy Station is also the first battle of the war's most famous campaign - Gettysburg.

The Confederates had planned for June 9, 1863, to be a day of maneuver rather than of battle. Two of the army's three infantry corps were near Culpeper, six miles southwest of Brandy Station, poised to move into the Shenandoah Valley and thence up to Pennsylvania. Major General J.E.B. Stuart, at Brandy Station, was to screen this movement with his 9,5000-man cavalry division, while the remaining infantry corps held the attention of the Union Army at Fredericksburg, 35 miles southeast of Brandy Station.

The Federals knew that Confederate cavalry was around Culpeper, but its intelligence had not gathered information of the sizeable infantry force behind the horsemen. Army of the Potomac commander, Major General Joseph Hooker, interpreted the enemy's cavalry presence around Culpeper to be indicative of preparations for a raid of his army's supply lines. Accordingly, he ordered his Cavalry Corps commander, Brigadier General Alfred Pleasonton, to "break up Stuart's raid in its incipiency."

The Confederates apparently did not expect any harassment from the enemy cavalry, for the day before the important screening mission was scheduled to take place, the Southern troops conducted a grand review for General Robert E. Lee at Inlet Station, just two miles southwest of Brandy Station. Meanwhile, 8,000 Federal cavalryman organized into three divisions, and about 3,000 Northern infantryman were preparing to disrupt the Confederate plans.

About 4:30 a.m. on June 9th, Brigadier General John Buford's column on 5,500 soldiers splashed across the fog-shrouded Rappahannock River surprising the Confederate pickets at Beverly's Ford. Nearby Southern horsemen from Brigadier General William "Grumble" Jones' brigade, awakened by the sound of gunfire, rode into the fray partially dressed and often riding bareback. They struck Buford's leading brigade, commanded by Colonel Benjamin F. "Grimes" Davis, near a bend in the Beverly's Ford Road and temporarily checked its progress. In the fighting Davis was killed.

Davis' brigade had been stopped just short of where the Confederate Horse Artillery was camped and was vulnerable to capture. Cannoneers swung one or two guns into position and fired down the road at Buford's men, enabling the other pieces to escape and establish the foundation for the subsequent Confederate line. The artillery unlimbered at the Gee House and at St. James Church -- structures located on two knolls on either side of the Beverly's Ford Road.

Most of Jones' command rallied to the left of this Confederate artillery line, while Brigadier General Wade Hampton's brigade formed to the right. The 6th Pennsylvania Cavalry suffered the greatest casualties of any regiment participating in the battle, when it unsuccessfully charged across a field to the very muzzles of the guns at St. James Church.

Realizing that the Southern artillery blocking the direct route to Brandy Station was a force to be dislodged, Buford determined to anchor his right on the Hazel River and try to turn the Confederate left. But he found Brigade General W.H.F. "Rooney" Lee's brigade blocking his advance with some troops on a piece of high ground called Yew Ridge and some dismounted troopers positioned along a stone wall in front. After sustaining heavy losses, the Federals wrestled the stone wall away from the Confederates. Then, to the amazement of Buford's men, the Confederates began pulling back.

The Southerners were shifting to meet a new threat, adjusting to their second surprise of the day. Brigadier General David M. Gregg's Union division of about 2,800 men had orders to cross the Rappahannock at Kelly's Ford and proceed on roads leading directly into Brandy Station, but discovered his way blocked by Brigadier General Beverly Robertson's brigade. However, Gregg determined that another road network leading to the battlefield by a more circuitous route was completely unguarded. Following these roads, his lead brigade under Colonel Percy Wyndham arrived in Brandy Station about 11 a.m. Between Gregg and the battle taking place between Buford and Stuart was a prominent ridge called Fleetwood Hill. The eminence had been Stuart's headquarters, but the general was at the front and the only force on Fleetwood when Gregg arrived was a 6-pounder howitzer, which had been sent to the rear for want of reliable ammunition. Major Henry B. McClellan of Stuart's staff pressed this gun into service and sent a desperate plea to his chief for reinforcements. Wyndham meanwhile formed his men into line and charged up the western slope of Fleetwood. As he neared the crest, the lead elements of Jones' brigade, which had just withdrawn from St. James Church, rode over the crown.

Gregg's next brigade, led by Colonel Judson Kilpatrick, swung around east of Brandy Station and attacked up the southern end and the eastern slope of Fleetwood Hill, only to discover that their appearance coincided with the arrival of Hampton's Confederates. A series of confusing charges and countercharges swept back and forth across the hill. The Confederates cleared the hill for the final time, capturing three guns and inflicting 30 casualties among the 36 men of the 6th New York Light Artillery, which had attempted to give close-range support to the Federal cavalry.

Colonel Alfred Duffie, with a small 1,2000-man division, was delayed by two Confederate regiments in the vicinity of Stevensburg and arrived on the field too late to participate in the action.

While Jones and Hampton withdrew from their initial positions to fight at Fleetwood Hill, "Rooney" Lee continued to confront Buford, falling back to the northern end of the hill. Reinforced by Colonel Thomas Munford, commanding the brigade of the ailing Fitzhugh Lee, "Rooney" Lee launched a counterattack against Buford at the same time as Pleasonton had called for a general withdrawal, and the battle was over.

Despite being surprised by his adversary twice in the same day, Stuart was able to retain the field. Union losses numbered 866; Confederate casualties were reported at 575. But the overwhelming superiority that the Confederate cavalry once enjoyed was gone.

DIRECTIONS TO THE BATTLEFIELD

Follow the directions and map carefully for a tour of the Brandy Station battlefield. please respect the rights of private landowners when visiting the field. To reach the battlefield from Fredericksburg or Chancellorsville, proceed west on Rt. 3 to Stevensburg, about 17 miles west of Chancellorsville. Turn right on Rt. 663 and go 3.8 miles to Brandy Station, where the main road will become Rt. 700. Follow Rt. 700 for only 0.2 mile. Turn left on Rt. 669 and go 0.1 mile. Turn left on Rt. 762. After traveling 0.5 mile, an historical marker (A) will be on the left side of the road. Another 1.5 miles farther, turn right on Rt. 342 and pull in the visitor parking area of the Virginia State Police area office.

Stop 1 - Grand Review Site. The site of two Confederate cavalry reviews, including the June 8th affair held for Robert E. Lee, occurred on the other side of the state police building. The fields trampled over by Southern horsemen were owned by the prominent Unionist John Minor Botts.

Turn left on Rt. 762 and backtrack to Brandy Station. Turn left on Rt. 663 and go 0.2 mile, carefully crossing Rt. 15/29. Turn right on Rt. 685 and go 0.3 mile, pulling off on the shoulder to the left, adjacent the carnival grounds.

Stop 2 - Gregg's Attack The ridge before you is Fleetwood Hill. The prominent building to your left is the Barbour house, called "Beauregard" (B). Gregg's lead brigade under Wyndham attacked over the ground in front of you -- primarily on the ground to the right of the road. Gunners of the 6th New York Light Artillery manning three cannon suffered heavy losses on the slight knoll (C) just across Flat Run.

Continue ahead for 0.6 mile and park on the right side of the road where steps lead up to a United Daughters of the Confederacy historical marker.

Stop 3 - Fleetwood Hill. Stuart's headquarters were on this site the eve of the battle, and it was here that H.B. McClellan ably directed reinforcements to counter Gregg's attack. While facing the marker, Kilpatrick's attack came from your left front, and the 1st Maine Regiment of that brigade charged all the way to the Barbour house 9B), at a time when General Robert E. Lee was observing the battle from the structure.

Continue straight ahead for 0.8 mile and turn left on Rt. 676. Then 06. down the road, Rt.

676 will turn to the left, and Rt. 677 will continue straight ahead. Follow Rt. 677 for 1.2 miles to a slight bend in the road. (Caution: The hard surface road will change to gravel, which can be muddy during wet weather.)

Stop 4 - Mortal Wounding of "Grimes" Davis This road continues across private property to Beverly's Ford. Buford's division, with "Grimes" Davis brigade in the lead, crossed the ford early on June 9th and advanced to this bend in the road, where it was assailed by "Grumble" Jones' Confederates. In the brief melee Davis was shot from the saddle. Startled and momentarily leaderless, Davis' men took cover, giving Stuart time to prepare a defensive line near St. James Church.

Turn around and drive 1.2 miles to the junction of Rt. 676. Turn right and go 0.2 mile, stopping at the far edge of the woods on your left.

Stop 5 - St. James Church. The church stood in the woods to your left-rear, and several pieces of Major Robert F. Beckham's horse artillery were posted here. The charge of the 6th Pennsylvania Cavalry was made across the field to your right. "Rooney" Lee's Yew Ridge position (D) is visible in the distance to your left-front.

Select a place to turn around and return to the intersection of Rts. 676 and 677. Ahead of you, as you face the intersection, is Gee House Hill (E), another key Confederate artillery position during the battle

This concludes your tour. The battlefields of Cedar Mountain, Bristoe Station, Kelly's Ford, Mine Run and Rappahannock Station are also in this area. Written guides are available for those as well at the visitor centers at Fredericksburg and Chancellorsville.

To return to Rt. 15/29, turn right and continue on Rt. 676, proceed to the end of the road, and turn left on Rt. 685. When you reach Rt. 15/29, turn right to reach Culpeper and left to go toward Warrenton.

For more information on the battle and preservation of the battlefield, see Brandy Station Foundation's website.

Map of Brandy Station Battlefield

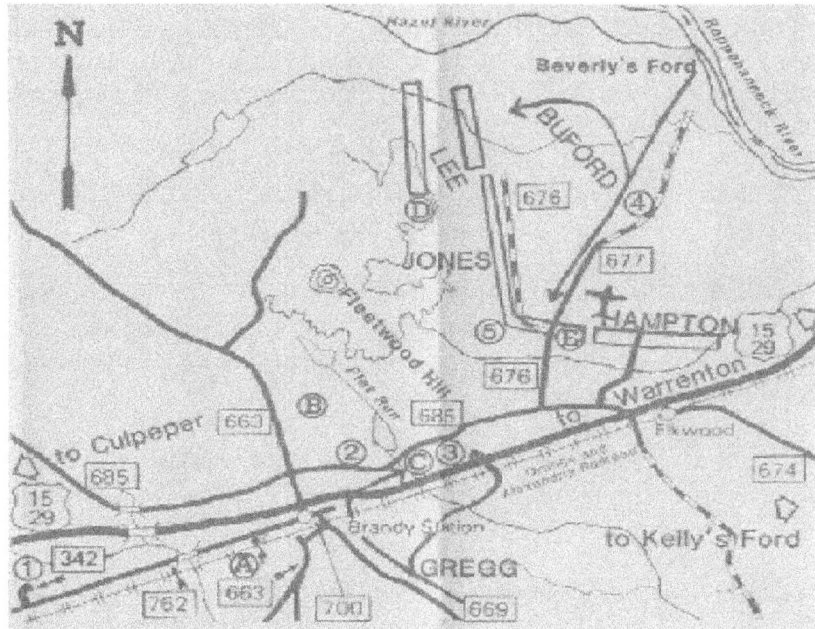

Fleetwood Hill on the Brandy Station Battlefield

Regimental History: 6th Infantry South Carolina

DRANESVILLE, VA. DEC. 20TH, 1861   Dranesville, Va., Dec. 20, 1861.

Ord's Brigade, Battery A, 1st Pennsylvania Artillery, and 1st Pennsylvania Cavalry.   While an expedition under Brig.-Gen. E. O. C. Ord was moving in the vicinity of Dranesville in search of forage, it was attacked by four regiments of Confederate infantry and a battery. The attack occurred on the Leesburg pike, just outside of the town of Dranesville, where the Federal column had halted to rest. Using the village as his right Ord deployed his forces and placed his battery so as to sweep the road. About 3:30 p.m., after the battle had been in progress some hours, Ord ordered an advance and at the point of the bayonet the Confederates were driven from their position.   Pursuit was given for some 4 or 5 miles and a battery captured. The Federal loss in the engagement was 7 killed and 61 wounded.

The Confederate casualties were heavier, 43 killed, 143 wounded and 8 missing. The greater part of the   enemy's doss came in the first charge on the Federal position.   Reynolds' brigade had been ordered to Ord's aid, but before it   arrived the enemy had fallen back. Brig.-Gen. J. E. B. Stuart   commanded the enemy's forces.

Source: The Union Army, vol. 5

The Battle of Williamsburg
May 5, 1862

In the first pitched battle of the Peninsula Campaign, nearly 41,000 Federals and 32,000 Confederates were engaged. Following up the Confederate retreat from Yorktown, Hooker's division encountered the Confederate rearguard near Williamsburg. Hooker assaulted Fort Magruder, an earthen fortification alongside the Williamsburg Road, but was repulsed. Confederate counterattacks, directed by Maj. Gen. James Longstreet, threatened to overwhelm the Union left flank, until Kearny's division arrived to stabilize the Federal position. Hancock's brigade then moved to threaten the

Confederate left flank, occupying two abandoned redoubts. The Confederates counterattacked unsuccessfully. Hancock's localized success was not exploited. The Confederate army continued its withdrawal during the night.

WILLIAMSBURG, VA   MAY 4TH - 5TH, 1862   Williamsburg, Va., May 4-5, 1862.

3rd and 4th Army Corps and Cavalry, Army of the Potomac. Upon the evacuation of Yorktown by the Confederates, Gen. McClellan, commanding the Army of the Potomac, ordered his cavalry, with four batteries of horse artillery, under the command of Brig.-Gen. George Stoneman, in pursuit, the infantry following as rapidly as   possible. The 3rd corps, commanded by Brig.-Gen. S. P Heintzelman, moved on the direct road from Yorktown to   Williamsburg with Hooker's division in advance closely   followed by Kearny's.

The 4th corps, under command of Brig.- Gen. E. D. Keyes, took the Lee's Mill road farther to the   left, Smith's division having the advance with the divisions   of Couch and Casey in supporting distance. Near the Half-way   house-so called because it was about half way between Yorktown   and Willliamsburg-Stoneman's advance encountered some of the enemy's cavalry and the skirmishing commenced. Knowing that the Confederates were moving on both roads, Stoneman sent Emory's brigade to cut off the enemy on the Lee's Mill road, while he engaged the force in his front, gradually pressing it   back to Fort Magruder, about a mile from Williamsburg. Fort   Magruder was the largest of a line of redoubts which had been constructed sometime before by Gen. Magruder, commanding the   Confederate forces on the lower peninsula. When Stoneman came   in sight this was the only one of the redoubts occupied, but   Gen. J. E. Johnston, who was conducting the retreat, hurried   troops to the rear to man the trenches before Stoneman's supports could come up.

Emory encountered a regiment of   Confederate cavalry on the Lee's Mill Toad, under the command   of Gen. Stuart himself, but without infantry could not corner   the enemy. Some confusion arose in the movements of the   Federal infantry. McClellan had remained at Yorktown to   direct the movements of Franklin's division of McDowell's   corps, which had been ordered to the peninsula, and Sumner was   assigned to the command of the forces in pursuit. Heintzelman   was in the advance before Sumner, and in his report states   that his instructions directed him to "take control, of the   entire movement." When Smith's division reached Skiff creek,   on the left-hand road, the bridge was found to have been   destroyed and Sumner ordered him to take a cross-road to the   one on which the other column was moving. This brought Smith   into the other road near the Half-way house just as Hooker's   troops came up, forcing Hooker to halt for about 3 hours until

Smith's command could get out of the way. Hooker then   followed Smith for some 3 miles, when he crossed over to the   road that the latter had left, and where Emory's cavalry was operating. Smith's division came up with Stoneman about 5:30 p.m. and by Sumner's direction was formed in three lines of battle to charge the enemy's works. About 6:30 the order was given to advance, but the dense undergrowth in the woods soon made it apparent that a charge over such ground was impracticable, and as darkness was coming on the troops were halted under instructions to attack at daylight the next morning. The attack on the 5th was commenced by Hooker's division, which had marched until 11 o'clock the night before, and at 5 :30 a.m. was within sight of the enemy's works before Williamsburg.

Two hours later Gen. Grover was ordered to begin the attack by sending the 1st Mass. to the left and the 2nd N. H. to the right of the road as skirmishers, under instructions to advance to the edge of the timber, where they were to turn their attention to the occupants of the rifle- pits in their front, as well as to the sharp-shooters and gunners in Fort Magruder. The 11th Mass. and 26th Pa. were then sent to the right of the 2nd N. H. and ordered to advance as skirmishers until they reached the Yorktown road. Webber's battery was next pushed forward into an open field on the right of the road, but before the guns could be brought into action it was subjected to such a heavy fire from Fort Magruder and a battery on the left that the cannoneers were forced to retire. Volunteers were called for to man the battery and the men of Osborn's battery dashed to the deserted guns, placed them in position and opened fire on the fort and the battery mentioned. Bramhall's battery was then brought up on the right of Webber's, and by 9 o'clock the guns of the forts were silenced the Confederates in the rifle- pits having in the meantime been driven back by the well-directed fire of Hooker's sharpshooters. Leaving the 5th N. J. to support the batteries, Gen. Patterson moved with the rest of his brigade to the left of the road in anticipation of an attack from that direction, and the heavy firing there soon demonstrated that the anticipation was being realized. Patterson found himself confronted by Pryor's and Pickett's brigades, outnumbering his own command five to one, and twice sent back for reinforcements, but receiving none gave the order to retire. The 73rd and 74th N. Y., the only remaining regiments of Hooker's reserve, were ordered to the left, and with their assistance Patterson rallied his men and repulsed the enemy three times after he had advanced to within 80 yards of the road, which was the center of operations. Hooker now ordered all his available troops to the left, and they arrived just in time to meet a fourth assault by Longstreet's whole division, which had just reached the field. At the same time the guns from Fort Magruder opened again and another body of Confederate troops advanced against Webber's and Bramhall's batteries, capturing 4 guns. Just then Berry's brigade of Kearny's division arrived on the field and repulsed the attack on the batteries, saving the remainder of the guns, the 5th Mich. charging with the bayonet and driving the enemy back to the rifle-pits with a loss of 143 killed and a large number wounded. Kearney's other two brigades-Birney's and Jameson's- now came up and relieved Hooker's men, who retired to the rear, where they replenished their ammunition and remained in reserve. The Confederates, seeing that the Union line had been strengthened by the arrival of these fresh troops gave up the attempt to turn Hooker's left and retired to their intrenchments.

Smith's attack, which was to begin at daylight, did not commence until about noon. Late on the evening of the 4th Sumner learned from a countryman that the redoubts on the Confederate left were unoccupied. A reconnaissance the next morning verified the information, and Hancock was ordered to move with his own brigade, part of Davidson's, and Cowan's M. Y. battery and occupy the redoubts. Hancock crossed Cub Dam creek on a narrow bridge, threw forward the 5th Wis. and 6th Me. as an assaulting party in case the redoubt should be occupied by the enemy. Finding it unoccupied he left three companies to hold it, formed a skirmish line in an open field to the rear, with the main body of his infantry behind in line of battle, the artillery in the center, and moved against another redoubt farther down the stream. This was also found to be unoccupied and was taken possession of by Hancock, who now sent back to Smith for reinforcements to enable him to hold the advantage he had gained. He then moved forward to drive the enemy from the two nearest works in his front and create a diversion in favor of Hooker, who was then seriously engaged in front of Fort Magruder. Deploying his line on a crest, with the artillery on the right and left of the redoubt, he threw forward a strong skirmish line and drove the enemy from his position, but did not take possession of it as the reinforcements had not arrived. Sumner had twice ordered reinforcements to Hancock, but each time had countermanded the order.

Upon a third request for reinforcements he ordered Hancock to fall back to his first position. Doubtful as to whether this meant the first fort occupied or to retire across the creek, Hancock determined to hold on until he could communicate with Sumner, and again sent back for reinforcements, directing the officer to state the importance of holding the position. In his report Hancock says: "While I was awaiting a reply to this message the crisis of the battle in front of Fort Magruder appeared to have arrived; and in order to furnish all the assistance possible our battery threw percussion shell into that fort." This action drew attention to Hancock. Artillery was turned on him and D. H. Hill advanced with a heavy force of infantry to drive him from his position. Hill soon occupied the redoubts and Hancock's skirmishers became engaged with this force while a cavalry column came out from behind a point of woods on the right. This was held in check by the skirmishers, however, and Hancock gave the order to fall back to the crest and form in line of battle. This was taken for a retreat by the enemy, who now advanced. Hancock's men behind the crest waited until the Confederates were within easy range, when they suddenly appeared over the top of the hill and poured a murderous volley of musketry into the line rushing up the opposite slope. "Now, gentlemen, the bayonet!" cried Hancock, and the whole brigade charged with a vigor that threw the enemy into utter rout and drove him from the field with a loss of about 400 men in killed, wounded and captured. McClellan, in his report, refers to this action of Hancock's as being "one of the most brilliant engagements of the war." It was the relieving feature of the battle of Williamsburg, an engagement fought without a plan, without unity of action on the part of the different commands, and practically. without a commander. The repulse of Hill came about 5:30 p.m. Before he could reform his shattered lines to renew the attack darkness came on and the Confederates in front of Hancock bivouacked in line of battle, expecting to be attacked during the night. Late in the afternoon Peck's brigade of Couch's division came up and took position on the right of Hooker, where he held his position until the action was over. Had he arrived sooner Sumner might have been able to reinforce Hancock, thus enabling him to press the advantage he had gained on the Confederate left, which would no doubt have resulted in a sweeping victory for the Union arms. About the time that Hill was driven back loud and prolonged cheering was heard at Sumner's front, announcing the arrival of McClellan on the field. The enemy, however, regarded it as a signal that heavy reinforcements had come up, and during the night Johnston evacuated his position, continuing his retreat toward Richmond. The Union losses in the battle of Williamsburg were 456 Killed, 1,410 wounded and 373 captured or missing. The Confederate reports show a loss of 288 killed, 975 wounded and 297 missing, but Heintzelman, in his report, says: "In the town the enemy abandoned all their severely wounded without attendance or the least provision for their sustenance. Counting them, the prisoners captured during the battle and the first day of the retreat, we got about 1,000 men; among them one colonel and several other officers. Up to Saturday 800 rebels were buried by our troops."

Source: The Union Army, vol. 6

ANTIETAM, MD. SEPT. 16-17TH, 1862   Antietam, Md., Sept. 16-17, 1862.

Army of the Potomac. In his report of the battle of South Mountain, which was fought on the 14th, Gen. Meade says: "The command rested on their arms during the night. The ammunition train was brought up and the men's cartridge-boxes were filled, and every preparation made to renew the contest at daylight the next morning should the enemy be in force.

Unfortunately, the morning opened with a heavy mist, which prevented any view being obtained, so that it was not until 7 a. m. that it was ascertained that the enemy had retired from the mountain." As soon as this discovery was made the whole Union army began pouring through the passes of South Mountain in pursuit. At Boonsboro Pleasonton's cavalry came up with the Confederate rear guard. The 8th Ill., which was in the advance, immediately charged and then pursued the retreating enemy for a distance of 2 miles. There the Illinois regiment was joined by a section of Tidball's battery, which threw a few shells into the Confederate lines, completely routing the enemy from the field. The Union loss in this skirmish was 1 killed and

15 wounded, while the Confederates left 30 killed and 50 wounded on the field, and a number of prisoners were taken. About the time this engagement commenced another was taking place on the Sharpsburg road, between the Confederate rear and the 5th N. H. infantry. This skirmish lasted until 9 p. m., when the New Hampshire troops were relieved, after losing 4 men in killed and wounded. T

The enemy's loss here was 12 killed and wounded and 60 prisoners. The 2nd Del. and 52nd N. Y. also skirmished with the rear guard at other points, and in the afternoon the Confederates opened a heavy artillery fire on the Federal advance near Antietam creek, keeping it up until after dark. This was replied to by Tidball's horse artillery and Battery B, 1st N. Y. light artillery, from the heights east of the creek.

McClellan's hope was to bring on an engagement before the Confederate forces could be united. Lee, on the other hand, was bending every effort to concentrate his army in time to resist the general attack which he now realized was imminent. Stonewall Jackson, with his own division and those of Ewell and A. P. Hill, was at Harper's Ferry. McLaws, after his defeat at Crampton's pass on the 14th, formed his forces across the lower end of Pleasant Valley, while the Union forces under Gen. Franklin confronted him at the upper end of the valley, about 2 miles distant. Here the two lay all day on the 15th, each supposing the other to be superior in strength and neither daring to attack. The morning of the 16th found Longstreet and D. H. Hill occupying a position on the west side of the Antietam, between that stream and the little town of Sharpsburg.

Here Lee personally directed the movements of his army, selecting the strongest possible ground to withstand an attack until the detachments under Jackson and McLaws could be united with the main body. Soon after crossing the Antietam Lee learned that the Federal garrison at Harper's Ferry had surrendered, and sent orders for the whole force near the ferry to move at once to Sharpsburg. The Army of the Potomac at this time was organized as follows: The 1st army corps, commanded by Maj.-Gen. Joseph Hooker, consisted of the divisions of Doubleday, Ricketts and Meade; the 2nd corps, Maj.Gen. Edwin V. Sumner, included Richardson's, Sedgwick's and French's divisions; Couch's division of the 4th corps, the 5th corps, Maj.-Gen. Fitz John Porter, was composed of the divisions of Morell Sykes and Humphreys; the 6th corps, Maj.-Gen. William B. Franklin, embraced the divisions of Slocum and W. F. Smith , the 9th corps, Maj.-Gen Ambrose E. Burnside consisted of the divisions of Willcox, Sturgis and Rodman, and the Kanawha division, commanded by Brig.-Gen. Jacob D. Cox , the 12th corps, Maj.- Gen. Joseph K. F. Mansfield, included the divisions of Williams and Greene; the cavalry division numbering five brigades and commanded by Brig.-Gen. Alfred Pleasonton, and over 50 batteries of artillery. In his report of the campaign McClellan gives the number of his forces at 87,164. Lee, in his official report on the battle of Antietam, says: "This great battle was fought by less than 40,000 men on our side "

The Confederate line of battle on the 16th extended from the Potomac, at a point a little below Mercersville, to the Antietam about a mile below Sharpsburg. It was nearly four miles long and occupied a broken country, the low hills being separated by narrow valleys, while almost everywhere the limestone cropped out above the surface, affording a natural shelter for the troops. In front the line was protected by the Antietam, which was crossed by three bridges and several fords, though the latter were all too difficult to attempt a crossing with artillery. Near the south end of Lee's line was the bridge afterward known as the "Burnside bridge;" on the Sharpsburg and Boonsboro road, near the center of the line, was the second bridge, while the third was the stone bridge on the Williamsport road still further north. Near the mouth of the stream was a fourth bridge, but it was not used during the operations, except by A. P. Hill in bringing up his division from Harper's Ferry. On the Hagerstown pike, about a mile from Sharpsburg, stood the Dunker church in the edge of a patch of timber, since known as the "West woods." At the church the Smoketown road leaves the pike, and about half a mile north on this road were some more timber patches called the "East woods."

In forming his line Lee posted Longstreet on the right, so as to cover the Burnside bridge, and D. H. Hill on the left, covering the bridge on the Boonsboro road. On the opposite side of the Antietam lay the Union army with the 1st corps on the extreme right and the 9th on the left. McClellan established his headquarters at the Pry house, a short distance northwest of the Boonsboro road and near the center of his line. Lee's headquarters were at the west side of Sharpsburg on the road leading to Shepherdstown.   Shortly after 1 p. m. on the 16th Hooker received orders to cross the Antietam and attack the Confederate left. Meade's and Ricketts, divisions crossed at the stone bridge and Doubleday's at the ford just below. Once across the stream he turned to the right in order to gain the watershed between the Antietam and Potomac, intending to follow the ridge until he gained the enemy's left flank. Some skirmishing occurred along the line of march, and information of Hooker's movements was at once carried to Lee. At the time the messenger arrived Lee was in council with Longstreet and Jackson, who had arrived from Harper's Ferry that morning. Lee immediately ordered Jackson to the command of the left wing and Hood's command was moved from the center to a position near the Dunker church. A little while before sunset Hooker pushed forward a battery and opened fire on Jackson's left. The fire was promptly returned and the artillery duel was continued until after dark, when the corps went into bivouac a short distance north of the East woods, where the men rested on their arms during the night, ready to begin the attack the next morning. All that night there was desultory firing between the pickets, who were so close to each other that at times their footsteps could be heard. During the night Mansfield's corps was sent over to the assistance of Hooker and about 2 a. m. on the 17th took up a position on the Poffenberger farm, about a mile in Hooker's rear. As soon as it was light enough to distinguish objects on the morning of the 17th the Federal skirmishers began their work in the East woods. Soon afterward the entire corps was thrown into line with Doubleday on the right, Ricketts on the left, and Meade in reserve in the center, with instructions to reinforce either of the other divisions as circumstances might require.

Thus formed the whole line moved forward and the real battle of Antietam was begun. In the triangular space between the Hagerstown and Smoketown roads, and directly in front of Hooker, was a 30-acre field of corn in which the enemy had stationed a large force of infantry during the night. Before this force fired a shot its presence was discovered by the sun's rays on the bayonets, and in his report Hooker says: "Instructions were immediately given for the assemblage of all my spare batteries, near at hand, of which I think there were five or six, to spring into battery, on the right of this field, and to open with canister at once. In the time 1 am writing every stalk of corn in the northern and greater part of the field was cut as closely as could have been done with a knife, and the slain lay in rows precisely as they had stood in their ranks a few moments before. It was never my fortune to witness a more bloody, dismal battle-field." The survivors beat a rapid retreat toward the church and there sought shelter behind rocks, trees and stone fences. The Union men pressed forward in close pursuit for some distance, but the Confederates were rallied and reinforced, when the Federals were in turn forced to fall back. At this juncture Mansfield arrived, but while deploying his men he fell mortally wounded and the command of the corps fell on Gen. Williams, who had barely time to receive a few general instructions from Hooker before he was forced to go into the fight. Not knowing the exact position of the 1st corps there was some lack of unity in the movements of the various division commanders, but after nearly two hours of hard fighting the enemy was driven back to the West woods.

Greene's division succeeded in turning Jackson's right and in gaining a position in the edge of the woods near the Dunker church, where he hung on tenaciously, repulsing several attempts to dislodge him. In this part of the engagement the Confederates suffered severely. J. .R Jones, who was in command of Jackson's division, was wounded. Starke, who succeeded him, was soon afterward killed. Lawton then took command of the division and was wounded and borne from the field. Nearly one-half the entire force on the Confederate left were killed or wounded, and it is probable that if Sumner had arrived at this time the entire Confederate army could have been crushed. It was nearly 10 o'clock, however, before Sumner's corps,

241

some 18,000 strong, reached the field, coming on in three columns. Sedgwick on the right occupied the position from which Hooker had been driven earlier in the action. Next came the divisions of French and Richardson, the Union line now being extended well down toward the Boonsboro road. Sedgwick's division went into battle in three lines. The first had hardly become engaged when the Confederates made a desperate rush, broke through the Union line and turned Sedgwick's left. The third line was quickly faced about to repel an attack from the rear, but the Confederate fire on the left was so effective that the entire division was forced to retire. Here Sedgwick was wounded, but he remained in the saddle until his command was rallied and placed in a strong position, where, under the command of Gen. Howard, it remained throughout the rest of the battle. The battle was gradually moving southward and after ten o'clock there was no more serious fighting north of the church. About half a mile south of the church a road leaves the pike and, following a zigzag course, strikes the Boonsboro road about half-way between Sharpsburg and the Antietam. For some distance after leaving the pike this road was lower than the ground on either side, forming a natural breastwork, and was known as the sunken road. It was toward this road that French and Richardson directed their movements. When Lee saw that his left was defeated and his center in danger of being broken, he brought up every available man from his right. In quick succession the divisions of Walker, Anderson and McLaws were hurled against Sumner's veterans. Sumner was reinforced by part of Mansfield's corps and the Confederates were slowly forced back every foot of the ground being stubbornly contested, until their final stand was made at the sunken road. In this part of the engagement the heavy guns of the Union batteries east of the Antietam rendered important service by preventing the enemy from using his artillery. D. H. Hill, who commanded this part of the Confederate line, says: "Our artillery could not cope with the superior weight, caliber, range and number of the Yankee guns. They were smashed up or withdrawn before they could be turned against the massive columns of attack." At last Col. Barlow, commanding the 1st brigade of Richardson's division, made a successful flank movement on the road and captured about 300 men who still clung to it, more as a place of shelter than in the hope of checking the Federal advance. The road was filled with Confederate dead and is referred to in all descriptions of the battle as the "Bloody Lane."

In his report of the battle of Antietam McClellan says: "My plan for the impending general engagement was to attack the enemy's left with the corps of Hooker and Mansfield, supported by Sumner's, and if necessary by Franklin's and as soon as matters looked favorably there to move the corps of Burnside against the enemy's extreme right upon the ridge running to the south and rear of Sharpsburg, and having carried their position, to press along the crest toward our right, and whenever either of these flank movements should be successful, to advance our center with all the forces then disposable." In pursuance of this plan the 9th corps was stationed on the Federal left, with instructions to assault and carry the

Burnside bridge whenever an order to that effect   should be issued from headquarters. McClellan says that this   order was sent to Burnside at 8 a. m. on the 17th, while the   latter says he received it "about ten o'clock." The bridge   was guarded by Toombs, brigade, which occupied a strong   position among the rocks and trees on the bluff commanding the   west end of the bridge, while the bridge, the ford below, and   in fact, the entire valley, were all effectually covered by   the Confederate batteries. The first attempt to carry the   bridge was made by Crook's brigade of the Kanawha division,   with the 11th Conn. deployed as skirmishers to cover the   advance. The plan was to move the brigade across the bridge   in two columns of fours, which were to turn to the right and   left as soon as they reached the opposite bank, Rodman's   division meanwhile to try to cross at a ford about a third of   a mile farther down the creek. This plan failed because Crook   missed his way and reached the stream some distance above the   bridge, where he became engaged with the enemy on the west   bank.

A second effort, made by the 2nd Md. and 6th N. H.   infantry, likewise proved a failure. The two regiments   charged across the bridge with fixed bayonets, but were met by   a withering fire of artillery and musketry and forced to fall   back. Gen. Cox, to whom Burnside had entrusted the work of   carrying the bridge, then directed Gen. Sturgis to select two   regiments from Ferrero,s brigade and push them across the   bridge in accordance with the first plan. Sturgis selected the 51st N. Y. and the 51st Penn. A howitzer from Simmonds,   battery was brought forward and placed where it covered the   west end of the bridge. When everything was in readiness the   strong skirmish line opened fire, the howitzer was operated   rapidly, throwing double charges of canister into the ranks of   Toombs' men, and under this protection the two regiments   advanced at the double-quick with fixed bayonets and dashed   across the bridge, the Confederates hastily retreating before   the impetuous charge. The remainder of Sturgis, division and   Crook's brigade were hurried over to the support of the two   gallant regiments, and these were soon further strengthened by   Rodman's division and Scammon's brigade, which had succeeded   in crossing at the ford. Here another delay ensued. Sturgis'   and Crook's men had almost exhausted their ammunition and a   halt was made necessary until their cartridge-boxes were   replenished. During the pause Willcox's division and several   light batteries were brought over, the remaining batteries   being planted on the hills east of the creek, and at 3 p.m.   the left wing began its advance on Sharpsburg.

The   Confederates under D. R. Jones were soon encountered, drawn up   diagonally across the ridge, screened by stone fences, etc., and well supported by artillery. Welsh's and Christ's brigades, which were in advance, drove them back after some   sharp fighting, until near the edge of the village, where   Jones made his final stand in an old orchard. From this   position he was routed by the batteries with Willcox's   division and the orchard was occupied by the infantry. In the   advance Rodman's division formed the extreme left, and as the   movement was made in the form of a right wheel he became   separated from Willcox, causing a break in the line and   throwing Rodman's brigades en echelon. To the south was a   field of tall corn, through which A. P. Hill's division, just   up from Harper's Ferry, was advancing in line of battle to   strike the left flank. They wore the blue uniforms captured   at the ferry and it was thought they were part of the Union   forces until they opened fire. Scammon quickly faced his   brigade to the left and held Hill in check until the line   could be reformed. In order to do this it was necessary for   Willcox and Crook to retire somewhat from their advanced   position, while Sturgis came up with his command to fill the   break in the line. This gave Jones an opportunity to retire   beyond Sharpsburg and take a position on the high ground where   the national cemetery is now located, but it no doubt saved   Rodman's division from being cut to pieces. This virtually   ended the battle of Antietam, and at the close the two armies   held the same relative positions they occupied at the   commencement of the fight.

The Union loss was 2,108 killed, 9,549 wounded and 753   captured or missing. According to Confederate reports Lee's   army lost 1,512 killed, 7,816 wounded and 1,844 captured or missing, a much greater loss in proportion to the number of   troops engaged than that inflicted on the Federal forces.   Both sides claimed a victory and the engagement might well be designated as a drawn battle. The 18th was spent by both   armies in resting the tired troops and in caring for the dead   and wounded. McClellan's intention was to renew the fight on   the 19th, but when the sun rose that morning it was discovered   that the enemy had evacuated his position during the night,   crossed the Potomac at a ford some distance below the Shepherdstown road, and retired into Virginia. Lee's invasion   of Maryland was ended.

Source: The Union Army, vol. 5

ANTIETAM, MD. ALLAN PINKERTON, PRESIDENT LINCOLN, AND MAJOR GENERAL JOHN A. MCCLERNAND;

Alexander Gardner

1862 October 3.

Photograph from the main eastern theater of the war, Battle of **Antietam**, September-October 1862.

NOTES
Reference: Civil War photographs, 1861-1865 / compiled by Hirst D. Milhollen and Donald H. Mugridge, Washington, D.C.

WILDERNESS, VA   MAY 5TH - 7TH, 1864   Wilderness, Va., May 5-7, 1864.

Army of the Potomac.

On   March 9, 1864, Maj.-Gen. U. S. Grant was raised to the rank of   lieutenant-general and placed in command of all the United States armies in the field. The interval from that time until the 1st of May was spent in planning campaigns, and in   strengthening, organizing and equipping the several armies in   the different military districts. Grant remained with the   Army of the Potomac, which was under the immediate command of   Maj.-Gen. George G. Meade, and which had for its objective the   destruction of the Confederate army under command of Gen.   Robert E. Lee. On May 1, the Army of the Potomac lay along   the north side of the Rapidan river and was organized as   follows: The 2nd corps Maj.Gen. W. S. Hancock commanding, was   composed of four divisions; the 1st commanded by Brig.-Gen. F.   C. Barlow, the 2nd by Brig.-Gen. John Gibbon, the 3rd by Maj.-   Gen. D. B. Birney, and the 4th by Brig-Gen. Gershom Mott. The   5th corps, commanded by Maj.-Gen. G. K Warren, consisted of   four divisions, respectively commanded by Brig Gens. Charles   Griffin, J. C. Robinson, S. W. Crawford and J. S. Wadsworth.   The 6th corps under command of Maj.-Gen. John Sedgwick   included the three divisions commanded by Brig.-Gens. H. G.   Wright, G. W. Getty and James B. Ricketts. The 9th corps,   Maj.-Gen. A. E. Burnside commanding, was composed of four   divisions, each of which was commanded by a brigadier-   general-the 1st by T. G. Stevenson, the 2nd by R B. Potter,   the 3rd by O. B. Willcox and the 4th by Edward Ferrero. The   cavalry corps, under command of Maj.-Gen. P. H. Sheridan,   consisted of three divisions, the 1st commanded by Brig.-Gen.   T. A. Torbert, the 2nd by Brig.-Gen. G. A. Custer and the   3rd by Brig-Gen. J. H. Wilson. With the 2nd corps was the   artillery brigade under Col John C. Tidball; the artillery of the 5th corps was in charge of Col. C. S. Wainwright; that of   the 6th corps under Col. C. H. Tompkins, and the artillery   reserve, composed of Kitching's, J. A. Tompkins' and Burton's brigades, was commanded by Brig.-Gen. Henry J. Hunt. Burnside   had 14 light and 2 heavy batteries. During the campaign the   18th corps, commanded by Maj.-Gen. W. F. Smith, was transferred from the Army of the James to the Army of the   Potomac. This corps was composed of three divisions,   commanded by Brig.-Gens. W. T. H. Brooks, Godfrey Weitzel and   E. W. Hinks, and the cavalry division under Brig-Gen. August   V. Kautz.

Lee's army-the Army of Northern Virginia-consisted of the 1st, 2nd and 3rd corps, respectively commanded by Lieut.-Gens.   James Longstreet, R. S. Ewell and A. P. Hill, and the cavalry   corps of Maj.-Gen. J. E. B. Stuart. Longstreet's corps   included the divisions of Kershaw and Field, and the artillery   brigade under Brig.-Gen. E. P. Alexander. Ewell's corps was   made up of the divisions of Early, Edward Johnson and Rodes,   and the artillery brigade of Brig.-Gen. A. L. Long Hill's   corps was composed of the divisions of R. H. Anderson, Heth   and Wilcox, and his artillery was commanded by Col. R. L.   Walker. Stuart's cavalry embraced three divisions, commanded by Wade Hampton, Fitzhugh Lee and W. H. F. Lee, and the horse artillery under Maj. R. P. Chew. The Union army numbered about 120,000 men of all arms, exclusive of Smith's corps. Lee's army numbered about 61,000 not including the forces under Beauregard on the Petersburg lines and the troops left in the defenses of Richmond, about 30,000 in all. Ewell's corps was intrenched along the south side of the Rapidan, his right resting near Morton's ford a short distance above the mouth of Mine run. The upper half of the intrenched line was held by Hill's corps, the left extending to Barnett's ford, about 5 miles west of the Orange & Alexandria railroad. Longstreet's command was at Gordonsville, the junction of the Orange & Alexandria and the Virginia Central railroads. Lee's headquarters were at Orange Court House, about half way between Longstreet and the line along the Rapidan, from which point he could easily communicate with his corps commanders, and detachments of cavalry watched the various fords and bridges along the river.

Grant's plan was to cross the Rapidan at the fords below the Confederate line of intrenchments move rapidly around Lee's right flank and force him either to give battle or retire to Richmond. As soon as this movement was well under way, Gen. Butler, with the Army of the James, was to advance up the James river from Fortress Monroe and attack Richmond from the south. The region known as the Wilderness, through which the Army of the Potomac was to move, lies between the Rapidan the north and the Mattapony on the south. It is about 12 miles wide from north to south and some 16 miles in extent from east to west. Near the center stood the Wilderness tavern, 8 miles west of Chancellorsville and 6 miles south of Culpeper Mine ford on the Rapidan. A short distance west of the tavern the plank road from ermanna ford crossed the Orange & Fredericksburg turnpike, and then running southeast for about 2 miles intersected the Orange plank road near the Hickman farmhouse. The Brock road left the Orange & Fredericksburg pike about a mile east of the tavern and ran southward to Spottsylvania Court House, via Todd's tavern. The first iron furnaces in the United States were established in the Wilderness, the original growth of timber had been cut off to furnish fuel for the furnaces, and the surface, much broken by ravines, ridges and old ore beds, was covered by a second growth of pines, scrub-oaks, etc., so dense in places that it was impossible to see a man at a distance of 50 yards. Between the Orange plank road and the Fredericksburg pike ran a little stream called Wilderness run, and north of the latter road was Flat run the general direction of both streams being northeast toward the Rapidan into which they emptied. On the Orange plank road, about 4 miles southwest from the Wilderness tavern, was Parker's store. From the Confederate signal station on Clark's mountain, near the right of Ewell's position, the Federal camps could be plainly seen. On May 2nd Lee, accompanied by several of his generals, made a personal observation, saw the commotion in the Union lines, and rightly conjectured that an early movement of some kind was in contemplation. He accordingly directed his officers to hold their commands in readiness to move against the flank of the Federal army whenever the orders were given from the signal station. It was on this same day that Meade, by Grant's instructions, issued his orders for the advance. Knowing that his every movement was observed by the enemy, he determined to cross the Rapidan during the night. At midnight on the 3rd the 5th and 6th corps, preceded by Wilson cavalry division, began crossing at Germanna ford. The 2nd corps, preceded by Gregg's cavalry, crossed at Ely's ford farther down the river. On the evening of the 4th Warren's corps went into bivouac near the Wilderness tavern, Sedgwick was between Warren and the Rapidan; Hancock was near the cross-roads at Chancellorsville and Burnside, with the 9th corps, was moving by a forced march from the Rappahannock river toward Germanna ford in response to a telegram from Grant. Wilson's cavalry covered both the plank road and the turnpike west of Warren's camp, the main body of the division being at Parker's store and a small force at Robertson's tavern on the pike. The orders issued that evening for the movements of the army on the 5th would indicate that both Grant and Meade believed that Lee would fall back toward Richmond upon finding his flank turned by a superior force. In this they were mistaken. Lee had outgeneraled Hooker on the same ground a year before, and he now decided to make an effort at least to drive the Federals back across the Rapidan. Therefore, as soon as he learned on the morning of the 4th that Meade's advance had crossed the river, Ewell was directed to move by the Orange turnpike, Hill by the plank road, and Longstreet was ordered to bring up his corps with all possible despatch. That night Ewell was bivouacked about 5 miles from Warren's camp, Hill was at Verdiersville, about 3 miles in the rear of Ewell, and Longstreet was at Brock's bridge, 10 miles east of Gordonsville. During the night Lee sent word to Ewell to "bring on the battle now as soon as possible," and ordered Hill to move forward at the same time as Ewell. Warren's orders were to move at 5 a.m on the 5th to Parker's store and extend his right toward the Wilderness tavern to connect with the 6th corps. He moved on time, Crawford's division in advance, Wadsworth's in the center and Griffin's in the rear. About 7 o'clock Meade received a despatch from Warren, announcing that the Confederates were in some force on the pike about 2 miles west of the tavern. Meade hurried to the front and directed Warren to attack with his entire corps to develop what part of Lee's army was there. Hancock, who was moving to take a position on Warren's left, was ordered to halt at Todd's tavern and await further orders. Sedgwick was ordered to move by a cross-road that left the Germanna road at Spottswood, attack any Confederate force he might find in his way, and connect with Warren's right on the pike. Grant joined Meade soon after these orders were issued and the two generals established their headquarters on the knoll around the Lacy house, a little west of the Wilderness tavern. At 8 o'clock Crawford was in a strong position on the Chewning farm, where he was directed to halt until Griffin and Wadsworth were ready to move against the enemy on the turnpike, when he was to send one of his brigades to join in the attack. About noon Griffin attacked vigorously striking Jones brigade of Johnson's division and driving it back in some confusion through the supporting line, after which he advanced against Battle's and Doles' brigades of Rodes' division. Wright of the 6th corps, was to have moved forward on Warren's right, but owing to the dense thickets and the uneven surface of the ground, he was unable to connect with Griffin's line in time to carry out the original plan of attack. As Griffin advanced, his right therefore became exposed and Ewell hurled the brigades of Gordon and Daniel against his flank forcing Ayres' brigade back across the pike. Seeing that his line was in danger of being broken, Griffin then gave the order to fall back. In executing this order his line was so closely pressed by the Confederates that he was compelled to abandon 2 pieces of artillery. Wadsworth, in moving forward through the thickets, lost his direction and exposed his left flank to Gordon and Daniel, just after they had forced Griffin to retire. These two brigades now attacked Wadsworth and drove back his left in disorder. The Confederates then poured through the gap thus formed and struck Dennison's brigade of Robinson's division in the flank as it was moving to Wadsworth's support. Pursuant to orders Crawford had sent McCandless' brigade to join Wadsworth's left, but the latter had begun his advance before McCandless could reach the position assigned him. The brigade was moved forward, however, in the direction that McCandless supposed would bring him into the desired place, and came up just in time to be engaged by Gordon's victorious forces after Dennison's defeat. A sharp fight ensued, but McCandless was greatly outnumbered and was finally forced to withdraw with a severe loss in killed and wounded and the capture of several hundred of his men. Ewell then reformed his line on the ground where he was first attacked and intrenched his position. Warren fell back about 300 yards and formed a new line with his right resting on the pike.

Early in the morning Wilson left Col. Hammond, with the 5th N. Y. at Parker's store and pushed on with the rest of his command toward the Craig meeting-house. Soon after Wilson's departure Hammond became engaged with Hill's advance and Crawford threw forward a skirmish line of his infantry to support the cavalry. This line soon encountered Kirkland's brigade of Heth's division and with Hammond's regiment was slowly forced back along the plank road toward the Wilderness tavern. Getty's division was hurried forward to the intersection of the Brock and Orange plank roads, and a despatch was sent to Hancock directing him to move up on the Brock road to Getty's support. Getty reached the cross-roads just in time to secure that important position, and formed his division in two lines of battle at right angles to the plank road, Wheaton's brigade in the center, Grant's on the left and Eustis' on the right. Hill advanced against this line, but received such a galling fire that he speedily retired and for the next two hours everything was quiet, except for the almost constant firing of the skirmishers. When Hancock received the order at 9 a.m. to halt at Todd's tavern his advance was already some 2 miles beyond that point, and this caused some delay when, two hours later, he was ordered to move to the support of Getty. At 2 p.m. Birney's division came up on the Brock road and formed on Getty's left in two lines of battle along that road. The divisions of Mott and Gibbon followed in order, as fast as the narrow road and dense undergrowth would permit, and also formed in two lines on the left of Birney. Barlow's division, on the extreme left, was thrown forward to some high, clear ground, which was the only place along the line where artillery could be used to advantage. Here Hancock massed all his batteries except Dow's and one section of Ricketts', the former of which was placed near Mott's left and the latter on the plank road. As fast as the different commands fell into position breastworks of logs and earth were thrown up. The second line also threw up works in the rear of the first, and later a third line was constructed behind the divisions of Mott and Birney. Before his troops were in position Hancock received orders to attack, and a little after 3 p.m. Getty was directed to attack at once, without waiting for Hancock. During the lull of two hours Hill had been industriously pushing his men into position and forming a junction with Ewell's right. He was anxiously awaiting and expecting the arrival of Longstreet, but that officer had delayed his advance, because he was unwilling to take the road assigned him by Lee, and waited for permission to select his own route. The result was that when darkness fell on the 5th he was still miles away from Hill's right.

Although Getty received orders about 3 o'clock to attack at once, his advance was delayed an hour, as he was engaged in shifting Wheaton's brigade to the right of the plank road to make more room for the 2nd corps. At 4:15 he moved forward down the plank roads, but had not proceeded more than 300 yards when he encountered Heth's division. Ricketts' guns had advanced with the line of infantry and did good service in forcing back the enemy's center, but Hill's line overlapped Getty's flanks and the slight advantage gained in the center was more than offset by the severe losses on both the right and left, where the Federal attacks were repulsed, Grant losing nearly 1,000 men, about one-half of his brigade. Seeing that Getty had met the enemy in force, Hancock ordered Birney's and Mott's divisions to his support, and a little later sent Carroll's brigade of Gibbon's division to the right of the plank road to support Eustis. About 5:30 the enemy charged and forced back the Union line for 50 yards. One of Ricketts' guns had to be abandoned on account of the horses being killed. Some of the Confederates reached this gun and planted their colors on it, but they were driven away before they could withdraw it. About the time that this charge was made Hancock had completed the formation of his line and attacked Hill's right with great vigor, Smyth's "Irish" brigade driving back the enemy's line for some distance. In his report Hancock says: "The battle raged with great severity and obstinacy until 8 p.m. without decided advantage to either party." While this was apparently true at the time an hour more of daylight would have witnessed Hill's defeat. He had extended his lines to the southward to cover the ground that had been assigned to Longstreet. This thin line was now shattered and disjointed, and had it been severely pressed for an hour longer it must inevitably have been broken at some point and the whole corps driven from the field. During the action Gen. Hays' commanding one of Hancock's brigades, was killed; Col. Carroll and Gen. Getty were both severely wounded, but neither left the field until the fighting was over for the day. In the afternoon some heavy skirmishing took place on the Federal right.

About 5 p.m. Ricketts' 2nd brigade, under the command of Brig.-Gen. Truman Seymour, who had relieved Col. B. F. Smith that morning, Neill's brigade of Getty's division, and part of Wrights's 1st brigade, under Col. W. H. Penrose, attacked the Confederate brigades of Hays and Pegram in a strongly intrenched position on the ridge south of net run. Pegram placed some artillery on his left, the fire from which enfiladed Neill's line, forcing him and Penrose to retire from the field with considerable loss. Seymour continued the contest until dark, but was unable to dislodge the enemy from his position. The Federal loss in killed and wounded was heavy on this part of the field, Col. Keifer, commanding Seymour's first line, being severely wounded. On the other side Gen. Pegram was wounded and compelled to leave the field. While these different infantry engagements were going on the cavalry was not idle. At the Craig meeting-house Chapman's brigade of Wilson's division encountered Rosser's brigade of Hampton's cavalry and drove it back about 2 miles. Rosser was then strongly reinforced and Chapman fell back on the 1st brigade at the junction of the Parker's store and Catharpin roads. Soon after this Wilson ordered his whole command to Todd's tavern, where he had been directed by Sheridan to meet Gregg's division. On the way to Todd's he was closely pressed by the Confederate cavalry. Gregg arrived at the tavern about the same time as Wilson, when the two divisions immediately assumed the offensive and drove the enemy beyond Corbin's bridge across the Po river. Immediately after the fighting ceased on the 5th, Hancock, Warren and Sedgwick received orders to attack at 5 o'clock the next morning. Burnside, then in the vicinity of Germanna ford, was instructed to march at 2 a.m., with Stevenson's, Potter's and Willcox's divisions, and be in position to join in the general advance at the hour designated. From prisoners captured during the day it was learned that Longstreet was hourly expected and Hancock was notified to keep a close watch on his left. Barlow's division, with all the artillery of the 2nd corps, was therefore placed in position to protect the left flank and a strong skirmish line was thrown out on the Brock road. The Federal attack was anticipated by the enemy, who began firing on both the left and right a few minutes before 5 o'clock. Soon after the firing commenced, Hancock attacked in two lines, extending across the plank road, Getty's division, with Eustis on the right, Wheaton in the center and Grant on the left, supporting the divisions of Mott and Birney, the latter being in command of Hancock's right wing. The Confederates were pushed back about a mile and a half from the cross-roads when Wadsworth's division came sweeping in from the right, which threw the enemy into confusion and resulted in the capture of several hundred prisoners. The whole line then pressed on after the almost routed enemy for nearly a mile farther; Lee's trains and headquarters were in full view and the battle was nearly won, when a heavy artillery fire was opened on the Union lines from Poague's batteries masked in the shrubbery on the south side of the road, and it was learned that one of Longstreet's divisions had finally connected with Hill's right. In the impetuous advance Hancock's line had become somewhat disordered and he ordered a halt to readjust his lines before engaging the fresh troops. Getty had been wounded during the action and turned over the command of the division to Wheaton. He was now relieved by Webb's brigade of Gibbon's division and formed his command along the original line of battle on the Brock road. At 7 a.m. Gibbon, commanding the left wing, was directed to attack the Confederate right with Barlow's division, but owing to the expected attack by Longstreet the order was but partially carried out. Frank's brigade only was thrown forward to feel the enemy's position and after some sharp fighting it connected with Mott's left. About 8 o'clock Stevenson's division of Burnside's corps reported to Hancock. Burnside, with his 2nd and 3rd divisions, had been expected to move by a cross-toad toward Parker's store, on Birney's right, and attack simultaneously with the rest of the line. About the time of Stevenson's arrival at the Brock road, Hancock received word from Meade that Burnside had then pushed forward nearly to the store and was ready to attack. This information proved to be erroneous and was in a measure contributory to the disaster that overtook Hancock later in the day. Burnside was delayed by a lack of definite information regarding the ground over which he was to move and the dense thickets he encountered, so that it was 2 p.m. before his attack was commenced. A few minutes before 9 o'clock Birney, Mott and Wadsworth, with part of Stevenson's division and three brigades of Gibbon's, resumed the attack along the plank road and were soon furiously engaged with the enemy. Just previous to this, rapid firing was heard in the direction of Todd's tavern, which Hancock supposed to be the threatened flank attack by Longstreet, and this caused him to send Brooke's brigade of Barlow's division out on the Brock road to occupy a line of breastworks there to hold Longstreet in check. Leasure's brigade of the 9th corps and Eustis' of the 6th were held in readiness to support Barlow. As a matter of fact Longstreet was at that moment in Hancock's front, the firing at Todd's being an engagement between Sheridan and the Confederate cavalry. In his report Hancock says: "The arrangements made on my extreme left to receive Longstreet prevented me from pushing my success at the time when Gen. Birney was driving Hill on the plank road." South of the plank road and nearly parallel to it was the unfinished Gordonsville & Fredericksburg railroad. About 10 o'clock Longstreet sent Gen. Mahone with four brigades to move along the line of this railroad and gain Hancock's flank and rear, while the brigades of Law, Gregg and Benning engaged the Federals in front. Mahone first encountered Frank's brigade, which had nearly exhausted its ammunition and was therefore compelled to retire before the vehement flank attack. He then struck the left of Mott's division, which in turn was forced back in some confusion. Heroic efforts were made to rally the men and reform the line along the plank road by throwing back the left, but the troops had been engaged all morning under a heavy fire in the dense forest and their formation was too irregular for such a movement. At Birney's suggestion the whole line was then withdrawn and reestablished in the breastworks along the Brock road. When Longstreet saw that Mahone's attack was successful he ordered a general advance along the plank road, hoping to crush Hancock's line. Mahone's men, upon seeing the head of the Confederate column, mistook it for a fresh body of Union troops and fired a volley, killing Gen. Jenkins and wounding Longstreet. Lee then assumed command of his right wing in person and ordered the attack to be postponed, although the Confederate line was then within a short distance of the Union works. About half an hour before Mahone struck the left of Hancock's line Cutler's brigade of Wadsworth's division was driven back to the open ground near the Lacy house, but Birney sent two brigades and recovered the lost ground, though at considerable loss. During this part of the battle Gen. Wadsworth was mortally and Gen. Baxter severely wounded. From 11 a.m. to 4 p.m. all was comparatively quiet along Hancock's front. About 2 o'clock Robinson's 1st brigade, under Col. Lyle, and two regiments of heavy artillery reported to Hancock and were massed near the cross-roads in reserve. At this time Burnside made an assault on the enemy's line near the Tapp house, north of the plank road, and drove it back in disorder, but part of Heth's division and Wofford's brigade of Kershaw's came up as reinforcements and regained all the lost ground. At 3 p.m. Hancock and Burnside both received orders to attack at 6 o'clock. They were not permitted to wait until that hour, however, for at 4:15 the enemy advanced against Hancock in force, pressing up to the edge of the abatis, less than 100 yards from the first line of works, where they halted and opened a fierce fire of musketry. This was continued for half an hour, during which time the Union line held firm. Then a portion of Mott's division and Ward's brigade of Birney's gave way. Concerning this break, Hancock says in his report: "The confusion and disorganization among a portion of the troops of Mott's and Birney's divisions on this occasion was greatly increased, if not originated, by the front line of breastworks having taken fire a short time before the enemy made his attack, the flames having been communicated to it from the forest in front (the battle-ground of the morning), which had been burning for some hours. The breastworks on this portion of my line were constructed entirely of logs, and at the critical moment of the enemy's advance were a mass of flames which it was impossible at that time to subdue, the fire extending for many hundred paces to the right and left. The intense heat and smoke, which was driven by the wind directly into the faces of the men, prevented them on portions of the line from firing over the parapet, and at some points compelled them to abandon the line."

As soon as Mott's men gave way the Confederates advanced And, some of them reached the breastworks and planted their colors thereon. But their victory was of short duration, for Carroll's brigade moved by the left flank, advancing at the double-quick with fixed bayonets, and drove the enemy back with heavy loss in killed and wounded, some of the dead being afterward found inside the works. Dow's battery, one section of which was near the plank road and the others in the second line near Mott's left, did good service in firing on the enemy, both during his advance and retreat. After the repulse of the Confederates by Carroll, Lee withdrew his troops from the contest, and there was no more fighting along the Brock road that day, the order for the attack being countermanded because Hancock's men were almost out of ammunition and it was too late to replenish the supply. When Burnside heard the firing in Hancock's front he advanced against the enemy before him, but his attacks were isolated and unsupported and the only important result attained was to prevent Heth and Wilcox from moving to Lee's support When the attack began in the morning Wright's division vigorously assaulted Early's intrenchments in his front, but was repulsed with heavy loss. A second attack met with no better success, and as the withdrawal of Burnside's corps had left Sedgwick's right exposed he was ordered to intrench his position and act on the defensive. Warren's attacks on Ewell were also unsuccessful, as the enemy's lines here had been strengthened during the night and several pieces of artillery added. During the day Sedgwick was reinforced by Shaler's brigade, which had been guarding the trains, and Johnston's brigade was sent to Early. Both sides were thus reinforced and some sharp fighting occurred during the afternoon, the attacks of Warren and Sedgwick serving to keep Lee from concentrating his entire force against Hancock. Just before sunset Gordon's brigade, supported by Johnston's, made an attack on Sedgwick's right flank, while Pegram engaged the Federals in front. Shaler's brigade was engaged in building breastworks and the sudden descent of the enemy threw it into confusion, rolling it back on Seymour's brigade, which also fell into some disorder. Seymour and Shaler, with several hundred of their men, were captured. Johnston passed to the left of Gordon and gained Wright's rear, where he captured a few prisoners. Wright promptly restored order among the troops and repulsed the attack of Johnston. Gordon's men were thrown into confusion and Early ordered both brigades to withdraw. In his Memoir Early says of this flank attack: "It was fortunate, however, that darkness came to close this affair, as the enemy, if he had been able to discover the disorder on our side, might have brought up fresh troops and availed himself of our condition." This flank attack of Early's was the last important event in the day's contest, and, in fact, closed the battle of the Wilderness, for when Federal pickets and skirmishing parties were sent out the next morning no trace of the enemy could be discovered on the field of the day before. The Army of Northern Virginia had retired to its line of intrenchments and the redoubtable Lee had evidently abandoned his offensive campaign. The Union loss in the battle of the Wilderness was 2,246 killed 12,037 wounded and 3,383 captured or missing. No doubt many of the wounded were burned to death or suffocated in the fire that raged through the woods on Hancock's front.

General Lee In The Wilderness Campaign
By
Charles S. Vernable, Lieutenant-Colonel, C. S. A., Of General Lee's Staff

DURING the winter of 1863-64 General Lee's headquarters were near Orange Court House. They were marked by the same bare simplicity and absence of military form and display which always characterized them.

Three or four tents of ordinary size, situated on the steep hillside, made the winter home of himself and his personal staff. It was without sentinels or guards. He used during the winter every exertion for filling up the thin ranks of his army and for obtaining the necessary supplies for his men.

There were times in which the situation seemed to be critical in regard to the commissariat. The supplies of meat were brought mainly from the states south of Virginia, and on some days the Army of Northern Virginia had not more than twenty-four hours' rations ahead. On one occasion the general received by mail an anonymous communication from a private soldier containing a very small slice of salt pork, carefully packed between two oak chips, and accompanied by a letter saying that this was the daily ration of meat, and that the writer having found it impossible to live on it had been, though he was a gentleman, reduced by the cravings of hunger to the necessity of stealing. The incident gave the commanding general great pain and anxiety, and led to some strong interviews and correspondence with the Commissary Department. During the winter General Lee neglected no interest of his soldiers. He consulted with their chaplains and attended their meetings, in which plans for the promotion of special religious services among the men were discussed and adopted.

While he was accessible at all times, and rarely had even one orderly before his tent, General Lee had certain wishes which his aides-d they must conform to. They did not allow any friend of soldiers condemned by court-martial (when once the decree of the court had been confirmed by him) to reach his tent for personal appeal, asking reprieve or remission of sentence.

He said that with the great responsibilities resting on him he could not bear the pain and distress of such applications, and to grant them when the judge advocate-general had attested the fairness and justice of the court's decision would be a serious injury to the proper discipline of the army.

Written complaints of officers as to injustice done them in regard to promotion he would sometimes turn over to an aide-de-camp, with the old-fashioned phrase, "'Suage him, Colonel, 'suage him " meaning thereby that a kind letter should be written in reply. But he disliked exceedingly that such disappointed men should be allowed to reach his tent and make complaints in person. On one occasion during the winter an officer came with a grievance and would not be satisfied without an interview with the commanding general. He went to the general's tent and remained some time. Immediately upon his departure General Lee came to the adjutant's tent with flushed face and said , warmly, " Why did you permit that man to come to my tent and make me show my temper ? "The views which prevail with many as to the gentle temper of the great soldier, derived from observing him in domestic and social life, in fondling of children, or in kind expostulation with erring youths, are not altogether correct. No man could see the flush come over that grand forehead and the temple veins swell on occasions of great trial ' of patience and doubt that Lee had the high, strong temper of a Washington, and habitually under the same strong control. Cruelty he hated. In that same early spring of 1864 I saw him stop when in full gallop to the front (on report of a demonstration of the enemy against his lines) to denounce scathingly and threaten with condign punishment a soldier who was brutally beating an artillery horse.

The quiet camp-life at Orange had been broken in upon for a brief season in November by Meade's Mine-Run campaign. In this General Lee, finding that Meade failed to attack the Confederate lines, made arrangements on the night of December 1st to bring on a general battle on the next morning by throwing two divisions against the Federal left, held by Warren's corps, which had been found by a close cavalry reconnaissance to present a fair occasion for successful attack. He had hoped to deal a severe blow to Mea very keenly his failure to carry out his designs. When he discovered that Meade had withdrawn, he exclaimed in the presence of his generals, "I am too old to command this army ; we should never have permitted these people to get away." Some who were standing by felt that in his heart he was sighing for that great " right arm " which he threw around Hooker at Chancellorsville. Both armies returned quietly to winter quarters and rested until May 4th, when Lee marched out in the early morning to meet the Federal army which had moved under its new commander, at midnight on the 3d, to turn his right flank. He took with him Ewell's corps (less two brigades which had been detached for duty elsewhere during the winter) and two divisions of Hill's corps -with artillery and cavalry-leaving Long street with two divisions at Gordonsville (Pickett's being absent below Richmond), Long street's third division and Anderson's division of Hill's corps, on the Rapidan heights, to follow him on the next day.

On the morning of the 5th General Lee, though generally reticent at table on military affairs, spoke very cheerfully of the situation, having learned that Grant was crossing at Germanna Ford and moving into the Wilderness. He expressed his pleasure that the Federal general had not profited by General Hooker's Wilderness experience, and that he seemed inclined to throw away to some extent the immense advantage which his great superiority in numbers in every arm of the service gave him. On the 5th Ewell marched on the old turnpike, and Hill on the Plank road, and the cavalry on a road still farther to the right into the Wilderness. Lee rode with Hill at the head of his column. He was at the front in the skirmish at Parker's Store and moved with the advance to the field on the edge of the forest which became the scene of the great conflict on the Plank road.

Riding on in advance of the troops, the party, consisting of Generals Lee, Hill, and Stuart and their stamounted and sat under the shade of the tree,, when a party of the enemy's skirmishers deployed from a grove of old-field pines on the left, thus revealing the close proximity of Grant's forces, and the ease of concealing movements in the Wilderness.

Hill's troops were soon up and in line, and then began on the Plank road a fierce struggle, nearly simultaneously with that of Ewell's forces on the old turnpike. Thus was inaugurated a contest of many battles, in which the almost daily deadly firing did not cease for eleven long months.

Heth's and Wilcox's divisions, under Lee's eye, maintained themselves well against the heavy assault of the Federal forces which greatly outnumbered them; Ewell's corps did good work on the old turnpike in its contest with Warren's corps, and Rosser's cavalry on the right had driven Wilson back. Lee slept on the field not far from his line of battle, sending orders to Long street to make a night march and reach the front by daybreak on the 6th.

On that morning serious disaster seemed imminent. Longstreet did not arrive in time to reenforce Lee's line of battle in the position it held at the close of the engagement of the preceding evening. Hancock's well-planned attack on our right forced the two Confederate divisions from their position, and it seemed at one moment that they would sweep the field. Lee gave orders to get his wagon trains ready for a movement in retreat, and sent an aide to quicken the march of Longstreet's two divisions. These came soon, a little after sunrise, at double-quick, in parallel columns, down the Plank road. Lee was in the midst of Hill's sullenly retreating troops, aiding in rallying them, and restoring confidence and order, when Longstreet's men came gallantly in and reformed the line of battle under his eye. Lee's presence at the front aroused his men to great enthusiasm. He was a superb figure as he sat on his spirited gray with the light of battle on his face. His presence was an inspiration. The retreating columns turned their face front once more, and the fresh divisions went forward under his eye with splendid spirit. It was on this occasion that the men of the Texas brigade (always favorites of the general), discovering that he was riding with them into the charge, shouted to him that they would not go on unless he went back. The battle line was restored early in the morning. Soon afterward, Anderson's division, which had been left on the Rapidan heights, arrived on the ground; and a successful assault, which carried everything before it, was made on Grant's left. The Federal troops were driven back, with heavy loss, to their intrenchments on the Brock road. Long street's wounding, and the necessary delay in the change of commanders, (1) caused loss of time in attacking them in this position. An attack made in the afternoon failed, after some partial successes, to gain possession of the Federal breastworks. The rumor which General Grant mentions in his " Memoirs " and , to which he seems to have given credence, that "Lee's men were in confusion after this attack and that his efforts failed to restore order," was without foundation in fact. On the same afternoon, of the 6th, a successful flank assault was made by Gordon, with three brigades of Ewell's corps, the results of which were not so great as hoped for, because night put a stop to his further successful rolling up of Sedgwick's line.

The Wilderness fighting closed with the night of the 6th of May.

Lee's grand tactics in these two days of battle had been a superb exhibition of military genius and skill in executing his plan of throwing his little army boldly against his opponent, where his great inferiority in numbers would place him at the least disadvantage ; where maneuvering of large bodies was most difficult, and where superiority in cavalry and artillery counted almost for nothing.

(1)R. H. Anderson was taken from Hill's corps to command Long street's, and Mahone assumed command of Anderson's division.-editors..

The failure to push rapidly the successful movement in which Longstreet was wounded was a serious disappointment to General Lee. I believe his daring spirit conceived the signal defeat of Grant's army, and the driving it back across the Rapidan, as a possibility within his immediate grasp. One thing remarkable in the position of the Confederate lines in these engagements is worthy of note, namely, the large gap between Ewell's right and Longstreet and Hill's left. I had occasion, on being sent with orders to General Ewell on the 6th, to ride across this lonesome interval of half a mile or more, and to meet or see no one, except two Federal soldiers, who had found it easier to desert to the front than to the rear.

The quiet on the 7th told Lee that Grant would move on around his left. When Grant did move, the Confederate general, with that firm reliance upon the steadfast courage of his men in fighting against odds which had never failed him, and in the consequent ability of a small body of his troops to hold superior forces in check until he could come to their support, sent Anderson with Long street's two divisions to support Stuart's cavalry in holding Spotsylvania Court House until he could come up with the rest of his army. This mutual confidence between the general and his men was a striking feature of the campaign, and, indeed, a prime necessity for any possibility of success. General Grant sent troops to occupy Spotsylvania Court House, but retained Hancock's corps to guard against the contingency of another attack from Lee in the Wilderness. Lee had evidently won the respect of his foes when, with his smaller force, reduced by two days' hard fighting, he could employ one part of his infantry to aid in checking the movement of the Army of the Potomac on Spotsylvania, Court House, and at the same time threaten its rear in the Wilderness.

Meanwhile General Grant was sending to Washington for reenforcement.

Lee sent an aide-de-camp with Anderson under orders to keep him constantly advised with the main body of his army, took up his position on the Spotsylvania lines in the afternoon of the 8th. And Grant again found himself in a position which required hard fighting and in which he could not use to great advantage his superiority in numbers and equipment.

The Spotsylvania campaign of twelve days was marked by almost daily combats. It was General Lee's habit in those days of physical and mental trial to retire about 10 or 11 at night, to rise at 3 A. M., breakfast by candle-light, and return to the front, spending the entire day on the lines. The 9th of May was spent by both armies mainly in strengthening their positions by throwing up intrenchments. The day was marked, however, by the death of General Sedgwick, who was killed by a Confederate sharp-shooter. He was much liked and respected by his old West Point comrades in the Confederate army, and his death was a real sorrow to them. Early on the morning of the 10th Hancock's corps made an effort to pass around Lee's left wing and gain a position on his flank and rear. This was repulsed by Early, commanding Hill's corps (Hill being ill). Almost simultaneously came fierce assaults on Lee's left wing, which were repulsed with terrible slaughter.

These were renewed again in the afternoon with the same result. The heaviest assault was made at 5 o'clock by Hancock and Warren, and again repulsed; again reorganized and hurled at Lee's lines only to meet with a still more bloody reception. In one of these attacks a small portion of the Confederate line was taken, but held for a short time only by the assailants. It was pitiful to see and hear the bravest of these brave men who had got up nearest to the Confederate lines as they lay the next day groaning with the pangs of thirst and pains of death, when to relieve them was impossible, on account of the active sharp-shooting of the Federal riflemen. One fair-haired New York youth lay thus twenty-four hours near the Confederate intrenchments before he was relieved from his sufferings by det to bring him in having been rendered unavailing by the sharp fire which his would-be rescuers met at the hands of his comrades, ignorant of their kind intentions.

About the same hour at which these last assaults were made, there was a heavy attack by the Sixth Corps on Ewell's front, near Lee's headquarters for the day, about 200 yards in rear of Doles's brigade, which captured and held a portion of the lines for a short time. This attack was repulsed and the line recaptured by Gordon, the men and officers, as in the Wilderness, again beseeching Lee to go to the rear, and shouting their promises to retake the line if he would only go back.

The 11th of May was a comparatively quiet day, as there were no regular assaults on the Confederate lines. But on that day the gallant J. E. B. Stuart met his death in an engagement with Sheridan, whom he had followed up from Spotsylvania and boldly attacked with greatly inferior numbers near Richmond. Stuart's loss was greatly mourned by General Lee, (1) who prized him highly both as a skillful soldier of splendid courage and energy, and a hearty, joyous, loving friend.

On the 12th, before dawn, came Hancock's famous assault on a weak salient in Ewell's front-the sole appreciable success in attack of all the hard fighting by the Federal troops since they crossed the Rapidan. The threatening attitude of Hancock's attacking column, as indicated by the noise of the preparations going on in front of the salient during the night, had not been communicated to General Lee. The announcement of the disaster was the first news which came to him of this movement of the enemy.

He galloped forward in the darkness of the morning and learned the extent of it from those engaged in rallying the remnants of Edward Johnson's division and in making arrangements to check Hancock.

The occasion aroused all the combative energies of his soldier nature, and he rode forward with his columns toward the captured angle. His general with him, and his men cried him back shouting their promises to retake the lines. The advance of Hancock's troops, after his successful assault, was checked by the brigades of Hill's corps, under Early, which held the lines on the right of the salient, and by Ewell's troops on the left of it.

A line of battle was formed making the base of the triangle of the salient, and the work on the retrenchment (which had been begun the day before as a new line to remedy this weak point in the lines) was pushed rapidly forward. During the day General Lee sent three brigades and a number of batteries of artillery to reenforce Rodez's division , on which fell the main task of holding the enemy in check and recovering, if practicable, the salient and the eighteen pieces of Confederate artillery which lay silent between the opposing lines (having arrived too late in the morning for effective use against Hancock's assault). In that narrow space of the salient captured before dawn raged the fiercest battle of the war. Lee's position during the day was near Early's lines, where he observed from time to time, the movements of the Federal troops in aid of Hancock's attack, and counter-movements of Early's troops. He was with the artillery when it broke Burnside's assault. Lee was present dictating notes and orders in the midst of his guns.

At one time he rode at the head of Harris's Mississippi brigade, which by his orders I was guiding down in column to the assistance of Rodez. The men marched steadily on until they noticed that Lee at their head was riding across a space swept by the artillery fire of the enemy. Then were renewed the same protesting shouts of "Go back, General Lee," and the same promises to do their duty. The firing in the battle of the salient did not cease until far into the night. Hancock had been compelled to retire behind the lines which he had captured, holding them as breastworks for the protection of his troops. The Confederate front at the close covered four of the eighteen pieces of artillery entrenchment in rear of our battle-line (which rendered the salient a useless capture) had been completed. The wearied and worn Confederate battalions were withdrawn to this line late at night, but the four recovered guns, after being dragged off, were left hopelessly stuck in a swamp outside of the new lines, and became Hancock's trophies after all. General Grant did not leave Hancock unaided in this fight, having sent the Sixth and Fifth corps to his support.

He expected much from Burnside also, but Early's counter-movements in part prevented the realization of these hopes. I have gone into some detail in this brief sketch of the battle of the salient, because, as perhaps the fiercest struggle of the war, it is illustrative of the valor of the troops on both sides.

On the 18th an attack was made on Early's left and easily repulsed, though some of the assailants reached the breastworks. On the 19th Ewell was sent to the north side of the NY to threaten Grant's communications. He met some Federal reenforcements, and, being without artillery (finding the ground impracticable for it), he regained his position on the south side of that stream with some loss. Hampton's cavalry brigade and battery of horse artillery proved of great assistance in his withdrawal from his hazardous position.

The battles of Spotsylvania Court House closed with the 19th of May. It gives a clearer idea of the nature of this tremendous contest to group by days and count its various combats from the beginning of the campaign : On May 5th three on May 6th, four ; on May 8th, two ; on May 10th, five ; on May 12th, repeated assaults during twenty hours in salient and two combats on another part of the line ; May 18th, one ; May 19th, one. It is no wonder that on these fields the Confederate ordnance officers gathered more than 120,000 pounds of lead, which was recast in bullets and did work again before the campaign of 1864 was closed.

(1) The news of Stuart's fall reached General Lee on the 12th.- C. S. V.

Lee, discovering that Grant had set out on the 20th of May on his flanking movement southward, immediately marched so as to throw his army between the Federal forces and Richmond.

He crossed the North Anna on the 21st. General Grant arrived on the 23rd. Lee would gladly have compelled battle in his position there. He was anxious now to strike a telling blow, as he was convinced that General Grant's men were dispirited by the bloody repulses of their repeated attacks on our lines. Lee had drawn Pickett and Breckinridge to him. But in the midst of the operations on the North Anna he succumbed to sickness, against which he had struggled for some days. As he lay in his tent he would say, in his impatience, `~ We must strike them!" "Wethem pass us again !" " We must strike them ! " He had reports brought to him constantly from the field. But Lee ill in his tent was not Lee at the front. He was much disappointed in not securing larger results from the attack which prevented the junction of Hancock's and Warren's columns after they had crossed the North Anna.

On May 26th Grant withdrew his army from its rather critical position on the south side of the North Anna, and moved again to the east, down the Pamunkey, which he crossed on the 28th, to find Lee confronting him on the Totopotomoy. Grant had received reenforcements from Washington, and had drawn Smith's corps from Butler in Bermuda Hundred. This corps reached him at Cold Harbor on June 1st. On the 30th the Confederate forces were in line of battle, with the left at Atlee's Station confronting the Federal army. General Lee was still sick, and occupied a house at night for the first time during the campaign. As one of his trusted lieutenants has well said : "In fact nothing but his own determined will kept him in the field; and it was then rendered more evident than ever that he was the head and front, the very life and soul of his army." Grant declined general battle and drew eastward; and after several lesser combats, with no serious results, the two armies confronted one another on the 3d of June at Cold Harbor. In these days Lee had drawn to himself Hoke's division from Beauregard, and had been reenforced by Finegan's Florida brigade and Keitt's South Carolina regiment.

The days from May 30th to June 2d were anxious ones for General Lee. For while General Grant had easy and safe communication with Petersburg and Bermuda Hundred, and commanded all the Federal troops north and south of Richmond, he commanded only the Army of Northern Virginia and was compelled to communicate his " suggestions" to General Beauregard through General Bragg and the War Department at Richmond.

This marred greatly the unity, secrecy, and celerity of action so absolutely essential to success. That he considered this separation of commands, and the consequent circuitous mode of communication with its uncertain results, a very grave matter is plain from the telegrams which he sent at this time. General Beauregard had telegraphed from Chester (half-way between Richmond and Petersburg), on May 30th, 5 : 15 P. M., as follows : " War Department must determine when and what troops to order from here. I send to General Bragg all information I obtain relative to movement of enemy's troops in front." This called forth the following telegrams: (1)

ATLEE'S, 71/2 P. M., 30th May, 1864.

" GENERAL G. T. Beauregard, Hancock's House : "

If you cannot determine what troops you can spare, the Department cannot. The result of your delay will be disaster. Butler's troops will be with Grant tomorrow.

R. E. LEE."

ATLEE's, 7 P. M., 30th May, 1864.

HIS EXCELLENCY JEFFERSON DAVIS, RICHMOND :

General Beauregard says the Department must determine What troops to send from him. He gives it all necessary information. The result of this delay will be disaster. Butler's troops (Smith's Corps) will be with Grant to-morrow. Hoke's division at least should be with me by light to-morrow.

R. E. LEE.

INDORSEMENT.

OPERATOR : Read last sentence by light to-morrow.C. S. V., A. A. G.

(1) The first dispatch is from the original in possession of General T.F.. Rodenbough. The dispatch to Jefferson Davis is from the original in possession of the Massachusetts Commandery of the Loyal Legion.-editors.

The battle of the 3d of June was a general assault by Grant along a front nearly six miles in length, and a complete and bloody repulse at all points, except at one weak salient on Breckinridge's line, which the brave assailants occupied for a short time only to be beaten back in a bloody hand-to-hand conflict on the works. The Federal losses were naturally, under the circumstances, very large, and those of the Confederates very smallg lay in front of the Confederate lines in triangles, of which the apexes were the bravest men who came nearest to the breastworks under the withering, deadly fire. The battle lasted little more than one brief hour, beginning between 5 and 6 A. M. The Federal troops spent the remainder of the day in strengthening their own lines in which they rested quietly. Lee's troops were in high spirits.

General Early, on the 6th and 7th of June, made two efforts to attack Grant's forces on his right flank and rear, but found him thoroughly protected with intrenchments. On the 12th General Hampton met Sheridan at Trevilian and turned him back from his march to the James River and Lynchburg.

General Grant lay in his lines until the night of June 12th.

On that night he moved rapidly across the peninsula. The overland campaign north of the James was at an end.

Except in the temporary driving back of Lee's right on the morning of May 6th before the arrival of Longstreet's divisions, the brief occupation of Rodez's front on May 10th, Hancock's morning assault on May 12th, and a few minor events, the campaign had been one series of severe and bloody repulses of Federal attacks. The campaign on the Confederate side was an illustration of Lee's genius, skill, and boldness. and as well of the steadiness, courage, and constancy of his greatly outnumbered forces, and of their sublime faith in their great commander.

After the battle of Cold Harbor, Lee felt strong enough to send Breckinridge toward the valley to meet Hunter's expedition, and on the 13th to detach Early with the Second Corps, now numbering some eight thousand muskets and twenty-four pieces of artillery, to join Breckinridge; he also restored Hoke's division to Beauregard.

When Grant set out for the James, Lee threw a corps of observation between him and Richmond.

Grant moved his troops rapidly in order to capture Petersburg by a coup de main. Smith's corps was in front of the advanced lines of Petersburg on the morning of the 15th. The first brigade of Hoke's division reached Beauregard on the evening of the 15th. On the night of the 15th Lee tented on the south side of the James, near Drewry's Bluff. On the 16th and 17th, his troops coming up, he superintended personally the recapture of Beauregard's Bermuda Hundred line., which he found to be held very feebly by the forces of General Butler, who had taken possession of them on the withdrawal of Bushrod Johnson's division by Beauregard to Petersburg on the 16th. On the 17th a very pretty thing occurred, in these lines, of which I was an eye-witness, and which evinced the high spirit of Lee's men, especially of a division which had been with him throughout the campaign, beginning at the Wilderness, namely, Field's division of Longstreet's corps. After the left of Beauregard's evacuated line had been taken up, there remained a portion the approach to which was more formidable. The order had been issued to General Anderson commanding the corps to retake this portion of the lines by a joint assault of Pickett's and Field's divisions. Soon afterward the engineers, upon a careful reconnaissance, decided that a good line could be occupied without the loss of life which might result from this recapture. The order to attack was therefore withdrawn by General Lee. This rescinding order reached Field but did not reach Pickett. Pickett's division began its assault under the first order. The men of Field's division, hearing the firing and seeing Pickett's men engaged, leaped from their trenches,-first the men, then the officers and flagbearers,-rushed forward and were soon in the formidable trenches, which were found to be held by a very small force. On the 15th, 16th, and 17th battle raged along the lines of intrenchments and forts east of Petersburg, between Grant's forces and Beauregard's troops, who made a splendid defense against enormous odds. About dark on the 17th grave disaster to the Confederates seemed imminent, when Gracie's brigade of Alabamians, justhaffin's Bluff on the north side of the James, gallantly leaped over the works and drove the assailants back, capturing a thousand or more prisoners. Hoke, too, on his part of the lines, had easily repulsed Smith's assaults.

This battle raged until near midnight. Meantime Beauregard's engineers were preparing an interior line, to which his wearied troops fell back during the night. A renewal of the attack on the lines held by the Confederate troops on the night of the 17th had been ordered by Grant along his whole front for an early hour on the 18th. But the withdrawal of the Confederates to interior lines necessarily caused delay, and, when the attack was made at noon, Lee and two of his divisions, Kershaw's and Field's had reached the Petersburg lines.

Tho attack made no impression on the lines, which were held until the evacuation on April 2d, 1865.

To some military critics General Lee seemed not to have taken in the full force of Beauregard's urgent telegrams in those critical days of June. But it must be remembered how easy it was for General Grant to make a forced march on Richmond from the north side of the James, accompanied by a strong feint on the Petersburg lines. Then, too, any strategist will see that Petersburg, cut off from Richmond by an enemy holding the railroad between the two cities (or holding an intrenched line so near it as to make its use hazardous), would not have been a very desirable possession. The fact is, that the defense of Richmond against an enemy so superior in numbers to the defending army, and in possession of the James River to City Point as a great water-way to its base of supplies, was surrounded with immense difficulties. And, in fact, in sending back Hoke's division to Beauregard, and in approving that general's withdrawing of Bushrod Johnson's division from the Bermuda Hundred line to Petersburg, Lee thereby sent him more reenforcements by far than he sent to Rodez on the 12th of May at Spotsylvania, when that general was holding the base of the salient and Wright and Warren. Besides this, Lee had already detached Breckinridge's division and Early's corps to meet Hunter at Lynchburg. And, after all, the result showed that Lee's reliance on his men to hold in check attacking forces greatly superior in numbers did not fail him in this instance; that he was bold to audacity was a characteristic of his military genius.

The campaign of 1864 now became the siege of Petersburg. On the night of June 18th Hunter retreated rapidly from before Lynchburg toward western Virginia, and Early, after a brief pursuit, marched into Maryland, and on July 11th his advance was before the outer defenses of Washington.

Source: "Battles and Leaders of the Civil War"

Concerning the enemy's casualties Badeau, in his Military History of U. S. Grant, says: "The losses of Lee no human being can tell. No official report of them exists, if any was ever made, and no statement that has been put forth in regard to them has any foundation but a guess. It seems however, fair to presume that as Lee fought outside of his works as often as Grant, and was as often repelled, the slaughter of the rebels equalled that in the national army. The grey coats lay as thick as the blue next day, when the national scouts pushed out over the entire battle-field and could discover no living enemy ."

Source: The Union Army, vol. 6

Battle of the Wilderness

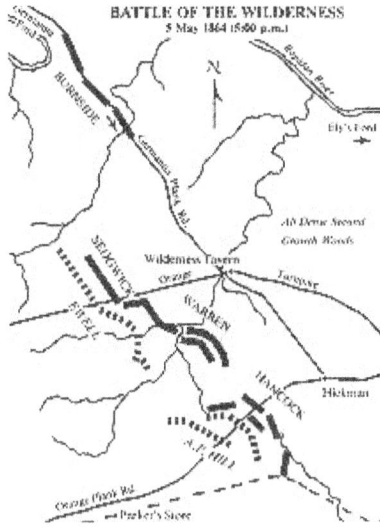

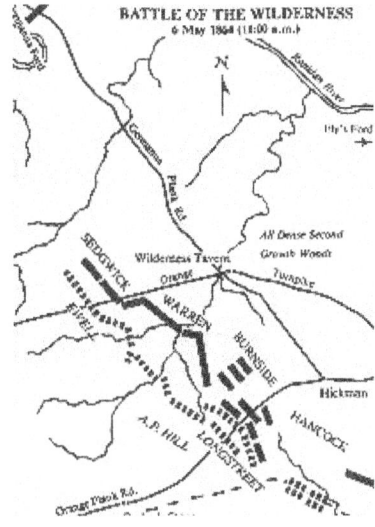

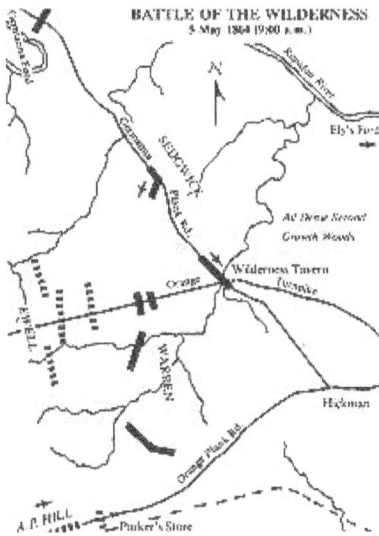

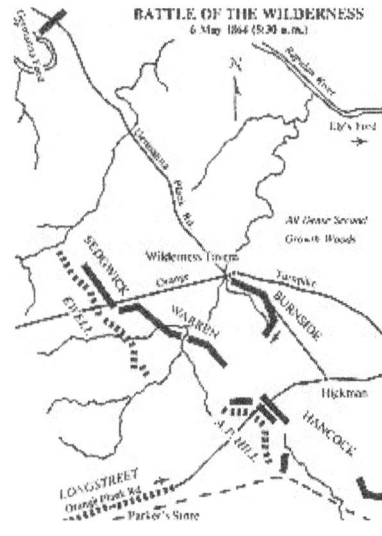

Through The Wilderness
By
Alexander S. Webb, Brevet Major-General, U.S.A.

In '61, '62, and '63, the Army of the Potomac, under McClellan, Hooker, and Meade, had by constant attrition worn down Lee's command until , in the minds of many officers and men who were actively engaged in the front, there was confidence that Lee would not hold out against our army another year.

On April 9th, 1864, General Grant instructed General Meade that Lee's army would be his objective. Meade had with him, according to his report of April 30th, 95,952 enlisted men, 3486 officers, and 274 guns. Hancock's corps contained 26,676 men; Warren's; 24,125 men; Sedgwick's, 22,584 men (1); while Sheridan controlled 12,525 in the cavalry. To guard all the trains there was a special detail of 1200 men. General Grant had also attached the Ninth Corps (an independent command) to the army operating under his eye. The total force under General Grant, including Burnside, was 4409 officers and 114,360 enlisted men. hor the artillery he had 9945 enlisted men and 285 officers ; in the cavalry, 11,839 enlisted men and 585 officers ; in the provost guards and engineers, 120 officers and 3274 enlisted men. His 118,000 men, properly disposed for battle, would have covered a front of 21 miles, two ranks deep, with one-third of them held in reserve ; while Lee, with his 62,000 men similarly disposed, would cover only 12 miles. Grant had a train which he states in his " Memoirs" would have reached from the Rapidan to Richmond, or sixty-five miles.

(1) These three corps had been increased by the consolidation with them of the First and Third corps. Besides causing great dissatisfaction throughout the army, this consolidation in my opinion, was the indirect cause of much of the confusion in the execution of orders, and in the handling of troops during the battles of the Wilderness.-A. S. W.

Of Lee's army, Longstreet's corps (two divisions) numbered about 10,000 ; Ewell's corps about 17,000. A. P. Hill went into the Wilderness with about 22,000 men for duty in the ranks ; "Jeb " Stuart's cavalry numbered about 8000, and the artillery about 4800. Lee's total strength, as estimated by General Humphreys, was 61,953 men, and the number of field-guns 224.

General Grant's aggregate over Lee was therefore 94 guns and 56,819 enlisted men ; but then Lee had, at the outset, his position in the Wilderness, and Grant did not know at that time, as did General Meade and General Hooker, to what advantage Lee could turn the Wilderness with its woods, ravines, plank roads and dirt roads.

The Army of the Potomac began to cross the Rapidan at midnight of May 3d, after due preparation on the part of Sheridan's cavalry to cover our front. A canvas and a wooden pontoon bridge were laid at Germanna Ford, similar bridges at Ely's Ford, and a wooden bridge at Culpeper Mine Ford. These three fords cover about seven miles of the Rapidan River, which in general flows southeast.

Hancock, preceded by Gregg's cavalry, crossed at Ely's Ford and moved to Chancellorsville, which placed him on the left, or south-east, side of the Wilderness battle-field. Warren, with Wilson's cavalry in front (and followed by Sedgwick), crossed at Germanna Ford and followed the Germanna Plank road, due south-east, to Wilderness Tavern. Sedgwick encamped for the night three miles south of the ford. The sixty-five miles of trains were until 2 P. M. of May 5th in passing over Culpeper Mine Ford and Germanna Ford. Generalwas Meade's chief-of-staff at the time, states that the halt of the infantry on the 4th at Chancellorsville and the Wilderness was caused by the difficulty in moving the trains across the Rapidan.

General Law, who commanded a brigade under Longstreet, states that on the 2d of May General Lee, in the presence of a number of his officers , expressed the opinion that the Union army would cross the river at Germanna or Ely's Ford. General Lee's headquarters were at Orange Court House ; Longstreet, with his corps, was distant at Gordonsville ; Ewell was near at hand on the Rapidan, above Mine Run ; and A. P. Hill was on his left, higher up the stream ; and it seems that Lee intended to move with his whole force against Grant's right flank as soon as Grant was far enough advanced into the Wilderness on the road to Richmond.

As for the Wilderness, it was uneven, with woods, thickets, and ravines right and left. Tangled thickets of pine, scrub-oak, and cedar prevented our seeing the enemy, and prevented any one in command of a large force from determining accurately the position of the troops he was ordering to and fro. The appalling rattle of the musketry, the yells of the enemy, and the cheers of our own men were constantly in our ears. At times, our lines while firing could not see the array of the enemy, not fifty yards distant. After the battle was fairly begun, both sides were protected by log or earth breastworks.

For an understanding of the roads which shaped the movements in the Wilderness, cross the Rapidan from the north and imagine your self standing on the Germanna Plank road, where the Brock road intersects it, a little south of Wilderness Tavern, and facing due west. In general, the Union right wing (Sedgwick) held the Germanna road, and the left wing (Hancock) the Brock road, while the center (Warren) stretched across the obtuse angle formed by them. At the Lacy house, in this angle, Grant, Meade, and Warren established their headquarters during the day of the 5th. If, standing at the intersection of these roads, you stretch forward your arms, the right will correspond with the Orange turnpike, the left with the Orange Plank road. Down the Orange turnpike, on May 5th, Lee sent Ewell against Warren, while two divisions of A. P. Hill advanced by the Orange Plank road to check Hancock. Nearly a day later, Longstreet reached the field on the same road as Hill. The engagements fought on May 5th by Ewell on the Orange turnpike, and by A. P. Hill on the Orange Plank road, must be regarded as entirely distinct battles.

Warren received orders from Meade at 7:15 in the morning to attack Ewell with his whole force. General Sedgwick, with Wright's division and Neill's brigade of Getty's division, was ordered to move out, west of the Germanna Plank road, connecting with the Fifth Corsposed across the turnpike in advance of Wilderness Tavern. At this time also, General Hancock, at Chancellorsville, was warned by General Meade that the enemy had been met on the turnpike, and he was directed to halt at Todd's tavern until further orders. Meantime Crawford's division of Warren's corps, between , the turnpike and plank road, in advancing, found Wilson's cavalry skirmishing with what he supposed to be the enemy's cavalry. At 8 A. M., under orders, Crawford halted, and, hearing that our cavalry, at Parker's store, almost directly south of him, was in need of support, he sent out skirmishers to assist them. Those skirmisher s struck Hill's corps, moving down the Orange Plank road toward the Brock road. Thus at 8 A. M. General Grant and General Meade had developed the presence of Hill on their left and Ewell on their right. Getty's division of Sedgwick had reached Wilderness Tavern ; and. when it was learned that Hill was coming down the Orange Plank road, Getty was directed to move out toward him, by way of the Brock road, and drive Hill back, it' possible, behind Parker's store.

On our right Johnson's division of Ewell was driven back along the Orange turnpike in confusion by General Griffin of Warren's corps. Ricketts and Wright of Sedgwick were delayed in reaching their position on the right of Warren, and for lack of such support Griffin's right brigade under Ayres was forced back and two guns were abandoned. Wadsworth, with his division of Warren's corps, supplemented by Dennison's brigade of Robinson's division, of the same corps, had started forward in a westerly direction, until he found himself with his left toward the enemy. McCandless's brigade of Crawford's division (also of Warren's corps) had endeavored to obtain a position on the left of Wadsworth, but lost its bearings in the entangled woods so that its left came in contact with Ewell's right, and it, as well as Wadas driven in by Daniel's and Gordon's brigades, forming the right of Ewell.

Thus Crawford was left with his left flank in the air, and he of necessity was drawn in about 2 o'clock and posted about a mile south-west from the Lacy house, facing toward his first position at Chewning's house. Wadsworth finally took position on the left of Crawford, facing toward the south and west, with his back toward the Lacy house. Griffin, on Crawford's right, reached to the Orange turnpike. Wright's division of Sedgwick formed on the right of Griffin, with the left of Upton's brigade resting on the pike ; then came the brigades of Penrose and Russell, then Neill's brigade of Getty's division. Soon after getting into position Neill and Russell were attacked by Johnson, who was repulsed. Still farther to the right, toward the Germanna Plank road, Seymour, of Ricketts's division, came up and took position. The entire Union front line was now intrenched At this time on the center and right Warren and Sedgwick were securely blocked by Ewell's single corps. On the left of the line the situation was this : At 11 A. M. Hancock, whose advance had passed Todd's tavern, received a dispatch stating that the enemy was coming down the Orange Plank road in full force, and he was directed to move his corps up to the Brock road, due north. He was further informed that Getty had been sent to drive the enemy back, and must be supported immediately ; that on the turnpike Griffin had been pushed back somewhat, and that he (Hancock) must push out on the Plank road and connect his right with Warren's left.

Hancock promptly started his column, and met General Getty at the junction of the Plank and Germanna roads. Getty's division Was then in line of battle, along the Brock road, With Grant's brigade on the left of the Plank road , and Wheaton's and Eustis's brigades on the right of the road which the troops were intrenching. This Was at 2 P. M. of the 5th. Getty informed Hancere two divisions of A. P. Hill out in his front, and Hancock directed the finishing of the Works that had been begun, before any advance should be made. Hancock placed Birney's division on the left of Getty, in two lines of battle along the Brock road, and Mott's and Gibbon's divisions on Birney's left; Barlow's division held the extreme left and formed an angle on the Brock road overlooking the bed of an unfinished railroad. Most of the artillery of Hancock's corps was posted with Barlow's division.(1) Frank's brigade of Barlow's division Was stationed partly across the Brock road, near the junction of the Brock road and a cross-road leading to the

Catharpin road.

All of Hancock's corps Were directed to throw up breastworks of logs and earth, the intrenched line beginning at Getty's left and extending to Barlow's left where it was refused to cover the flank. The second line of the Second Corps, also threw up earth-works, and a third intrenched line was formed behind Birney and Mott nearest the Plank road.

At 4:30 P. M. Getty started to the attack, and marched but four hundred yards When he struck Heth's division of Hill's corps, and found the enemy in force, his right having been reenforced by Wilcox's division. Hancock threw forward Birney and Mott on the left of Getty, and put a section of Ricketts's old battery on the Plank road. General Hancock says in his report : " The fight her e became very fierce at once the lines of battle Were , exceedingly close, the musketry continuous and deadly along the entire line."(2) Carroll's and Owen's brigades of Gibbon's division Were sent in to support Getty, upon the Plank road. Colonel Carroll, an excellent fighting man Was Wounded, but remained on the field. More to the left, Brooke and Smyth, of Barlow's division, attacked the right of Hill, and forced it back.

About 4 o'clock, also, Wadsworth, w ho had been sent from his position near the Lacy house to strike across the country toward the Plank road, halted for the nightle, facing nearly south between Tapp's house and the Brock road. (3) This ended the operations of May 5th, leaving the Army of the Potomac in close contact with Ewell and Hill.

(1) According to General Francis A. Walker's account, in the " History of the Second Army Corps," Dow's 6th Maine Battery was placed in the second line on Mott's left and a section of Ricketts's "F " , 1st Pennsylvania Artillery was posted with the troops of General Getty.-EDITORS.

(2) Colonel Theodore Lyman informs me that on a visit he made to the battle-field of the Wilderness after the war, in going over the ground where on May 6th, the next day, the 20th Massachusetts, of my brigade, lost a third of its numbers, he found the line occupied by the enemy to be just behind the crest of a slight elevation, where they had placed a row of logs, by which they were effectually screened from the bullets and the sight of our troops; for in front of and around them was a dense forest of saplings, the 20th Massachusetts and other of our troops were in the thicket, not more than twenty or thirty yards distant. Their presence was made known by their advance through the brush, and their return fire, aimed as they supposed at the enemy, had cut off the saplings four and five feet above the ground, as regularly as if they had been cut by a machine. Many of the broken tree-tops were still hanging when Colonel Lyman visited the ground.-A. S. W.

(3) Humphreys, to show how bewildering was the dense forest growth, says, " Many men from both armies, looking for water during the night, found themselves within the opposite lines."-A. S. W.

During the night of the 5th orders were given for a general attack by Sedgwick, Warren, and Hancock at 5 o'clock the next morning.

Burnside, who, with his corps, had been holding the line of the Orange and Alexandria railroad back to Bull Run, set his corps in motion the afternoon of the 4th and made a forced march to the field. The leading division, under Stm Brandy Station, crossed at Germanna Ford the night of the 5th, was held in reserve at Wilderness Tavern, and joined Hancock on the Brock road at 8 A. M. of the 6th. Potter and Willcox, coming from Bealton and Rappahannock Station, reached the field about daylight, and were ordered to fill the gap between Warren and Hancock and join in the general attack. (1) Ferrero's colored division, after a forced march of forty miles, was held in the rear to guard the trains.

Longstreet's arrival on the field was known and reported by General Hancock to General Meade at 7 A. M. on the 6th; indeed, it was found that Longstreet was present when, at 5 o'clock, my brigade (of Gibbon's division) was ordered to relieve General Getty. When I advanced I immediately became engaged with Field's division, consisting of Gregg's, Benning's, Law's, and Jenkins's brigades, on the north side of the Orange Plank road.

Just before 5 o'clock the right of the line under Sedgwick was attacked by the Confederates, and gradually the firing extended along the whole front.

Wadsworth's division fought its way across Hancock's front to the Plank road, and advanced along that road. Hancock pushed forward Birney with his own and Mott's divisions, Gibbon's division supporting, on the left of the Plank road, and soon drove his opponents from their rifle-pits, and for the time being appeared to have won a victory. His left, however, under Barlow, had not advanced. From information derived from prisoners and from the cavalry operating in the vicinity of Todd's tavern, it was believed at this time that Longstreet was working around the left to attack the line along the Brock road. Instead of attacking there, Longstreet moved to the support of Hill, and just as the Confederates gave way before Birney's assault, Longstreet's leading division, under General C. W. Field, reached Birney's battle-ground and engaged my line.

Thus at 8 o'clock Hancock was battling against both Hill and Longstreet. General Gibbon had comm Hancock himself was looking out for the Plank road.

Warren's Fifth Corps, in front of Ewell, had obeyed the orders of General Grant, in making frequent and persistent attacks throughout the morning, without success. The same may be said of Wright, of Sedgwick's Sixth Corps, who was attacking Ewell's left; but Ewell was too strongly intrenched to be driven back from his line by the combined Fifth and Sixth corps.

(1) General Humphreys remarks in his account as follows : " For, so far as could be ascertained, the gap between Hill and Ewell was not yet closed, neither was that between Hancock and Warren." As I held the right of Hancock on May 6th until 1 o'clock, I can state that it was never closed on the part of the Union troops. My aide, Colonel W. T. Simms, was badly wounded, on my right, while seeking to form a junction with the Ninth Corps or with Crawford of the Fifth Corps.-A. S. W.

General Burnside, with the divisions of Willcox and Potter, attempted to relieve Hancock by passing up between the turnpike and the Plank road to Chewning's farm, connecting his right with Warren and joining the right of Hancock, now held by my brigade.(1) Burnside's other division, under Stevenson, moved up the Plank road in our support, and I placed four of his regiments, taken from the head of his column, on my right, then pressed to the rear and changed my Whole line, Which had been driven back to the Plank road, forward to its original line, holding Field's division in check With the twelve regiments now under my command. Now, at this very moment, General Wadsworth (Who had assumed command over me because he stated that Stevenson ranked me, and he must take us both in his command) had given to me the most astonishing and bewildering order, -- which was to leave

(1) The right of the column under Willcox advanced beyond the Lacy house to Wilderness Run, and found the enemy well posted on high ground, behind the swamps along the creek. An attack here was deemed impracticable, and Willcox was moved to the left toward the Tapp house in support of Potter, who had gone in near the Plank. road.-Editors.

the twelve regiments under my command at his (Wadsworth's) disposal, and to go to the left, find four regiments, and stop the retreat of those troops of the left of our line who were flying to the Brock road. (1) When I rode off to obey this unfortunate order, General Wadsworth, in order to stop the enemy's attack upon Birney upon his left, went to the 20th Massachusetts of my brigade and ordered that regiment to leave its log-works and charge the enemy's line, a strong breastwork on the west side of a ravine on Wadsworth's front.

General Wadsworth was told that the regiment could not safely be moved, that I had changed my front on that regiment and held the line by means of it. Wadsworth answered that the men were afraid, leaped his horse over the logs and led them in the charge himself. He was mortally wounded, (2) and my line was broken by Field, and swept off as by a whirlwind. Birney's line, as a consequence, was broken to pieces, and back to the Brock road went the troops. This attack was directed by Lee in person. [See also p. 124.] When I came back from endeavoring to carry out the order that Wadsworth had given me, I found the 19th Maine, under Colonel Seedless Connor, on the Plank road. Another regiment also staid with me to hold the Plank road and to deceive the Confederates, by fighting as though they had a continuous line. Colonel Connor was shot in the leg after a long skirmish ; I offered him my horse, but his wounds being such as to render him unable to mount, he had to be carried to the logworks. His regiment staid there until I gave the order to break like partridges through the woods for the Brock road.

(1) Of this incident, Col. C. H. Banes, in his " History of the Philadelphia Brigade" (Owen's), says

"Webb's First Brigade of the Second Division was moved from its position on the Brock road, and quickly advanced on either side of the Plank road. By 8 o'clock the fighting had become continuous along the entire front of the Second Corps, and was raging at some points with great fury. . . . Toward 9 o'clock there was an almost entire cessation, followed soon after by furious assaults that expended their force before anything definite was accomplished, and these were followed in turn by desultory firing. . . . A few moments before 12 o'clock, General Wadsworth, whose division had pushed its way during the morning until it conne . . rode through the woods to the Plank road, and began to ascertain the location of the corps with a view to concerted action. While General

Wadsworth was on the edge of the road, near the line of battle, and engaged in making these observations, and before his command was really assured of its position, there occurred one of the strangest scenes of army experience. Without any apparent cause that could be been from the position of the brigade, the troops on our left began to give way, and commenced falling back toward the Brock road. Those pressing past the left flank of the Second Division did not seem to be demoralized in manner, nor did they present the appearance of soldiers moving under orders, but rather of a throng of armed men who were returning dissatisfied from a muster. Occasionally some fellow, terror stricken, would rush past as if his life depended on speed, but by far the larger number acted with the utmost deliberation in their movements. In vain were efforts put forth to atop this retrograde movement; the men were alike indifferent to commands or entreaties.

. . . The division of Wadsworth, being on the right of the Plank road, was the last to feel this influence; but, in spite of the most gallant efforts of its commander, it soon joined with the other troops in moving to the rear, leaving the brave Wadsworth mortally wounded." A. S. W.

(2) General Wadsworth and myself had been discussing why I did not have certain men carried off the field who had been shot in the head. I told him that from my observation I had never considered it worth while to carry a man off the field if, wounded in the head, he slowly lost his vertical position and was incapable of making a movement of his head from the ground. I considered such cases as past cure. When I was shot in the head in the works at Spotsylvania Court House on the morning of the 12th, at the Bloody Angle, the bullet passed through the corner of my eye and came out behind my ear. While falling from the horse to the ground I recation with General Wadsworth; when I struck the ground I made an effort to raise my head, and when I found I could do so I made up my mind I was not going to die of that wound, and then I fainted.- A. S. W.

Burnside had finally become engaged far out on our right front ; Potter's division came upon the enemy intrenched on the west side of a little ravine extending from Ewell's right. General Burnside says that after considerable fighting he connected his left with Hancock's right and intrenched.

Hancock was out of ammunition, and had to replenish the best way he could from the rear. At 3:45 P. M. the enemy advanced in force against him to within a hundred yards of his log-works on the left of the Plank road.

The attack was of course the heaviest here. Anderson's division came forward and took possession of our line of intrenchments, but Carroll's brigade was at hand and drove them out at a double-quick. .

Now let us return to our right, and stand where General Meade and General Grant .were, at the Lacy house. The battle was finished over on the left so far as Hancock and Burnside were concerned. Grant had been thoroughly defeated in his attempt to walk past General Lee on the way to Richmond. Shaler's brigade of Wright's division of Sedgwick's corps had been guarding the wagon-trains, but was now needed for the fight and had returned to the Sixth Corps lines. It was placed on the extreme right on the Germanna Plank road, due north from where General Grant was standing. Shaler's brigade was close up to the enemy, as indeed was our whole line. Shaler was busy building breastworks, when it was struck in the flank, rolled up in confusion, and General Seymour and General Shaler and some hundreds of his men were taken prisoners. But the brigade was not destroyed: A part of it stood, and, darkness helping them, the assailants were prevented from destroying Wright's division. Wright kept his men in order.

This is in fact the end of the battle of the Wilderness, so far as relates to the infantry. Our cavalry was drawn in from Todd's tavern and the Brock road. The enemy's cavalry followed them. They were all intrenched, and General Grant decided that night that he would continue the movement to the left, as it was impossible to attack a position held by the enemy in such force in a tangled forest. To add to the horrors of war, we had the woods on fire all around us, and Humphreys estimates that about two hundred of our men were burned to death. The best possible proof that this was an accidental battle can be found in the movements of the troops. There was no intention to attack Lee in the Wilderness.

May was the last day of the battle of the Wilderness. Ewell had most effectually stopped the forward movement of the right wing of Meade's army, and Hill and Longstreet defeated our left under Hancock.

The fact is that the whole of the left was disorganized. From Hancock down through Birney and Gibbon, each general commanded something not strictly in his command. Hancock had "the left" Gibbon "the left" of Hancock ; Birney had his own and Mott's divisions, and Wadsworth had Webb and Stevenson. The troops of these division commanders were without proper leaders.

We had seen the mixed Second and Ninth corps driven in, in detail, on our left. We knew that the Fifth and Sixth corps were blocked, and we felt deeply the mortification consequent upon our being driven back to the Brock road. From personal contact with the regiments who did the hardest fighting, I declare that the individual men had no longer that confidence in their commanders which had been their best and strongest trait during the past year. We are told by General Badeau in his history that at the very time our men were being tossed about on the Plank road " General Grant lay under the trees awaiting Burnside's advance, and revolving the idea of a movement still farther to the Union left, thrusting his whole force between Lee and Richmond." We did move toward Spotsylvania. Warren's Fifth Corps was directed to withdraw from the Wilderness after dark on the 7th of May, and to move by the left behind Hancock on the Brock road, with Sedgwick (the Sixth Corps) following him, and to proceed toward the court house.

This was attempted, but Warren found that he was required with his corps to help Sheridan's cavalry, which was detained by J. E. B. Stuart at Todd's tavern, or near that point. Warren gave the required assistance, driving out of his way Stuart, who was assisted by infantry.

At 8: 30 P. M. Warren moved by the Brock road to the left of the Second Corp pike and Germanna Plank road to Chancellorsville, thence by the Piney Branch Church road to the intersection of that road with the Brock road. At this point Sedgwick was ordered to leave a division, with another at Piney Branch Church, and a third midway between these two. Burnside started to follow Sedgwick, but early on the morning of the 8th he was ordered to halt at Aldrich's, where the Piney Church road leaves the main Fredericksburg Plank road, to guard the trains. Ferrero's division of this corps was now detached for this service.

Warren was delayed by the blocking of the Brock road by the mounted troops of the provost guard, and this delay gave Longstreet's men, under R. H. Anderson, the opportunity to reach Spotsylvania in advance of Warren.

When Warren reached Todd's tavern at 3 A. M., he found Merritt's cavalry engaging the Confederates. Hancock had waited for the whole army to pass, and reached the tavern at 9 o'clock on the 8th. (1). At 11 A. M., say s General Humphreys, "Hancock sent his leading brigade under Miles to make a reconnaissance down the Catharpin road toward Corbin's Bridge, about two miles distant." Miles had his own brigade, one battery, and one brigade of Gregg's cavalry. He found Hampton's cavalry, and held them at bay until 5:30 P.M. While returning, Miles was attacked by Mahone's infantry, and was compelled to call up reenforcements. At 1:30 P. M. Hancock sent Gibbon east ten miles to support Warren and Sedgwick.

(1) My notes show that we of the Second Corps obeyed orders implicitly. We waited to cover the movements of the rest of the army, and then took our place at 4 P.M. of the 8th of May on the Brock road, about one mile south-east of Todd's tavern.- A. S. W.

About 8 A.M. on the 8th Warren's leading division, under General John C. Robinson, deployed into the clearing north of Spotsylvania Court House, and was fired upon by Confederates upon Spotsylvania Ridge. General Robinson was severest fire. Griffin's division advanced on the right of Robinson's ; but the line, being unable to sustain itself soon fell back until it was succored by the divisions of Crawford and Wadsworth, which now reached the front. A line was taken up east of the Brock road, near Alsop's. Sedgwick came up about noon and the Fifth Corps, supported by , Sedgwick, were at 1 P. M. directed to storm the Confederate position on Spotsylvania Ridge. Sedgwick moved south to join Warren's left; but it was late in the day when Crawford's division of the Fifth and one of Wright's brigades under Penrose assaulted what proved to be Rodes's division of Ewell's corps in position and intrenched.

On the morning of the 9th Burnside's corps moved across from the Plank road to the Fredericksburg road at the crossing of the Ny River . This brought him east of the court house one and a half miles. He pushed over the river one division under O. B. Willcox. Stevenson's division came up at noon. Potter's division remained a mile in rear on the Fredericksburg road. Willcox fought a brigade of R. H. Anderson and some dismounted cavalry. Hancock moved east to the right of Warren, and intrenched overlooking the Po. On the morning of the 9th Sheridan started on a raid around Lee's army.

In front of Hancock the Po River ran from west to east, then it turned due south opposite Warren's right. The Confederate left rested for a time on this south bend, and the bridge over it at the crossing of the Shady Grove Church road was fortified by Longstreet. While the several corps were adjusting their lines on the 9th, General Sedgwick; our most esteemed general, was killed by a sharp-shooter, and Horatio G. Wright took command of the Sixth Corps.

General Burnside had reported to General Grant on the 9th that he had met the enemy on the east of Spotsylvania Court House, and he had added to his report that he judged, from the indications in his front, that Lee was about to move north toward Fredericksburg. It was theed that Hancock should make a reconnaissance toward Lee's left, crossing the east and west bend of the Po River, moving south as far as the Shady Grove road, turning the enemy's left then to move east and cross the Po River , again by the Block House road bridge. Hancock crossed three of his divisions (Mott was with Wright) at different points at 6 o'clock in the morning, forcing the crossing, and meeting a very stubborn resistance in front of Barlow, who was on his left, and but little in front of Gibbon who was on , his right. He now laid three pontoon-bridges over the river, it being fifty feet wide and not fordable, and then pushed due south toward the Block House bridge, but reached that point too late that night to attempt a crossing.

During this night orders were issued from Meade for the operations of the next day : Hancock was to endeavor to find the position of the enemy's left, to force him from the position of his (Hancock's) front. The Sixth Corps was ordered to feel the intrenchments near the center. Mott's division of Hancock's corps, still kept north of the Po River with Wright, and on the left of the Sixth Corps, was to prepare to join Burnside, who with his corps (the Ninth) was to attack Early from the east on the morning of the 10th.

But at dawn on the 10th an examination of the Block House bridge, made by Hancock, showed that the enemy was strongly intrenched on the east side of the Po at that point. However, Brooke's brigade of Barlow's division was sent down the Po River to a point half a mile below the bridge.

Brooke discovered the enemy in strong force holding intrenchments extending nearly half a mile below the bridge, their left resting on the Po River.

But other arrangements had been made f or the movement of the army, and Meade now ordered Hancock back. Meade was directed to arrange for the assault at 5 o'clock, under General Hancock's command in the front of Warren and Wright.

Birney, while withdrawing, was attacked ; Hancock, who had started ahead with Gibbon to prepare for the attack, recrossed to the south bank of the Po and joined Barlow. Barlow was half a mile south of his bridges. His left, composed of Miles's and Smyth's brigades, was along the Shady Grove road, facing south, their left rested at the bridge. Brooke's and Brown's brigades were in front or south of the Shady Grove road. North-east and to their , rear one and a half miles, Field's guns were planted in intrenchments, sweeping the ground behind them and covering the pontoon-bridge over the Po.

Hancock drew back Brooke and Brown to the right and to the rear; . and then Miles and Smyth retired to the crest south of the pontoon-bridges.

These troops formed a tête-du-pont facing south. Heth's division, of Hill's corps, attacked the two right brigades with vigor, but was twice repulsed. The Union loss was very heavy.

Hancock, finding the enemy repulsed and the woods on fire in the rear of his line, crossed to the north side of the Po River. One gun, the first ever lost by the Second Corps, was Jammed between two trees in the midst of this fire , and was abandoned by Birney's men. Many of our wounded perished in the flames.

Of this battle on our right, General Hancock said "The enemy regarded this as a considerable victory. Had not Barlow's division received imperative orders to withdraw, Heth's division would have had no cause for congratulation."

Meanwhile, Warren had determined to make the attack, and at 3:45 he did so, directing it personally and leading in full uniform.(1) The assaulting column was composed of Crawford's division, Cutler's division (formerly Wadsworth's), and Webb's and Carroll's brigades of the Second Corps. The official diary of Longstreet's corps says that "some of the enemy succeeded in gaining the works, but were killed in them." We were driven back, however, with heavy loss, including Brigadier-General James C. Rice, of Cutler's division killed.

(1) Warren had made reconnaissances in force, with division front twice. He knew his ground, as he always did.-A. S. W.

General Hancock returned to us at half-past five, and we were ordered to make another attack at 7 P. M. with Birney's and Gibbon's divisions and part of the Fifth Corps. We made the assault, but we were driven back a second time. Our men were demoralized by fruitless work. Over on our left, in the Sixth Corps, General Wright had found what he deemed to be a vulnerable place in the Confederate line. It was on the right of Rodes's rebel division and on the west face of the salient. Colonel Emory Upton was selected to lead this attack. Upton's brigade was of the First Division, Sixth Corps. He had four regiments to his command ; and General Mott, commanding a division of the Second Corps, had been ordered by General Wright to assault the works in his front at 5 o'clock to assist and support Upton's left.

BATTLE OF HAW'S SHOP

View east across the battlefield from Enon Church

Date	May 28, 1864
Location	Hanover County, Virginia
Result	Inconclusive[1]

Belligerents	
United States (Union)	CSA (Confederacy)

Commanders	
David McM. Gregg Alfred T.A. Torbert	Wade Hampton

| Strength | |

2 cavalry divisions	3 cavalry brigades, 800 mounted infantry
Casualties and losses	
~300	~320 (27 killed)

Wilderness – Todds Tavern – Spotsylvania Court House – Yellow Tavern – Meadow Bridge – Wilson's Wharf – North Anna – **Haw's Shop** – Totopotomoy Creek – Old Church – Cold Harbor – Trevilian Station – Saint Mary's Church

- The **Battle of Haw's Shop** (also called **Hawe's Shop**—the historic spelling[2]—or **Enon Church**) was fought on May 28, 1864, in Hanover County, Virginia, as part of Union Lt. Gen. Ulysses S. Grant's Overland Campaign against Confederate Gen. Robert E. Lee's Army of Northern Virginia during the American Civil War. It was the second significant cavalry engagement of the 1864 campaign and one of the bloodiest of the war.

BACKGROUND

After Grant's army escaped from the trap that Lee had set for it at the Battle of North Anna, it began to move again around the right flank of Lee's army, in a continuation of the maneuvering that had characterized the campaign throughout May 1864. Lee gave orders for his army to fall back 12 miles to Atlee's Station, only 9 miles north of the Confederate capital of Richmond, and near the site of the start of the Seven Days Battles of 1862.

On May 27, Union cavalry established a bridgehead on the south side of the Pamunkey River, near the Hanovertown Ford. Brig. Gen. George A. Custer's Michigan cavalry brigade (from the division of Brig. Gen. Alfred T. A. Torbert in Maj. Gen. Philip Sheridan's Cavalry Corps of the Army of the Potomac) scattered the mounted Confederate pickets guarding the ford and an engineer regiment constructed a pontoon bridge. The rest of Torbert's division then crossed the river, followed by the cavalry division of Brig. Gen. David McM. Gregg and a division of Union infantry.

Lee knew that his best defensive position against Grant would be the low ridge on the southern bank of Totopotomoy Creek, but he was not certain of Grant's specific plans; if Grant was not intending to cross the Pamunkey in force at Hanovertown, the Union army could outflank him and head directly to Richmond. Lee ordered cavalry under Maj. Gen. Wade Hampton to make a reconnaissance in force, break through the Union cavalry screen, and find the Union infantry.

BATTLE

On May 28, Hampton rode off with three veteran cavalry brigades, a battery of horse artillery, and three regiments of mounted infantry, green troops from South Carolina. As more of Grant's troops crossed the pontoon bridge over the Pamunkey, Gregg led his Union cavalry division probing west from Hanovertown, searching for Lee. (Torbert's division began to picket along Crump's Creek in the direction of Hanover Courthouse.) Three miles west of Hanovertown, and a mile beyond a large blacksmith shop called Haw's Shop, Gregg's troopers ran into Hampton at Enon Church, finding the Confederate cavalrymen dismounted in a wooden area behind a swamp, hurriedly erecting breastworks made of logs and rails, and well covered by artillery. Brig. Gen. Henry E. Davies, Jr., of Gregg's division deployed pickets from the 10th New York Cavalry to Hampton's front. Hampton reportedly exclaimed, "We've got the Yankees where we want them now."[3] It was impossible to turn the position, due to a stream to the north and a mill pond to the south, so Gregg, despite being outnumbered, launched a frontal assault.

The Confederates met the Union charge with a wall of fire. The South Carolina mounted infantry carried Enfield rifles, which outranged the carbines carried by the Federal cavalry, killing or wounding 256 men. As Davies rode into the fighting, his saber was cut in half by a Minié ball and his horse's tail was shot off. Union return fire was heavy as well, because the troopers were armed with seven-shot Spencer repeating carbines. One Pennsylvania trooper estimated that the 200 men in his unit fired 18,000 rounds. Their carbines got so hot that from time to time the men had to pause to let them cool.[4]

As Gregg's first attack ground to a halt, and his second brigade attack under J. Irvin Gregg failed to dislodge the Confederates, Hampton's men moved out from their works and started a series of counterattacks. Gregg sent for reinforcements from Sheridan, who released two brigades from Torbert's division. (There was plenty of infantry nearby, but Maj. Gen. George G. Meade refused Sheridan's request for two brigades.) Torbert's brigade under Brig. Gen. Wesley Merritt extended Greg's line to the right, thwarting Hampton's attempted flanking maneuver. Sheridan also threw Custer's brigade into the fight. He pointed toward the Confederates and commanded, "Custer, I want you to go in and give those fellows hell!"[5]

Due to the heavily wooded terrain, Custer had his brigade dismount and deploy in a long, double-ranked line of battle, as if they were infantrymen. However, Custer inspired his men by staying mounted as he led them forward, waving his hat in full view of the enemy. Some of the relatively inexperienced South Carolina infantry mistook a Union shift in position for a retreat and charged after them, only to run into Custer's men, who captured 80 of the Confederates. Forty one of the Union cavalrymen fell in the attack, as did Custer's horse, but their enthusiastic charge caused Hampton's men to withdraw. (Another factor was that Hampton had just received intelligence from prisoners on the location of two Union corps, which meant that his reconnaissance mission had been successfully completed.)

Aftermath

The Battle of Haw's Shop lasted for over seven hours and was the bloodiest cavalry battle since Brandy Station in 1863. Union casualties were 256 men in Gregg's division and another 41 from Custer's brigade, including Private John Huff, the cavalryman from the 5th Michigan who had fatally shot Maj. Gen. J.E.B. Stuart at Yellow Tavern. Confederate losses were never tabulated officially, but Union reports claimed they buried 187 enemy bodies after the battle, recovered 40 to 50 wounded men, and captured 80 South Carolinians.[6] Gregg paid tribute to the Confederates "who resisted with courage and desperation unsurpassed." He later wrote that the battle "has always been regarded by the Second Division as one of its severest."[7]

Since the Confederates withdrew, the battle was a technical Union victory, but at a high cost. Hampton had delayed the Union advance for seven hours and General Lee received the valuable intelligence he had sought. This information caused him to shift the Army of Northern Virginia to a new blocking position at Cold Harbor.

Notes

1. NPS
2. All of the references for this article use the more modern spelling. Numerous regimental histories written in the 19th century refer to "Hawe's." Historian Bruce Catton, in his 1953 work *A Stillness at Appomattox*, spells it "Hawes's Shop."
3. Rhea, p. 25.
4. Grimsley, p. 151.
5. Heidler, p. 952.
6. Grimsley, p. 152.
7. Jaynes, p. 149.

References

- Grimsley, Mark, *And Keep Moving On: The Virginia Campaign, May-June 1864*, University of Nebraska Press, 2002, ISBN 0-8032-2162-2.
- Heidler, David S., and Heidler, Jeanne T., eds., *Encyclopedia of the American Civil War: A Political, Social, and Military History*, W. W. Norton & Company, 2000, ISBN 0-393-04758-X.
- Jaynes, Gregory, and the Editors of Time-Life Books, *The Killing Ground: Wilderness to Cold Harbor*, Time-Life Books, 1986, ISBN 0-8094-4768-1.
- Rhea, Gordon C., *The Battle of Cold Harbor*, National Park Service Civil War Series, Eastern National, 2001, ISBN 1-888213-70-1.
- National Park Service battle description

Coordinates: 37°40′34″N 77°18′42″W37.6760°N 77.3118°W

Cold Harbor, VA June 1-3, 1864

Early on June 1, relying heavily on their new repeating carbines and shallow entrenchments, Sheridan's troopers threw back an attack by Confederate infantry.

Confederate reinforcements arrived from Richmond and from the Totopotomoy Creek lines. Late on June 1, the Union VI and XVIII Corps reached Cold Harbor and assaulted the Confederate works with some success.

By June 2, both armies were on the field, forming on a seven-mile front that extended from Bethesda Church to the Chickahominy River.

At dawn June 3, the II and XVIII Corps, followed later by the IX Corps, assaulted along the Bethesda Church-Cold Harbor line and were slaughtered at all points. Grant commented in his memoirs that this was the only attack he wished he had never ordered.

The armies confronted each other on these lines until the night of June 12, when Grant again advanced by his left flank, marching to James River.

On June 14, the II Corps was ferried across the river at Wilcox's Landing by transports.

On June 15, the rest of the army began crossing on a 2,200-foot long pontoon bridge at Weyanoke.

Abandoning the well-defended approaches to Richmond, Grant sought to shift his army south of the river to threaten Petersburg.

Result(s): Confederate victory

Location: Hanover County

Campaign: Grant's Overland Campaign (May-June 1864)

Date(s): May 31-June 12, 1864

Principal Commanders: Lieutenant General Ulysses S. Grant and Major General George G. Meade [US]; General Robert E. Lee [CS]

Forces Engaged: 170,000 total (US 108,000; CS 62,000)

Estimated Casualties: 15,500 total (US 13,000; CS 2,500)

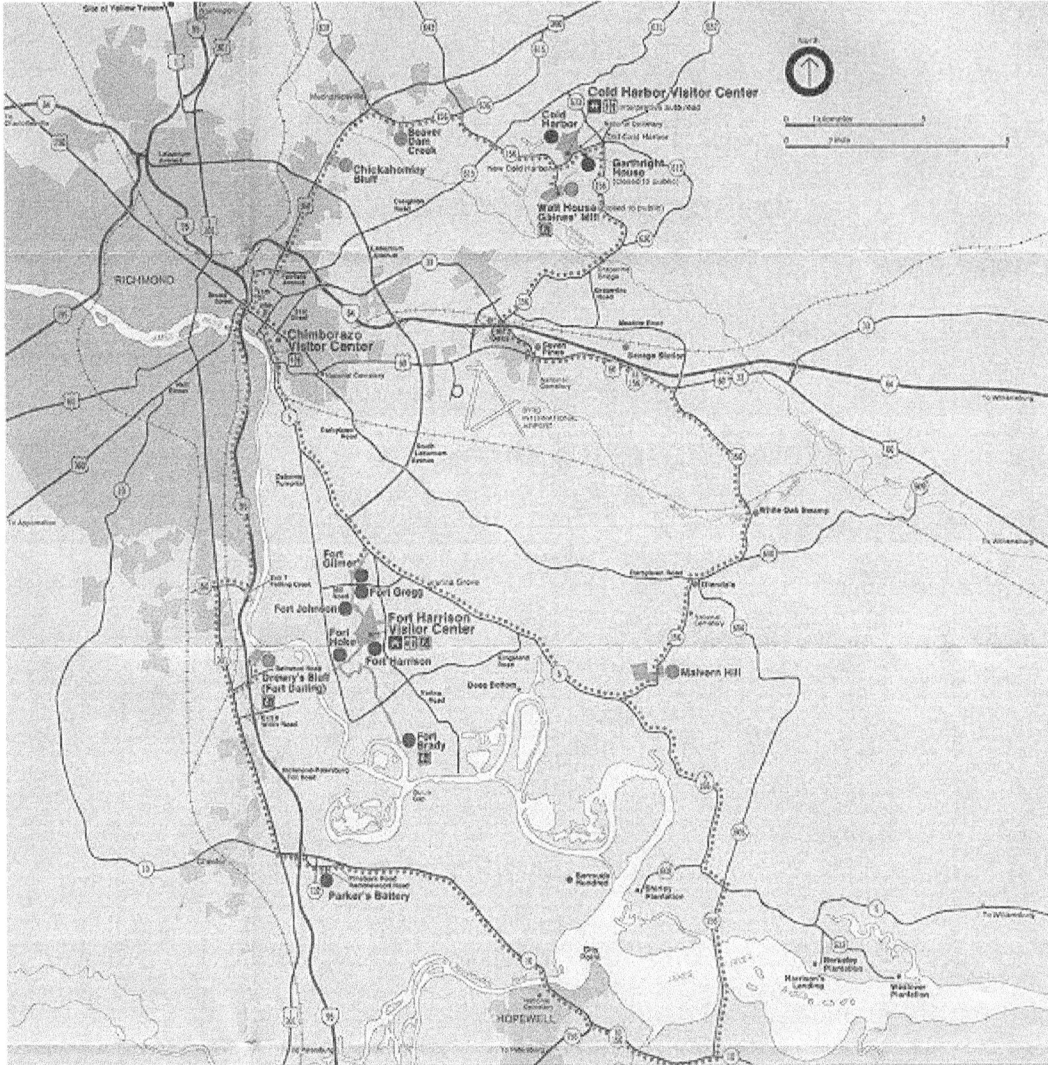

The enigmatic commander in chief of the Union forces through the last year and a half of the Civil War. It is both a revelatory portrait of Ulysses S. Grant and the dramatic story of how the war was won.

Trevilian Station

The Battle of Trevilian Station
Trevilians
June 11-12, 1864

To draw off the Confederate cavalry and open the door for a general movement to the James River, Maj. Gen. Philip Sheridan mounted a large-scale cavalry raid into Louisa County, threatening to cut the Virginia Central Railroad. On June 11, Sheridan with the Gregg's and Torbert's divisions attacked Hampton's and Fitzhugh Lee's cavalry divisions at Trevilian Station. Sheridan drove a wedge between the Confederate divisions, throwing them into confusion. On the 12th, fortunes were reversed. Hampton and Lee dismounted their troopers and drew a defensive line across the railroad and the road to Gordonsville. From this advantageous position, they beat back several determined dismounted assaults. Sheridan withdrew after destroying about six miles of the Virginia Central Railroad. Confederate victory at Trevilian prevented Sheridan from reaching Charlottesville and cooperating with Hunter's army in the Valley. This was one of the bloodiest cavalry battles of the war.

HISTORY ARTICLES

Custer's First Last Stand: The Battle of Trevilian Station by Eric Wittenberg

The Battle of Trevilian Station (Trevilian Station Battlefield Foundation)

Battle of Trevilian Station (NPS)

- CWPT Maps: Battle of Trevilian Station
- Historical Maps: Battle of Trevilian Station

RECOMMENDED BOOKS

Glory Enough for All: Sheridan's Second Raid and the Battle of Trevilian StationBy Eric J. Wittenberg
 Recommended Reading List: Battle of Trevilian Station

ONLINE RESOURCES

Fredericksburg and Spotsylvania County National Battlefields Park - Trevilian Station (NPS)
Wikipedia: Battle of Trevilian Station
Wikipedia: Wade Hampton
Wikipedia: George Custer
Trevilian Station Battlefield Foundation
Trevilian Station Driving Tour
Historic Markers: Battle of Trevilian Station

BATTLE FACTS

CAMPAIGN

- Grant's Overland Campaign

BATTLES IN THIS CAMPAIGN
- The Wilderness
- Spotsylvania Court House
- North Anna
- Cold Harbor

LOCATION
- Louisa County, Virginia

DATES

- June 11 - 12, 1864

UNION COMMANDER
- Philip Sheridan

CONFEDERATE COMMANDER

- Wade Hampton

FORCES ENGAGED
- 9,216 Union
- 6,700 Confederate

ESTIMATED CASUALTIES

- 1,000 Union
- 1,000 Confederate

SOUTH CAROLINA CIVIL WAR MAP OF BATTLES

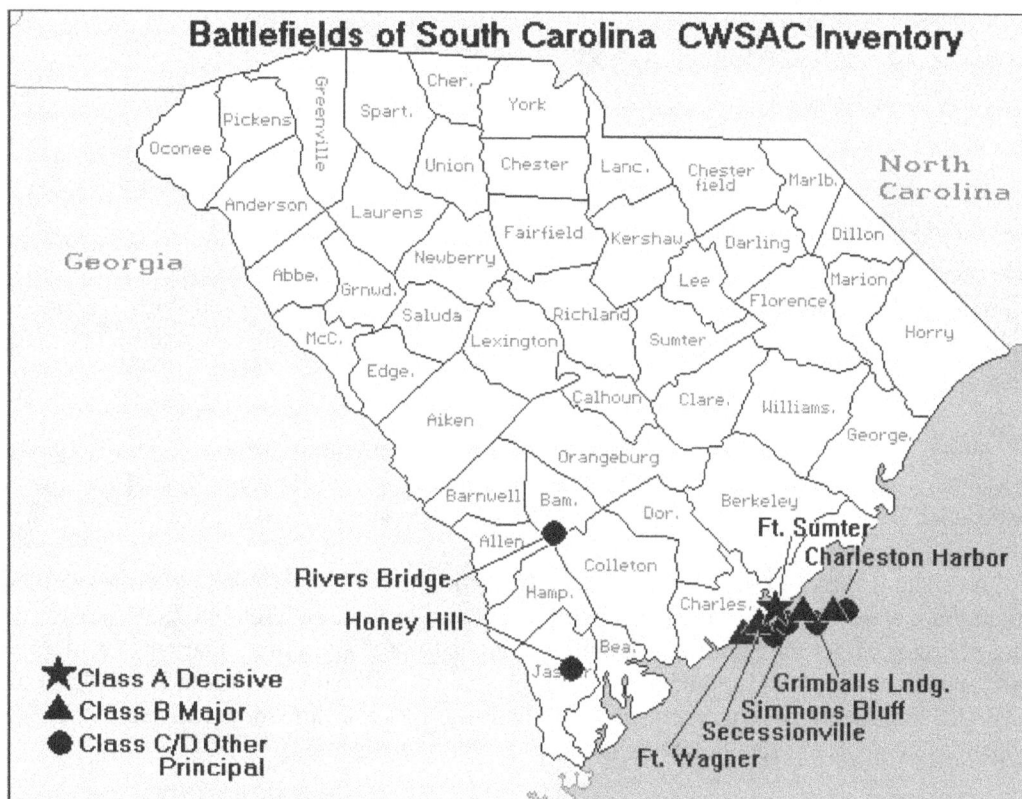

April 12-14, 1861 Fort Sumter

June 16, 1862 Secessionville / Ft. Lamar / James Island

June 21, 1862 Simmon's Bluff

April 7, 1863 Charleston Harbor / Fort Sumter

July 10-11, 1863 Fort Wagner / Morris Island

July 16, 1863 Grimball's Landing / Secessionville / James Island

July 18-September 7, 1863 Fort Wagner / Morris Island

Aug 17-Aug 23, 1863 Fort Sumter / Charleston Harbor / Morris Island

The South Carolina Flag

Though the South Carolina State Flag harkens back to the crescent worn by her troops in the American Revolution, and the palmetto tree is a reminder of the palmetto logs that stopped British cannon balls in the bombardment of Ft. Moultrie during the same war, it is still very much a Confederate flag for its current incarnation.

While the flag in some variation was adopted under the South Carolina Militia Act of 1838, the flag as shown today was not officially adopted as the state flag until January, 1861. Then it was the flag of the seceded Republic of South Carolina - the first of the states to leave the Union.

As such, it is indeed every bit as much a Confederate flag as any other pattern of Confederate flag (and there were many). In fact, the palmetto flag, as it became called at the time, was far more the symbol of secession for the South than the more famous Bonnie Blue flag - that gets far more publicity than it deserves based on an examination of the newspapers of the time (but it did have the song). I have found FAR more mentions of palmetto flags being hoisted all over the South (as well as out West and in the North) as symbols of secession than the lone star/Bonnie Blue flags.

South Carolina troops also fought under their state flag -the state providing flags to the first ten regiments raised for its defense. Other palmetto flags were issued to local military companies as well which saw early combat use.

The palmetto flag of South Carolina is, therefore, a Confederate battle flag, just like those that were created to be as such during the war by the various CSA commanders.

This is a version of an early flag raised over South Carolina shortly after its secession from the Union in 1860 (it was also supposed to have been raised over Yale University by sympathizers). It was called the South Carolina Sovereignty Flag and was supposed to have been an inspiration for the Confederate flag in its later form.

Brice Family Served in the Following Major Battles
as Well as Others not listed

More information on each battle can be accessed on line by typing in the name of the battle and location.

Fort Wagner

Other Names: First Assault, Morris Island

Location: City of Charleston

Campaign: Operations against Defenses of Charleston (1863)

Date(s): July 10-11, 1863

Principal Commanders: Brig. Gen. Qunicy Gillmore [US]; Gen. P.G.T. Beauregard [CS]

Forces Engaged: Brigades

Estimated Casualties: 351 total (US 339; CS 12)

Description: On July 10, Union artillery on Folly Island together with Rear Adm. John Dahlgren's fleet of ironclads opened fire on Confederate defenses of Morris Island. The bombardment provided cover for Brig. Gen. George C. Strong's brigade, which crossed Light House Inlet and landed by boats on the southern tip of the island. Strong's troops advanced, capturing several batteries, to within range of Confederate Fort Wagner. At dawn, July 11, Strong attacked the fort. Soldiers of the 7th Connecticut reached the parapet but, unsupported, were thrown back.

Result(s): Confederate victory

Petersburg

Other Names: Assault on Petersburg

Location: City of Petersburg

Campaign: Richmond-Petersburg Campaign (June 1864-March 1865)

Date(s): June 15-18, 1864

Principal Commanders: Lt. Gen. Ulysses S. Grant and Maj. Gen. George G. Meade [US]; Gen. Robert E. Lee and Gen. P.G.T. Beauregard [CS]

Forces Engaged: 104,000 total (US 62,000; CS 42,000)

Estimated Casualties: 11,386 total (US 8,150; CS 3,236)

Description: Marching from Cold Harbor, Meade's Army of the Potomac crossed the James River on transports and a 2,200-foot long pontoon bridge at Windmill Point. Butler's leading elements (XVIII Corps and Kautz's cavalry) crossed the Appomattox River at Broadway Landing and attacked the Petersburg defenses on June 15. The 5,400 defenders of Petersburg under command of Gen. P.G.T. Beauregard were driven from their first line of entrenchments back to Harrison Creek. After dark the XVIII Corps was relieved by the II Corps. On June 16, the II Corps captured another section of the Confederate line; on the 17th, the IX Corps gained more ground. Beauregard stripped the Howlett Line (Bermuda Hundred) to defend the city, and Lee rushed reinforcements to Petersburg from the Army of Northern Virginia. The II, XI, and V Corps from right to left attacked on June 18 but was repulsed with heavy casualties. By now the Confederate works were heavily manned and the greatest opportunity to capture Petersburg without a siege was lost. The siege of Petersburg began. Union Gen. James St. Clair Morton, chief engineer of the IX Corps, was killed on June 17.

Result(s): Confederate victory

Globe Tavern

Other Names: Second Battle of Weldon Railroad, Yellow Tavern, Yellow House, Blick's Station

Location: Dinwiddie County

Campaign: Richmond-Petersburg Campaign (June 1864-March 1865)

Date(s): August 18-21, 1864

Principal Commanders: Maj. Gen. G.K. Warren [US]; Gen. Robert E. Lee, Lt. Gen. A.P. Hill, Maj. Gen. Henry Heth, and Maj. Gen. William Mahone [CS]

Forces Engaged: Corps (34,300 total)

Estimated Casualties: 5,879 total (4,279 US; 1,600 CS)

Description: While Hancock's command demonstrated north of the James River at Deep Bottom, the Union V Corps and elements of the IX and II Corps under command of Maj. Gen. G.K. Warren were withdrawn from the Petersburg entrenchments to operate against the Weldon Railroad. At dawn August 18, Warren advanced, driving back Confederate pickets until reaching the railroad at Globe Tavern. In the afternoon, Maj. Gen. Henry Heth's division attacked driving Ayres's division back toward the tavern. Both sides entrenched during the night. On August 19, Maj. Gen. William Mahone, whose division had been hastily returned from north of James River, attacked with five infantry brigades, rolling up the right flank of Crawford's division. Heavily reinforced, Warren counterattacked and by nightfall had retaken most of the ground lost during the afternoon's fighting. On the 20th, the Federals laid out and entrenched a strong defensive line covering the Blick House and Globe Tavern and extending east to connect with the main Federal lines at Jerusalem Plank Road. On August 21, Hill probed the new Federal line for weaknesses but could not penetrate the Union defenses. With the fighting at Globe Tavern, Grant succeeded in extending his siege lines to the west and cutting Petersburg's primary rail connection with Wilmington, North Carolina. The Confederates were now forced to off-load rail cars at Stony Creek Station for a 30-mile wagon haul up Boydton Plank Road to reach Petersburg. Confederate general John C.C. Sanders was killed on August 21.

Result(s): Union victory

Chaffin's Farm/New Market Heights

Other Names: Combats at New Market Heights, Forts Harrison, Johnson, and Gilmer; Laurel Hill

Location: Henrico County

Campaign: Richmond–Petersburg Campaign (June 1864-March 1865)

Date(s): September 29-30, 1864

Principal Commanders: Maj. Gen. Benjamin Butler [US]; Gen. Robert E. Lee and Lt. Gen. Richard S. Ewell [CS]

Forces Engaged: Armies

Estimated Casualties: 4,430 total

Description: During the night of September 28-29, Maj. Gen. Benjamin Butler's Army of the James crossed James River to assault the Richmond defenses north of the river. The columns attacked at dawn. After initial Union successes at New Market Heights and Fort Harrison, the Confederates rallied and contained the breakthrough. Lee reinforced his lines north of the James and, on September 30, he counterattacked unsuccessfully. The Federals entrenched, and the Confederates erected a new line of works cutting off the captured forts. Union general Burnham was killed. As Grant anticipated, Lee shifted troops to meet the threat against Richmond, weakening his lines at Petersburg.

Result(s): Union victory

Fort Fisher

Other Names: None

Location: New Hanover County

Campaign: Expedition against Fort Fisher (December 1864)

Date(s): December 7-27, 1864

Principal Commanders: Rear Adm. David D. Porter and Maj. Gen. Benjamin Butler [US]; Maj. Gen. Robert Hoke [CS]

Forces Engaged: Expeditionary Corps, Army of the James [US]; Hoke's Division and Fort Fisher Garrison [CS]

Estimated Casualties: 320 total

Description: Maj. Gen. Benjamin Butler was relieved of command of the Army of the James and assigned to lead an amphibious expedition against Fort Fisher, which protected Wilmington, the South's last open seaport on the Atlantic coast. Learning that large numbers of Union troops had embarked from Hampton Roads on December 13, Lee dispatched Hoke's Division to meet the expected attack on Fort Fisher. On December 24, the Union fleet under Rear Adm. David D. Porter arrived to begin shelling the fort. An infantry division disembarked from transports to test the fort's defenses. The Federal assault on the fort had already begun when Hoke approached, discouraging further Union attempts. Butler called off the expedition on December 27 and returned to Fort Monroe.

Result(s): Confederate victory

Hanover Court House

Other Names: Slash Church

Location: Hanover County

Campaign: Peninsula Campaign (March-September 1862)

Date(s): May 27, 1862

Principal Commanders: Brig. Gen. Fitz John Porter [US]; Brig. Gen. Lawrence O'B. Branch [CS]

Forces Engaged: Divisions

Estimated Casualties: 1,327 total (US 397; CS 930)

Description: On May 27, 1862, elements of Brig. Gen. Fitz John Porter's V Corps extended north to protect the right flank of McClellan's Union army that now straddled the Chickahominy River. Porter's objective was to cut the railroad and to open the Telegraph Road for Union reinforcements under Maj. Gen. Irvin McDowell that were marching south from Fredericksburg. Confederate forces, attempting to prevent this maneuver, were defeated just south of Hanover Courthouse after a stiff fight. The Union victory was moot, however, for McDowell's reinforcements were recalled to Fredericksburg upon word of Banks's rout at First Winchester.

Result(s): Union victory

Chancellorsville

Other Names: None

Location: Spotsylvania County

Campaign: Chancellorsville Campaign (April-May 1863)

Date(s): April 30-May 6, 1863

Principal Commanders: Maj. Gen. Joseph Hooker [US]; Gen. Robert E. Lee and Maj. Gen. Thomas J. Jackson [CS]

Forces Engaged: 154,734 total (US 97,382; CS 57,352)

Estimated Casualties: 24,000 total (US 14,000; CS 10,000)

Description: On April 27, Maj. Gen. Joseph Hooker led the V, XI, and XII Corps on a campaign to turn the Confederate left flank by crossing the Rappahannock and Rapidan Rivers above Fredericksburg. Passing the Rapidan via Germanna and Ely's Fords, the Federals concentrated near Chancellorsville on April 30 and May 1. The III Corps was ordered to join the army via United States Ford. Sedgwick's VI Corps and Gibbon's division remained to demonstrate against the Confederates at Fredericksburg. In the meantime, Lee left a covering force under Maj. Gen. Jubal Early in Fredericksburg and marched with the rest of the army to confront the Federals. As Hooker's army moved toward Fredericksburg on the Orange Turnpike, they encountered increasing Confederate resistance. Hearing reports of overwhelming Confederate force, Hooker ordered his army to suspend the advance and to concentrate again at Chancellorsville. Pressed closely by Lee's advance, Hooker adopted a defensive posture, thus giving Lee the initiative. On the morning of May 2, Lt. Gen. T.J. Jackson directed his corps on a march against the Federal left flank, which was reported to be "hanging in the air." Fighting was sporadic on other portions of the field throughout the day, as Jackson's column reached its jump-off point. At 5:20 pm, Jackson's line surged forward in an overwhelming attack that crushed the Union XI Corps. Federal troops rallied, resisted the advance, and counterattacked. Disorganization on both sides and darkness ended the fighting. While making a night reconnaissance, Jackson was mortally wounded by his own men and carried from the field. J.E.B. Stuart took temporary command of Jackson's Corps. On May 3, the Confederates attacked with both wings of the army and massed their artillery at Hazel Grove. This finally broke the Federal line at Chancellorsville. Hooker withdrew a mile and entrenched in a defensive "U" with his back to the river at United States Ford. Union generals Berry and Whipple and Confederate general Paxton were killed; Stonewall Jackson was mortally wounded. On the night of May 5-6, after Union reverses at Salem Church, Hooker recrossed to the north bank of the Rappahannock. This battle was considered by many historians to be Lee's greatest victory.

Result(s): Confederate victory

Spotsylvania Court House

Other Names: Combats at Laurel Hill and Corbin's Bridge (May 8); Ni River (May 9); Laurel Hill, Po River, and Bloody Angle (May 10); Salient or Bloody Angle (May 12-13); Piney Branch Church (May 15); Harrison House (May 18); Harris Farm (May 19)

Location: Spotsylvania County

Campaign: Grant's Overland Campaign (May-June 1864)

Date(s): May 8-21, 1864

Principal Commanders: Lt. Gen. Ulysses S. Grant and Maj. Gen. George G. Meade [US]; Gen. Robert E. Lee [CS]

Forces Engaged: 152,000 total (US 100,000; CS 52,000)

Estimated Casualties: 30,000 total (US 18,000; CS 12,000)

Description: After the Wilderness, Grant's and Meade's advance on Richmond by the left flank was stalled at Spotsylvania Court House on May 8. This two-week battle was a series of combats along the Spotsylvania front. The Union attack against the Bloody Angle at dawn, May 12-13, captured nearly a division of Lee's army and came near to cutting the Confederate army in half. Confederate counterattacks plugged the gap, and fighting continued unabated for nearly 20 hours in what may well have been the most ferociously sustained combat of the Civil War. On May 19, a Confederate attempt to turn the Union right flank at Harris Farm was beaten back with severe casualties. Union generals Sedgwick (VI Corps commander) and Rice were killed. Confederate generals Johnson and Steuart were captured, Daniel and Perrin mortally wounded. On May 21, Grant disengaged and continued his advance on Richmond.

Result(s): Inconclusive (Grant continued his offensive.)

Confederate Monument, First Presbyterian Churchyard

In the Churchyard of the First Presbyterian Church in Columbia is a Column from the South Carolina Statehouse, that was damaged in February of 1865 when Major General William T. Sherman's Union Army bombarded the City of Columbia. This Column was later removed from the Statehouse and a plaque was placed on it at the First Presbyterian Church for the members of that church that served in the American Civil War. The Plauqe reads as follows:

*"Men who served in the Confederate States Army from the Congreation of the First Presbyterian Church, Columbia, South Carolina, 1861-1865. Dedicated in Pride to those who Died; In Gratitude to those who served. *Robert C. Beck, Charles C. Beck, *Josiah Beden, *C.C. Brice, John Brice, *S.C. Burkett, *DeSaussure Burroughs, James Cathcart, William J. Cathcart, *Robert Crawford, *William Crawford, Andrew Oates, Douglas DeSaussure, *William DeSaussure - Colonel, *William Elkins, Albert Elmore, Frank H. Elmore, *Frank English, George Howe, *William Howe, *Arthur Kennedy, *Robert Kenedy, James P. MaCre - Captain, John Matthews, Jonathan Maxcy, *W. Ashley Maxcy, * James McDonald, *George McKenzie, Frank L. McKenzie, *James McMahan, Fitz Wm. McMaster - Colonel, *Beverly W. Meas, Arthur C. Moore, *J.R. Moore, *William Moore, James M. Mooris, Shannon Morrison, Henry D. Muller, F. Belton Orchard, Henry M. Orchard, *James D. Owens, Benjamin M. Palmer - D.D., William D. Peck - Major; John T. Rhett - Lt. Colonel, James R. Scott, John Scott, *Thornwell Scott, William Scott, James Sloan, John C.B. Smith - Colonel, John C. Suber, William R. Suber, B. Frazer Subert, Lamar Stark, Eben Stenhouse, GEorge Taylor, *James H. Taylor, Lawrence W. Taylor, William A. Taylor, *Gillespie Thornwell, James H. Thornwell, Charles S. Venable - Colonel, James Woodrow, Ph D. * * * * * * * * * * * * * Died in Service * * * * * * * * * * * * Members of the Congregation after 1865, who served in the Confederate Army. Alexander R. Banks, William E. Boggs - Chaplain, John W. Brinson - Chaplain, David Cardwell, Washington A. Clarke, John O.M. Clarkson, William L. Duffie, David R. Flennikey, J. William Flinky, John L. Girardeua - Chaplina, John H. Kinard, Robert G. Lamar - Colonel, William B. Lowrance - Captain, Rufus N. Lowrance - Major, Preston A. Lorick, Joseph B. ___ - Chaplain, Luthur _____ - ____, Issac H. Means - Colonel, Thomas T. Moore, Richard O'Neale, Wesley E. S_____, William Wallace - Colonel."*

- Confederate Monument, South Carolina Statehouse, along Gervais Street

Battle of Brice's Crossroads

Brice's Cross Roads – Tupelo – 2nd Memphis

The **Battle of Brice's Crossroads** was fought on June 10, 1864, near Baldwyn in Lee County, Mississippi, during the American Civil War. It pitted a 4,787-man contingent led by Confederate Major General Nathan Bedford Forrest against an 8,100-strong Union force led by Brigadier General Samuel D. Sturgis. The battle ended in a rout of the Union forces and cemented Forrest's reputation as one of the great cavalrymen.

The battle remains a textbook example of an outnumbered force prevailing through better tactics, terrain mastery, and aggressive offensive action. Despite this, the Confederates gained little through the victory other than temporarily keeping the Union out of Alabama and Mississippi.

Situation

Union Gen. William Tecumseh Sherman had long known that his fragile supply and communication lines through Tennessee were in serious jeopardy because of depredations by Forrest's cavalry raids. To effect a halt to Forrest's activities, he ordered Gen. Sturgis to conduct a penetration into northern Mississippi and Alabama with a force of around 8,500 troops to destroy Forrest and his command. Sturgis, after some doubts and trepidation, departed Memphis on June 1. Gen. Stephen D. Lee, alerted of Sturgis's movement, warned Forrest. Lee had also planned a rendezvous at Okolona, Mississippi, with Forrest and his own troops but told Forrest to do as he saw fit. Already in transit to Tennessee, Forrest moved his cavalry (less one division) toward Sturgis, but remained unsure of Union intentions.

Forrest soon surmised, correctly, that the Union had actually targeted Tupelo, Mississippi, located in Lee County, about 15 miles (24 km) south of Brice's Crossroads. Although badly outnumbered, he decided to repulse Sturgis instead of waiting for Lee, and selected an area to attack ahead on Sturgis's projected path. He chose Brice's Crossroads, in what is now Lee County, which featured four muddy roads, heavily wooded areas, and the natural boundary of Tishomingo Creek, which had only one bridge going east to west. Forrest, seeing that the Union cavalry moved three hours ahead of its own infantry, devised a plan that called for an attack on the Union cavalry first, with the idea of forcing the enemy infantry to hurry to assist them. Their infantry would be too tired to offer real help and the Confederates planned to push the entire Union force against the creek to the west. Forrest dispatched most of his men to two nearby towns to wait.

Battle

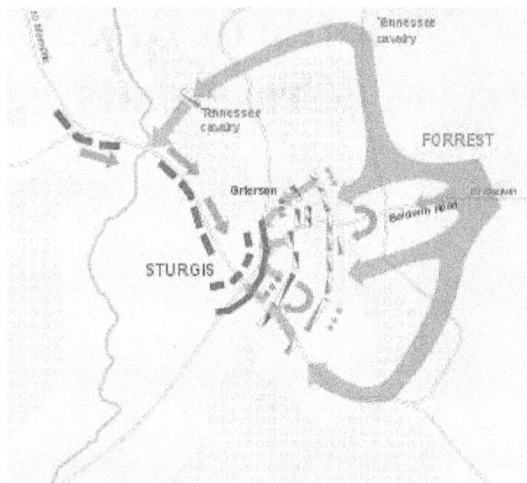

Battle of Brice's Crossroads

At 9:45 a.m. on June 10, a brigade of Benjamin H. Grierson's Union cavalry division reached Brice's Crossroads and the battle started at 10:30 a.m. when the Confederates performed a stalling operation with a brigade of their own. Forrest then ordered the rest of his cavalry to converge around the crossroads. The remainder of the Union cavalry arrived in support, but a strong Confederate assault soon pushed them back at 11:30 a.m., when the balance of Forrest's cavalry arrived on the scene. Grierson called for infantry support and Sturgis obliged. The line held until 1:30 p.m. when the first regiments of Federal infantry arrived.

The Union line, initially bolstered by the infantry, briefly seized the momentum and attacked the Confederate left flank, but Forrest launched an attack from his extreme right and left wings, before the rest of the federal infantry could take to the field. In this phase of the battle, Forrest commanded his artillery to unlimber, unprotected, only yards from the Federal position, and to shell the Union line with grapeshot. The massive damage caused Sturgis to re-order the line in a tighter semicircle around the crossroads, facing east.

At 3:30, the Confederates in the 2nd Tennessee Cavalry assaulted the bridge across the Tishomingo. Although the attack failed, it caused severe confusion among the Federal troops and Sturgis ordered a general retreat. With the Tennesseans still pressing, the retreat bottlenecked at the bridge and a panicked rout developed instead. The ensuing wild flight and pursuit back to Memphis carried across six counties before the exhausted Confederates retired.

Aftermath

The Confederates suffered 492 casualties to the Union's 2,164 (including 1,500 prisoners). Forrest captured huge supplies of arms, artillery, and ammunition as well as plenty of stores. Sturgis suffered demotion and exile to the far West. After the battle, the Union Army again accused Forrest of massacring black soldiers. However, historians believe that charge unwarranted, because later prisoner exchanges undermined the Union claim of disproportionate death.

The following is a list of artillery pieces captured by Forrest:[1]

- One 3-inch steel gun, rifled
- Three 6-pounder James bronze guns, rifled
- Two 3.8-inch James bronze guns, rifled
- Five 6-pounder bronze guns
- Two 12-pounder bronze howitzers
- Three 12-pounder Napoleon bronze guns

Factors leading to the Union loss

In correspondence with General Sturgis, Colonel Alex Wilkin, commander of the 9th Minnesota Volunteer Infantry Regiment gave several reasons for the loss of the battle.[2] He stated that General Sturgis, knowing that his men were under-supplied, having been on less than half rations, had been hesitant to advance on the enemy, but had done so against his better judgment because he had been ordered to do so. When the cavalry had engaged the enemy, many of the infantry had been ordered to advance double-time to support the cavalry, and in their weakened condition, many had fallen out in the advance. Those who did arrive were exhausted at the beginning of the battle, while the Confederates were fresh, and well fed owing to a large supply in their rear.

The roads were also wet due to a recent rain storm, that slowed the advance of the supply wagons and ammunition train, and several men were employed to try to make the roads passable. Additionally, the horses pulling the trains were poorly fed because there was little in the way of forage for them to eat along the way. This accounted for Forrest's capture of the artillery and supplies.

Intelligence had entirely favored the South, because the Confederates had been constantly fed information about the position and strength of the Union army from civilians in the area, while Sturgis had received no such intelligence. Because of this information, the South had been able meet the Union Army at a place where they could ambush Sturgis and make retreat as difficult as possible (Tishomingo Creek was in their rear with only a single bridge as a crossing point.) This place was close to the Confederate supply depot, and very far from the Union's.

When the retreat had occurred, with food and supplies exhausted, many of the Union soldiers were unable to retreat with the rest because of fatigue. This was much of the reason why so many Union soldiers were captured during the battle.

Finally, Wilkin stated that the rumors that Sturgis had been intoxicated during the battle were entirely false.

Battlefield today

The battle is commemorated at Brices Cross Roads National Battlefield Site, established in 1929. The National Park Service erected and maintains monuments and interpretive panels on a small 1-acre (4,000 m²) plot at the crossroads. This is the spot where the Brice family house once stood. The Brice's Crossroads Museum is in Baldwyn, Mississippi, just over a mile from the battlefield. Brice's Crossroads is considered one of the most beautifully preserved battlefields of the Civil War.

In 1994 concerned local citizens formed the Brice's Crossroads National Battlefield Commission, Inc., to protect and preserve additional battlefield land. With assistance from the Civil War Preservation Trust (formerly the APCWS and the Civil War Trust), and the support of Federal, State, and local governments, the BCNBC, Inc. has purchased for preservation over 800 acres (3.2 km²) of the original battlefield. Much of the land purchased came from the Agnew Family in Tupelo who still owns some of the battlefield property.

The modern Bethany Presbyterian Church sits on the southeast side of the crossroads. At the time of the battle this congregation's meeting house was located further south along the Baldwyn Road. However, the Bethany Cemetery adjacent to the Park Service monument site predates the Civil War. Many of the area's earliest settlers are buried here. The graves of more than 90 Confederate soldiers killed in the battle are also located in this cemetery. Union dead from the battle were buried in common graves on the battlefield, but were later reinterred in the National Cemetery at Memphis, Tennessee.

The roads that form Brice's Crossroads lead to Baldwyn, Tupelo, Ripley, and Pontotoc, Mississippi. Tupelo is the county seat for historic Lee County, Mississippi. The roads, paved today, are still a major route into Lee, Prentiss, and Union counties, with thousands of cars traveling through the national battlefield to reach other destinations.

Notes
1. O.R., Series I, Vol. XXXIX, Part 1, p. 227.
2. "Minnesota in the Civil and Indian Wars, 1861-1865 pp.473".
   http://books.google.com/books?id=gLAEVluEQCcC&pg=PA464&dq=Battle+of+Tishomingo+Creek&as_brr=1#PPA473,M1.

References
- National Park Service battle description
- U.S. War Department, *The War of the Rebellion*: *a Compilation of the Official Records of the Union and Confederate Armies*, U.S. Government Printing Office, 1880–1901.

Confederate Cemetery

The modern Bethany Presbyterian Church sits on the southeast side of the crossroads. At the time of the battle this congregation's meeting house was located further south along the Baldwyn Road. However, the Bethany Cemetery adjacent to the Park Service monument site predates the Civil War. Many of the area's earliest settlers are buried here. The graves of more than 90 Confederate soldiers killed in the battle are also located in this cemetery. Union dead from the battle were buried in common graves on the battlefield, but were later reintured in the National Cemetery at Memphis.

History of the Battle

In the spring of 1864 General William Tecumseh Sherman led more that 100,000 Union soldiers into northern Georgia. His mission was to capture the city of Atlanta, a vital center of transportation and industry. The city's fall would be a staggering blow to the already faltering southern Confederacy. To protect his army's vulnerable supply lines, Sherman ordered Union forces at Memphis, Tennessee to march into North Mississippi. Their job was to find and, if possible, destroy Major General Nathan Bedford Forrest and his Confederate cavalry.

On the morning of June 10, 1864, Union and Confederate troops clashed near Baldwyn, Mississippi along the sleepy wooded lanes around Brice's Crossroads. Forrest led elements of his cavalry corps in a bloody day-long battle against a much larger Union army commanded by Brigadier General Samuel D. Sturgis. Fighting in the sweltering heat, Forrest used his superior knowledge of the enemy, aggressive tactics and favorable terrain to win one of the most decisive victories of the American Civil War, completely routing Sturgis' expeditionary force, and capturing most of their weapons and supplies.

Forrest had won a stunning victory, but it was not complete. Despite the high cost, Sherman had in fact successfully diverted Forrest away from his supply lines. The Atlanta campaign could continue.

The Battlefield Today

In 1929 Brice's Crossroads was declared a "National Battlefield Site." To commemorate the battle the National Park Service erected, and maintains, monuments and interpretive panels on a small one-acre plot at the crossroads. This is the spot where the Brice family house once stood.

In 1994 concerned local citizens formed the Brice's Crossroads National Battlefield Commission, Inc. and began working to protect and preserve additional battlefield land. With assistance from the Civil War Preservation Trust (formerly the APCWS and the Civil War Trust), and the support of Federal, State and local governments, the BCNBC, Inc. has purchased for preservation over 800 acres of the original battlefield.

Today the site hosts the Agnew-Ford Group Use Area, which is available upon approval to scouts and organizations for primitive camping. The site is named for Todd Agnew and Dr. J.M. Ford. For reservations or more information contact the visitors' center at 662-365-3969 or by e-mail at bcr@dixie-net.com.

The modern Bethany Presbyterian Church sits on the southeast side of the crossroads. At the time of the battle this congregation's meeting house was located further south along the Baldwyn Road. However, the Bethany Cemetery adjacent to the park Service monument site predates the Civil War. Many of the area's earliest settlers are buried here. The graves of more than 90 Confederate soldiers killed in the battle are also located in this cemetery. Union dead from the battle were buried in common graves on the battlefield, but were later reintured in the National Cemetery at Memphis.

In the second half of 1863 Union armies won important victories at Vicksburg, Gettysburg, and Chattanooga. Four of the 11 Confederate States were completely in Union hands. The strong positions Union armies held all around the Confederacy were further strengthened when Lincoln unified all the various commands and named Ulysses Grant supreme commander on March 9, 1864. Grant took command of the Army of the Potomac and placed William T. Sherman in charge of the Union war effort in the west. This coordination of the Union war effort resulted in two great armies poised for the simultaneous invasion of the South.

The Battle of Brices Cross Roads

The Union plan for war in the west was to bisect the South east of the Mississippi with Sherman's army working out of Chattanooga and Nashville. His task was to destroy the Confederate Army led by Joseph E. Johnston, occupy Atlanta, and if possible, go on to Savannah and Charleston. From May to September, Sherman fought doggedly through northern Georgia, finally forcing, with the aid of a change in the Confederate command, the evacuation of Atlanta.

Early in the Atlanta campaign, the Confederate high command had considered the possibility of attacking from Mississippi Sherman's vulnerable supply line—the one-track railroad from Nashville to Chattanooga. Late in May, Gen. Stephen D. Lee, who commanded the Department of Alabama, Mississippi, and East Louisiana, directed Gen. Nathan Bedford Forrest, an unschooled farmboy

who had become a millionaire before he was 40 and had risen from private to major general, to strike Sherman's line of communications in middle Tennessee. Forrest had distinguished himself by his ability to move fast and fight hard. He lacked formal training in military science, but he acted on the simple maxim that in warfare it was all-important to get to the decisive point of the battle first with the most men. Gifted with daring and inspirational leadership, he had an uncanny ability to carry into execution his theory of successful warfare. So on June 1 Forrest put his columns in motion at Tupelo, Miss., and three days later was in Russellville, Ala., a day's march from the Tennessee River.

Sherman knew that his supply line was vulnerable and therefore charged Gen. Samuel D. Sturgis to move out of Memphis into northern Mississippi and hold Forrest there. Alerted by Lee of Sturgis' moves, Forrest hurried back to Tupelo.

Forrest began concentrating his forces, which numbered approximately 3,500 men, along the railroad between Guntown, Baldwyn, and Booneville.

On the evening of June 9, he knew from his scouts that Sturgis, with about 8,100 men, was in camp at Stubbs Farm 13 to 16 kilometers (8 to 10 miles) from Brices Cross Roads. Both armies marched at dawn.

Forrest, who had scouted his enemy well, planned to attack at Brices. But Sturgis' cavalry reached and passed the crossroads before the Confederates got there. Forrest, approaching along the Baldwyn Road, met the Union patrols about 1.5 kilometers (1 mile) east of Brices. The Confederates checked the Union advance and by noon, with rapid reinforcement, were attacking vigorously. The Union forces, called up on the

double, were exhausted from the march along the muddy roads made almost impassable by torrential rains the night before. Many never even crossed Tishomingo Creek.

Forrest pressed his attack and by midafternoon pushed the Union lines back to the crossroads. Sturgis began a careful withdrawal. But at Tishomingo Creek bridge there was trouble when a wagon overturned as the Federals recrossed the stream. Some 8 miles up the road, as they crossed the treacherous Hatchie River bottom, many of the soldiers panicked and the retreat became a rout. Most of the artillery and wagon train were abandoned, and, in the wild flight to Memphis, more than 1,500 Federals were captured.

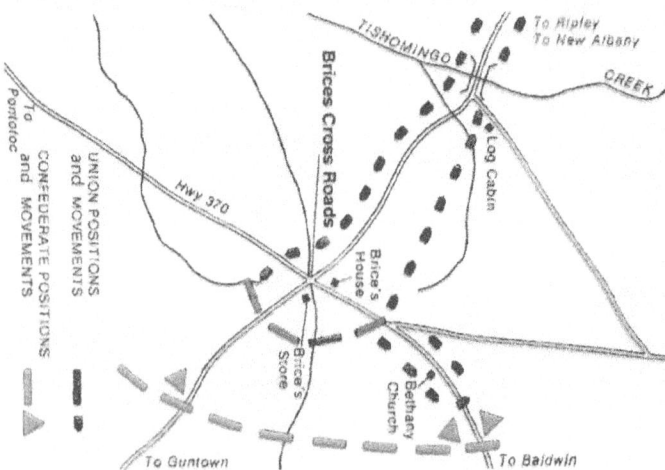

Brices Cross Roads

TISHOMINGO CREEK
To Ripley
To New Albany
Log Cabin
Hwy 370
Brice's House
Brice's Store
Bethany Church
To Guntown
To Baldwin
To Pontotoc

UNION POSITIONS and MOVEMENTS
CONFEDERATE POSITIONS and MOVEMENTS

BATTLE OF BRICES CROSS ROADS
JUNE 10, 1864

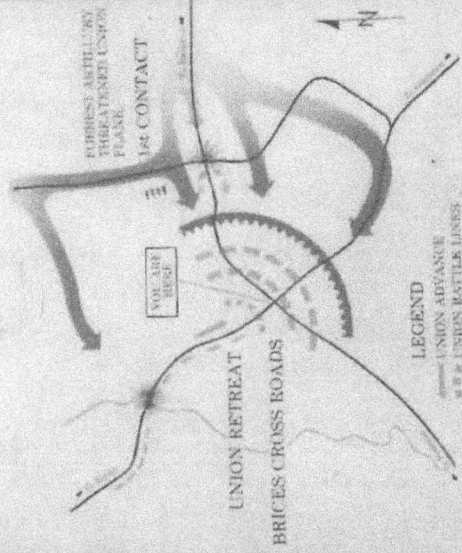

FORREST ARTILLERY THREATENED UNION FLANK

1st CONTACT

YOU ARE HERE

UNION RETREAT

BRICES CROSS ROADS

LEGEND
- UNION ADVANCE
- UNION BATTLE LINES
- UNION RETREAT
- CONFEDERATE ADVANCE
- MAIN CONFEDERATE BATTLE LINE

NATIONAL PARK SERVICE
UNITED STATES DEPARTMENT OF THE INTERIOR

THE WESTERN CAMPAIGN, 1864

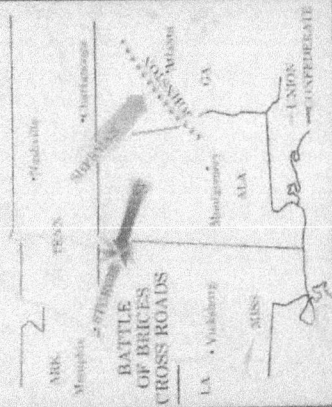

Nashville

Chattanooga

GA

ARK.
Memphis

TENN.

Montgomery
ALA.

UNION

CONFEDERATE

BATTLE OF BRICES CROSS ROADS

LA. Vicksburg

MISS.

300

296

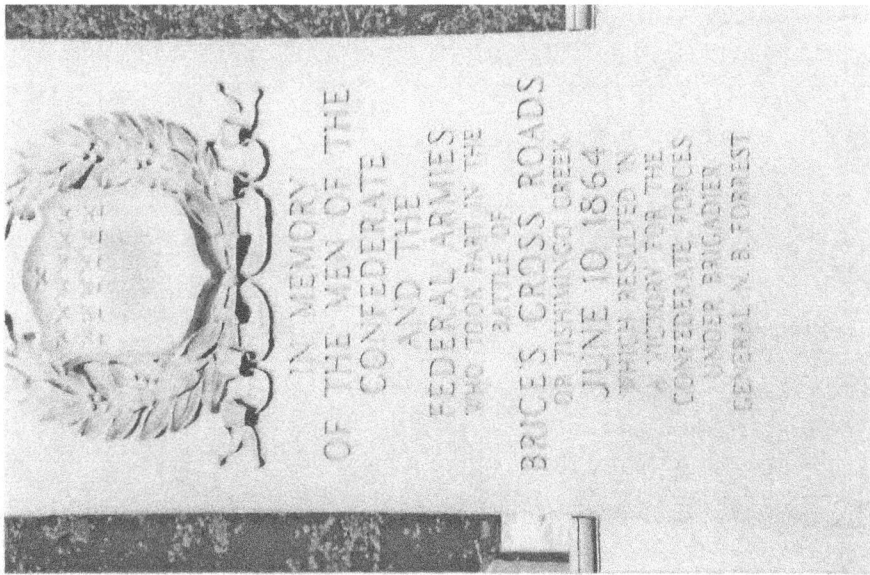

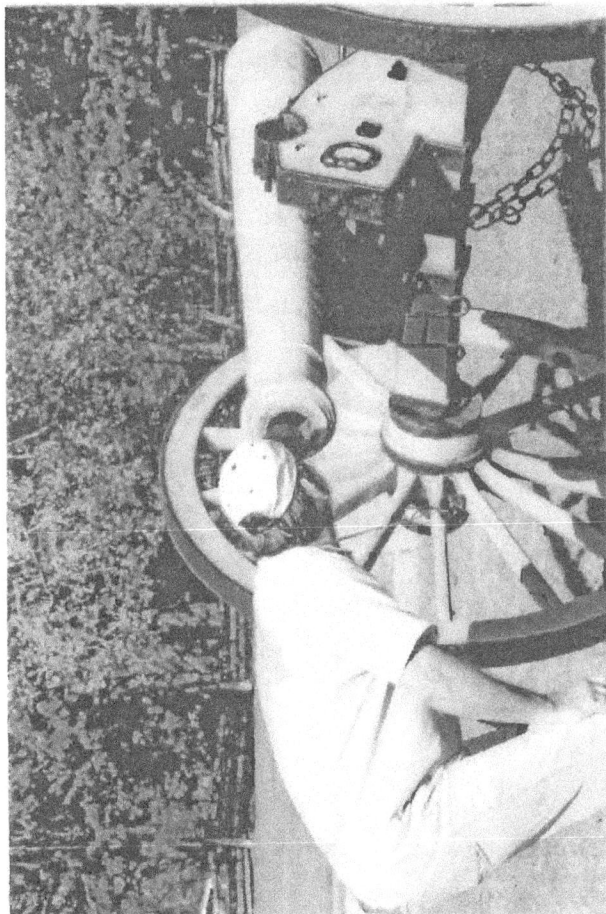

AGNES JEANNETTE
Dau. of
L. R. & C. S. BRICE
Born
Sept 9, 1901
Died
Nov 7, 1904

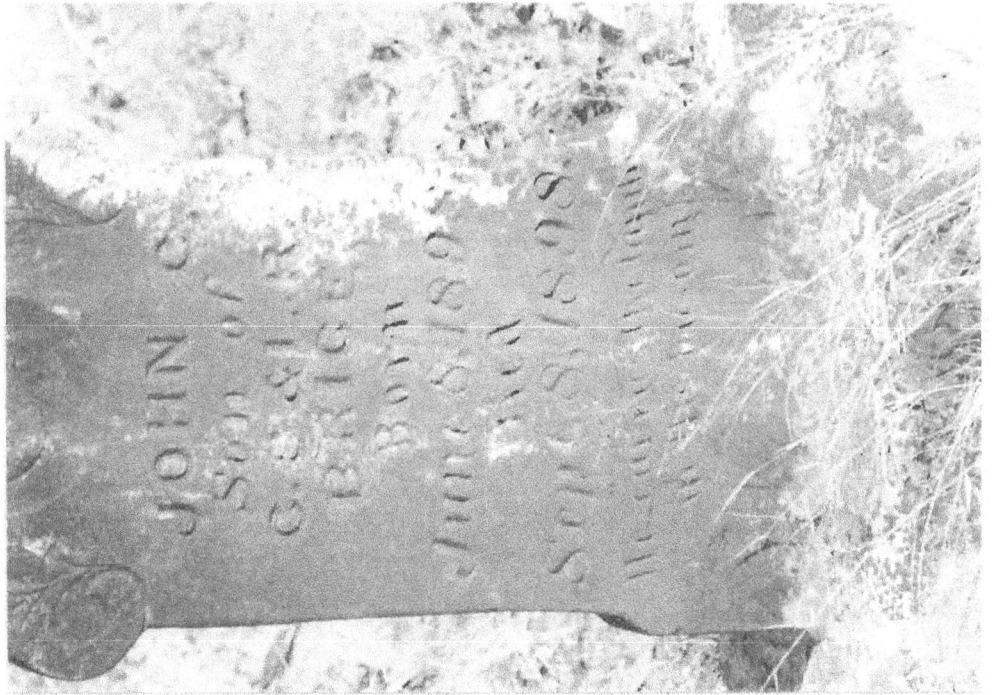

JOHN C.
Son of
C. S. & L. R.
BRICE
Born
June 6, 189_

Charles, 66

Burnside
Maj. Gen. A. E., 258
Maj. Gen. Ambrose E., 232, 253

Butler
Maj. Gen. Benjamin, 282, 283

C

Cailean (Nicol) Mac Donnachaldh, 14

Caldwell
Alexander M., 168
Anna Brice, 108
Carrie, 79
Eliza, 166, 168
Florence McCalla, 109
Henry S., 168
James, 166, 168
James B., 194
James McCalla, 108, 109
Jane S., 166, 167, 168, 169
Janie Bothia, 109
John, 174
John Steele, 109
Kate, 109
Leila Latham, 109
Mary McKenzie, 109
Mary Simmons, 109
Nellie Caroline, 109
Robert, 166, 168
Robert Brice, 109
Robert Brice, Jr., 109
Susan Hemphill, 109
Susie Meek, 109
William, 167, 168
William Frederick, 109
William Joseph, 109

Calhoun
John C., 100
Rebecca, 99
Sen. John C., 99

Calvin
John, 47

Cameron
T. J., 90

Campbell
Sir Neil, 7

Carroll
Col., 249
Frances Theus, 191
Jennie Clare, 191
Ruth Louise Theus, 191
Sally Keith, 191

Carson
Tench C., 174

Castle Chichester, 30

Castlelaw
Rev. Edward, 50

Castler Chichester, 31

Castles
Henry, Jr., 177
J. R., 177

Cathcart
James, 286
Mary, 72, 104, 124
William, 286

Cato
Meynel Clowney, 69, 71

Cessions
Edward, 191

Chalmers
Charlie Brice, 91
Eva, 91
James C., 91
John T., Jr., 91
Mary Agnes, 91
Palmer, 91
Rev. J. T., 92
Rev. John T., 91

Chambliss
Col., 226

Chaplin
Willoughby, 29

Cherry
Sarah Pauline, 76

Chew
Maj. R. P., 238

Chichester
Sir Arthur, 32, 40, 44, 46

Chisolm
Thomas, 165

Cl
Julean, 67

Clowney
Alice Brice, 67
Alice Irene, 67
Anna Boyd, 70
Benjamin Brice, 67
Capt. Samuel Boyd, 71
Eliza, 167
Eunice Marie, 67
Ida, 67
James Brice, 66
James Edward, 67
Jane Louise, 67
Joe, 66
John, 68, 70
John, Jr., 71
John Spratt, 66, 67, 68
John Spratt III, 67
Julia Adelia, 67
Lenora Baker, 67
Lois, 67
Lt. Robert Cheyne, 71
Margaret, 66, 176
Margaret Jennette, 66
Margaret Rebecca, 69
Mary Julian, 67
Mary Sue, 67
Mildred, 67
Moses, 68, 69, 70, 71
Robert Cheyne, 70
Robert Yongue, 69
Roland, 67
S. B., 82
Samuel Boyd, 67
Samuel Stanley, 67
Samuel Thomas, 70
Sgt. William James, 71
Susannah Yongue, 68
Susie, 66
Thomas, 67

William Brice, 67
William E., 67
William M., Jr., 67
William Meador, 67

Cockrel
Samuel, 82

Cockrell
John, 83

Cole
Sir William, 57

Coleman
Henry F. F., 83
Jonathan, 93
Wiley W., 83

Collins
Capt. John, 184

Colwert
Rev. Henry, 48

Comyn
John, 4, 5, 6, 7, 11
Sir John, 58

Cork
Daniel H., 90
David H., 90

Coulter
Sarah, 185

Countess of Carrick
Marjorie, 3

Cox
Brig. Gen. Jacob D., 232, 237, 253
Gen., 242

Crawford
David, 123
David A., 123
Maj. Gen. S. W., 258

Cross
Kathryn, 109

Crowder
Marie, 67

Cunningham
Rev. Robert, 48, 51

Curry
Miss, 29

Custer
Brig. Gen. G. A., 237, 258
Brig. Gen. George A., 269

D

Dabney
Lt. C., 225

Dahlgren
Rear Adm. John, 280

Daily
Samuel, 67

David I, 6

David Of Scotland, 12

Davies
Brig. Gen. Henry E., Jr., 269

de Braose
Isabella, 3

de Brus
Adam, 1
Christina, 12
Isabella Of Gloucester, 13
Robert, 1, 3, 12, 13

William, 12
de Bruys
Robert, 1
de Burgh
Elizabeth, 5
de Clare
Gilbert, 13
Isabel, 14
Richard, 13
de Courcy
John, 37
de Montgomerie
Roger, 36
de Warenne
John, 4
Dean
Rev. Virgil A., 76
DeBrus
Robert, 5th Lord Of Annandale, 3
Dickson
Rev. David, 50, 51, 55
Dobbins
Annas, 39
John, 201
Dobbs
Arthur, 199
Jane, 29, 62
Richard, 29, 62
Domhnall I
Earl Of Mars, 3
Helen, 3
Isabella, 3
Donald III, 6, 11
Donesan
John, 198
Donnchadh, Earl Of Carrick, 14
Dougass
Alexander, 72
Doughtery
Elizabeth, 123
Douglas
Alexander, 92
Alexander Brown, 81
Alexander Brown, Jr., 81
Alexander S., 89
Arch Alexander, 91
Archabald Alexander, 91
Charles, 92
Dorothy, 81
Dr. John, 153
Elizabeth, 92, 94
Grace Jane, 92
James, 7, 8, 92
Jane, 94
John, 92
Martin Alexander, 91
Mrs. A. B. (Katherine Brice), 72
Robert Leroy, 92
Sir James, 11
William, 92
Douglass
Albert Gilmore, 176
Alexander, 176, 195
Alexander, Jr., 195
Alexander S., 176
Alexander Scott, 195

C. A., 177
C. M., 177
Charles Alexander, 176
Charles Brown, 195
Ebenezer Erskine, 176
Edgar Scott, 176
Grace Jane, 195
J. C., 177
J. E., Jr., 177
J. E., Sr, 177
J. W., 177
James, 195
James Calvin, 176
Jane G., 176
John, 172, 195
John S., 176
John Scott, 176
John Simonton, 195
John W., 177
John Walkup, 176
Joseph Simonton, 176
Laura Jennette, 176
Lois Emeline, 176
Margaret S., 176
Martha Eugenia, 176
Martha Simonton, 176, 195
Mary, 172, 195
Mary E., 176
Mary Emeline, 72, 76
Mary Emmeline, 195
R. T., 177
Samuel, 195
Sara E., 195
Sarah E., 176
Scott, 177
W. B., 177
William, 195
William B., 176
Drysdale
John, 59
Duffie
Col. Alfred, 228
Dunbar
Rev. George, 48, 51

E

Earl of Carrick
Niall, 3
Earnhart
John, 67
East
David Ponder, 191
Eckin
Robert, 29
Edmondstone
William, 27
Edmonston
Sir James, 45
Sir William, 45
Edward I, 3, 4, 5
Edwards
John, 199
Elder
F. M., 180
Ellison

Robert, 191
Enloe
Maj. A. B., 111
Ennis
Mr., 29
Eubanks
James, 128
Eve
Dr. Philip Henry, 81
Edward Armstrong, 81
Helen Caldwell, 81
Katherine Brice, 81
Philip Henry, Jr., 81
Walter Brice, 81
Ewell
Lt. Gen. R. S., 238
Lt. Gen. Richard S., 282

F

Faris
S. J., 82
Ferrero
Brig. Gen. Edward, 237, 258
Fischer
Prof. David Hackett, 42
Flenniken
Carrie McMaster, 114
Flourney
Maj. C. E., 225
Forrest
Maj. Gen. Nathan Bedford, 287, 290
Foster
Joseph, 201
Fox
Capt. J. R. P., 225
Lt. Frederick, 226
Frame
Hetty, 186
Polly, 186
Franklin
Benjamin, 99
Gen., 237
Maj. Gen. William B., 232, 237
William B., 253
Frier
Hilory, 126
Maurice Walter, 126
Warren Walter "Mack", 127
Fuller
Genevieve, 110
Fullerton
Sir James, 39

G

Galloway
Dr. J. C., 110
J. M., 115
John C., 115
Julia, 110
L., 115
Louis C., 115
Mary E., 115
Robert S., 115
William B., 115

9 780788 455797 *